The HOME VISITOR'S Guidebook

3RD Edition

The **HOME**
VISITOR'S
Guidebook

Promoting
Optimal
Parent
& Child
Development

by

Carol S. Klass, Ph.D.

Baltimore • London • Sydney

Paul H. Brookes Publishing Co.
Post Office Box 10624
Baltimore, Maryland 21285-0624
USA

www.brookespublishing.com

"Paul H. Brookes Publishing Co." is a registered trademark
of Paul H. Brookes Publishing Co., Inc.

Typeset by Maryland Composition, Inc., Laurel, Maryland.
Manufactured in the United States of America by
Sheridan Books, Inc., Chelsea, Michigan.

The individuals described in this book are composites or real people whose situations are masked and are based on the author's experiences. In all instances, names and identifying details have been changed to protect confidentiality.

Photographs on pages xxiii, 3, 31, 97, 143, 173, 227, 257, 287, and 313 are courtesy of Marilyn Nolt, 508 Noble Street, Souderton, PA 18964. Phone/fax: 215-721-9055. e-mail: noltphotos@mail.com

Library of Congress Cataloging-in-Publication Data

Klass, Carol Speekman.
   The home visitor's guidebook : promoting optimal parent and child development / by Carol S. Klass. – 3rd ed.
      p.   cm.
   Includes bibliographical references and index.
   ISBN-13: 978-1-55766-903-2 (pbk.)
   ISBN-10: 1-55766-903-1
   1. Parenting—Study and teaching.   2. Child development—Study and teaching.
    3. Home-based family services. 4. Social case work. I. Title.
   HQ755.7.K59 2008
   649'.1–dc22   2008007253

British Library Cataloguing in Publication data are available from the British Library.

2020 2019 2018 2017 2016
10   9   8   7   6   5   4   3

Contents

About the Author

In her long career, Carol S. Klass, Ph.D., has taught college, worked as an early intervention specialist and mental health consultant, and served as a field-based mentor of early educators. She has designed and directed two early intervention programs for young children with high needs and three professional development programs for early childhood educators.

Dr. Klass has used ethnographic action research to improve her own practice and the practice of the early educators with whom she has worked.

Her books include *The Autonomous Child: Day Care and the Transmission of Values* (Falmer Press, 1986) and *The Child Care Provider: Promoting Young Children's Development* (Paul H. Brookes Publishing Co., 1999).

Her works in progress include a book of oral narratives of early childhood educators and a book for parents. Dr. Klass provides training seminars and keynotes and teaches as an adjunct professor. She is a sunrise walker, cook, gardener, mother of two sons, and grandmother of one granddaughter and one grandson, and she always knows the phase of the moon.

Foreword

This third edition of Carol Klass's valuable book is as welcome as were the first two editions. The dilemmas, delights, and challenges experienced by a practitioner entering a family home are again set forth recognizably and articulately. This basic, yet sophisticated, primer is of great value to anyone attempting work with parents and their young children in a home visiting model. Whether the reader is an occupational therapist, a childhood educator, a mental health professional, or a professional from another background, this book—overall and in specific chapters—makes welcome contributions to understanding the complex nature of home visiting. It addresses the expected struggles involved in learning how to do this work well and comfortably.

The continuing need for services that support families is often met through home visiting. In this new edition, Dr. Klass yet again expands considerably on descriptions of the many aspects of environments, situations, and internal and external stressors that place young children and their families at risk. The material presented is wide ranging and includes discussion of such disparate topics as maternal depression, drug exposure and drug use, community and domestic violence, parental discord and absence, general societal toxicity, and other obstacles to a child's optimal development. She has included a chapter on grandparents partly in response to the increasingly large role they play in the lives of their grandchildren, sometimes as their primary caregivers and often as the providers of daily care. Even in a lesser role as possible support to parent and/or child, grandparents may be included by the home visitor in his or her work. These are important variables of which practitioners need to be aware.

The numbers of children developing in vulnerable environments grow larger, while economic support for the services they need shrinks. This is true despite the fact that research since the 1970s has made it abundantly clear that the experiences infants and toddlers have within their caregiving relationships and within the social and cultural contexts in which their families are embedded make crucial contributions to the children's development, affecting their developing sense of self and sense of others, their internal beliefs and values, their general competencies, and their sense of possibility. Children developing in stressful, unresponsive, understimulating, or violent environments, whose parents must struggle to achieve any sense of stability for their family, require many kinds of services. Offering needed services competently can enhance and shift the climate of relationships within which a child grows and even some aspects of the environment in which the family is embedded. These services constitute a serious and hopeful response to infants', toddlers', and parents' personal needs; community needs; national needs; and overarching human needs.

The most promising and frequent effort offered to meet this need has been home visiting programs that are universally accessible and programs that serve at-risk families. They are designed to nurture, educate, treat, support, and care about young children and their families. Healthy Start, Even Start, Smart Start, and Early Start programs of various kinds with different goals are reaching into communities across the country. The rapid proliferation of these programs highlights the need to support and promote their best functioning. Home visitors—with a range of motivations, skills, supports, training, and knowledge—are central in providing these services. Whatever the explicit goals of these programs, and they are myriad, they are all devoted to working with parents to make positive differences in their lives and in the lives of their small children. At its best, the work is intended to create a personal world and way of relating that is more positive and rewarding for parent and child than existed when the visitor first entered their lives.

This book speaks to all of these different practitioners with their particular goals and illuminates what they have in common, including challenges. Both in overall concept and in revealing, detailed vignettes, Dr. Klass has something useful, insightful, or practical to say. Whether she is focusing on the complexities of parent–child–visitor relationships or on child development, the book is clear and useful. Her chapters on child development are models. They present developmental progression from the point of view of both the child and the parent. She shows simultaneously what each emerging level of development in an area means to the child's skills, understanding, and sense of self and what each emerging developmental level might mean to or demand of the parent (and whether it might enrage or engage the parent).

As she describes aspects of the mutual experiences of parent, child, and home visitor, Dr. Klass thoughtfully describes the repeated dilemmas posed to the home visitor. She understands the simultaneous and sometimes conflicting needs of all the parties, including the home visitor. How can the home visitor attend effectively to both parent and child, and how can the home visitor support the efforts of the parent to do the same with the home visitor and the child? Dr. Klass's insights are complemented by practical ideas on how to solve such dilemmas. This perspective is threaded throughout the book and simultaneously acknowledges the difficulty of the work and offers help.

This updated edition specifically expands the discussion of culture, particularly as it shapes families' beliefs and values and integrates the many important ways these values and beliefs are expressed. It emphasizes the need to recognize and acknowledge the roots of difference and an appreciation of these differences. Discussions of ethnicity, economic status, cultural transition, and the definitions of *family* and *role* are among the many aspects of diversity included. All of these inform, but also underline, the need for home visitors not only to appreciate these things in others but also to become highly aware of their own, often unarticulated, systems of belief. The addition of an evaluation/assessment component to the chapter on professional development usefully organizes the ways in which a practitioner showed development and how this self-awareness and increasing understanding of the work influences her ability to be effective.

The expansion of the chapter on social-emotional development in this new edition is highly informative and useful. It includes a more detailed description of the nature of specific capacities that coalesce in a child's general functioning. This includes discussion of memory, conscience, and morality, among other aspects of development, and further contributes to the understanding of a child's important sense of self, including effectiveness and competence. An additional new chapter highlights basic care and prevention in the overall context of illness. Typical issues potentially facing parents include dealing with a "fussy" baby as well as maintaining appropriate dental care and nutrition and avoiding dental problems and obesity. It addresses concerns ranging from ear infections to serious illness and emphasizes the need for daily health routines and appropriate medical care. These are basic issues for the home visitor to engage in during his or her work with parents.

Dr. Klass's book stems from her more than 30 years of experience with young children and their various caregivers, from her supervision in a variety of programs, and from her ability to make keen observations. It stems as well from her splendid knowledge of infant–toddler development and infant–parent interaction; from her thoughtful understanding and articulation of the experiences of doing this work; and from her careful analysis of the complex relationships between the parent(s), the child, and the home visitor. She uses this understanding of the relationship context to portray in vivid and useful ways the many aspects of the parent–home visitor relationship. She does this skillfully enough that the book is relevant to the beginner with little specialized training and also to those professionally trained in some or many of the required skills.

The book is coherent and flows from the author's understanding of well-researched bodies of knowledge. In addition, it represents a useful distillation of a wide range of thinking about supportive therapy, interpretive therapy, and therapeutic intervention. The same useful distillation is true for the book's developmental material. All of the information is supported by a sound and thorough literature review.

Dr. Klass offers an opportunity for practitioners to reflect on what they do and why and how they might do it better in a wholly engaging and available form. Her informed perspective also stresses the need for the clarification of limits and possibilities of what a particular home visitor should feel reasonably responsible for and competent to provide in terms of skills, training, and goals.

Overall, Dr. Klass's book offers a source of understanding, knowledge, and support to home visitors. At the same time, it offers a model for how seriously and carefully the role of the home visitor must be conceptualized, delimited, and supported by supervision. It is only by being as thorough and as careful about home visiting as Dr. Klass is that these efforts can be of as much benefit as possible and do no harm.

This new edition will not only prove useful to individual practitioners but also contribute to the spirited discussion in this burgeoning field. It is a strong voice for the need to provide appropriate, ongoing, thorough training; a sound knowledge base; and the crucially necessary supervisory support to the home visitor working with children and their families.

The work of helping parents and children find new strengths, new hopes, and new possibilities could not be more important. It needs to be treated as well and as seriously in the world as it is in this book.

Jeree H. Pawl, Ph.D.
Former Director
Infant–Parent Program
University of California
San Francisco

Preface to the Second Edition

Kaon arrives at the home of Jamal, age 13 months, who lives with his mother, Djuanna. This is Kaon's second year as a home visitor for Jamal and Djuanna. Kaon takes Jamal's file, which lists his birth date and his mother's name on the outside. In her bag, Kaon has two hard-paged books, a canister with a slit on its top, and two dozen poker chips.

As Kaon walks toward this family's front door, she thinks about her plans and wonders if Djuanna has settled her dispute with her mother-in-law. Will she once again need to use time in this visit to process this dispute? She knows that no matter how carefully she has planned this visit, she cannot anticipate what will happen until after she enters that front door. She sees Djuanna peeking from the living room curtain as she walks toward the front door.

Experienced home visitors know that each home visit is unique. In fact, with the same family, each visit is different from the last one. They know that their consistent challenge is to balance their interactions with the parents and with the child or children. They also know that family events between visits may be positive and productive but may also be problematic. The parent might need to process these events instead of focusing on the child's development. Some parents and children live in extended families, so a grandparent or sibling might join the visit. If a family has multiple stresses, home visitors do not know if anyone will be home when they arrive. Kaon likes her job. She likes that home visiting can be messy and unpredictable but knows that she makes a difference in families and their children's future.

As I wrote this book, my aim was to try to make sense of the ever-changing, complex nature of the home visitor's work. I wanted to demonstrate how over time, home visitors can develop close, personal relationships with parents and, in fact, make a difference in the lives of young children and their families. I have been very fortunate to have spent several years working with talented home visitors who I repeatedly observed and interviewed both informally and formally. This book is grounded in several years of home visits, interviews with home visitors and parents, extensive reading in child development theory and literature on home visitors, and my own professional experience in the field of child development.

I use a developmental frame to guide the discussion in this book. Five assumptions are central to home visiting. First and most important is that development occurs within and through relationships. Babies and young children develop within their relationships with their parents. When home visitors are effective, parent development also occurs within the relationship with the home visitor.

Second, all relationships involve mutuality. Parents influence their young children, and their children influence them. Home visitors influence parents, and parents also influence home visitors. A mother's soft voice soothes her baby, and her baby's smile and cooing stimulates her to sing softly. A home visitor's support and guidance may encourage a parent to give her toddler some clear limits, and the parent's success may give the home visitor confidence to initiate new topics.

Third, young children develop as a whole. There is unity in development. No developmental realm—communicative, cognitive, social-emotional, physical, moral, or spiritual—can be understood apart from other realms. Development is an integrated process. Each domain of development has significant implications for development in other domains.

Fourth, development is characterized by increasing complexity and qualitative change. As babies and young children develop, new and more complex behavior builds on previous behavior. Development is not linear. Rather, qualitative changes in development occur. For example, at 3 months, babies begin to coo, smile, and have extended periods of alertness; between 7 and 9 months, babies share attention and intention—they experience intersubjectivity.

Finally, child and parent development are intertwined with their social environment beyond the family.[1] Friends and relatives, neighborhood and workplace, child care center, local community resources, and national economy and policy all have an impact on the everyday life of young families. Thus, an effective home visitor's perspective includes not only the specific family visited but also the family's informal and formal support systems.

As I was writing the second edition of this book, I realized how much of my own professional history was coming into play. Since the mid-1960s, I have helped adults in their work with babies and young children in several roles and programs. Working with parents, teachers, family child care providers, and home visitors, I have had the opportunity to observe the subtleties and complexities of adults' everyday interactions with young children. As I reflected on what I observed, I began to understand the meanings of these ever-changing interactions. I have seen wide differences, but along with these differences, I have seen commonalities in patterns of adult–child interactions across contexts.

Since the late 1970s, I have combined work with parents, child care providers, and teachers with qualitative research, much of which has focused on adult–child interactions. When I conducted a participant observation case study of child care programs, I found that patterns of child care teachers' interactions with young children emphasized individual as opposed to social learning and, on a small scale, reproduced our nation's ethic of individualism.[2] In an early intervention program for the Illinois Department of Children and Family services, I hired and provided ongoing training in rural counties and factory towns to women, who, in their homes, cared for babies and young children at risk of maltreatment. In this project, I found that I could understand how the life history of talented family child care staff intersected with their skill in relating to young children.[3]

In 1988, as research coordinator for the Parents as Teachers (PAT) national center, I began observing several PAT home visitors conduct home visits and wrote a case study on the parent educator's role.[4] That was the beginning of the work that led directly to this book. When I left PAT, I took a job as an early intervention specialist at a children's hospital. I helped child care providers and parents of young children who had behavior difficulties at home and in the classroom. In my work with parents and child care providers, I learned that the taken-for-granted daily routines and adult–child interactions could be adapted so that young children could succeed. As I revised this book for the second edition, I participated in reflective one-to-one supervision with urban child care providers of children 2 weeks to 3 years old. I never get tired of observing and assisting adults learning to interact meaningfully with children in ways that may influence the children's developmental potential.

In all these positions, I have shuttled back and forth between scholarly literature and my own clinical experience and research. Core themes have been relationship, child and parent development, and the complex interplay between child development, parent development, and the social environment. As I read scholarly work, I could see the ideas being worked out in the nitty-gritty reality of parenting and early education. Problems that perplexed parents, child care providers, and home visitors were addressed in scholarly literature, but I found that scholarly information usually was not easily accessible to parents or people in early education.

I have tried to integrate my clinical and research experience, developmental theory and research, and the everyday encounters between young children, home visitors, and parents. If I am successful, home visitors will be able to see themselves in some of the vignettes and learn new ways to understand and practice home visiting.

NOTES

1. Current literature uses the term *ecological* to describe the reciprocal relationship between people and their environment. Bronfenbrenner, Garbarino, and Cochran have each conducted extensive research on the interplay of child and parent development, and multiple levels of environment—personal, community, and national. Bronfenbrenner, 1979; Cochran, Larner, Riley, Gunnarsson, & Henderson, 1990; Garbarino, 1992; Garbarino, Dubro, Kostelny, & Pardo, 1992.

2. Klass, 1986, pp. 99–117.
3. Klass, 1985.
4. Klass, 1990.

REFERENCES

Bronfenbrenner, U. (1979). *The ecology of human development: Experiments by nature and design.* Cambridge, MA: Harvard University Press.

Cochran, M., Larner, M., Riley, D., Gunnarsson, L., & Henderson, C.R., Jr. (1990). *Extending families: The social networks of parents and their children.* New York: Cambridge University Press.

Garbarino, J. (1992). *Children and families in the social environment.* New York: Aldine de Gruyter.

Garbarino, J., Dubrow, N., Kostelny, K., & Pardo, C. (1992). *Children in danger: Coping with the consequences of community violence.* San Francisco: Jossey-Bass.

Klass, C.S. (1985). *A profile of caregiving: Life history interviews of family day care providers.* Paper presented at the American Education Research Association annual meeting, New Orleans.

Klass, C.S. (1986). *The autonomous child: Day care and the transmission of values.* London: Falmer Press.

Klass, C.S. (1990). *Anatomy of the personal visit: A case study of the Missouri Parents as Teachers Program.* St. Louis: The Missouri Parents as Teachers National Center.

Acknowledgments

I am very grateful for the emotional, cognitive, and editorial support my husband Dennis gave me as I was revising this book.

I also appreciate the assistance that Sarah Shepke, my editor, provided during all phases of this revision.

Credits

For my grandchildren,

Asha and Nikhil

Introduction

Marquisha is a 39-year-old mother of six children, ages 3–21 years. I interviewed her after she had completed 2 years in Even Start. During these 2 years, her home visitor, Cynthia, visited her and her children twice a month. Marquisha was deeply affected by her experience with Cynthia and told me the following.

The home visiting program has made a wonderful difference in how I feel about myself. Talking to Cynthia, she treats you like a bigger sister, more or less, like your friend. She's just like the big sister I never had. Talking to her, I can talk about my problems if I'm going through any problems. I know Cynthia respects me and cares a lot. I told her, "You know something, I needed somebody a long time ago that cared about me the way you care about me. Care enough to boost me up instead of letting me down." Cynthia is a person you can talk to because she's looking at you. You can see that she is understanding your feelings from the expression that she shows, that she really cares. A person that you can look straight in the face and talk to. You know, when I talk to people, I don't hold my head down. Cynthia is a person you can look at, talk to because she's looking at you. You can see that she really cares. I had never really met nobody that cares about me, other than my mother. I knew my mother loved me and everything else. I knew she loved me with all her heart—but a person that I can talk to and tell my problems to, Cynthia knows how to answer me. Maybe it's not everything I want to hear, but I know what Cynthia's saying is true.

Before this program, I mean, I had little reason to live. I was just like in my bed all the time, just grogging around. Then, I signed up for this program with Cynthia. If it wasn't for Cynthia, I'm telling you, I wouldn't have a business. The day Cynthia walked in that door, I still think about it. I mean, even when I'm laying down sometimes at night, I think if Cynthia had never come, I would never be where I'm at right now. I look at Cynthia sometimes and say, "Boy, that is a woman!" Made a big difference in my life, and for my kids, for every last one of them. I love the way my kids love to play with Cynthia. I learn something about my kids every time she comes over. And my 3-year-old says, "Come on Mom, let's play like Cynthia did." I'm learning every day.

Later, I told Cynthia how Marquisha had said that she was an important person in her and her children's lives. "Yes," Cynthia replied, "She often tells me that. And I know that Marquisha is probably one of the two people in my life that I truly have influenced in a way that allowed them to make dramatic changes." Cynthia knows that very few of her families will respond as dramatically as did Marquisha. She said that it is harder to know what her visits mean to some people. But she does know that she is making a difference.

This book is about home visiting, an evolving profession in which adults strive to assist other adults in improving their everyday family lives. Modern home visiting began in the 1960s as one part of America's "war on poverty." In the early 1960s, child development research gave evidence that the first 5 years of life are the years of most rapid intellectual development and have great consequences for later development. Developmental literature moved from a unidimensional focus on the child's development to a bidirectional focus on parent and child. At the same time, literature on cultural deprivation claimed that our nation's poverty cycle might be broken by compensatory education that would allow children living in poverty to be better prepared for schooling. This social science literature coincided with the civil rights movement and President Johnson's anti-poverty political agenda. Federal assistance became available for impoverished families with young children in the form of federal grants to states for child care programs, Head Start, and early intervention programs.[1] Home visiting became a central program component of early intervention programs such as the Child and Family Resource Program sponsored by the Administration for Children, Youth and Families; Ira Gordon's Home Learning Center Approach to Early Stimulation in Gainesville, Florida; and David Weikart's Ypsilanti Perry Preschool Project in Ypsilanti, Michigan.

The 1970s brought a marked increase in single-parent homes, teenage parenting, and employed mothers of children younger than age 6. As a response to qualitative changes in social values, economic realities, and changes in the traditional family, family support programs have grown across the United States.[2] Home visiting became a primary means of service delivery in many of these programs. Most home visiting programs have the child as their primary focus and have prevention and intervention goals such as preventing low birth weight newborns, preventing child abuse and neglect, promoting healthy child development, and improving school readiness.

Although home visiting is a relatively new profession, it was a part of earlier United States history. The latter half of the 19th century was marked by increasing industrialization, massive European immigration to America, and rapid urbanization. As a response to this immigration and urbanization, settlement houses emerged and developed programs to support the family. Settlement houses were one of the first movements of the Progressive era. Wealthy women raised funds for these centers. Supervised matrons who maintained day nurseries regularly visited children's homes and taught night classes in English, homemaking skills, and child care. The settlement house programs were the beginning of America's family support movement, dedicated to socializing recent immigrants to normative American values of middle class family life.

By the beginning of the 20th century, the hallmark of the Progressive era was social reform. The first White House Conference on Children in 1909 was part of this movement toward social reform. G. Stanley Hall had begun the child study movement, and Hall's ideas were integrated into the newly begun Parent–Teacher Associations (PTAs). When they began, PTAs primarily focused on parent education. In the 1920s, with the popularization of the progressive education theory of Dewey and the psychological theories of Freud, Gesell, and Watson, parent education flourished. As parent education expanded, family support for immigrants declined. The 1920s also was the decade when nursery schools, which embraced parent education, were begun for middle class children. Until the 1970s, parent education focused on current social scientific theory; parent educators were experts teaching parents what was needed if parents were to raise successful children.

Today, our theory is different. We recognize that parents are the experts about their own children and that effective home visiting is a partnership between professional and parent, not the expert teaching the parent.

APPROACH

This book attempts to portray the complexity and the developmental possibilities in home visiting. Home visiting programs vary according to the population served, the program agenda, the strategies used to implement the agenda, the intensity and duration of service, and the types of people who conduct the home visits.[3] The vast majority of home visiting programs are primarily prevention-oriented and serve families with children, from pregnancy through age 5 years. This book discusses home visiting that helps parents to understand child development and to develop appropriate parenting skills. Home visiting programs with other goals can benefit from many parts of this book, especially the first three and last two chapters.

This book integrates theory and research from the field of infant mental health. Charles and Paula Zeanah identified several key concepts in infant mental health:

- Multiple interrelated context within which infants develop
- Process and content of infant development
- Risk and protective factors as they impact developmental trajectories
- Infant psychopathology
- Social competence and resilience[4]

Emde (2000) wrote of two important perspectives on the developmental contexts for infant mental health.

> *First, we must think about infant mental health in terms of the development of competencies. It involves, for example, increasingly organized complexity in the acquisition of abilities to learn and to accumulate knowledge, to regulate one's emotions, and to build social skills within relationships. It also involves the child's ability to gain satisfaction during exploration, social exchanges, and play. Second, we must think about infant mental health in terms of successful adaptation in the midst of challenges and opportunities. Successful behavioral adaptation involves the ability to respond meaningfully to changing circumstances across time—simply put, the ability to be flexible.[5]*

These key concepts and perspectives are prevalent in this book.

Quality programs are family centered because they believe that parents are the true experts regarding their child's and their family's needs. Families are treated with dignity and respected as implementers strive to create partnerships with parents. When programs can be community based, they are delivered in both physical and psychological proximity to where young children live. Effective programs coordinate their services with those of other agencies and organizations in the community.

This book is designed for home visitors and those adults involved in supervision, preservice, and in-service professional development of home visitors. I have tried to write this book in a manner in which home visitors can see themselves in the vignettes and conversations with home visitors; the vignettes illustrate the key ideas and practices discussed. As readers understand the home visitors whose work is described in the book, they may understand themselves better. Many of the vignettes are based on my extended study of one home visitor, Janice. For 2 years, I observed Janice as she completed monthly home visits with two families. Then, for 2 additional years, I observed her as she conducted home visits with three additional families. Please note that the vignettes are taken from interviews conducted in the early 1990s and may not always reflect current terminology and practices.

As I began writing this book, I also began working with Cynthia, the director of an Even Start program. Cynthia also is an exceptionally skilled and insightful home visitor, and I have included vignettes from my work with Cynthia, primarily in the first two chapters.

Because I have been engaged in professional development of adults since the 1980s, I am aware that one learns best when highly skilled models are available to the learner. Janice and Cynthia are exemplary home visitors whom I believe can make the home visiting process most clear. I have observed many other home visitors, not all of whom are as skilled as Janice and Cynthia. Some vignettes in the book depict additional home visitors, and some vignettes depict child care providers or other caregivers with whom I have studied in the past. Everyone can learn to improve his or her understanding and skill.

Home visiting can be unpredictable, messy, difficult work. Some families are not able to relate to friendly home visitors, whether they are professional or paraprofessional home visitors. Both Janice and Cynthia have had families in their caseloads who refused home visits, and each has experienced an array of struggles with families that remain in their program. Success is not a given, even for experienced, talented home visitors. Though I did not witness these struggles, these women's descriptions of some of these difficulties are included in this book. In addition, each chapter ends with a description of difficulties and dilemmas that home visitors may encounter in their work.

Parents as Teachers (PAT) is a partnership between home and school that is based on the belief that experiences in the early years are critical in laying the foundation for later school success. PAT aims to support parents in their role as their child's first and most influential teacher. In my home state of Missouri, the legislature has mandated and appropriated funds for each of the 543 school districts to serve 40% of district families with children who are birth to 3 years. PAT is a universally accessible nondeficit program. The program entails regularly scheduled home visits by trained parent educators, group meetings with other parents, periodic monitoring, and formal developmental screening of children from birth to 36 months.

In the United States, a large proportion of home visiting programs serve at-risk families such as low-income families and teen parents. This book primarily discusses home visiting for all families, for our basic assumption is that the primary principles and approaches of home visiting are the same for everyone, across social class, age, ethnicity, or any other distinguishing characteristic of a family. For example, effective home visitors show respect, develop rapport, empathically listen, and support every family with whom they work. I acknowledge that the home visitor's task often becomes more complex and challenging when working with families with multiple, complex problems, a pattern that occurs with greater frequency in low-income, teen, and minority families. I address these complexities as part of the first chapter on parent–home visitor relationships and the second chapter on home visiting approaches. In addition, chapters in Section I and II end with a discussion of difficulties and dilemmas that home visitors experience. Home visitors can experience these difficulties and dilemmas with any family; however, not surprisingly, they will confront many of these challenges more often with at-risk families.

OVERVIEW OF TOPICS

Section I, Home Visiting: The Basics, focuses on the complexities of the home visitor role. The first chapter, The Parent–Home Visitor Relationship, discusses the relationship between the parent and the home visitor, which is the scaffolding that makes it possible for parents to gain new understanding of their child and to strengthen their parenting practices through their home visiting experience. Chapter 2, The Home Visitor's Approach, discusses two levels of skills needed for effective home visiting. First, the chapter discusses communication and interpersonal skills that encourage, maintain, and promote the parent–home visitor relationship. The later portion of this chapter examines the complexities and difficulties of working with families at greatest risk in our society—minority, low-income, and teen families. The chapter also examines a collection of knowledge and skills that are less process-oriented, but essential to the home visiting process.

Throughout each chapter, I discuss effective home visiting with culturally diverse families. After defining the meaning of culture, race, and ethnicity in Chapter 1, other chapters contain discussion of ethnic differences, bilingual families, poverty, and difficulties and dilemmas in working with this population. Because my professional work over the past 25 years has been mainly with Caucasian and African American families, I have limited my discussion of minority families to African Americans, but home visiting programs can support families of all populations. Because of the target population with whom I have worked, the people discussed in this book are primarily urban and suburban families; however, home visiting is a needed form of family support in rural areas, as well.

Chapter 3, The Home Visitor's Professional Development, ends Section I with a discussion of ways in which home visitors can gain greater knowledge, understanding, and skill. Professional education and supervision are discussed as contexts for gaining new knowledge, understanding, and reflection on one's practice, individually and through sharing with peers, mentors, and supervisors.

Section II, Promoting Healthy Parent and Child Development, covers the topics that home visitors find most important for effective home visiting to occur. The discussion has a developmental thrust, for regardless of program agenda, every home visitor of families with young children needs a strong developmental knowledge base. At the same time, not all areas of development are detailed, for there are many excellent child development texts available.

The organization of Chapters 4–7 is three tiered. First, the chapters trace child development from birth to 5 years. Then, the chapters discuss appropriate understanding and parenting skills, and finally, how home visitors can promote parents' understanding of their children and appropriate parenting practices. Chapter 4, Developing a Sense of Self: The Foundation of Social and Emotional Development, discusses how sense of self encompasses social and emotional development and affects all other developmental areas.

Once their infant becomes a toddler, parents often are most interested in talking about guidance and discipline, the topic of Chapter 5. Mundane, everyday routines often are the setting for many parents' difficulties in guidance and discipline, yet it is an area that often is taken for granted and unexamined. Chapter 6, Communication and Language, examines how children learn to talk and communicate. Chapter 7, Play, Learning, and Development, explains how play is the primary way of learning for infants and young children.

Section II continues with a discussion of routines, rituals, and celebrations in Chapter 8; children's illnesses in Chapter 9; and sibling relationships in Chapter 10. Chapter 11 discusses salient factors that cause a family to be psychologically vulnerable: marital discord, separation and divorce, mental illness, domestic and community violence, and child maltreatment. Patterns of parent action as well as family dynamics as they affect young children are discussed. There is also a discussion of resilient children.

Section III, Person and Profession, asks the question: What kind of people are these home visitors? In my work, I consistently find that very skilled professionals often are people who experience their work life as being very meaningful, who express themselves creatively in their work; and interestingly, their work often intersects with dominant strands of their childhood history. Chapter 12 briefly portrays themes that characterize the personal history of Janice and Cynthia, two PAT home visitors, their values and attitudes, and the meaning they find in their work.

Working with caregivers of infants and young children has helped me to better understand the subtle, ever-changing nature of early development and the caregiving process. Throughout this book, I have tried to be mindful of how young children, parents, and home visitors each are developing, and in turn, how each can influence the other's development. I designed this book to be useful to home visitors, their supervisors, and teachers. At the same time, I know that the discussion is not complete. I hope that it can be a useful step in the growth of an evolving profession in our society.

NOTES

1. Lazar and Darlington provided an overview of early intervention programs of the 1960s and 1970s and of accompanying research on these programs. Lazar & Darlington, 1982.

2. Weissbourd provided a provocative overview of traditional parent education and a history of the development of family support programs. Weissbourd, 1987.
3. Varying dimensions of home visiting and different types of programming were discussed in Behrman, 1993.
4. Zeanah & Zeanah, 2001, p. 14.
5. Emde, 2000, p. 22.

REFERENCES

Behrman, R.E. (Ed.). (1993). *Home visiting: The future of our children.* Los Altos, CA: Center for the Future of Children, David and Lucile Packard Foundation.

Emde, R.N. (2001). A developmental psychiatrist looks at infant mental health challenges for Early Head Start: Understanding context and overcoming avoidance, *Zero to Three, 22*(1), 21–24.

Lazar, I., & Darlington, R. (1982). Lasting effects of early education: A report from the Consortium for Longitudinal Studies, *Monographs of the Society for Research in Child Development, 47*(2, Serial No. 195), 2–3.

Weissbourd, B. (1987). A brief history of family support programs. In S.L. Kagan, D.P. Powell, B. Weissbourd, & E.F. Zigler (Eds.), *America's family support programs* (pp. 38–56). New Haven, CT: Yale University Press.

Zeanah, C.H., & Zeanah, P.D. (2001). Towards a definition of infant mental health. *Zero to Three, 22*(1), 13–20.

Home Visiting

The Basics

The Parent–Home Visitor Relationship

The true community does not arise through people's having feelings for one another (though indeed not without it), but through first, their taking their stand in living in mutual relations with a living Center, and second, their being in living mutual relation with one another.

Martin Buber (1923/1958, p. 45)

THE CORE OF HOME VISITING is the relationship between the parents and the home visitor. Parents' development enhances their relationship with the child, which is the foundation for the child's development. A basic premise of this book is that development occurs both through and within these relationships, which consist of patterns of interaction over time. Just as the everyday patterns of parent–child interaction are the most powerful influences on baby and child development,[1,2] the parent–home visitor relationship is pivotal to parent development. This chapter examines the components of the parent–home visitor relationship that maximize the chance for promoting parent development.

A central characteristic within the parent–child and the parent–home visitor relationships is that each person influences the other at every moment and in important ways over time. Two words characterize these relationships: *mutuality* and *reciprocity*. What *A* does influences *B*, and what *B* does influences *A*. For example, when a young baby is very irritable and difficult to soothe, the parent's feelings of competency are affected, which in turn can decrease the parent's ability to provide calm, warm, loving care. The baby then feels the parent's tension and becomes more irritable. Thus, the cycle continues.

The parent–home visitor relationship is dynamic. It varies both in nature and in effect as a result of the personal characteristics of the parents and the home visitor, as well as the dynamics of the larger environment. The personality, values, and attitudes of the parents and home visitor affect their relationship. Furthermore, the parent–home visitor relationship is influenced by characteristics of larger social systems, such as race, ethnicity, schooling, neighborhood, and the socioeconomic status (SES) of the parents and the home visitor.[3] All of these factors are in play as the parents and the home visitor cocreate their relationship.

This chapter first reviews the importance of cultural sensitivity and recognition. Then it discusses key elements in forming the parent–home visitor relationship. Next, the chapter examines the progression of the relationship and discusses the meaning and significance of the personal relationship for the parent. Finally, it explores dimensions of home visitors' relationships with teenage parents and their families.

CULTURAL SENSITIVITY AND RECOGNITION

Daily interactions in the home and among family members reinforce the values and beliefs of culture. Families are the primary vehicle for the transmission of culture. Culture includes beliefs about child rearing, children's growth and development, the role of the family, and the meaning of child and parent behavior.[4] Cross-cultural research indicates that maternal sensitivity and contingent responsiveness to babies' cues varies based on parental cultural beliefs.[5] For example, cultural models for caregiving related to a baby's crying exist around the world; however, the caregiving may vary according to the beliefs of each culture.

Home visitors bring knowledge of the universal aspects of child development to their practice. However, they also need to consider each family's cultural beliefs, practices, and attitudes as they work with parents.

Approximately 40% of American children are not Caucasian. Therefore, children of other cultures are being raised in families who may have different socialization goals and value different traits than Anglo-American families.[6] These factors, identified by Lynch and Hanson, can help determine how much cultural variation to anticipate:

1. Socioeducational level
2. Time of arrival in the United States
3. Premigration and migration experiences
4. Proximity to other members of their cultural or ethnic community
5. Proximity to other cultural groups
6. Age
7. Gender
8. Language proficiency
9. Sociopolitical climate, including the extent of societal bias, distrust, and racism[7]

Sensitivity is the key to working with parents from diverse cultures. Home visitors must respect cultural differences in feeding practices, sleeping, toilet learning, discipline, and the role of family members as well as beliefs about holding, cuddling, and spoiling babies and young children. Home visitors need to be sensitive when interpreting babies' needs, responding to babies, and considering their parents' points of view.

When home visitors work with families of cultural backgrounds different from their own, respect, rapport building, empathic listening, and support are especially important. The home visitor may have assumptions about other cultures, which could lead to stereotyping. Therefore, to provide effective service when working with families of different cultures, home visitors need to be flexible and open minded to avoid stereotyping.

What one sees, hears, and understands is filtered through his or her cultural background. Home visitors' sensitivity to how their own behaviors, attitudes, and values reflect their age, gender, ethnicity, and SES is the first step in the ability to relate to families of a different culture. In other words, competent home visitors are dual minded—aware of their own actions, thoughts, and feelings as well as the actions, thoughts, and feelings of the families with whom they work.

When home visitors work with families of a different culture, they try to do several important tasks at the same time: 1) be aware of their own cultural biases; 2) work to understand and respect each family's cultural patterns; 3) try to recognize differences within and not just between different cultures; and 4) see the uniqueness of each family, regardless of its culture. For example, the home visitor understands that the discipline values and practices of the Tsai family represent their Japanese American heritage; however, the Tsai family also have developed patterns of relating to their children that are uniquely their own, not just typically Japanese American.

BILINGUAL FAMILIES

When young children learn two languages from birth, they have a special advantage. If infants hear two languages and then keep using the languages as they grow, they will be able to speak both languages fluently, like native speakers. Early childhood is the best time to learn more than one language because young children automatically develop second speech centers. Young children learn two languages easiest if they hear each language from a consistent source (e.g., if the mother speaks English and the father speaks Chinese).

Talking to bilingual parents often requires tact because some parents may feel that their English skills are poor. Home visitors can help bilingual parents recognize that their children's goal is to develop strong communication skills, regardless of the language. Young children learning two languages may need some extra time to reach certain language milestones. As a result, on early language screenings, these children may have a slight language delay in expressive skills, but home visitors can stress that the long-term advantage of being bilingual is worth the short-term delay in expressive skills. When finances allow, home visiting programs hire staff that are bilingual.

FORMING THE PARENT–HOME VISITOR RELATIONSHIP

In the home visitor's work with a family, four elements are central:

1. *Expectations:* Home visitors discuss with parents their expectations and the parents' expectations.

2. *Agenda:* Home visitors describe what they hope to accomplish with the parent and child.

3. *Roles:* Home visitors and parents clarify their roles of parent and home visitor in the context of their relationship.

4. *Setting:* Both home visitor and parent need to be comfortable working in a parent's home. However, the setting of a home visitor's work in the parent's personal space raises issues different from other work settings such as an office, classroom, or clinic.

In good home visiting, these elements are made explicit in initial contact with a family.

Expectations: Parent and Home Visitor

All relationships include expectations of ourselves and of other people. The home visitor's role is fairly new in our society, so what people think might happen during and after the visit can be ambiguous. It is therefore important for the home visitor to clearly state expectations and to invite parents to share their own. Expectations are multiple. The home visitor should ask, "What do I expect of myself, what do I expect of the parent, and what do I think the parent expects of me?" The parent should ask, "What do I expect of myself, what do I expect of the home visitor, and what do I think the home visitor expects of me?" Intertwined with these expectations are the parent's and home visitor's expectations for the child and what will happen to the child as a result of their work together. As they work together, parents and home visitors will want to clarify what they are experiencing in relation to their expectations of each other.

Sometimes home visitors and parents may have different ideas about where the authority lies. In the family support programs described in this book, the home visitor assumes that parents are the experts in their child's development; the home visitor should therefore aim to support, affirm, and promote the parents' relationship with their child. Some parents may assume that the home visitor is the expert and is coming into their home to teach them the right way to parent. In other words, parents may give total authority to their home visitor as teacher and put themselves in a subordinate role. This expectation violates the kind of relationship that makes the parent–home visitor partnership work. In these situations, it is not the task of home visitors to challenge the parents' expectations; however, home visitors do not have to accept the authority that the parents project onto them. Rather, home visitors may need to adjust their approach. For example, the home visitor can be very specific about goals and the approach to take while trusting that, over time, the parents' experience in working with the home visitor will influence the parents to accept authority.

During the initial phase of home visiting, the home visitor can encourage parents to express their expectations for their child and talk about their priorities regarding the child's behavior and skills. It also can be helpful to ask specifically how parents would like to use their time with the home visitor. The home visitor uses what the parents say to establish rapport and to build a partnership with the parents. If parents' goals or priorities seem developmentally unrealistic, home visitors can discuss these issues with the parents in an open and respectful manner as they share developmental information. Within these discussions, the home visitor can communicate clearly that parents are always the decision makers in matters about their child, and that all conversation during a home visit is confidential.

Because the home visitor's role is ambiguous, many parents enter the relationship with uncertainties. Some parents have little experience with opening their home to others. They may worry about their privacy being violated or about the adequacy of their home being judged, as in the cases of Sally and Rob.

Sally is a young mother with learning disabilities who joined Even Start (a family support program) when her son was 3 months old. Sally was in and out of juvenile detention centers as an adolescent and quit school in the eighth grade. Given her troubled background in her family of origin and adolescence, she had misgivings about being visited at her home. She shared her concerns about her adequacy as a parent with her home visitor and indicated that as a first-time mother she was exceptionally nervous. She babysat when she was younger, but she was not prepared to be around a baby 24 hours a day. Sally didn't know if what she was doing with the baby was right, which made her feel like she was bad at parenting and could not raise a child. After joining Even Start, Sally gained the confidence she needed and now thinks she's just as good as—if not better than—any other parent.

Similarly, Rob, a parent in a Parents as Teachers (PAT) program, expressed his initial wariness of the home visiting program. As a firefighter who's often involved with the school district, Rob was skeptical about the program, thinking the tax dollars used to support it may be a ploy to get more employment for the school district staff. He also thought having to schedule time for the home visits would be a pain. In reality, Rob was able to attend almost all home visitor meetings and added a great deal to each meeting.

Because parents initially may have uncertainties, home visitors need to clearly state their purpose and expectations. Experienced home visitors are confident. They trust the power of the process of relationship development. When beginning in this role, however, home visitors also may have uncertainties. The comments of Janice, a home visitor in a PAT program, illustrate initial discomforts and developing skills.

It is always difficult to begin a relationship, no matter how long you have been doing this, no matter how comfortable you feel with all the families you have been serving over the years. Your heart beats a little faster when you walk into someone's home for the first time because you want to be accepted by them, and you are never sure what it is going to take to have that happen. When I first began, I was a motor mouth, but in the past couple of years, I've learned that it is okay to have quiet time when no conversation is going on between the parent and me, or between the child and me. And this helps the parent feel a sense of calm. And when they feel that you are calm with whatever is going on in their family, they feel more calm about what is going on—for example, being calm when the baby starts crying or the toddler starts being negative. If we act like this is something we expect kids to do, that it's no big deal, then the parent does not feel embarrassed and nervous about it. [Of all] the changes we have felt [the most important is] one of comfort with what we are doing—our own self-confidence.

Before the birth of Janice's children, she taught third grade. Given the newness of the home visitor role when she started, Janice's own expectations were not very clear. She did not have the self-confidence that she had in her teaching, where she knew what she was supposed to do. With experience, she began to understand her relationships with parents and to trust her skills. Then, she could maintain a slower, calmer pace during her home visits.

Home visitors bring their prior work experiences into their new role as home visitor, which influences their interactions with parents. All adults experience uncertainty in new occupations, and home visiting is no exception. Having a clear understanding of the program agenda and the tasks involved assists the home visitor's transition into this new role.

The Agenda: What Is My Job?

One of the first tasks of home visitors is to clearly understand their program agenda. The program agenda varies depending on the population being served, the overall agenda of the agency or institution, and whether professionals or paraprofessionals do the home visiting.[8] Is the program universally accessible? Is it for teenage parents only? Is it for parents with low incomes who are at risk? Is it for families with low birth weight babies? Is the agenda primarily to lessen existing difficulties or to prevent the occurrence of problems? Possible agendas might be to promote the health of babies and young children, to ensure the child's physical and psychological safety, to promote the cognitive skills of at-risk children in low-income families, to help parents develop an understanding of child development and appropriate parenting skills, or to work toward prevention of child abuse and neglect. Still, regardless of the agenda, nothing can be accomplished until a trusting relationship is formed between the parent and visitor.

Within program agendas, the home visitor chooses activities determined by a continuum of priorities such as giving information, understanding how a family is doing, deciding what resources can be brought to bear, or being a surrogate parent to a teenage mother. Competent home visitors know their agenda when they are in the home because it is impossible to pay attention to everything. Home visitor Janice explains her goals and the agenda that she sees as basic to her work:

I think parents appreciate someone coming in who sees lots of children the age of theirs and who can help them be objective, but who also helps them appreciate that these are really great kids. And even though they are great, I think parents want to be sure that they are great. Parents also appreciate the screening we do and knowing appropriate kinds of things for themselves and their children to do—things that will maintain their children's interest, things that nurture their development without pushing. I think they really are looking for appropriate ways to nurture their child.

Janice understands that parents can take in information when they are affirmed, and the strongest affirmation is taking pleasure in their child.

Respective Roles: Who Is Responsible for What?

In forming a relationship with parents, home visitors try to ensure that parents understand the behaviors associated with the roles of home visitor and parent. The most important dynamic of family support programs is developing mutual respect and partnership between parents and home visitors, because a successful home visiting relationship is defined by a collaboration between the home visitor and the parents. Historically in parent education programs, the parent educators are the experts in children's development.[9] In contrast, the home visitor is an empathic listener, consultant, resource, guide, advocate, and partner. For example, when focusing on sleeping, the home visitor first learns how the baby or young child is sleeping and how the parent assists the child's sleep. Then the home visitor shares developmental information and possible parenting strategies as related to the lived experience of the parents and child. The topic may be the home visitor's or the parent's choice. The directives of traditional parent education are replaced in home visiting by joint problem solving—a working alliance.

Parents are the experts in their children's development, active participants in home visits, and the final decision makers with regard to nurturing their children. Home visiting is a helping relationship defined by collaboration between the home visitor and the parents.

Competent home visitors work on two levels. They are completely engaged in interactions with the parents and child, while at the same time they are aware of their own reactions and feelings, such as excitement at a new accomplishment, frustration in parenting skills, or growing to like the family. When home visitors can relate to the family while being aware of their own feelings and making decisions based on these feelings, they are more likely to be successful. Cynthia describes this concept of working on two levels:

For over 2 years, I have been working with Marquisha and her large family, her sister, and [between them] their 12 children, between 2 and 22 years old. I was sitting on the couch with Marquisha. Her 18-year-old daughter [Rashonda] stood next to us with several envelopes in her hand. She took the envelopes and held them up to the light and read the dollar amounts. Well, then it occurred to me, they were welfare checks, and she was looking at hers and reading the amount— and her mother's and her aunt's and her cousin's. Her mother knew I was there to visit and was very embarrassed. She said, "Rashonda, stop doing that. Quit reading other people's mail." But Rashonda kept doing it.

By that time, I was aware of my own feelings. I was irritated with the 18-year-old. It's like, "Why are you doing this? Why are you embarrassing your mother? Rashonda, go in the back of the room, and just leave us alone." And she kept doing it, and then she'd look at me and say, "I'm not opening the mail, am I, Cynthia?"

Well at this point, I was aware of feeling baited. "Okay, Cynthia, what are you going to do about it? How are you going to handle this?" In my head, I knew I had to decide: "What am I going to do? I know I have a good relationship with this family, a decent relationship, but it's not the strongest in the world. I was being challenged by the 18-year-old. Her mother is embarrassed. So what do I do?"

I just stuck with what I know best, which is to be myself, and I answered honestly, but I was conscious of, "Don't let your anger show. Just be honest." So what I said to Rashonda was, "Nope. You are not opening up the envelopes, but you still are invading people's privacy." And that is all I said. Then, I turned back to her mom, and we continued our conversation. Rashonda put the envelopes down. She didn't leave the room. She sat down and just kind of listened and played with her baby. By the time I left, it was okay. We were back on track.

Cynthia feels secure in her relationship with this family. A professional with 20 years of experience, she is confident and trusts her judgment, even when everything seems to be falling apart. Had she scolded Rashonda, Rashonda probably would have fled the room, enraged. Her honest, respectful reply not only ended Rashonda's behavior, but also gave Rashonda permission to remain and learn what Cynthia had to offer. This two-level process using internal and external dialogue is a skill that develops over time, with experience and ongoing supervision.

The Setting: Working in the Parents' Space

Home visitors enter into a family's private space, of which many families are protective. Some parents may not understand why the home visitor is there and may not feel safe. Given their uneasiness, some parents carefully watch their home visitor from the moment he or she gets out of the car. Home visitors can help parents feel comfortable when they themselves are relaxed, genuine, and able to find a common ground on which to make their first contact. Once the adults are able to have a relaxed exchange, home visitors can describe their role and begin to learn what the parent would like from their visits. Home visitors should understand that they cannot accomplish anything until they know the family, the family knows them, and a relationship is established. This process takes time.

As guests in parents' homes, effective home visitors take cues from parents, such as asking the parents' permission before touching or picking up their baby. Similarly, it would be inappropriate to enter other rooms in the home unless the home visitor is invited to do so. Janice explained how she follows the parents' lead:

I try to come in as the guest in the home, not as somebody that is in charge of this hour. I always try to keep in mind that it is the parent's home; thus, as much as possible, I try to follow the parent's lead. If the parent sits on the floor first, I sit on the floor. Wherever she sits first is where I sit first. Once I introduce an activity, usually we both sit on the floor with the child. But, if the parent initially is most comfortable remaining on the chair, I'll respect that decision. Then, in a few minutes, I'll invite the parent to join the child and me.

But just as important as my own agenda and planned activity, I invite parents to share observations of their child, happenings within the family, concerns, or questions. The visit always is for the family, and I try and keep foremost that I am interested in how parents would like to use our time together.

Janice's behavior shows respect and genuine interest. Janice knows that her words and behavior will communicate who she is and what the visits will entail.

When home visiting is not sought out by a family, a first visit can be very difficult, as Cynthia describes.

I have been working with two sisters in their late thirties and their children, who range in age from 19 years to, when I first met them, a newborn. So there are 12 children between the sisters who live in this household, and the older children of these sisters also have children. So, at any given moment, there are up to 20 people in and out of this household.

On my first visit, I knocked on the door. This was a referral from the child protection agency. They [the sisters] did not want to see me. They did not want me in their home. They did let me in. It was dark in the home. There was a couch and a loveseat in this fairly large room, a small TV on the shelf. One of the moms let me in, and I introduced myself. I did my spiel about [how] I am from Parents as Teachers, and this is what we do. I'll bring these games, and we are going to talk about development—the whole spiel.

She kind of looked at me and turned about and walked away. And she didn't come back for 5 minutes. You know, you are just kind of standing there. [I was] like, "Well, now what do I do?"

So pretty soon she comes back with her other sister, and I had to go through this spiel again. She wanted her sister to know about this, but she really wanted somebody there with her while I was there.

It didn't take long for Cynthia to realize that this was not going to be a typical visit, and her planned agenda had to be disregarded. Although she felt awful, she persevered.

And no one asked me to sit down. I had been told to take my cue from the parent. They just left me standing there. So, I finally thought, "That's not going to work. I'm not going to be able to take my cue here." Either I leave or I ask to sit down, which is what I did. "Would it be okay if I sat down?" They replied, "Oh well, all right. Go ahead."

Well, then they brought the kids out, and the sisters sat on one side of the room. And I was over on the other side with the children. The TV was blaring. I didn't have the nerve to ask them to turn it down because I thought, "You know, I'm just getting started with this. I'm not going to ask them to do that." So I kind of sat there and played with the children, a 3- and a 4-year-old. We talked, and I got some books out and read some books. The parents sat on the other side of the room, and they watched me.

Then, someone knocked at the door. A third adult came in, and the three of them sat over there and had their own conversation and said things I couldn't quite hear. They would laugh, and I thought, "I'm not paranoid, but I know they're talking about me, and they don't want me here. I'm going to leave and never come back." And so I read stories, played with the children, and watched a little TV.

Cynthia described this family's life as being on the edge of chaos, but she knew she was making a difference.

Now the family has moved from Parents as Teachers into Even Start. Neither mom had finished high school. They are in adult education; they bring their children to the child care center, and I make two visits a month.

At the end of the my second year working with this family, the evaluator asked one of these parents, "Why are you in this program?" and she said, "Because Cynthia just won't go away." And I think there is some truth in that. I just wouldn't give up. There were a lot of times I wanted to, but I saw that spark of interest. I know they wanted to do something for themselves and for their kids. I just kept coming back. Last year, they only attended the adult education center 1 out of 4 days. This year, one of the sisters has been attending 3 out of 4 days and even has gotten several attendance awards for perfect weekly attendance.

Over time, Cynthia communicated to the sisters that she cares and that they and their children are important. Cynthia knows that parents, regardless of how problematic their behavior may seem, want the best for their children and for themselves. This knowledge gives Cynthia the commitment and courage to persevere. In turn, the sisters have learned that they have a friend who truly cares. They have experienced what Jeree Pawl stated is "one of life's greatest privileges—the experience of being held in someone's mind."[10]

PROGRESSION OF THE
PARENT–HOME VISITOR RELATIONSHIP

Establishing Appropriate Boundaries

Each home visiting program has its own goals, agenda, and time limitations. Regardless of the program agenda, it should be implemented through an extended relationship between the parent and home visitor. However, such types of relationships can lead to a blurring of the appropriate boundaries of parent–home visitor interaction; working in a family's home adds to the role ambiguity. Once parents feel they have a trusting relationship with their home visitor within the privacy of their own home, the parents may extend discussion beyond the explicit goals and tasks of the home visiting program to include personal problems. These topics may range from family conflict with a spouse or parents; internal stresses such as depression; or external problems such as housing, inadequate income, or employment.

Some home visitors have a hard time distinguishing what they can do and what they are unprepared to handle, as well as how to carefully maintain their boundaries of involvement with families. Some home visitors try to solve others' problems when they lack the expertise; this violates the family support program goal of empowering parents. Some complicated family problems interfere with parents' attention to their child; these situations are often beyond a home visiting program that does not include broader social services.[11] When parents discuss highly personal matters or external problems beyond the home visiting agenda, home visitors can listen empathetically and, when appropriate, help the parents seek other services in the community to meet their needs.[12] When a home visitor encounters a parent who shares his or her personal troubles, the home visitor should seek advice or help from peers and/or supervisors while keeping the family's issues confidential. A mature home visitor is aware of his or her professional limitations. Cynthia describes how she maintains boundaries:

I see myself in a helping relationship without taking over. I listen because if the parent brings something up, it is foremost on the parent's mind, so you at least listen to it. A lot of times, home visitors get hooked up trying to solve everything. But most people don't want you to tell them what to do anyway. So, I'll listen to the parent, and sometimes you can tell they just needed to get that off their chest, and then they can go on. And sometimes you need to let them talk about it more and explore options with them. When you are working with families, you are there to help them problem solve, not do things for them.

Cynthia understands that one of her most effective approaches is listening to parents, even when they go beyond the planned agenda of discussing their child and their parenting. At the same time, she understands that her role is not to rescue parents who are immersed in problems.

Carol: In those families in which there are substantial problems, like serious emotional problems or external problems like housing, do you find that you also are making decisions about when is it time to get a professional with expertise that you don't have?

Cynthia: Oh sure! But I still listen. I make the decision that this is not my realm of expertise, and I need to help this family get other resources. I'll say to the parent, "You know, I am not really experienced with this kind of thing. I am not a counselor. I don't feel I really can help you with this, but I know someone who can." Then, I offer possible services. I'll tell them that if they would like to talk more about this—because it really seems to be bothering them—here is the number of someone who can help. For the most part, I give them the information and let them self-refer. On a few occasions, I thought the situation was really bad, and I called the psychologist who works with families in our district, and he then called the parent.

Cynthia knows specifically what her agenda is and what her areas of expertise are. If a parent shares a problem beyond the scope of Even Start, Cynthia is able to think on two levels: talking with the parent while thinking through whether the parent's problem is a situation requiring just listening and support, listening and helping with problem solving, or listening and networking with community resources. Having built trust into her relationships with parents, Cynthia actively listens to whatever the parent chooses to share, but still lets parents know when they have entered areas beyond her expertise. In turn, parents appreciate Cynthia's honest statements regarding her own limitations, for this acknowledgment communicates genuineness and respect of the parent.

Janice, who has been a home visitor since 1986, shared her perspective:

When a parent puts out something that I don't feel equipped to discuss, I have to remember sometimes all she wants me to do is listen and that I can provide an important service to her by just listening very empathetically and not offering anything other than my ears, really; a friendly gesture; and a suggestion of whom she might contact.

We have to be real honest with parents and let them know where we are good and where we are not. And that the things I know, I know pretty well. I really know child development and understand parenting, but I don't know anything about housing. And if they have a housing issue, they need to call Mrs. Smith at such-and-such bureau because I know she is good and can help them. I think when parents hear that we are real honest on that, they will trust us more on the issues where we do have expertise.

Like Cynthia, Janice understands that when a parent is troubled, listening empathetically can be the support needed. At the same time, Janice is quick to recognize when a parent's problem is beyond her expertise, at which point she tells the parent who could be of assistance.

Experienced early educators across program types share their successes with and obstacles to boundary issues in Table 1.1.

Table 1.1.   Boundary issues in home visiting

Successes	Barriers
Home visitors set clear goals.	Parents are not accessible.
Home visitors are nonjudgmental.	Parents have low self-esteem.
Home visitors are active listeners.	Home visitors have unmanageable case-
Home visitors are supportive and empathic.	loads.
Home visitors are persistent and don't give up.	Parents do not follow through with home visitors' suggestions.
Home visitors know who and where to refer parents to and explain to parents available community resources.	Parents experience difficulties with extended family members.
	Physicians say the child is fine, but home visitors know this is not true.
Programs have bilingual staff members.	Parents are overwhelmed because their homes are a revolving door for profes-
Programs have a lending library of books with DVDs/videotapes, audiotapes, DVD/video players, and audio players.	sionals helping their children.
	Homes have inadequate space and are filthy with rats and cockroaches.
Programs budget for a taxi service for parents.	Parents' homes are in dangerous neighborhoods and pose safety issues.
Home visitors work with grandparents.	Parents have unrealistic expectations for their children or spouses.
Home visitors give parents options.	Home visitors don't understand the fam-
Home visitors are culturally and ethnically sensitive.	ily's culture or ethnicity.
Home visitors help parents develop a list to use when talking to a professional of another discipline.	Home visitors impose their own personal or social values on parents.
	Home visitors do too much for parents.
Home visitors employ role play with parents to practice calling a professional of another discipline.	Home visitors need an interpreter to communicate with parents.
	Parents deny a child's special needs.
Home visitors help parents schedule needed visits with professionals of other disciplines.	Parents refuse to admit a family problem.
Programs feature effective mentoring and supervision.	
Home visitors help parents read confusing documents, such as legal documents.	

Building on Strengths

Home visitors should recognize the important job of parenting and should acknowledge that parents are the experts regarding their own children. From the outset, home visitors should identify parents' strengths, affirm them, and strive to use these strengths as the building blocks for their relationship and for the parents' development. Janice describes her approach:

Especially in early parts of my relationship, I make sure I can praise things the parent does. And that makes them realize right up front that not only do I enjoy their baby, but I think they are doing a good job. Even if there are some things they are not doing, I really praise the things they are. And at the end of my visit, when I give them our handouts, I'll say, "You probably are doing this already." In as many subtle ways as possible, I try to find the strength of the parent and build on that.

My goal is for parents to trust themselves, to trust what they know, and to trust their judgment because they have a foundation of child development information and parenting information that our program provides for them so that they feel strong in what they do. And you know, interestingly, when parents feel strong in what they do, they are more likely to ask for help when they need it.

Karyn, a first-time mother of a 24-month-old, described what Janice's home visits meant to her:

She never left the house without telling me, "You are doing an important job. It is very hard work, and you are doing it well." I always waited for her to say that.

When working with troubled families, home visitors can feel uneasy, even overwhelmed, with a family's many difficulties, making it difficult to spot the positive elements on which to build. In these situations, home visitors may need to give themselves and the parents time to get to know one another and to build a relationship. The child can often serve as common ground to begin a conversation, although initially the only common ground may be a television show or community event. When home visitors are genuine and interested, over time they develop a relationship in which they can see, acknowledge, and affirm parents' interests and strengths.

Sharing One's Own Family Life

Just as home visitors learn to develop boundaries for areas they can address and those that are beyond their expertise, so too should home visitors develop sensitivities about when sharing their own family life is appropriate. When a parent expresses a concern or asks a question, a home visitor's brief vignette from his or her own family life can communicate understanding, support, and validation of the parent. The effective home visitor tries to keep the child's and parent's development as the focus; thus, any personal sharing must remain integral to ongoing concerns, questions, or happenings within the family being visited. Janice's discussion with Shelly is illustrative:

Shelly: Erin [age 24 months] loves the playground at the park. She's getting better with the slides. She holds on pretty good. But on the swing, she doesn't have the concept to wait until the swing stops to get off.

Janice: I remember it was hard for me when my boys were small. I used to find myself saying, "Be careful" again and again and again. It's hard because I also wanted them to try and to be competent.

Shelly: I try and remember to say to Erin, "Pay attention to what you are doing."

Once Janice shared this personal vignette, Shelly then elaborated on her concern. The two adults brainstormed together how Shelly could ensure Erin's safety while encouraging her to climb and swing competently. Janice explained to me her rationale for sharing her own family life with parents:

I think personal sharing helps rapport. Not that I am always spinning off about my family, but every now and then I am willing to share about my own life or about my own child that matches up with something in their lives. I mean, I don't care what family it is, I try to pull something out of my life. For example, this week… the mother was working as a nurse's aide part time in a nursing home. And I didn't have anything in common with this woman except that my husband's aunt is in a nursing home. And I was able to say to her how important the people are to our family that do the kind of work that she does. And just pulling together that nursing home experience, validating her importance to my life, did something for us. It made her see me as a person, which is what I think I need to be to parents for them to pay attention. I heard a phrase at one of our staff meetings that I really believe—that parents need to know that we care before they care what we know.

Janice wants the parents she works with to know that she cares and respects them. When something in a parent and child's life together triggers Janice's thoughts of her own family, her sharing is another way she communicates the meaningfulness of this family's life. Janice aims to have mutuality in her relationship with parents, in which parents' comments have meaning to her in the same way that she hopes her comments are meaningful to them.

Parents are disclosing so much of their private life to me that if I don't disclose something about me to them, they are going to think it is too one-sided. I am in their home, asking about their baby, asking about their opinions, and if I don't share something, if I don't let them at least partway into my life, it seems like there is too much distance. And that's not fair to them. I don't go overboard and talk a lot about my kids, but I want them to know that I am a mother and that I have experienced some of these things. And as I get the sense that there is some closeness developing between us, then I feel more comfortable discussing some touchy issues. I am not as comfortable getting into problem areas with somebody I do not know very well, and I don't think it works either.

Janice accepts and trusts her own family experience. She is sensitive to balancing the parents' levels of disclosure with her own sensitive disclosures so that she matches what the parents are sharing. As she shares her own experience, she is assisting parents in accepting and trusting their experience.

ESTABLISHING RECIPROCAL, POSITIVE FEELINGS BETWEEN PARENTS AND HOME VISITORS: A PERSONAL RELATIONSHIP

Whether or not they know it, parents make decisions every moment they interact with their babies and young children. The child is affected by the decisions the parents make in the morning, at bedtime, when the television is on, or when at the store. The child is affected by decisions parents make about what to say to the child or to others when the parent is diapering or feeding the child. Home visitors, on the other hand, are only in the home for an hour per week or month. So, it is not what home visitors tell parents, or the decisions home visitors think are best for the child, that will make a difference in the end. The parents need to make decisions that help the child's development for the program to be successful.

Regardless of a home visiting program's agenda, parents are the final decision makers in their child-rearing practices. When home visiting programs are successful, parents' new understanding and skills allow them to be informed when making deliberate decisions such as what kind of toys to buy for their child; everyday decisions should become habitual. Parents' informed decision making emerges from their extended interactions and personal relationship with their home visitor.[13] In personal relationships, each person influences the other continuously over time. Just as the toddler learns to say "please" and "thank you" from her parents, the parents become comfortable talking to their 4-month-old son as they change and feed him as a result of their relationship with the parent educator. Shelly talked about her home visitor's continued influence:

We always look forward to Janice coming—oh, what is she going to tell us this month, and what is going to be going on [in the visit]? And I can't wait to show her what we can do. And, you know, Janice will say something and then leave. And in a few days, Erin would be doing it, and I will think, "Oh, I knew she was going to do this."

Janice has been visiting Shelly, Rob, and their daughter Erin for 2 years, since Shelly's third trimester of pregnancy. Patterns have developed in Shelly and Rob's relationship with Janice. They look forward to her visit when they can share Erin's new skills, and they sense that Janice truly enjoys relating to them and their child. They remember Janice's descriptions of the new developmental strides they can expect in their child. In her discussions with Janice, Shelly sometimes describes an experience she and Erin had and then tells Janice what she remembered that Janice had told her during a prior home visit—sometimes as long ago as the previous year.

How does this personal relationship between parents and home visitors develop? The relationship evolves from extended interactions over time. Several home visitors in a PAT program identified key themes in forming their relationship with parents. Lela explains:

First, parents have to trust you, and that takes time. I try and build a rapport so that they can talk to me about things they are concerned about, topics like sleep problems, discipline, or toilet training, with comfort, and not feeling like they are being failures as parents. And they need to know that I am not there to judge them, that I'm there as a support person. And if there is any information I can get them that they need, I'll be glad to do that. And sometimes I even bring in personal experiences in my own life so that they'll know that, hey, a lot of other parents experienced this problem too.

Several themes emerge in Lela's description. Parents need to feel comfortable enough to talk about whatever is going on in their lives. They can do this if Lela has developed rapport with them and they trust her. Like Janice, Lela feels that occasional sharing of her personal experience supports parents in the knowledge that they are not alone in their concerns.

Ernestine explained her relationships with parents as follows:

I think I gave genuine concern and even sometimes stated, "I am concerned" or "I care." And what we focus on often depends on the family. What is going on in that family? And I try to be available to listen to whatever is going on in that family's life that the parent chooses to tell me. As I listen, I make sure I give them eye contact and sometimes even restate what they have said to help them know I understand.

Ernestine sees genuineness, concern, caring, and active listening as central to her relationships with parents. The parents feel her genuine concern and caring because often they share whatever is going on in their family life—a clear sign of their trust. Although she always enters a home with activities and ideas to discuss with parents, she is quick to adjust her agenda when parents want to share their concerns. Mutuality is a part of these relationships, as both parent and home visitor control the agenda of the visit.

Janice discussed how she tries to praise the family members while she strives to help them trust themselves and "feel strong in what they do." Extended observations of Janice's home visits illustrate her approach:

Greg (age 19 months) is playing with a large tub of beans and assorted spoons and cups. As he puts a spoon into a cup, he says, "Spoon in cup." His mother, Karyn, repeats his statement.

Janice says, "You are so good at saying his words." As she praises Karyn, Janice provides developmental information and developmental interpretation: "Then, he hears the correct pronunciation. He knows you understand him, and you are encouraging him to talk."

Greg's parents explained how they would describe Janice to a friend who knew nothing about PAT.

Karyn: She is the best, like a surrogate mother to me. She is warm, and I always feel comfortable with her. She is so encouraging. And I feel free to call her when I need her helpful knowledge, even though we have moved out of the district. I don't have enough words for her. She is very warm—like a friend. And she gives information in a way that you can accept or reject it.

Don: And she has a genuine interest in Greg. She doesn't lecture. She tells you what she thinks—not "go do this or that." And when playing with Greg, I used to take the lead. Now, Greg takes the lead, for Janice taught me that he could feel more connected and accepted if he took the lead.

Karyn and Don described Janice as warm, comfortable, and easy to talk to; they see her as a friend who has a genuine interest in their child and some-one who they can call when needing help. They acknowledge that Janice shares a wealth of information, yet the parents choose what they think is relevant for their family. Although Karyn and Don are aware that Janice has influenced their parenting, they also feel that they are the decision makers.

From this discussion of home visiting, several themes arise that are impor-tant to forming personal relationships between parents and home visitors. In good parent–home visitor relationships, the home visitor should

- Show genuine concern and caring
- Be "warm," as if relating to a friend
- Actively listen to whatever the parents choose to discuss
- Be nonjudgmental and validating, praising the parents' actions when appro-priate
- Allow and encourage the parents to be the decision makers[14]

SHARED DELIGHT IN THE CHILD

When home visitors show they enjoy playing with a child or delight in a child's new skill, parents experience it as affirmation of themselves. Janice consistently expresses her delight in a baby's or young child's achievement. As Erin easily puts together a puzzle, Janice tells Erin's mother and father, "I can't tell you how exciting it is to see how she just does it with such ease for her young age!" Erin's father, Rob, shared his experiences with Janice:

[Janice] is so enthused about what Erin is doing. It's not like a job to her, I don't think. I think it's just something she really enjoys doing, and she gets paid for it. The last time you both [Janice and Carol] were here, and Erin [age 25 months] started jumping rope—and the surprise that came over both of your faces when she started jumping. When you left, we were like, "Did you see their faces?" Like it was no big deal to us.

Janice spoke of how important it is for parents to know that she enjoys their child as much as they do; she sees this enjoyment as helping them feel closer to her. When she has her final visit with each family, Janice shares her pleasure and appreciation with parents. On this last visit, she gives parents a summary sheet that highlights one thing from each of her visits. She explained this process to me:

On the summary sheet, I write, "Thank you for sharing this special time in your life with me," and then some little blurb about their child and that they are doing a good job as a parent. I'm really sincere in saying that. I enjoy going and seeing them. And it is a special time in their lives. And they have every right to keep it private, but they have shared it with me, and I appreciate that.

Janice understands that she can connect most readily with young parents through her genuine enjoyment of their children. As she celebrates a baby's or young child's accomplishment with parents, she also is encouraging the parents' skill in observing their child's development.

When parents consistently experience a home visitor's enjoyment and delight in their child, they often enjoy telling their home visitor stories of happenings between visits. Several parents have told me that they always can tell Janice stories about their child because they do not feel as if they are bragging. As Shelly stated, "If I tell somebody else, they'll just think I'm trying to show off my child, but I know Janice really cares and really enjoys Erin in the same way as I do." Given the close bond Rob and Shelly feel toward Janice, they eagerly tell her about family happenings—a trip to their uncle's farm, a family birthday party, a parent's illness—in a manner reminiscent of sharing with a relative who has stopped by for a visit. As they describe these events, they often invite Erin to tell Janice about some specific aspect of the event, and Erin usually does so in a simple manner typical of toddlers.

GRANDPARENTS

As families have changed, so has the role of the grandparent in the family. Grandparents may have to relate to their child and grandchildren in ways their own grandparents never imagined. Their child may be a homosexual parent, unmarried, divorced, living in a blended family with stepchildren, or living with someone who is not the biological parent. The grandparents may even be the primary caregivers for their grandchildren. Home visitors often can assist parents and grandparents in defining roles, understanding each other, and learning ways of positive interaction.

In recent decades, many fathers have assumed new roles. So, too, grandfathers may have adopted new roles. Contemporary grandfathers understand that being nurturing is a positive virtue. They wish to and do show love to their grandchildren, and are often indulgent in ways they never would have been with their own children. Often the special role of grandparents in children's lives can be limited by geographical distance, but ingenious ways have been created to ensure connectedness when living far away from grandchildren. The telephone and Internet are often a vital link. Grandparents can send letters or audio and video recordings or can even have live video conversations via the computer. Home visitors can assist both parents and grandparents in devising ways to stay connected across distances.

In a study of 4-year-old children's contact with grandparents of biological parents, single mothers, and stepparents,[15] no differences in how often children saw their grandparents were found between family types. Children who had greatest closeness to their grandparents showed fewer emotional and behavior problems in all three types of family systems. Closeness to maternal grandparents was linked to better child adjustment than closeness to paternal grandparents. Closeness to grandparents was found to be especially protective for young children born at risk.

The joy of grandparenting includes seeing your own child parent. Wightman illustrated:

> The privilege of watching your own child interact with her baby is unlike any other.... Watching my daughter as a mother and witnessing her capacity to be available, responsive, and sensitive to her baby—without any help from me—has become a deep pleasure.[16]

Today more grandparents than ever are raising their grandchildren. Home visitors may have these grandparents, who are often of low income,[17] in their caseload. In fact, the median income of families in which grandparents raise their grandchildren is half the median income of traditional households with children.[18] Often these grandparents can qualify for Temporary Assistance for Needy Families (TANF) and other government programs such as Medicaid; Special Supplemental Nutrition Program for Women, Infants, and Children (WIC); and Head Start.

Regardless of their economic status, for grandparents to comfort a small child at 2 a.m., assemble a toy, or supervise playing children may be more challenging at age 60 or 70 years than it was at age 25 or 30 years. Just as home visitors work with young parents, they can work with these grandparents to provide them with both child development information and appropriate parenting information.

FATHERS

Home visitors do not always find it easy to include fathers in their home visits. Children can have biological fathers or social fathers (e.g., male relatives, friends, their mother's romantic partner) who vary widely in their levels of involvement with the children. Fathers in one study spoke about enjoying their children and feeling that being a father made them become better men.[19] They tried to steer their children in the right direction, and they genuinely wanted to be there for their children, something that did not occur in the childhood of several of the men. Divorced fathers felt obligated to provide financial support for their children, often "in-kind" support such as paying rent, buying food, and buying clothing. Unemployment prevented some fathers from meeting their financial obligations, which they blamed on themselves.

Janice always tries to conduct her first home visit at a time when both mother and father can be present. When she gives just the mother the handout, she urges her to share it with the child's father. Some mothers who I observed during Janice's home visits enjoy telling Janice about how the father plays with the baby or what concerns the father may have. Many home visitors work in the evening or on Saturdays so that they can meet with both mothers and fathers. Given the increasing number of working mothers of children younger than 3 years of age, evening and Saturday visits may be essential. When a father is involved in a visit, he should be actively involved in conversation with the home visitor and playing with the child along with the mother.

WORKING WITH PREGNANT MOTHERS AND THEIR FAMILIES

Becoming pregnant and having a baby is one of the most transforming experiences a woman can have. Throughout pregnancy, selfhood is often redefined. Women experience changes in their relationships with their body, partner, parents, and other significant people in their lives. If a woman is working, she is confronted with a host of decisions regarding whether she will continue to work and in what manner.

Prenatal Care

Primary goals of prenatal care are the health of the mother, prevention of preterm labor, and prevention of infant low birth weight. Home visitors' first task with pregnant mothers is to provide support, encouragement, and shared delight. They can also be a source of very helpful information. They can help pregnant mothers learn how to safeguard their own health, such as by avoiding alcohol, tobacco, and other drugs; getting regular exercise; attending prenatal visits; and eating nutritious meals. The home visitor can encourage parents to learn about any family history of birth defects, hereditary conditions, miscarriages, or unexplained stillbirths.

Home visitors also can tell parents that their attachment to their baby begins as soon as they begin to feel a connection to their fetus. The stronger the parents' attachment is to their baby prenatally, the more secure the baby will be after birth. By the 24th week of gestation, babies begin hearing.[20] It has been shown that relaxing music can calm both mothers and their fetuses.[21] Home visitors can help parents understand that fetal hearing can be a direct avenue for attachment.

When home visitors begin working with families in the early stages of pregnancy, they can ensure that mothers gain appropriate prenatal care. As they visit the pregnant mother, they can discuss physician's visits and the baby's development in utero. They can also ask open-ended questions to motivate pregnant mothers to share any stresses or changes they may be experiencing. For first-time pregnant mothers, the home visitor can explain the usual schedule of visits to the physician.

HOME VISITORS' RELATIONSHIP WITH TEEN PARENTS

The United States has the highest teenage birth rate of any Western industrialized nation,[22] with almost 1 of 10 girls between 15 and 19 years old becoming pregnant each year.[23] Home visitors are thus very likely to encounter families with teen parents, so they need to understand the developmental characteristics of both the adolescent parents and their children. Many teens lack adult under-standing and skills, whereas others had to grow up early and may be wise be-yond their years. While being a parent to their baby or young child, teenage parents are in the midst of characteristic adolescent issues, such as striving for independence from their families and longing for peer companionship.

Teens often have difficulties establishing appropriate boundaries with their babies and young children. The teen mother's mental health and intelli-gence are two factors that affect her maternal skills, responsiveness to her baby, and perceptions of the baby.[24] Poorer quality parenting is also associated with rapid subsequent pregnancy.[25] Having a baby often interferes with a teenager's education, and so limits his or her economic self-sufficiency. Teenage parents often share the characteristics of lower SES families,[26] such as difficulties of ac-cessibility and multiple external and internal problems. Many home-visiting ap-proaches with teenagers, such as the PAT approach, are similar to those used when working with families with lower SES. Like lower SES families, teenager-parented families are not all alike, with some managing better than others.

Such as with parents experiencing multiple stresses, a teenage parent's im-maturity and needs may be so great that he or she may not recognize the child's needs. Especially at the outset, a home visitor's conversation may have to be teen centered rather than baby centered. The home visitor's role often expands to include counselor, referral source to community resources, friend, role model, and surrogate parent,[27] as Carrie explains:

We wear two hats—surrogate parents and parent educators aiming to provide developmental guidance. We have a dual approach, but both are one. Our teens always have their own agenda. They mostly are interested in meeting their own needs, which can be gigantic. One of our most difficult challenges is to move from parent need to focus on the parent's child. We understand that as we move mother along, we bring her baby along. As we help moms feel their feelings, they can recognize their babies' feelings—that the best way to understand their tod-dlers' fear is to understand their own fear. And whenever a teen is in crisis, we are their referral source. Recently, a pregnant girl was badly malnourished, her hair was coming out, and she had massive headaches. Six months ago, she had had an abortion [and now was pregnant again]. Addressing this teen's immediate needs took me 2 hours. These crises make our work very episodic.

Many teen parents' childhood homes often have characteristics of trou-bled families: disorganization, family conflict, poverty, and/or substance abuse.[28] Given their immaturity and social-emotional problems, many of these teens have difficulty reading the language of their babies' behavior. Is the baby crying because he is hungry, tired, or merely trying to make the teen upset? Cynthia knows that if she is going to help a teen parent, she must have a per-sonal relationship with that parent.[29]

In working with these teen families, the key is time and number of contacts, be-cause the more you are there, and the more you get to know that parent, and the more you can connect with the parent as a person in her own right, not as the mother of a child, the more you can have a personal relationship. The relationship is the key. And once you can establish that you see them as a person and one of their roles as a human being is to be a mother of this child, but that they have other things that they do that you care about, that helps.

Changing Family Roles

Adolescence is a time of transition. Teen parents must redefine themselves as parents at the same time they redefine their relationships with their own parents and siblings. Because most teen mothers have limited money,[30] they tend to live with members of their childhood family and do not marry their babies' fathers.[31] Strain is added when a teenage daughter adds a newborn to the family, and conflicts arise.

Although home visitors strive to focus their work on the teen mother, it is important that they also relate to the grandparent(s) whose home they are visiting and who often is a central player in child rearing. This process is a difficult balance of strengthening the young mother's role while respecting and affirming the grandparent's role. Cynthia discussed how she approaches these families:

When you have a teen parent and her mother at odds, in conflict over how to raise that baby, that gets real sticky, and you have to be very careful. One of my rules of thumb is always talk to the parent of the child, the teen. I will direct my talking to the teen parent. If the grandmother is there and offers things, I will interact with the grandmother. But I always try to come back to the parent of the baby and reinforce that role. A lot of times teenagers really don't want to be the parent of that baby, and it is easier to let grandmother take over—and grandma takes over, and sometimes that causes tension. Yet, there are some extended families where everyone works pretty well together to raise that child.

The task becomes even more difficult when the home visitor's views contradict those of the grandparents. Home visitors do not want the teen mother to feel caught in the middle or for the grandparent to feel threatened. There is no ready solution in these situations. Expressing respect and genuine interest and actively listening to all family members is helpful. Janice shared her approach in these situations:

I try and help parents recognize and value the grandparent's perspective because many times young parents will talk with you about the frustration they feel about the grandparent spoiling their baby or being overly intrusive or any number of things. What I always try to do is to frame it in terms of the grandparent's love and interest... if there is a way the parent can think about it in terms of a loving relationship, even if it is an uncomfortable loving relationship, if they can think about it as love. And yes, it is still their baby, and they still have the power to do things their own way, but acknowledge the grandparent's perspective.

I remember one teenage mom whose child was getting to the age of wanting to touch and explore, and the grandmother was determined that this coffee table was going to stay where it was with the artificial flowers on top, and the child would learn not to touch it. I empathized with the mother, and as it played out over several months, the mom would say to me, "When I am here by myself with the baby, I move all that stuff up. When my mom is here, we have to have it down. But those are the times that I try to take the baby somewhere else to play or try to stay closer to her." Then, after several months, I went back, and everything was gone. The grandmother just joked about it, "Yeah, we just sort of got rid of the whole thing." How they worked that out internally in their family, I don't know, but I felt my role was to try to encourage the mom to talk continually with her parent and make this a mutual decision allowing for the child's safety and exploration in whatever way they could work it out in that family.

Janice knew that the baby's grandmother was engaged in the baby's care and needed to be recognized and valued. Janice gave the teen mother support and developmental information and encouraged her to discuss her baby's needs with her mother when there was a disagreement between them. With Janice's help, the teen was able to be the decision maker regarding her baby.

Because problems of overcrowded space and the many extended family members interrupting a home visit can be common with teen families, it may be more effective to conduct visits out of the teen's home. In these situations, often the most productive work with the teenage parent is in more neutral territory, such as the teen's high school or the home visiting program's office. At the same time, effective home-visiting programs also try to reach the extended family members. Some home-visiting programs have found that grandparent support groups are useful for giving grandparents a setting to meet each other, express their frustrations, and gain support and possible ideas to improve their relationships with their teenage children. One home-visiting program has monthly meetings for teens and their entire extended families with transportation, dinner, and child care. Then, adults attend three 20-minute sessions offered by a variety of social service and health professionals in the community, such as one session on health resources in the community, one session on guidance and discipline of young children, and one session on sibling rivalry.

Need for Expression

Teenagers often do not express themselves in mature ways and need help with social skills. Beyond home visiting, home visitors may meet weekly in small groups with the teens at their school. Carrie and Diane described their work with teens.

Carrie: They have a real difficult time expressing themselves and usually are not sure what the problem is, so one of our jobs often is just to observe behaviors. For example, a mother who normally talks all of a sudden seems very quiet and is kind of off by herself, away from her friends. That usually indicates she is dealing with a pretty heavy problem. So we might approach her and ask an open-ended question, and then she shares with us her problem.

You usually can tell that they are trying to express themselves, but often there is so much anger in their family that they start screaming at each other. Mother, the daughter, and the baby's daddy will start hollering, and then they get real depressed because they never have been able to convey what they needed to express. So, in group we talk a lot about what did you really want to say, and we talk about the different ways of being able to say it.

Diane: And with many of our mothers, we try to get them counseling. Social skills play a big part in what we do—what is the appropriate way to act. You know, a lot of our teen mothers feel like they don't have a family. The majority of these kids sort of have been left on their own to raise themselves, and it is amazing! When you talk to them about how they want to raise their babies differently, their ideas often are more structured than the home life they came from.

Work with teen parents can be astonishingly draining, and Carrie appreciates having another teen-parent home visitor, Diane, with whom she can share problems, strategies, and successes. Carrie and Diane also gain assistance and support in their weekly 2-hour staff meetings. Providing support and professional development to home visitors is essential for providing quality service.[32] Even though the job can seem endless, teenage parents do benefit greatly from home visiting. Terry, a teen parent, explained how home visiting has helped her.

They understand you. At first, you think you are just the bad kid, and everyone is looking down on you. But they support you and tell you you're still normal. PAT has made a difference in my feelings about my son, Nicholas (24 months), because now when I think he has done something wrong, I just know that it is to be expected, and that he is not a mean kid or trying to be rotten. That's what he's supposed to be doing.

It is also important to remember that teenage parents are not a unified group in our society; some teen parents are more mature and better able to handle the responsibility of parenting than others. Cynthia sees the fact that a teen parent joined Even Start as indicative of some maturity because Even Start focuses on gaining a high school diploma in addition to parenting a young child.

The teens I am working with are ready to leave and are trying to get out of their [childhood] home. They are 17 or 18, for the most part. Many of the teens we have in Even Start are not living with their parents; rather, they are bouncing from house to house. In these instances, they are in control and are assuming the role of parent, in the sense of making a decision of where that child is going to be.

But what they tend to do is drop their child off at different places, a friend watches the child for a day, an aunt watches the baby for a day, or a boyfriend, which is difficult for the child as well as the teen parent, yet it is hard to generalize. We have another teen mom who moved out of her home because her mother is an alcoholic and abusive, so the teen took her two kids and left. She is 18 years old. She tried living in shelters for a short period of time, got a part-time job, and now has her own apartment.

MOTHERS AND CHILDBEARING DAUGHTERS

Families with multiple generations of early childbearing usually have 13–17 years between parent and child.[33] The adolescent is legally and developmentally a child, but with the birth of her baby, she is also a young adult. Similarly, her younger adult mother has prematurely moved to the status of grandmother. This premature shifting of stages sometimes leads to mothers and their adolescent daughters relating to each other like siblings. These mother–daughter relationships often become tense because the mothers struggle with simultaneously maintaining emotional closeness with their daughters while pushing them into adulthood. The mother's anticipation of additional child care responsibility may affect her perceptions of closeness and introduce conflict in her relationship with her adolescent child-mother.

Poverty is associated with more physical and psychological dangers.[34] Extended families with grandparents, aunts, and/or uncles complicate relationships. Low-income families often have to deal with violence within their community and are more likely to engage in domestic violence. When home visitors work with at-risk low-income families, they need to ensure their own safety. It is important to notify their administrator before and after a visit, have a cell phone, and have all materials ready immediately on arrival to the home.

DIFFICULTIES AND DILEMMAS

Home visitors encounter some parents with whom it is very difficult to develop a meaningful relationship and thereby assist them. Two types of parents who are very challenging to work with are 1) parents who are unmotivated and minimally involved with their child and 2) parents whose inner turmoil impedes their awareness of their baby's emotional and developmental needs.

When a parent is unmotivated and minimally involved with his or her child, this parent also probably will not remain in the room during a home visit. Working with these parents can be very demoralizing to a home visitor, who has to be ingenious to capture the parents' attention. In reality, these often are parents who themselves were reared in a troubled family with minimal parenting and probably are somewhat depressed or in some other way overwhelmed by their ongoing problems.[35] For these parents, their young toddler may be viewed as intrusive and they get little joy from parenting.

With unmotivated, minimally involved parents, forming a trusting personal relationship can take extended time and repeated visits. Without a personal relationship, the home visitor will never gain the parent's trust or involvement in the home visit. Cynthia's discussion of her experience with unmotivated, minimally involved parents provides some guidelines for working with this type of family.

You may have a parent who sees the child as a burden and wants nothing to do with the child. I have worked with some moms, especially younger moms, who have that attitude but not so much that at some point I can't get them to interact with their child. It all depends on time and the number of contacts you have with the parent. As you get to know that parent, you care more about her as a person and get more involved in your visit.

As I get to know the parent and establish the relationship, and as trust builds, I sometimes get real directive. If they walk out of the room, I just yell, "I need you in here. Help!"—that kind of thing. I may say, "This child is driving me nuts. You need to come help me"—something that is kind of funny. And they'll come back and not leave me.

Last year, I worked with a mom who saw her child as a pain in the rear, an imposition. It was a real challenge to work with her. Often, I had to say, "I need you to come back in here with me. This is for you, too, and not just for your child." I would have to be directive. Once I got her back in, I would find a way to relate to her, not necessarily as a mother, but "How is your job?" I have found that when both child and parent are together, the child usually is trying to relate to the parent, whether the parent is connecting or not. And I can use that, "Did you see the way she looked at you? Look at that. Look, she wants you to see what she is doing." Most parents can't resist that.

And sometimes I speak for the child. For example, this mother would deliberately hurt the child. When the child put her hand down to feel the xylophone, the mother took the stick and hit the child's hand with it. And I said, "Oh, mom, that hurt me. I was just trying to feel what this was like." And the mom looked at me and said, "That tap didn't hurt her." But what it did was stop the child's play, so I talked about that a little. I said, "It may not have hurt her but, you know, she is not interested in it any more." You have to be careful and not say, "What did you do that for?" or "Look at what you did." At the same time, you have to help parents see how their actions and interactions with their child make a difference. It is difficult, but you have to keep working at it.

Cynthia understands that when she works with an unmotivated, uninvolved parent, she first must connect with the parent as a person, not as a parent. She lets the parent know that she knows the parent does other things and has other interests and problems. She is interested in relating to the parent as a person. Once she develops a personal relationship, she uses several strategies to work with the parent. At times, she is directive. She speaks for the child because she knows that some parents do not understand that their behavior has an effect on their child. Other times, she points out when the child is approaching the parent. Often, these parents are so shut down that they are not aware that their child seeks their attention. Most important, Cynthia is persistent and confident that, with time, she can develop a personal relationship with most parents and thereby begin to help the parent. At the same time, Cynthia recognizes that some parents never will be open to working with a home visitor. Despite her extensive experience, Cynthia finds accepting this reality to be very difficult.

Some parents rarely focus on the baby as a separate individual because their inner turmoil impedes their awareness of the baby's emotional and developmental needs. Unwittingly, the baby becomes a participant in the parent's conflictual experience. In other words, the baby becomes representative of a figure within the parent's childhood. Most often, the parent has negated or repudiated this figure, possibly a very harsh mother or a father who sexually abused the child.[36] Fraiberg used the metaphor "ghosts in the nursery" to speak of this parent–baby dynamic.[37] During psychotherapy, the therapist provides for the parent a corrective attachment that can be a vehicle for the parent's conflictual internal representations of self in relationship to the parent's original problematic attachment figure.[38] In this type of therapy, the baby always is present, most often on the mother's lap. The baby's behavior is a powerful aspect of the therapeutic intervention.

CONCLUSION

This chapter has discussed the formation and progression of parent–home visitor relationships. Two very skilled home visitors, Janice and Cynthia, shared their experiences in establishing and developing relationships with parents, and several parents shared how they view these women. These parents spoke of Janice and Cynthia as their friends, their surrogate mothers, and their confidantes. Janice and Cynthia related that in their work it is the parents who are the experts about their child and who are the decision makers regarding how they parent their child. These home visitors explained that they can assist parents' decision making only if they have a personal relationship with them. Parent development occurs through and within parents' relationship with their home visitor, just as child development occurs through and within the child's relationship with his or her parent.

The process of developing relationships is different for different people, but this chapter points out some common themes: the importance of a trusting relationship between parent and home visitor; discussing expectations, tasks, and roles; and maintaining boundaries of involvement. Also discussed is working with families who are parented by teenage mothers. Beyond developing a personal relationship, home visitors use many different approaches to promote parenting. Chapter 2 discusses approaches in effective home visiting.

The Home Visitor's Approach

In our endeavor to understand reality we are somewhat like a man trying to understand the mechanism of a closed watch. He sees the face and the moving hands, even hears its ticking, but he has no way of opening the case. If he is ingenious he may form some picture of a mechanism which could be responsible for all the things he observes, but he may never be quite sure his picture is the only one which could explain his observations.

Albert Einstein and Leopold Infeld
(1938/1996, p. 31)

ONCE THE HOME VISITOR has developed the personal relationship with parents that is described in Chapter 1, he or she can effectively approach the primary purpose of most home visiting programs—helping parents to understand their child's development and improve their parenting skills. When home visiting is effective, parents see themselves and their child from a whole new perspective and interact with their child in new ways.

This chapter discusses approaches that promote effective home visiting in three parts. The first part explores communication and interpersonal skills that encourage, maintain, and promote the parent–home visitor relationship:

1. Individualizing across families

2. Establishing respect and rapport

3. Providing empathic listening and support

4. Listening actively

5. Using I-messages

6. Engaging in observation and offering descriptive affirmation

7. Modeling

8. Sharing developmental information

9.   Making developmental interpretations

10. Offering suggestions within context

11. Questioning

12. Solving problems

13. Promoting active parent involvement

14. Being comfortable with silence

15. Achieving streams of interaction: balancing and initiating

The second part of the chapter discusses five additional skill areas that are essential to effective home visiting:

1.   Promoting informal support through social networks

2.   Networking with community agencies, institutions, and organizations

3.   Promoting the program agenda

4.   Maintaining efficient organization and management

5.   Being aware of legal and ethical issues

The chapter concludes with the third part, which focuses on difficulties and dilemmas that emerge when working with parents who are concrete thinkers or with families who live in chaotic conditions.

COMMUNICATION AND INTERPERSONAL SKILLS

This section describes 15 aspects of communication; however, in reality, these aspects often work together to form the whole. For example, home visitors cannot listen empathically unless they respect parents; they cannot give helpful developmental interpretation of a child's action unless they are keen observers and are knowledgeable about child development. Furthermore, communication is more than just language. For babies and young children to learn to communicate, they must have experienced repetitive daily give-and-take exchanges with their parents and other caregivers. For parents and home visitors to communicate, they must have a relationship grounded in mutual respect and trust and their conversations must express such mutuality.

The home visiting process is the organic unfolding of a relationship. Recipes do not work. Even for the experienced home visitor, the home visiting process is unique to each family as it develops over time. Home visitors can improve their skills through experience, reflection, and constructive feedback from peers, mentors, and supervisors. Thus, underlying this discussion is a paradox. Some of these communication and interpersonal skills are essential to forming the parent–home visitor relationship, yet a relationship takes time to develop; the parents and home visitor need to have a trusting relationship before some of these approaches can be effective.

Individualizing Across Families

Effective home visiting requires an individualized approach to address each family's distinctive patterns. Each family has its own routines, problems, values, standards of behavior, and priorities. When home visitors understand that each family is unique, they can use their observation skills and extended conversations with parents to guide their work. For example, once a home visitor becomes aware of a mother's unique style of interaction with her baby and the activities that they enjoy, then the home visitor can support the mother's participation in these activities with her child.

To individualize, home visitors also look beyond the everyday patterns of the family to understand the family's connection with extended family members, their neighborhood, workplaces, and so forth. For example, when a grandmother is very close to the baby's mother and regularly provides child care, the home visitor should encourage the grandmother to participate in the visits and include discussion of the grandmother in conversations with the baby's mother. When a child is enrolled in a child care program, the home visitor can invite parents to talk about their experiences with and feelings about the program. Not only do home visitors make adaptations in their approaches for different families, but they must also make adjustments as families change and require a new approach. Janice spoke with me about her perspective on individualizing across families.

Janice: You have to know that when you step through the door, you may find something that is totally different than what you anticipated. It could even be a family that you have visited for 2 years, and you can walk in, and the mom may look different, she talks different, she may simply be different from what she has ever been before. The child may be behaving differently and you know that something is going on with her. I have to change. I have to step back and listen, listen to what it is that is happening in this home right now.

The cues usually come from the parents. You must be able to read their signals. You also must be able to read what the child's needs are at the time. Development may be entirely different than what you anticipated when you came through the door. This is especially true when you are working with a family that has had a premature baby because those babies really are on a different time schedule. You may think that they are going to be developmentally at such a stage because the child was age 3 a month ago, and that is what you expected. And they may be far more advanced than you had expected. There is an incredible call for flexibility.

If you have not been able to blend the parent's agenda with your agenda, you might as well not be there. There are certain things that you want the parent to have access to, such as appropriate expectations for a child at this stage of development. But if that's not what is high on her agenda, pick out the one or two key points you want to get through and forget the rest, and spend most of your time addressing what are her issues for that day, and do the best you can with that. That's why it is incredibly important to be prepared and to know the range of things that are likely to come up with parents and their whole family, really.

Carol: As I listen to you, I sense the ever-expanding lens that your have from your extended experience with a large range of parents and your understanding of the range of parent development and not just child development.

Janice: That's true, but on the other hand, you can pretty quickly pull in the range of things likely to come up. Because it is just not that much. You know, if I think about what it takes to work with families that have 2-year-olds, there are likely to be only so many issues that they are going to be facing. I may go to a visit thinking that I am going to talk about toilet training, and the issue the parent wants to discuss is about the child's nightmares. Well, I'll put my issue aside for the next visit, for we are going to talk about nightmares. And I know that this is an appropriate topic within the 2-year-old time frame; so I shift topics.

Although home visitors should enter each home with a planned agenda, they need to be able to quickly adjust when either the child is behaving unusually or the parents have issues they want to discuss. Parent-initiated agendas always need to come first; acknowledging this communicates respect, affirmation, and support. Parents integrate knowledge into their decision making most readily when they raise the issue themselves. A home visitor who is experienced and knowledgeable in child development knows the range of behavior and potentially problematic issues for each period of development. When parents introduce a concern not on the home visitor's initial plan, the visitor needs to work with the parent to understand that concern and assist the parent spontaneously. At the same time, the home visitor needs to realize that when parents initiate discussion of a concern that the visitor does not feel equipped to address, he or she should listen, support, and when appropriate, suggest another professional with expertise in the area of the parent's concern. This issue of professional boundaries is discussed in Chapter 1.

Establishing Respect and Rapport

When home visitors communicate that they value and accept parents, parents feel they are respected. When parents feel some mutual understanding, agreement, and connection with their home visitor, the home visitor has established rapport. A home visitor's first task is thus to find a common ground with the parent and thereby begin to develop rapport. Cynthia described the various topics she discusses in a first visit: she may comment on something she sees in the home, what the parent or child is wearing, or even television programs or movies. When home visitors have informal conversations with parents, they help parents feel at ease and connected with them. In this process, home visitors convey respect and genuine interest in parents.

When a home visitor has been working with a family for some time, the first few minutes of conversation often are a continuation of a topic discussed in a previous session. For example, Cynthia knew that Sally's mother-in-law, who lives with Sally, just began a new job. On arrival, Cynthia asked Sally, "How does your mother-in-law, Donna, like her new job?" Her question sparked a brief conversation about Donna's new job. Then, Sally told Cynthia about how Willy's child care teachers are trying to address the problem of him biting the other children. Cynthia first renews her bond with Sally, then discusses Sally's concern.

When Cynthia enters a home, she also strives to let the parents know that she understands she is a guest there.

When I first walk in, it's a little awkward because the parents are not sure what to do with me or where to put me. I am aware that this is their home. I want to be invited to sit down or be told where to sit down. In my first home visits, I usually will introduce myself and tell the parents why I am there. Then, I'll say, "Where would you like me to sit?" Then, I am saying, "This is your home; you make the choice of where you want us to meet." I am somewhat direct. Then, I talk to them about some common ground like the weather, or if the child is there, we talk about the child.

Cynthia communicates respect and genuineness in her own way to the parents with whom she works. She is skilled at removing the emotional distance between herself and the parents and thereby develops trust and rapport with them.

Empathic Listening and Support

Empathic listening and support are intertwined in home visitors' interactions with parents throughout their home visits. As they carefully listen, home visitors try to see things from the parent's perspective and recognize the parent's feelings. When Sally tells Cynthia that her 20-month-old son, Willy, had a 104-degree fever over the weekend, Cynthia comments, "That's scary." When Karyn told Janice that she took Greg (age 9 months) to the eye specialist because he had been scratching his eyes, but the specialist could discover no cause, Janice comments, "All kinds of medical things occur this first year. And when you are concerned, it is good to trust yourself and call the doctor." Janice and Cynthia's empathic responses give support to these mothers and communicate that they understand and value what the parent is sharing.

Once a personal relationship is formed, parents share their frustrations, ambivalence, or anxiety about their child or their parenting. As they listen, home visitors suspend judgment. Sometimes they can help parents understand that these are normal feelings experienced by many parents. Parents then feel accepted and can be more at ease knowing that their feelings are universal. Sharing one's own personal life experiences is another way of showing empathy and support. Visiting Karyn 5 weeks after her baby Greg was born, Janice had the following conversation:

Janice: How was your delivery?

Karyn: It was a C-section. He was so big. They did not give me realistic expectations of my recovery.

Janice: That was one of my big surprises! I was told what to expect of my baby, but nobody told me what my body would feel like.

Karyn: My husband, Don, took off work for 3 weeks, and that helped.

Janice: Do you have any relatives nearby?

Karyn: No, except for Don's sister, who has a 3-month-old and a 3-year-old.

Janice: That's tough, really tough. When my first was born, my mother was with me for 3 weeks. I can still remember when she drove off. Bill and I looked at each other. I almost can feel that now because my feelings were so strong.

Janice expressed to Karyn that she hears her and understands her feelings. This conversation occurred during her second visit with Karyn. Janice's empathic support and personal sharing are significant threads in establishing the rapport that is essential to her effectiveness.

When home visitors value listening, they allow ample time for parents to talk about what is concerning them, share what has happened since the last visit, respond to the home visitor's questions, or ask questions themselves. Home visiting demands total focus. A home visitor's attentiveness and body language communicate support and interest just as words do. As parents talk, home visitors sort through what is being said so that they can respond appropriately. Sometimes what the parent leaves unsaid is just as important as what is said.

Much of our talking includes telling stories. In the telling of stories, we give meaning to our lives.[1] That is, as we talk, we are thinking about our experiences and weaving our experiences into the meanings we make of our lives. When parents and home visitors have developed a personal relationship, parents talk about their child, experiences they have had with their child, and family life in general. The home visitor's ability to listen actively and empathically to what is being said not only affirms the parent's sense of well-being, but also contributes to the parent's understanding of themselves and their family. Sometimes it is even helpful to ask parents to explain a word they have used or to invite the parent to say more; this both supports and assists the parent's thinking. For example, a mother says that her new baby is well behaved. When asked to say more, the mother describes how helpful it is that her baby can sleep through the night and is not colicky, as was her first child. As she talks, the mother realizes that the issue is not her first baby's behavior, but rather that her second baby's calm temperament allows her to sleep more and to be more relaxed.

Active Listening

When the home visitor is actively listening, he or she repeats the speaker's content in different words. By doing this, the parent knows that the home visitor has heard what she is saying. For example, when a mother describes her husband's long work hours and the emerging dilemmas these work hours cause, the home visitor might say, "It sounds like you are quite concerned that Damon's work hours are so very long." In some situations, it can be helpful for the home visitor to respond to a parent's comment with a "wonderment," which is a statement that rephrases but also asks a question to encourage the parent to continue talking. For example, when a parent tells the home visitor that her baby is always bad, the home visitor can say, "I wonder when Justin is bad, what specifically does he do to make you feel he is being bad?" It might be that this young parent thinks that crying means that her baby is misbehaving. The home visitor then can help the parent understand that all babies cry and suggest what normally triggers a baby's cry.

I-Messages

Home visitors communicate effectively when they use I-messages, that is, begin a statement with "I" followed by a verb (e.g., "I am eager to know what new skills Jamal has learned during the past few weeks."). When parents hear I-messages, they do not have to second-guess what the home visitor means in her statement. When a parent tells her home visitor that her son is having problems, it is important that the home visitor respond appropriately. When the home visitor asks a closed-ended question such as "Is he fussy?" the discussion ends by the parent answering yes or no. In contrast, when the home visitor responds, "I hear that Joey is having some difficulty," she is inviting a conversation.

Observation and Descriptive Affirmation

Keen observation of both parent and child actions serves three purposes. First, by observing, the home visitor can identify positive parenting behaviors and build on these strengths. In recognizing the parents' strengths, home visitors support the parents' self-confidence and lessen any feelings of discomfort. Second, home visitors need to observe to assess the developmental level of the child and adjust their interactions appropriately. Being in the home provides an opportunity to be aware of the family's neighborhood and physical resources within their home, such as the amount of space or quality of toys. Third, home visitors can use their observations to verbally describe positive parent and child actions and, in this way, affirm the parent and child. Describing positive interactions is a more powerful and specific form of encouragement than using evaluative words such as "good" or "nice job." Drawing attention to specific positive behavior helps parents and children understand their successes rather than merely recognizing that they are pleasing the home visitor. This use of observation is termed *descriptive affirmation*. Descriptive affirmation also models an effective strategy for parents—verbally recognizing the child's positive behavior and thereby fostering the child's sense of self-worth. In other words, the home visitor builds on the parent's strengths in the same manner that the home visitor strives to help parents build on their child's strengths.

Within each home visit, Janice describes the positive behavior of both parent and child as she interacts with them.

Erin (age 31 months) is hammering golf tees into a square of Styrofoam. Her mother, Shelly, comments, "You did a good job hammering that one in."

Janice says, "That's a good way you have praised her, telling her what you are pleased about. You are hooking a little description onto your praise so that she can develop her own concept of what she did. What we want is for her to develop her own sense of pride—helping her recognize her successes."

Later in the session, Erin picks up her toy phone and gives it to her mother as she says, "Call Robbie."

Shelly says, "You want me to call Robbie."

Janice responds, "You are so good at automatically repeating and expanding Erin's speech. You probably are not even aware you are doing it. But Erin knows she is being heard and that you understand her."

Shelly says, "I remember last year when Erin began talking, you suggested I repeat but not correct her."

"That's it," Janice explains. "You are encouraging her speech and at the same time she hears the correct way to speak."

Janice has visited Shelly, Rob, and their daughter Erin monthly since Shelly's third trimester of pregnancy. Her relationship with Shelly continues, even when she is not present in the couple's home. Although Shelly no longer is aware of repeating and expanding her daughter's speech, she does remember that she had learned the skill from Janice the previous year. As Erin plays, Shelly positively describes her action. In turn, Janice affirms Shelly's parenting. When Shelly repeats and expands Erin's speech, Janice again affirms Shelly's action. Then, Janice interprets the meaning of Shelly's action in terms of Erin's development. During one home visit, my written observations documented that Janice had provided a positive description of the child's action 12 times and had given 4 examples of positive description of the parent's action. Janice explained this technique.

It comes naturally now. I don't even realize I am doing it a lot of the time. To me, it is a combination of parallel descriptive talk to support the child's action or language, but it also helps the child recognize her accomplishment. I always try to point out strong points of the parent and build on that. They are more likely to hear and remember my developmental information when I "hook it" to what they are doing.

Modeling

Modeling refers to the way the home visitor plays with the child, speaks to the child, asks the child questions, or reads to the child so that the parent can choose to imitate the home visitor. Modeling can help parents feel safe trying out new ways of relating to their child. Modeling is most effective when it is spontaneous rather than an explicit demonstration. Demonstrations implicitly place the home visitor in the expert role, thereby leaving parents feeling less than adequate. As home visitors interact with a child, they can talk with the parents about what they see happening. They can explain the meaning of the child's actions developmentally or comment positively on the child's involvement. In this way, the parents are involved and are not just observing passively.

During each visit, Janice provides a developmentally appropriate play activity for the young child. Janice actively participates in play with the child and, at the same time, maintains a dialogue with the child's parent as to the developmental meaning of the child's actions.

Janice sits on the floor with Mia (age 20 months). Janice gives Mia a cloth bag, and Mia dumps out toy kitchen items—cups, plates, utensils, pots, and pans. Mia hands Janice a plastic cup and metal lid. Janice remarks, "This lid doesn't fit on the cup. There's a pan. I wonder if it'll fit on the pan." Mia puts the lid on the pan. Janice exclaims, "The lid does fit on the pan!"

Mia picks up a fork as she says, "Fork."

Janice says, "A fork. You can take a bite." Mia puts the fork to her mouth as Janice says, "It tastes pretty good." Mia picks up the knife also, but only puts the fork to her mouth.

Janice comments to Tracy (Mia's mother), "It's interesting to note that Mia puts only the fork to her mouth."

Tracy answers, "We usually don't let her have knives."

Janice explains, "She's picked that up."

Janice picks up a cup as she suggests to Mia, "We can pretend to pour juice into my cup and drink it." Mia pours the juice and pretends to drink.

Janice continues, "Can you give Mommy some juice, too?" Janice pretends to drink from the cup as Mia pretends to pour juice into a cup for her mother.

Janice comments to Tracy, "A lot of imitating goes on at this age. Children love to role-play family activities like cooking. It's a time when they can be in charge. Pretend play is a natural way small children learn. When she gets a little older, she'll love to dress up in grown-up clothes."

Mia holds up a bottle as she says, "Open."

Janice says, "Can you open it?"

Mia answers, "I can't." Then Mia says, "Juice."

Janice says, "You are pouring juice into the cup." She asks Mia, "May I have some in my glass, please?" Mia pretends to pour into Janice's glass. Janice smiles and says, "It tastes good." Mia pretends to pour some in her cup and drink from it, and Janice comments, "You're having some, too. Let's give some to Mommy, too." Mia pretends to pour into her mother's cup. Janice then suggests that Mia cook her mother some eggs for breakfast, and the role play continues.

Throughout Janice's play with Mia, she models ways to promote Mia's emerging language: repeating Mia's words and extending them into complete sentences. She also models positive reinforcement. She describes Mia's actions and thereby affirms Mia's competence. As they play, she explains to Tracy the developmental importance of pretend play. She makes certain that Tracy also is included in the play. When Janice writes notes on this visit, she reminds herself to continue discussing Mia's spontaneous pretend play with Tracy.

Developmental Information Sharing

Effective home visitors provide information about child development and appropriate parenting practices, but do so within the context of the parent's observation of the child playing. Parents hear and remember this information when it relates to ongoing conversations or activities, such as when the information is part of a conversation the parents initiated or as part of the home visitor's observation of parent or child action. Developmental information helps parents understand their child's current behavior and anticipate the next steps in their child's development.[2] Tracy, the young mother in the previous example, explained.

Now I know the things that are going on. And things that aren't happening shouldn't be happening yet. Like, for instance, when I was worried about Mia [age 25 months] with potty training and that she wasn't doing good, Janice reassured me that they go through stages like that. Things that I don't know, she kinda helps clear up. And it's reassuring with Mia, who now is going through bad times with her temper. And Janice reassures me that they go through stages. And you will have bad times and good times. That kind of stuff reassures me.

Many parents experience concern when their child is behaving in bothersome ways or is not progressing as fast as the parent expected. When Janice explains that children go through stages that can be hard on parents but do not last forever, parents like Tracy are reassured.

Janice frequently provides developmental information as she positively comments on a child or on a parent's action.

Janice just arrived at Marta's home. As she and Marta chat about Thanksgiving, Brianna (age 7 months) crawls about the living room. Marta shares that Brianna began crawling 2 weeks ago. Janice gives Brianna an infant toy, and Brianna sits on the living room floor and begins exploring the toy.

Janice commented, "Brianna sits up so smoothly from that position. 'Miss Motor.' Her motor skills are just wonderful! One of the things that makes crawling challenging when it begins this early is that Brianna's memory is not up to her motor skills. You tell her not to touch, and she won't remember. You will need to have quite a repertoire of distraction tools to redirect her when she moves at this young age."

Janice observes Brianna's skill in moving from a crawling to a sitting position. She delights in Brianna's early motor development, and her delight communicates that she cares and enjoys this infant. Within these comments, she shares developmental information—that Brianna's memory is not as advanced as her motor development, so she will not remember her mother's directives. She also makes a simple suggestion that Marta can use distraction to redirect Brianna.

Developmental Interpretations

Within the activities and conversations of a visit, home visitors can interpret the meaning of a parent's or child's action as another way of promoting the parent's understanding. When a parent describes her toddler's new constant climbing, the home visitor can explain the developmental significance of this climbing—how the toddler's exploration is a sign of healthy curiosity and a primary way she learns about the world. Similarly, when a home visitor observes a parent's interaction with her child, the home visitor can explain the significance of this interaction. When the visitor hears a parent repeatedly state the rules, she can explain how the parent's consistent guidance is giving her toddler security so that he is able to explore and develop increasing independence. Providing developmental interpretations within the context of a home visit is a skill that develops with experience and supervision. Janice is very skilled in making interpretive comments, as she does with Natalie and her daughter Jene (age 5 months).

Natalie: Jene puts her lips out and pouts when upset.

Janice: Jene is saying, "I'm learning how to communicate. I can let you know when I'm unhappy. I don't have lots of tools yet, but I'm good with my mouth."

When Jene is lying on her back, holding a toy ring that she has in her mouth, Janice says:

Everything in her mouth. It's so good. She is curious and first learns about items through mouthing them. And there is a connection between mouthing toys and eating later on. She is getting used to different things in her mouth. It will be easier to have different kinds of table foods. Babies who are not used to lots of toys in their mouths may want only milk and mush.

Janice's interpretations of Jene's actions help her mother understand the developmental significance of these actions. Parents' understanding of the developmental meaning of their child's behavior can guide their child-rearing interactions and deepen their enjoyment of the child. When there is more than one child in the home, making interpretive comments to the children about their sibling often helps them understand one another's feelings and actions. Beyond helping the children's understanding, the home visitor is modeling effective parenting.

Janice does not educate parents in an abstract way; rather, she informs parents as she interacts with them and their children. The central focus of her visits is play activities that she initiates with the child, activities in which she is an active participant. Then, she invites the parent to join the activity.[3] Parents usually enjoy their children's delight in having two adult playmates; these positive feelings promote learning.

Contextual Suggestions

Different ways of offering suggestions communicate different messages. How parents hear a message influences their relationship with the home visitor and the effectiveness of the process. When a person gives a direct suggestion, the listener may hear authority and expertise. When a suggestion is given that does not relate to ongoing events, the listener may feel a lack of connectedness. When the home visitor wants to respect and support parents while assuring the parents that they are the final decision makers in child rearing, the visitor should be very sensitive to the manner in which suggestions are given. Janice discussed her method.

I try not to make a lot of suggestions, especially direct suggestions. Rather, I try to point out strong points of the parents and build on that. They are more likely to use these comments rather than a suggestion. If I were to give a lot of suggestions, I doubt if they would be remembered. My primary task is empowerment. I might frame a suggestion as, "Some parents have found that it helps if... " I don't want them to think I am coming in as the expert; rather, I am coming in to support them. I am under, supporting, not on top of you.

Janice strives to relate to parents as a partner, not as an expert. She often discusses a variety of methods other parents have used in similar situations. When Janice does give a suggestion, she either is answering a parent's question or concern or the suggestion is part of her observation. As Janice watches Greg (age 7 months) roll over and then get into a sitting position, she comments, "He has excellent motor coordination, the way he went from rolling to sitting. You really no longer can leave him. Have you purchased a gate?"

As their relationship develops, Greg's mother, Karyn, feels comfortable sharing her concerns about Greg (now age 27 months) with Janice.

Karyn: Greg loves to dump things into the trash, like my cookbooks. He broke one of my $30 frying pans.

Janice: It's a difficult age. He will get through this. You will get through this. He doesn't have much inner control. He is into "I want it my way."

Karyn: It's driving me crazy.

Janice: Give him his own trash can. He is at the age where he loves to put things into containers.

Janice gives Karyn support and offers a suggestion with developmental information to help Karyn understand Greg's actions. Janice described her growth in this area.

Initially, especially in my first year, when a parent would ask, "What should I do about this?" I would be quick to tell them what I thought they ought to do. I don't do that anymore. I have found it is much more effective to ask, "What have you tried?" using a whole series of questions, and then, "What else have you tried?" And very often one of the things they have tried is something that I can say, "Well that is really a good idea. I hope you take that one up." And then we talk about it. It makes them feel better if they can have ownership of the idea, if I can reinforce something that they have tried. It has more power than if I would say, "I think you should do… " And another method I use is I speak in terms of children in general: "Some children usually benefit from this, others benefit from that, and so on." Then, parents can pick out what they want without feeling threatened or without seeing me as the expert. On the other hand, if there is an issue of the child's safety, such as wearing a seatbelt in the car, I will be very direct.

In asking parents to share prior methods, Janice shows parents that they know many good ways to handle situations. When she speaks of how children benefit from different kinds of experiences, the parents become the decision makers who merely need some additional information.

Questioning

Questions are a natural part of conversation. In home visiting, open-ended questions encourage parents to talk more. Questions are open-ended when more than a yes-or-no answer is possible, such as, "What are some of the things you enjoy doing with your baby?" When a parent makes a statement, home visitors can ask a question to make sure they understand the parent, such as asking the parent to give an example. Sometimes a question can help a parent focus on specific issues that are a concern. For example, when a parent says, "He's bad all the time," the home visitor can ask the parent to give an example of this behavior. The parent hears that the home visitor is listening and wants to understand. Once examples are given, the parent and the home visitor can discuss the issue.

Especially during a baby's first year, Janice asks questions that track the baby's development. Her first few visits with Marta and her baby Brianna illustrate this pattern.

On Janice's first visit, Brianna was 4 weeks old. On her second visit, Brianna was 4 months old. Janice asked Marta, "How is she sleeping? Does Brianna turn over? How does she respond when you read her books?" On the third visit, Brianna was 5 months old. Janice asked Marta, "What sounds is she making? How does she sleep? What is her feeding schedule?" On her fourth visit, Brianna was 7 months old. Janice asked Marta, "What is her favorite thing to do? How is her eating? How does she fall asleep?"

As Janice asks these questions, she is assessing the baby's developmental strides. Often one of these questions leads to an extended conversation, for example, discussing how the baby's nighttime awakenings cause the parents' drowsiness and impatience during the day, or how the family has needed to adapt to the baby's need for regular feedings.

Problem Solving

When parents ask the home visitor a question, they often put the home visitor in the expert role and expect a quick answer. Rather than accept the expert role, home visitors can use the parents' questions or concerns as the first step in joint problem solving.[4] Not only does this joint problem solving help parents address their concern or question, but their participation increases the likelihood that they will remember the information discussed. When a parent shares a concern with Janice, she uses the situation for joint problem solving.

Shelly told Janice that Erin (age 31 months) recently had been very negative, always saying "No" when Shelly asked her to do something. Interspersed with play and conversations with Erin, the adults discussed her new pattern of negativism around toileting and hair washing.

Janice: How do you respond to Erin?

Shelly: I started the star routine on the calendar, and that's helping a little bit. Sometimes, I'm real patient, but other days [I'm not]... I finally said to Rob, "When she wants to go, she'll go." Now, I hold a star and say, "Do you want a star?" and she'll say yes, and go to the bathroom.

Janice: That's real smart.

Shelly then described the battle she and Erin had over washing Erin's hair.

Shelly: I don't want to fight with her, but I want to keep the discipline.

Janice: I think you have handled both situations positively. Kids need to understand that their parents understand their feelings, but rules are rules. The trick is to know when to ease up and when to stay firm. Are there enough situations where you can give her some space?

Shelly then described situations when she has given Erin choices and comments that she remembered how the previous year Janice had emphasized the value of giving children choices.

When parents share a concern, Janice always asks the parents how they deal with the issue. In this way, Janice has some time to think and she gains information. Furthermore, being included in the problem solving means the parent will have ownership of the solution, as Janice explains.

I always begin with "What have you tried?" And sometimes the question may change the direction of the discussion. The first issue may not be the most important issue for the parent.

Often some of the parents' actions are appropriate and Janice can affirm them. As they talk, she provides developmental information and gives suggestions.

When both parents are present, home visitors can invite each parent to share his or her understanding of the problem. Sometimes, a few questions help the parents look at the problem from a larger perspective. For example, if one parent is complaining that her son does not remain at the table during dinner, the home visitor can ask questions to frame the discussion around the family's patterns of eating dinner. The home visitor can ask parents what they would like to have happen. When focusing on desired solutions to the problem, the conversation becomes positive. During a discussion, the home visitor can help the parent understand that there usually are several ways to handle every situation. Sharing how other parents have handled a similar situation can be helpful and reassuring. As possible solutions are discussed, both short- and long-term benefits and liabilities can be identified.

Active Parent Involvement

One of the challenges of home visiting is balancing involvement with both parent(s) and child(ren). Active parental involvement increases the likelihood that parents will learn and remember child development information and child-rearing strategies presented during the visit. As parents play with their child, home visitors can help them understand the developmental meaning of a play activity and how young children learn through play. Parents will learn best through their own and their home visitor's interactions with the child and through their observations of their child engaged in activities during the visit. They will understand child development best by having it related to what their child is doing at any given moment. Janice discussed her approach as follows.

I initiate the activity with the child to provide an opportunity for modeling. Then, usually I invite the parent to join us, unless the activity is built around the child exploring something. But even then, I always end my visits with a book, and in these situations, I'll invite the parent to read the book. I want parents to feel that they are a real integral part of the visit. And also, I want to see how they interact with their child. And if a parent is very immature or developmentally slow, I take her down the path a little more slowly and with much smaller steps.

Janice understands that she promotes the parent's learning when she interacts with the parent and child. The process reinforces the mutuality of the relationship that Janice strives to maintain, as in the case of Mia.

Janice takes toy musical instruments out of a bag and says to Mia (age 36 months), "Now we're going to hear a song, and then after the song, we'll play the instruments." Janice has a small tape recorder on her lap. She helps Mia's little sister, Maggie (age 18 months), push the button and the Itsy Bitsy Spider song plays. As the song plays, Janice and the children's mother, Tracy, sing. Mia and the adults do the hand motions with the song. During the second song, Janice gives Mia cymbals, Maggie maracas, and Tracy a tambourine. She does the hand motions to the song as Tracy and the children play the instruments. The two adults and children continue the activity for about 15 minutes. As the children play their instruments, Janice comments, "Anything that promotes a sense of rhythm is really valuable. Children love this kind of activity."

Janice understands that it is important for play activities to be simple and inviting, yet having parents be active participants during a home visit is not a simple matter. First, a trusting personal relationship with the home visitor must be in place for parents to feel comfortable playing; this relationship takes time to develop. Second, many parents do not expect to play during a home visit and may feel a little clumsy at first. In fact, some parents will never play, despite of their home visitor's skill, because their definition of parenting does not include play. Promoting active involvement of the parent is another skill that takes experience to develop.

Comfort with Silence

With experience, a home visitor learns to be comfortable with periods of silence when the parent and home visitor observe the child. When parents learn that their home visitor is comfortable with silence, they know that the home visitor is relaxed, at ease, and at home with them. During these quiet times, parents often make specific observations of their child, similar to what they have seen the home visitor do on previous visits. The home visitor can affirm the parent's observation, as in the case of Asha.

Home visitor Rachel sits on the floor with 14-month-old Asha and her parents, Ronnie and Tuni. Rachel has been visiting this family since Tuni's third trimester. All three adults are silent as they watch Asha put chips into a canister with a slit in the top. After a few moments, Tuni says, "I'm amazed at how well she grasps these thin chips."

Rachel says, "It's an excellent indication that Asha has learned the pincer grasp: thumb and forefinger. That learning is important for her later learning in holding a crayon and pencil."

Streams of Interaction: Balancing and Initiating

A consistent challenge for home visitors is balancing their interactions with the parents and their interactions with the children. Home visiting involves multiple tasks, such as discussing developmental characteristics and emerging skills of the child, discussing parenting practices and issues, initiating activities with the child, and involving parents in these activities. For each visit, home visitors plan a specific activity and a developmental topic related to that activity. At the same time, however, parents and/or children may initiate a topic or activity unrelated to the home visitor's plan. Home visitors should then adjust their plans to integrate what the parent or child has initiated.

Interaction with Parents   Janice described a situation in which the mother's agenda became the theme of her visit. Her planned activity was to invite the toddler's exploration of a bag filled with assorted items and to discuss the child's curiosity and intellectual development with the mother.

This was the fifth home visit with a 2-year-old child, and his language... well he just wasn't talking very much at all. And all year long I had been very frustrated because I felt like the mother never was involved in really hearing what I was saying. Finally, yesterday his language was something she brought up, and I was thinking, "Thank goodness."

Language didn't quite fit my intent of the activities I brought, but I shifted gears to make the activity a language activity because now this was something she finally was ready to discuss and listen and try things out. And it was great! It was wonderful! I had started out using the bag of items to explore and had intended to talk about intellectual development and the value of exploration.

Well, my original intent to talk about curiosity and intellectual development became a very minor piece. I emphasized instead the adult's parallel talk and naming for the child, naming what he was pulling out of the bag and describing what he was doing with what he pulled out. I demonstrated naming and parallel talk and then got her to try it. She was a mom that was very much into asking her child questions and giving directives. Just an incredible number of questions. She couldn't even make a statement without putting it in the tone of a question.

This is not an activity I ever used in this way, but I thought, "I don't care. I'm going to have a language emphasis because finally she is ready to talk about language. She finally is ready to look at herself and see how she can encourage language development with her little boy who really needs to be talking more."

Janice was able to be flexible and adjust her original plan to accommodate the mother's expressed interest. Because Janice knows child development, she could immediately shift her topic to helping this mother learn how she could facilitate her son's language development. As the toddler pulled items out of the bag, Janice modeled methods to stimulate language. For example, she described what the child was doing as he played and encouraged the child to name the items. Given the interest and concern this mother had expressed, Janice was able to encourage her to try some new parenting approaches. Janice has a goal that her work encompasses a partnership between parents and herself. If parents are to benefit from a home visitor's work, the visitor must be ready to work with the parents to deal with the concerns they are expressing at the moment, as Janice is.

When I go into a visit, I will have a generalized plan for what I hope will happen, but I always think that it has to fit in terms also of the parents' agenda. I really don't come in with lots of details about what I am going to do in a visit, and my reason is that I want to have some control in the visit but only an element. I want a lot of control to be with the parents. If I've got in my head that I've got to talk about their toddler sharing, that might not exactly fit. I would rather talk about sharing when the mother brings up that the child cannot share with other children. I like to respond to, rather than initiate, these issues.

I can click off developmental information, but I don't think that's nearly as meaningful as pointing it out when I see it, as talking about it when the mother sees it and letting her really believe, as is the case many times, that she is seeing something first, and then we get to talking about it. However, there is also this tricky balance between having the parent bring up an issue and my letting them know in advance that a particular development is likely to occur. The difference is the scope: I mention in advance developments the parents can anticipate. We discuss it in depth when they see it and bring up the issue themselves.

Janice is steeped in developmental knowledge and appropriate parenting strategies. She knows what topics need to be covered for each developmental period, but she also understands that she can be an effective promoter of parents' understanding and skills only when the parents' lived experience gives them reason to be interested in the topic.

Interaction with Children   In addition to their involvement with parents, home visitors also must relate to young children. Beyond the activities and discussions that the home visitor and parent initiate, children also initiate activities. Child-initiated activities most often occur either at the outset of a visit or after the child is finished with the activity the home visitor has introduced. When Janice enters a home, a child may be playing with a toy or might go get a toy specifically to share with her. Janice frequently engages in play using this toys, as with Erin.

Erin (age 20 months) comes into the living room with a large plastic beach ball that she throws to Janice, who is seated on the floor. As she rolls the ball to Erin, Janice suggests, "Let's roll it." After a few exchanges with the ball, Janice asks Shelly if she has a laundry basket.

Shelly returns with a circular laundry basket that Janice places in front of her. Standing a few feet from the basket, Erin throws the ball into the basket several times. Each time she is successful, Erin jumps up and down as she says, "I got it! I got it!" Her mother hugs her as she says, "I'm so proud of you."

Janice then suggests, "Let's give Mommy a turn." Shelly first playfully bounces the ball as she says, "I have to dribble a bit." Then, she shoots a few baskets.

Janice holds the basket high as she says to Erin, "Do you want it high or low?" Erin replies, "Low" and then successfully throws the ball into the basket. As Janice raises the basket, she says to Shelly, "It's a totally different game when I put it on the floor and then lift it higher."

Janice now puts the basket on its side as she suggests to Erin, "How about rolling it like when Mommy goes bowling?" Erin does as Janice has suggested, and when the ball goes into the basket, she again jumps up and down saying, "I did it! I did it!" Janice then asks Erin to get a little ball, which Erin does. She throws it into the basket and then suggests, "Mommy's turn."

In this last sequence, Janice improvises to extend the activity with new ideas—introducing the basket, using the basket in several ways, and suggesting a different-sized ball. She encourages Erin's mother to join the play, and both mother and child express delight in the activity.[5] Janice explains her rationale for using children's toys during home visits.

One of the reasons that I like to use the children's toys is that I think I sometimes can expand on what the child does with that toy in ways that the parent might not have thought about—give them new ideas for stuff that has been around for a while. The other thing it does is it helps parents to further believe that they have made good choices in the toys they have bought for their child. Further, it lets the family realize that the things they want to be a part of the home visit are certainly as important as the things I choose. All along we are trying to promote the idea of following the child's lead, of paying attention to the child's cue. Thus, if I ignore what the child brings in, I am not practicing what I preach, so to speak.

Even the most disadvantaged family has something that their child has been playing with before I arrive. If I can, I'll use it in some way or observe the child playing with it. In cases where the toys are not appropriate, I use safe household objects that the parent probably has but hasn't designated as toys.

Achieving a balance in interacting with parents and their children is a progressively developed skill. Often, the home visitor feels that a child's initiative or a parent's question interrupts the flow. After observing how Janice was able to maintain a discussion with Tracy while having several sequences of exchanges with Tracy's 20-month-old baby, Mia, Janice explains what was going on in her mind during her discussion with Tracy.

Well, I do this deliberately, for I want the parent to see that you can acknowledge the child's desire to be a part of it and still get your point across without telling the child, "Be quiet. Wait a minute until I am finished," and so forth... that you really can juggle both roles—an adult role and interacting with the child as well. And it is a way to help the child feel a sense of being included. Because if you tell the child, "Wait a minute," the child is going to keep bugging you and bugging you and bugging you, and they're coming out looking bad instead of coming out looking good. You play with her doll for a couple minutes. They are satisfied, having been included, and then you go on with your adult conversation.

Janice knows that during each moment she is relating to parent and child, she is modeling for the parent. Often, parents have difficulty with their young child's persistent interruptions. In modeling, Janice exposes parents to a way of dealing with a child's interruptions. As parents watch, they see how their child responds. Then, the parents can decide whether what they are observing would be something they would like to try.

Inner Dialogue   When home visitors engage in conversation with parents, they should not only be aware of the content of the discussion, but also 1) their own personal feelings and reactions to the ongoing process and contact, 2) the parent's and child's feelings, and 3) whether the home visitor's culture or gender is interfering with their response. For example, when a parent describes when her 2-year-old woke up in her bed crying during the night, the home visitor should recognize her own bias about children sleeping with or separate from their parents. The bias may be based on cultural assumptions or other beliefs that the home visitor does not share with the parent.

ESSENTIAL KNOWLEDGE AND SKILLS

The second part of the chapter discusses the knowledge and skills that are essential for promoting the home visiting process. Unlike communication and interpersonal skills, these skills do not occur or interact together; therefore, each area is discussed separately.

Informal Support Through Social Networks

Social ties among parents become networks that are powerful influences in motivating behavior, beliefs, and development. Parents' social networks can provide information, emotional and material assistance, and support and encouragement of certain child-rearing attitudes and behavior, as well as role models. For infants or young children to flourish, their parents need access to support, encouragement, and assistance—all of which can be provided through social networks.[6] In other words, for parents to optimally fulfill their child's developmental needs, they need the support not only of family members within the household, but also of people in their larger network of social relations. Through these relationships, parents learn that they are not alone in their child-rearing responsibilities.

As they work with families, home visitors become sensitive to the differences in social networks of their families and the varied influences these networks have in a family's functioning.[7] Social networks can include extended family, neighbors, friends in the workplace, people who access blogs or message boards on the internet, and others with whom parents associate socially. Both relatives and friends can offer informal support and companionship to parents.[8] The size of parents' personal networks may vary greatly. A parent who is a full-time homemaker with very small children may experience isolation and accompanying loneliness. Many young parents in our society are quite mobile and may be relatively new to the community and, therefore, have minimal personal networks. In these situations, home visitors often can assist parents in developing relationships. For example, home visitors could inform parents of neighborhood playgroup possibilities, community playgroups, or "parents' day out" programs. Some home visiting programs also offer parent group meetings or parent–child sessions, both of which are excellent settings for parents to develop peer relationships. Janice described a method she has used to promote parents' social networking.

I have done a small group meeting about infancy, and mothers have come together in somebody's home, and we would talk about babies. And we would plan, maybe or maybe not, another similar meeting for this group. But what is more likely to happen is they make it happen for themselves. The kids in one of these groups are 8 or 9 years old now. I had no idea they would continue as a group. Their parents continue to get together as couples for a card club and that was strictly through their contacts in these infant groups.

The family's social network can expand to include child care staff. The demand for child care has mushroomed with the increase in single parenting and working mothers of children from birth to age 6.[9] When the infant or toddler is enrolled in a child care program, the connections between parents and child care staff become central to the child's healthy development. Young children feel secure when they hear similar messages from parents and their child care teachers. When home visitors value families' social networks, they can sensitively respond to parents' discussion of these experiences. For example, when a parent is having difficulty relating to her infant's child care teacher, the home visitor can listen empathically and engage in joint problem solving with the parent to discover possible strategies to resolve the parent's difficulty.

Extended Family and Social Support   Often, home visitors work with young parents living with their extended family in the same house, next door, or within the same neighborhood. Extended families can offer young children multiple strong emotional attachments with adults committed to their well-being.[10] For families at risk, extended families often can buffer parents and their young children from the impact of stress through, for example, the availability of child care and pooling of money for food and housing. When home visitors work with several extended families, they recognize that there are considerable differences in the way extended families are organized and relate to each other.

The home visitor's task becomes more difficult when families are more complex, as the home visit may include the extended family members. Cynthia discussed her experience.

When parents are living with extended family members, sometimes I go on a home visit, and I'll have the grandmother there or an aunt or sister there. What I usually do is leave it to the parent to decide whether or not that person stays, and it also is up to the other person who is there if she or he wants to stay. Sometimes they elect to leave. But what I find is if someone is there, especially if it is the grandmother or the aunt who is helping to raise the child, they'll stay. One of my rules of thumb is always to talk to the parent of the child. When the grandmother is there and offers things, I'll interact with the grandmother, but I always try to come back to the parent of the baby and reinforce that role. Or if it is the father, sometimes the father will be in the bathroom listening but won't come out because he doesn't want to participate actively but will stay in the bathroom and listen. And I respect his decision.

As she relates to young parents, Cynthia remembers that her role is to strengthen the parents' role as decision makers. Thus, Cynthia invites the parents to decide whether extended family members participate in the home visit. She also respects how family members may choose to be involved, whether actively or passively. When extended family members do participate, Cynthia accepts this extension; yet, she maintains her primary focus with the parent. She communicates that she values all family members' roles in rearing the child and at the same time communicates that she understands that the primary responsibility belongs to the parent.

Sometimes parents disagree with other family members about their childrearing practices and share these disagreements with their home visitor. Cynthia discussed her approach in these situations.

I have encountered families where everyone has a different approach. As I am working with the family and getting to know the people, I get a better sense of where they are coming from and what they consider important in child rearing. Any time the family has a conflict and I am working with people who have opposing views on something, I try to find a common ground. And if they are coming from the same family, there usually is a common ground. They have shared experiences, and so there is something that they both believe in when it comes to raising that child, and I try to use that as the beginning point.

Cynthia begins with the assumption that all family members have shared experiences that give them a common ground on which they all can agree. Once Cynthia and parents identify this common ground, Cynthia is able to assist family members in working through their differences. As she discusses differences with family members, Cynthia also helps them understand that young children feel secure when hearing similar messages from their family caregivers.

Janice also confronts these situations.

Parents are very likely to talk about grandparents somewhere along the line. Some do it much more often than others. Some will do it in a positive mode; some will do it feeling frustrated about their experiences.

Regardless of the parent's approach to the grandparent, I try to lay the groundwork of the grandparent's perspective. I even did that before I became a grandparent myself because I think it is important to establish that we really honor the whole family, and we understand that grandparents have a different perspective and show their love in a different way. But it doesn't mean that they should be ignored just because you have a home visitor coming in with different ideas. I try to help pull it all together, instead of pulling it apart. You can affirm the parents' role but also help them understand where the grandparents are coming from.

Janice tries to avoid making parents feel caught in the middle between their interest in the home visiting program philosophy and the rest of the family's beliefs, even though she may be providing new information and new suggestions that may be contrary to the family's beliefs.

I try to back out of that whenever and as much as is possible and let that be the parents' decision as to how to deal with the information. I might sympathize with the parent when she is going through this… As far as discipline is concerned, parents can feel caught in the middle when Dad does not agree with what Mom is doing, and Grandmother certainly doesn't agree with what Mom is doing. And Mom thinks she is trying to do something that she has learned through our program. It is easier when a parent can learn a new technique and practice that new technique on her own, before Dad is home or when Grandma is not around, and get pretty good at it. And then when Dad sees it, Mom feels very confident in passing along that suggestion because it has become her suggestion. It is not her home visitor's suggestion. It is something she has seen work with the baby, and she now wants to convince Dad.

Janice strives to help parents respect the grandparents' perspective, even when it is different from their own. Sorting through differences about discipline approaches is not an academic exercise and there is no hierarchical value to different people's perspectives. Like Cynthia, Janice always strives to build on the parent's strength. She knows that parents can approach differences best when speaking in their own voice, based on their own successful experience.

Social Supports in the Neighborhood and Workplace   In certain settings, such as the family's neighborhood or parent's workplace, the child does not participate directly but they are significant to the parent and thus have an effect on the child. When parents have neighbors who offer companionship, support, nurturance, feedback, and connectedness, the parents then have social resources on which to draw. With this support, parents are more able to meet the needs of their infants and toddlers. With a strong neighborhood connectedness, parents feel a sense of security, belonging, and peace of mind that translates into an ease with which they relate to their young. Osofsky and Thompson identified three ways that social networks benefit parents:

1. Parents are able to gain additional information about developmentally appropriate methods.

2. Supportive networks offer tangible resources such as child care and money.
3. Networks serve as buffers against maladaptive parenting and stress from life situations.[11]

When parents experience support and affirmation at their workplace, they are able to return home and give full attention to their family. When they experience tension or vulnerability at work, they are not as well equipped to relate spontaneously to the day-to-day patterns of life with their spouse and young child.[12] Also, when parents have limited access to employment and safe neighborhoods, they also have limited opportunities for social networking. In other words, social networks can spark stress as well as support. When parents' stress is increased, this stress influences their child's development. In their conversations with parents, home visitors can explore the social support that the parent has or does not have in the neighborhood, workplace, or a religious organization.

Networking with Community Agencies, Institutions, and Organizations

Informal social networks such as extended family, friends, and neighbors provide young families with many different services. At the same time, however, families sometimes need services from more formal support systems such as child care, mental health and physical health services, public aid and housing, juvenile justice, or shelters for homeless families or battered women. These resources are formal services offered both by government agencies (e.g., the Women, Infants, and Children program), private nonprofit organizations (e.g., Alcoholics Anonymous), and private for-profit companies (e.g., a child care center run as a for-profit business).

Chapter 1 examined the need for home visitors to know what they can do and what they are unprepared to handle, recognizing the boundaries of the program's agenda and the home visitor's expertise. When parents initiate discussion about personal troubles or external difficulties beyond the home visiting agenda and home visitors' expertise, home visitors can listen empathically and assist the parent in getting help from resources within the community. Before home visitors can connect parents with the appropriate community resources, they must become familiar with community resources.

If the administration of a home visiting program is committed to community networking, the home visitor should already have information and resources available. One Parents as Teachers (PAT) program in a suburban, multicultural, multi-income district illustrates integrating community resources into a home visiting program. Mariam Skoten, Director of Early Education, discussed her program's use of community human services.

I believe our district's early childhood programs are simply part of a big pie. Therefore, we often become a hub of referrals. Sitting on my staff now is a social worker [Jill] who has an adjunct position with the county department of mental health. This department offers services free of charge to school districts. And this social worker is housed at the well-baby clinic in our area. Thus, she serves as an intermediary to the health care provider that many of our families utilize.

It's neat because when a home visitor discovers some health concerns, either vocalized by the family or a concern of the home visitor, they immediately call Jill. And Jill can network expediency of health care, for example. She can break through the bureaucratic system of public health provisions.

Also, we have used on our staff in adjunct positions, our Division of Family Service [DFS]. When a family identifies for us that they have a case worker in this agency, we alert the case worker that we now also are included, and the family gives us permission in writing to do this. And then the case worker and home visitor work together. We have had some situations where our families have been under abuse or neglect with court orders, and again, with the family's written permission, we have become involved in providing alternatives to discipline. We have had DFS workers who actually have transported parents to parent education seminars.

Another tangent that has been really interesting to us is for our teen parents to work in tandem with the public health nurse, who has been identified through the county's department of health to see teen parents judged [to be] at high risk. We work in tandem with them.

We also have connections with our local out-of-home child care centers and nursery schools. We have gotten some scholarships for our PAT general population. There are very few [special programs] in our area that offer out-of-home child care for infants, but we have gotten some scholarships.

Coordination with businesses in the community is an area [where] we need to experience growth. Kiwanis has supported us by financial contributions and increasing the community's awareness of our program. They bought our first VCR. Because we are so included in the total community, when we have a need, we just express that need to our community, and it is often filled through church contributions or donations from civic organizations such as the Kiwanis.

In order to get known, I, and our staff, did a lot of workshops. For example, I did a workshop on PAT for all out-of-home child care center directors and their guests to alert the community to what we were about. And we've sent letters to all the ministers, to all the physicians, in the community. In staff meetings, we keep emphasizing that awareness must be comprehensive, intensive, and ongoing—the community's awareness of us and our awareness of the community.

Mariam sees her district's PAT program as an integral part of the community and as a hub of referrals to human service agencies in her community. She and her staff have developed relationships with professionals in an array of agencies that potentially can serve their young families. Given her close relationships with many agencies, she is able to hire professionals from these agencies as consultants to serve as a bridge between families and the agencies. Just as an agency can provide services to promote the PAT program (e.g., providing transportation so that a parent can attend a group meeting), the PAT staff can promote an agency's goals (e.g., by helping parents learn positive discipline strategies). When community resources are integral to a home visiting program, home visitors gain needed information and support in their work.

Program Agenda

The agenda of home visiting programs varies for different program sponsors and different populations being served.[13] For example, the agenda of Boston's Patrick O'Hearn Elementary School's home visiting program, implemented by parents, is to increase parental involvement.[14] Programs with a primary health focus—such as the Prenatal/Early Infancy Project—use nurses to serve young at-risk mothers. Some programs focus on promoting the parent's role as teacher of their child, such as the Head Start home visiting program

Home visiting programs vary as to their methods of instructing home visitors on tasks and goals. Effective programs have some explicit structuring of services, ongoing supervision, and professional development meetings. PAT and the Portage Project provide home visitors with very concrete lesson plans and home visiting observation record forms.[15] In these two projects, home visitors have a lesson plan for each developmental period from birth through 60 months. When home visitors are just beginning their work, these lesson plans can be helpful guides, as they were for home visitor Lela.

When I first began, the lesson plans were my bible, and I kept them right on my desk beside the families' folders. Every time I planned a visit, I used them almost to the letter. Now that I have worked a few years, I may go back to them, especially with young babies, to check to see that I didn't miss anything. Now, I have a developmental framework and know what is appropriate for the different ages of the children.

Experienced, skilled home visitors usually have an agenda based on a developmental framework, as Janice explained.

I like [to have] an overall structure of the things I would like to cover, the major issues of each developmental phase. For example, in Phase IV (8–14 months), the major issues are parallel talk and independence. I always try to hook the developmental information to something the baby is doing. I always have a play activity and spend time playing with the child and then inviting the parent to join the play. I believe that the mom gains the most information through the child as we are doing something with that child. But my focus always is interaction.

Lesson plans initially are important tools to assist PAT home visitors. With time, their primary tool is their developmental framework. Experienced home visitors such as Janice understand that their primary tool and focus always is interaction in the context of a strong personal relationship with parents and their young children. A primary premise of this book is that no home visiting agenda can be successfully implemented without a strong personal relationship between parent and home visitor.

Efficient Organization and Management

Home visitors work with a wide range of people in a variety of settings. Given the complexity of their work, organization and careful use of time, materials, and record keeping become essential skills.

Use of Time   Home visitors coordinate home visits with schedules of individual families while allowing time for their other responsibilities, such as completion of home visit reports, supervision and staff meetings, and community networking. Given the multiple tasks and different daily schedules of parents, home visitors can benefit from careful time management. This scheduling needs to allow time for travel and record keeping. Documentation of a home visit is most accurate if done soon after the visit. At the same time, a schedule needs built-in flexibility to adapt to necessary cancellations, such as when an infant is ill.

Janice explained the rationale for limiting the number of consecutive home visits on the same day.

Doing home visiting is a very intensive thing to do... I can do four [visits in one day] as an experienced home visitor. But beyond that I do not believe I am giving a high-quality visit to the last family. In fact, I don't even feel that I am giving as good a quality to the fourth family as I did to the first. You cannot retool your own head to go from one family to another because this is intense work. Even when there are no problems brought forward, it is intense work.

The thing about a home visit [is that] you are essentially on stage every minute you are on the visit. In the classroom, you even get little children occupied for a few moments, and you can turn around and take a deep breath. In home visits with a parent and child, you have no time to take a deep breath. You must be ready to answer, ready to respond, to observe, and to interact.

Janice understands that the attention demanded during 1 hour of interaction with parents and their young children is a focus that cannot be maintained indefinitely. Over years of experience, she has discovered the maximum number of visits (four) that she can effectively complete within 1 day.

Organization of Materials   To give a family total focus, home visitors need to have organized and prepared all materials in advance of their visits. Materials can include toys for different developmental periods, parent handouts, and individual family folders. Given the variety of materials for different families, as well as materials for use within the agency, home visitors need a very clear, organized system. Not surprisingly, car trunks often provide an easy-access file, especially for toys and family folders. Janice explained her system.

I spend a lot of time at the beginning of my program year doing initial organization that will make my day-to-day work flow more smoothly. For example, I organize my individual folders for the year for each family that I am going to see. If the child is 6 months old at the beginning of a program year, I will put in not just the handouts I want to use for my very next visit but also the standard handouts I know I will be giving that family for at least 6 months, maybe 10 months. I want to get a whole set of materials in one place so that I don't have to search for handouts each time.

I know there are certain handouts I am going to use time and time again. And also, I will put key information, such as the mother's first name, readily accessible. I don't want to drive up to the house and say, "Uh-oh, what is her first name?" I make certain I know the child's name, the family's name, the young siblings' names, and the mom's first name. I take a glance at the outside of the folder and there it is, along with their telephone number and directions to the house, right on the front.

I also put on the outside of the folder the dates that the child will enter a different developmental phase, so that I will know the key changes in development I can expect. I also color-code with dots on the folder different ages of the children. I also keep certain key handouts addressing certain issues. I would put all my good discipline handouts in, say, an orange folder and all my good language handouts in a blue folder, so that when I want it fast, I can get it. Issues like sleeping, eating, setting limits, [and] toilet training [are] key issues that appear again and again, across families.

Home visitors figure out their own system of organizing their materials. As long as they have some system that allows them to enter the home unencumbered with a mind full of details, they can give total focus on their interactions with parents and their young children.

Record Keeping   Home visitors will save time in the long run by updating their records shortly after each visit—specifically what they did during the home visit, any parent concerns, their observations of parents and child, and reminders for the next visit. For example, they might ask themselves, "What information do I need to give the parent next time? What topic did we leave unfinished?" This task needs to occur after the home visit because taking notes during the visit is distracting. Visitors can use these written records as a guide for evaluating one's relationship with a family, planning for the next visit, and as a resource during supervision and staff's professional developmental meetings. In some situations, the written descriptions of the child's developmental progress can be of invaluable assistance when a referral is needed, such as for an evaluation for special education services.

Legal and Ethical Issues

Confidentiality   For parents to trust their home visitor, they need to feel confident that the home visitor will not discuss their child or their parenting with other people. Thus, when home visitors illustrate how other parents handle a parenting issue or how a child has learned a specific skill, they speak in general terms so that no parent could recognize the people described. In this manner, home visitors demonstrate in their actions and words that they honor confidentiality with all their families.

As discussed previously, the role of the home visitor can be ambiguous to parents. Meeting in the parents' home invites the parent to relate on a more personal level than in a public setting. The combination of role ambiguity and the personal nature of the parent–home visitor relationship sometimes invites parents to share personal information that is outside the boundaries of the home visiting program agenda. *Any* personal sharing introduces issues of confidentiality. Although each home visiting program has its own policy regarding confidentiality, several guidelines crossover all program agendas, as described below.

Confidentiality is an ethical obligation in all home visiting. At the outset, home visitors can tell parents that personal information discussed during a visit will remain confidential unless a child or parent is in danger, such as indications of child maltreatment or a parent's suicidal thinking. Home visitors should never discuss clients in settings outside of supervision or team meetings. Some home visiting programs are part of a larger social service delivery system with other professionals such as physicians, nurses, and therapists. In these situations, home visitors need to share appropriate family information, yet they should offer only that information needed by the other service professional and in a confidential manner. Knowing what information is appropriate to share can be difficult. Before home visitors contact community agencies to link families with their services, they need the parents' written permission. Often, home visitors are unsure of how much confidential information is necessary for a specific referral.

Maintaining confidentiality also extends to any written materials about a family. Janice explained her approach.

When parents share personal information, I do not include it in my written records. I may put a key phrase related to the discussion to trigger my memory in future visits, but I never add any details or subjective interpretations about what they talked about. My written records are public records that can be subpoenaed, thus, I try and keep them as objective as possible. I believe every home visitor needs to do their written records with the assumption that every single piece of paper could be subpoenaed for a child custody battle, for example.

Janice is rigorous in maintaining written observations of what she did in each visit, observations of child and parent action, any parent concerns, and reminders to herself for her next visit. She maintains these records as objectively as possible and excludes any personal family data or her own subjective interpretation. In this manner, she maintains confidentiality.

Child Maltreatment   Child abuse and neglect are not protected by the ethical obligation of confidentiality because the home visitor's duty to the welfare of the child comes before the duty to the child's parent. Therefore, home visitors are mandated to report evidence of child abuse and neglect. Each home visiting program has its own procedure for reporting child maltreatment. When home visiting programs have a primary intent to develop a partnership with parents, home visitors need to inform parents of their forthcoming report to the child protection agency. Although it is difficult for the first few times, experienced home visitors with strong personal relationships with parents find it most helpful to make the reporting call while they are in the parents' home and with the parents present. In this manner, the home visitor makes certain that parents know there are no secrets and that the call is based on the visitor's efforts to assist the family. Knowing that they have the strong support of their administrators can give home visitors the courage to relate openly to parents about the child maltreatment report. When this is possible, the home visitor often becomes part of the child protection agency's team in offering help to the family. Home visitors may encounter other family situations in which they do not have a strong personal relationship and may even suspect that making a hotline call could put them in danger. In these situations, administrators usually make the call, or, in states that allow hotline calls to be anonymous, an anonymous call may be appropriate.

It can be harder for a home visitor to report child maltreatment than for a teacher because home visitors have developed a trusting, personal relationship with the parents. Often, the most difficult situations are in the gray areas when there is no concrete physical evidence of maltreatment, such as neglect in supervision or emotional abuse. Cynthia described an example.

We had a situation this year where there were many—entirely too many—people living in a home. The water was shut off for a period of time, and I reported it as a situation that had implications of health hazards. The child protection agency then was aware of it and began working with the family to try to get the water turned back on. This home is not the best place for these kids. It is chaos. I really struggle going in there. It's not like I see someone get hit with a belt, or I see a black eye or big bruise; it's just that I know that every day, this home is not a good environment for those kids. I struggle with that on each visit, and then when something happens like the water getting turned off and the adults in the home don't seem to be doing anything about it, I report it because in my mind, maybe now someone will do something about this situation.

Twice a month, Cynthia visited this family. On each visit, she left knowing that the children were living in a very dysfunctional home environment with too many people coming and going. Once Cynthia had a concrete basis to call the child protection agency because of no running water in the home, she was able to help this family get resources to improve their daily life. Many home visitors will feel most comfortable having their program director call the child protection agency.

DIFFICULTIES AND DILEMMAS

Two types of parents may be difficult to work with: concrete thinkers who have difficulty generalizing (i.e., parents who need a specific example to understand an abstract idea) and those living in chaotic conditions.

Concrete Thinkers

Lela described her frustrations in working with four parents in her caseload who were concrete thinkers.

A frustrating thing I am feeling right now is how to deal with the parent who seems to be a concrete thinker. For example, a mother does not grasp statements I make unless I give her a clear example. I share information with the parent on one visit and the very next visit they ask me about the same issue. Sometimes, I am at a loss as to how to you get through with some parents.

Lela made these comments during a weekly staff meeting, when her coworkers were able to offer several helpful suggestions. For instance, Cynthia finds that it is helpful to be concrete and directive when working with this type of parent. Cynthia visits Sally twice a month. Sally has difficulty managing her very active 18-month-old son, so Cynthia used a sensory activity as the setting in which to guide Sally.

Cynthia places a large plastic tub filled with birdseed, assorted spoons, and plastic containers in front of Willy. As Cynthia removes the lid, she says to Sally, "I brought this for a couple reasons. You know last time you told me Willy was doing so well with spoons, and you and I have been talking about setting limits. You know how he loves to throw things. Plus, sensory play is fun."

Willy immediately picks up some seed and tosses it out of the tub. Sally says, "In the box, baby." Willy begins putting seed into a small container with his hands as Sally softly says, "Good boy! You are so smart! You are taking the seed and putting it into the tub."

Cynthia says, "That describing what he is doing is wonderful. That is what he needs to learn—language."

Cynthia knows that parents who think very concretely learn best from their own experience. In her twice-monthly visits, she frequently describes Willy's actions and then tells Sally how important these descriptions are for Willy's language development as well as his self-esteem. When Sally spontaneously described her child's actions, Cynthia reinforced this important skill as it happened.

Willy throws a small amount of seed, and Cynthia says, "He's still throwing, right?"

Sally responds, "You can tell! Yeah."

"We have to set limits for him," Cynthia says. "When he throws things, what do you do?" Sally shrugs. Cynthia suggests it might help if Cynthia put Willy on her side of the tub so that it would be easier for her to guide him. "It will be easier to catch his hand if you do not want him to throw the seed," she says, "and when you are with him, you are helping him to keep calm. You can take his hand to show him how to use the spoon, too."

Cynthia gives a specific directive with a simple explanation that Sally can understand. However, Sally usually does not remember Cynthia's specific guidance, so Cynthia knows that it will take time and repetition for Sally to spontaneously show her son what she wants him to do.

As Sally watches her son play in the seed, Cynthia explains how this play is a calming activity that helps his eye–hand and small-muscle coordination as he dumps and fills. The experience of the moment becomes the teaching moment. Cynthia further described how she works with parents who are concrete thinkers.

Basically, what I do is work at two different levels. I work with the parents at whatever level the parents are. When they are at very concrete levels, I do a lot of demonstration of hands-on activities where the parents practice in order to help them understand a concept or skill.

After I have known the parent for a while, I get better at knowing how the parent learns, whether they need to be told to watch it or to do it themselves, or whether they do better watching a video. Usually, I will demonstrate and then have them try it and then coach them through. I talk about what the parent is doing and how the child reacts, and how that relates to the child's learning and development. Because that is what they often have trouble understanding—how their actions help their child learn, not what their child learns but how their child learns.

And in group meetings, we have to have something the parents can hold and touch in order to understand. So, when we are working with self-concept of the children, and how words and negative interactions impact a child, we take a paper doll. And each negative statement becomes a bruise or a tear in the doll. We told them things that they might say to their child, and then they had to judge whether or not that was something that supports the child's self-esteem.

I think the parents [with low intelligence] have to experience for themselves before they are able to provide that kind of activity for their child, let alone relate the activity to child development. Some of them never really quite get it. Most of the people we serve do not live alone; rather they live in an extended family, and that extended family helps to raise that child. So, we do not limit ourselves to just working with the parent during our home visit. We also work with the father, the aunty, the grandmother or grandfather, whoever is home and helps with child rearing.

Cynthia understands that for some of her parents to understand a concept or a skill, they must have direct experience; then, the home visitor can talk about the meaning of that experience. Cynthia often models for parents and then invites the parents to participate in the activity, coaching them as they play with their children. Some parents need more time than others, as well as repeated concrete experiences; home visitors need to exercise patience and persistence. Nothing will happen if the parent and home visitor do not have a trusting personal relationship.

Chaotic Lifestyles

It is very difficult to work with families that seem to be on the edge of chaos, such as large extended families coming and going throughout the day or families with multiple, complex external problems and little ability to cope with them. Given Cynthia's respect for each family, once she arrives, she invites the parents to decide whether they wish her to enter into their chaotic world. Cynthia described how she relates to those families who seem to live in perpetual chaos.

I went into a home with 12 children ranging in age from 18 months to 9 years, two mothers, and three adult men who were visiting the mothers. The men did not want me there, and they tried to intimidate me by singing nasty songs. I know these moms well enough that I thought, "Nope, I am not going to leave. These moms do not want me to leave. They do not think that this is not a good time for me to visit," so I stayed. And finally, one man in particular finally gave up and went outside to smoke.

[When I cannot get the mom's focused attention because of so many kids] I hang out and play with the kids. It does not matter if I have Mom's attention. I mean it does matter in the long run, but I will stay. I know that I am the only constant in these women's lives. With this family, I spent the first 6 months playing with the kids, and neither mom would talk to me. Often, they would go to another room and half-listen. This went on for 3 months before they would sit with me and their children. And then they could not sit with me the whole hour. They would get up and go have a cigarette or make a phone call.

Cynthia's persistence was unwavering; eventually, the parents understood that she does want and expect them to be with her and their children. But first they need to experience Cynthia's care and commitment by her persistent visiting, active play with their children, and consistent invitation for them to join her, even when they do not for so many months. For these two mothers, Cynthia was the first adult who had been absolutely predictable.

I know they want me to come. Their friends in Even Start teased them for only coming to Even Start 1 in 4 days on most weeks. They replied, "We do not need to come because Cynthia always visits us at home!" It is now so different [from] when I first started visiting them. They screen all their phone calls, but they always answer when I call them.

People see you in a certain light and expect you to do the same thing they are used to. One of the things I do for these chaotic families is that I provide a routine within the time frame that I am in their home. They know we are going to play some kind of game, and I am going to read a story, and then I am going to ask them to read. And the longer I have been there, the more successes I have in getting them on the floor to play with their child. Not every time, but it is much better than at the beginning.

Cynthia is secure in her competence and the parents' desire to give their children the best that they can. Thus, she is willing to try new strategies, even though she does not know whether they will work. What she does know is that she cares and that the parents eventually will understand that she cares. Then, with her guidance, they can move forward. Cynthia described a poignant example of her creative initiative.

One of the moms seemed so depressed that I changed my mode of operation one day. These are not women who would tell me about personal problems such as having a fight with their boyfriend. But I went to this mom's home and decided to change what I normally do. When I got to this home, I said, "I don't want to see the kids. Do you have someone who can watch them while you and I go to McDonald's?" We went to McDonald's, and I bought her a soda. And I just talked to her like a person and said, "You really have been down. Is there some way that I can help?"

And she cried and talked about how she has to do everything for her family and her sister's family [who all live with her]. Everyone is in and out of this house, and the teenagers and boyfriends come in and eat all the food that she has bought for the small children. And she goes to bed at night wondering if they will have food in the morning, and often they do not. And this happens almost every night. There are a lot of people in this home, up to 20 people, and she is tired, tired of trying to swim up river when there is this current the other way.

That was the only time that she talked to me like that. And what I did for her was to try to hook her up with the child abuse network because they do in-home counseling. I do not know if she will do it. But on the positive side, this mom tested on the sixth- or seventh-grade level last fall. And after 1 year, she now is at the eleventh-grade level. She only comes to Adult Basic Education 1 day instead of 4 days a week, but this is a parent who told me, "The reason I am still here is because you won't leave me alone."

But it is hard. I sometimes feel like I have been in a washing machine being pulled in all directions. One time, I arrived in her home and the 3-year-old was fingerpainting the baby's head. The mom was screaming at him, which did not help. Then, we could not find anything in the house to wipe the paint off with—no rags, tissues, nothing.

When I am with this family, I try to bring order, the only order this family experiences. In that living room, for 10 minutes, if I can get everyone around me listening to that book, I have brought order for a small amount of time. And that to me is powerful because I can show it can be done, and for the first time they experience order. These parents are not stupid. They experience this with me, and they remember, and the next time, maybe they will pick up the book and sit down to bring that order.

Cynthia believes that parents can give their child improved parenting if they experience a personal relationship with a caring adult who gives them support and guidance. She understands that some of the parents she works with had troubled childhoods and live in extreme chaos with no support. Although she often feels as if she is being pulled in too many directions when visiting these families, she knows that the parents feel overwhelmed with responsibilities and have little support. Her persistence and predictable, unswerving respect and care allow these parents to know that their struggles to care for their children are valued and that they can make a difference in their young children's lives.

CONCLUSION

This chapter examined two levels of home visiting skills. First, the chapter identified 15 high-level skills that improve through experience over an extended time. Improved practice stems from self-reflection on that experience and through constructive feedback from professional peers and supervisors. These 15 skills encourage, maintain, and promote the parent–home visitor relationship. Regardless of home visitors' extended experience and skills, forming a relationship can be very messy.

Second, the chapter identified five areas of knowledge and skill also essential to the home visiting process. Unlike the first 15 skills, these areas do not overlap or occur together. They are more like a collection that can be taught, at least partially. This is knowledge involving societal rules and resources. To illustrate these two levels of skills, two exemplary home visitors, Janice and Cynthia, shared their experiences with families and their understanding of these experiences. To gain clarity, the chapter discussed different approaches separately, even though home visiting is an organic, unfolding process in which visitors use several approaches simultaneously.

The chapter concluded with a discussion of difficulties and dilemmas encountered when working with parents who are concrete thinkers and those families who live in chaotic conditions.

The Home Visitor's Professional Development

> The starting point of any process of thinking is something going on, something which just as it stands is incomplete or unfulfilled.
>
> John Dewey (1916, pp. 146–147)

BECAUSE THE QUALITY of the relationship between the home visitor and the parent can determine whether the parent gains an understanding of child development and learns effective parenting skills, it is important to perfect the skills discussed in Chapter 2. Home visiting is a craft and home visitors are thus artisans. Much of a home visitor's craft is learned on the job through experience. Home visiting can be understood only as it evolves in each visitor's practice, which takes place in many unpredictable and unique situations.[1] Thus, much of home visitors' knowledge is tacit. The knowing is in the action; thinking and doing are interwoven.

The home visitor's continued professional growth parallels the parental development that occurs during home visits. As in parenting, professional development is an unfolding process learned on the job. There are no recipes or formulas. Often, the job seems untidy and unpredictable. Like parenting, the home visitor's work involves both feelings and thoughts—emotion and intellect.[2] The relationships between home visitors and their professional peers, mentors, and supervisors are essential to continued growth; these relationships should be based on mutual respect and collaboration. We will explore these relationships further in this chapter.

Other powerful learning mechanisms for home visitors are 1) professional education, 2) reflection on action, and 3) learning by doing and practicing.

When home visitors reflect on action, they stop and think about their work, recognizing that each home visit is new. Each parent will have his or her own way of thinking and goals for their child. With practice, visitors learn to think about what they are doing while they are doing it. They become more aware of both the uniqueness of each family and common themes across families. As their relationship with a family evolves, home visitors develop a series of expectations of parent, child, and self. They become more aware of both successful and problematic approaches. Through education, home visitors integrate new information into their experience and learn new approaches to their work.

The home visitor experience is complex. Through reflection, home visitors can learn to focus on what is important in the moment. With experience, home visitors are able to help parents develop their own skills. Six successful strategies for professional development of home visitors are:

1. Sharing ownership and having active involvement from all levels of the organization

2. Understanding that a culture of continuous improvement leads to excellence

3. Forming significant, reciprocal community collaborations and productive partnerships

4. Taking time to plan and implement, to develop new skills and strategies, and to practice and follow up

5. Having administrative support

6. Having a clear purpose and direction[3]

This chapter will discuss some approaches and challenges to the home visitor's professional development.

EDUCATION

This book promotes an educational approach that is different from didactic ("traditional") teaching and instead follows the style of Rogers, Dewey, and Bruner.[4] This education takes place in a climate of inquiry; here, learners actively think about their lived experiences, integrate new information into them, and discover new meaning to them.

New information can help home visitors see actions and relationships in a new way and thereby reconstruct their experiences. This approach is not linear but rather experiential. Janice explains how she learned something new through discussions with occupational therapists during her weekly staff meetings.

Occupational therapists have been very helpful. They can break down motor development in a way you don't see, for example, how a child gets in an out of a sitting position, how they reach for things—the detail that makes a difference in how a child functions. I didn't have a clue about these details until occupational therapists came to staff meetings on a regular basis. In a program like [Parents as Teachers (PAT)] with a strong focus on language and cognition, we can let motor development happen rather than pay attention to it. Paying attention to motor development makes a difference, especially if visiting a child whose development takes a different twist, for example a "mushy" feeling child or one really slow in walking. I have learned what are the very small signs of progress. I can help the parent see these signs and encourage ways to promote the development.

Janice was able to integrate the direct information received from occupational therapists so she could see more in a child's movement and provide additional information and guidance to the child's parents. Because of what Janice has learned, she is sensitive to movement and incorporates this education in her home visitations. For example, as Erin (18 months) watches Janice take toys out of her bag, she backs up and sits on her mother's lap. Janice comments, "It's interesting to see how she backs up into you. She has a good sense of body space." Janice's statement involves content (new information from occupational therapists) and reflective action (her application of this information to her work with families).

Home visitors' work is planned, but not predictable. In addition, home visitors have a limited backup system. In contrast, teachers go to work in a classroom with set of textbooks for a given set of specific subjects to teach, with a principal who can help in a crisis. Nurses work in hospitals with a predictable set of protocols and procedures, with physicians who are in charge. In contrast, home visitors carry a small bag with materials they have chosen and go into homes of young families, each of which is different and has its own patterns and problems. The home visitor has no given authority or support system within the parent's home.

Because home visiting is so personal, it is also inescapably individual. The home visitor's personal history influences how they understand and value their work.[5] In addition, the home visitor's methods are deeply rooted in learned ways of seeing, thinking, and acting. These ways were learned through relationships with others beginning in infancy. This complexity of self—both individual and social—creates provocative challenges for educating home visitors. Effective in-service education thus involves a dual process: every individual's way of working needs to be valued and nurtured while the individual's growth remains within a social setting. Therefore, the process of professional development is as important as the content.

The Structure and Process of Continued Education

Continuing education is an integral part of a home visitor's professional life and active, reflective learning is the core of home-visiting continuing education. Administrators of a program can structure this active learning within their team meetings. Cynthia, director of an Even Start program, discusses this need.

The program is a place for growth, not just for our children and our parents, but for ourselves. Everyone needs to know that this is a place for growth. When home visitors are hired, we tell them they are expected to actively learn new knowledge and skills. For this to happen, it takes a leader who is able to forge relationships of respect and support in working together. The art is to know how to help people become active, reflective learners.

Last month I gave everyone a reading I thought was very helpful because it clearly described effective approaches with families. No one touched it. Then last week, I shared this material in terms of concrete happenings with everyone's families. I made it come alive—in the context of peoples' work with their families. There has to be engagement, and people need to learn to reflect on how new knowledge relates directly to work with their families.

Cynthia provides clear administrative expectations of professional development in a community of respect and support.

Team Meetings   To ensure active reflective learning, administrators should schedule regular team meetings. These meetings are an informal setting in which home visitors can learn new information to directly apply to their everyday work with families. Opportunities for home visitors to actively process any provided content in terms of their visiting experiences will not only have an impact on their work, but promote their ability to be reflective.

It takes time for colleagues to trust each other, share their experiences, and respond honestly and helpfully to what others are saying. Not all home visitors are introspective by nature; some will need team meetings to promote this ability. When team meetings become a safe setting for home visitors to openly share their work with each other, each person is able to compare their own style to that of the other visitors. Exploring differences can increase sensitivity to the particularities of the home visitor's own way of working; it can also provoke questions about practices or beliefs. Home visitors have their own unique styles, personalities, interests, beliefs, biases, and distortions. Therefore, any new changes or approaches will be personal, made by an individual to address his or her work patterns.

Given the solitary work of home visiting, team meetings can provide opportunities for support and encouragement.[6] Home visitors are bonded together by shared commitments and experience. Janice describes the importance of sharing with colleagues.

Colleagues that do the same kind of work that I do, other home visitors, are important to me, because we share similar experiences. So that when I run into a problem, I know that I can talk with one of my colleagues, that the conversation will be maintained as confidential. With them I can sort-of brainstorm and process things that I need to work on to help a family. We can share how each of us has dealt with similar situations with different families, and what the outcomes have been. In reality, there are few problems that are really unique to family. That is the nice thing about having a fairly large staff, the sharing among team members.

You need to have a way, among your colleagues in a protected environment, that you can work through some of the difficulties that you confront.

Together, home visitors can collaborate in solving problems—in expanding notions of what is possible. This mutuality of interest, respect, and support provides encouragement for individuals to take risks and attempt new approaches.

Earnestine, an experienced home visitor, discusses a problem she is having with her team members. Earnestine describes her frustration in working with a directive mother, Kamera, who seems only to be interested in promoting academic learning of her 26-month-old son. Regardless of the play activity or Earnestine's interactions, Kamera focuses on color, shape, or number.

"I'm out of control. It seems no matter what I do or say, Kamera remains directive," Ernestine commented. Individual home visitors shared similar frustrations and then brainstormed together about possible strategies. They suggested that Earnestine could choose only very open-ended activities, such as sensory play in birdseed or sculpting with play dough. In fact, introducing sensory play with birdseed did provide a setting for Kamera to interact in a new way with her son. Over extended additional visits with Earnestine's support and assistance, Kamera learned to value her son's actions as a 26-month-old and to encourage developmentally appropriate play. Earnestine gave brief reports in team meetings, after which the team explored both the meaning of ongoing happenings and additional possible approaches with this family.

When Earnestine stepped back from her involvement with Kamara and shared her concerns with her peers, she gained new perspectives of possible approaches. As she heard individual home visitors share similar frustrations, she gained support and encouragement. Earnestine had felt out of control during her visits with Kamera. After discussing these visits with her colleagues, she returned feeling hopeful that she had a new possibility of making contact with this mother.

When a team has over 10–12 members, the total group is probably too large to have mutual, reflective sharing. For large staffs, structuring part of each team meeting into small groups, pairs, or triplets will be necessary to ensure this open sharing of practice, its significance, and brainstorming of additional approaches. There always will be some need for total group presentations or videos. For example, a video depicting a home visitor effectively working with a nonverbal mother can clarify a common situation. These total group activities are most productive when home visitors can reflect on how the topic relates to their own practice in small groups, followed by a total group "wrap up" to conclude the meeting.

Most programs have home visitors of different ages with different levels of experience. With increased experience comes a greater understanding of the meaning of the home visiting process. Regular informal team meetings with open sharing allow the more experienced home visitors to share insights and discuss their own changes. These visitors can be models of learning and may expand the perspectives of the less experienced visitors. When less experienced home visitors feel supported and safe, they can actively question their practices and gain assistance from their experienced colleagues. In this way, a climate of inquiry develops.

Seminars, Workshops, and Conferences   Other venues for learning are seminars, workshops, and conferences sponsored by outside organizations and agencies. When a home visitor meets people in related professions and learns from these professionals, his or her own knowledge and understanding are expanded. This multidisciplinary experience is especially important for home visitors because their work encompasses education, health care, and social service. Janice explains how conferences help her to develop new knowledge and skill.

I like conferences because they give me the opportunity to hear people from other fields, such as a physician or child protection worker. It broadens my perspective. It also is stimulating to meet other conferees who are in related fields. And I get ideas for reading. For I also like to read—to dig into books for new perspectives or depth of understanding.

Janice understands that her work cuts across disciplines, so she actively seeks new learning opportunities from professionals in other related disciplines. Her home visiting program supports her by funding this form of continuing education.

Programs should create an educational structure and process that provides sharing of experience and support so home visitors can pursue their craft with confidence and enthusiasm. Learning is a continual, fluid, individual, and collaborative process that is a natural part of the culture of a home visiting program.

The Content of Continued Education

Home visiting is a complex, dynamic process based on skills, knowledge, and reflection. Home visitors' actions are a blend of their personal abilities, style, experiences, professional education, and the requirements of a particular program. Skills and the different domains of knowledge overlap and often are interdependent.[7] Arranging for the content of home visitors' continued professional development thus involves the challenge of providing education across a variety of disciplines.

Child Development   Regardless of whether home visitors are nurses, social workers, or educators, when they work with families with young children, a solid foundation in child development is the first priority of professional education. Indeed, although this book is about home visiting, large sections focus on child development. As home visitors learn about the development of cognition and language, biology and physicality, society and culture, and psychological and emotional development, the emphasis should be on the intertwining of all these developmental realms. For example, when cognitive development is discussed, Janice relates how she needed to provide different activities for Erin than for Molly, children the same age with different abilities. Cynthia describes how she structured a toddler's play with birdseed so that his mother, who is a concrete learner, could have simple concrete experiences in managing her child's behavior. When in-service sessions combine child development *content with process*—that is, home visitors talking about their families—learning becomes more active and reflective. This method results in a higher probability that home visitors will use the learning in their everyday work with families.

Education to Broaden One's Perspective   Every parent–child relationship has its own style of interaction, representations, and meanings. The home visitor selects among her or his relevant knowledge base, then applies the knowledge to the unique family situation. Often the home visitor has to make sense of unfamiliar situations and family configurations, which means there is a wide range of knowledge and skills that can potentially be useful to each home visitor.

Weston[8] identifies key concepts that should be part of the training of practitioners working with very young children and their families:

1. Endowment, maturation, and individual differences in the first 3 years of life
2. The power of human relationships
3. Transactions between the baby and the environment
4. Developmental processes and their interrelationships
5. Risk, coping, adaptation, and mastering
6. Parenthood as a developmental process
7. The helping relationship

Education for home visitors cuts across many disciplines beyond child development: health and nutrition, language and communication, occupational and physical therapy, special education, and social service. Given this complexity, the regular use of outside consultants for staff in-service meetings can assist home visitors in gaining new tools beyond their personal and professional experience. Margaret is Director of Early Education in a large district that has had a home visiting program for 14 years. In Margaret's program, outside consultants from several disciplines regularly lead the weekly staff meetings. A child psychologist who has a family therapy practice leads two sessions each month—one group supervision session for staff to discuss difficulties they are having with specific families and one to share child development or family systems information. Consultants representing other disciplines, including health and nutrition, occupational therapy, pediatrics, and community agencies such as the child protection bureau and the substance abuse clinic, also lead sessions. Margaret discusses these staff meetings.

We need to bring in people with different lenses, different expertise, to broaden the staff's knowledge. People such as social workers, child psychologists, pediatricians, occupational therapists, people knowledgeable in drug and alcohol abuse, children's learning problems, and people representing community agencies. But we also need a balance. Sessions also need to involve the staff in issues directly related to their tasks, such as parenting skills for helping your baby go to sleep, baby massage, movement and music, even nitty-gritty kinds of things like toy making.

Home visitors gain a deeper, broader, richer understanding of what they do when consultants provide a variety of perspectives on the home visiting process. At the same time, Margaret understands that in many meetings, staff can work together on improving their skills. In these sessions, staff can think aloud about their work, building on their own expertise and the expertise of their professional peers. Colleagues become a source of new information and insight, while providing new ways of working with families and expanding ideas of what is possible. The process is interactive, involving personal and collaborative reflection.

Jeree Pawl provides guidelines for those who work with parents and babies to create a "crucial interpersonal center."

1. Trust in parents, be hopeful, and communicate your belief in impossibilities.
2. Work toward a mutual understanding with the family about purpose, goals, and objectives.
3. Hear and represent all voices within a family, not just the baby's voice.
4. Think of your knowledge about a particular family as a hypothesis, not the truth.
5. Maintain an appropriate role and adhere to boundaries, but be comfortable and flexible.
6. Recognize your own knowledge, beliefs, and biases, while remaining respectful of any differences.
7. Practice proactive inclusive interaction, which is "the capacity to continue to embrace and hold all of those with whom we are involved together at a particular time."[9]

Beyond child development knowledge, the home visitor's best resource is his or her own experience. Thus, active learning is enhanced by a close connection between the educational topic and the professional experiences of home visitors. At the same time, professional education should expand the home visitor's lens to enable an understanding of the complexities of their work and an openness to new perspectives. Four areas of knowledge and skill that are useful in expanding these horizons are

1. Using an ecological approach to social systems
2. Working with culturally diverse and at-risk families

3. Understanding family systems, family life cycle, and adult development

4. Networking with community agencies

The Ecological Approach   Discussion of home visiting may often focus on the enhancement of parent–child relationships. Using an ecological approach, home visitors understand that child development results from the interplay of the characteristics of children and the way the world affects them. When home visitors use an ecological approach, they also consider young children in their total family environment, especially the interplay of family with other social systems such as community, church, and workplace.[10]

To help a child or a family, you cannot do just one thing because the quality of a family's life is interconnected with the quality of their social environment. As Garbarino noted:

> We measure the social richness of an individual's life by the availability of enduring, reciprocal, multifaceted relationships that emphasize playing, working and loving... One of the most useful aspects of the ecological approach is its ability to highlight situations in which the actions of people with whom the individual has no direct contact significant affect development.[11]

Or as my cabinet-maker father would say, "If the only tool you have is a hammer, you tend to treat every problem as if it were a nail."

Taking an ecological perspective, home visitors look inside to the everyday patterns of parent–child interactions and outside to the social systems and settings that support or constrain these everyday patterns. There is a give-and-take mutuality between these external social systems and the child and family. For example, the manner in which child care providers and parents greet each other as the young child arrives influences not only the parent's feeling of trust in this caregiver, but the caregiver's feeling of support and affirmation. In turn, the child feels secure in the similarity between home and child care program or feels insecure because of mixed messages or tension between parent and child care provider.

In an ecological approach, home visitors locate each family in their social environment in terms of ethnicity, race, religion, education, and occupation. With this perspective, they are sensitive to a family's access to resources, personal/social networks, and potential constraints, all of which influence the family's everyday lifestyle. This knowledge and sensitivity allows home visitors to individualize their approach so that they communicate respect, support, and affirmation to each family they serve.

Because contemporary culture is so individualistic, no one should assume that the average home visitor will use an ecological approach. Thus, staff development sessions can expand perspectives by providing informational sessions on the notion of ecology, social systems, and how home visitors can approach a family accordingly. With this understanding, home visitors will be more sensitive to the messages parents receive from various parts of their environment—neighborhood, church, elementary school, workplace, television—and that parents sometimes receive mixed or contradictory messages from different parts of their environment. In team meetings, staff members can share how the social environment affects their families and gain new understanding through this sharing.

Culturally Diverse and At-Risk Families   By paying attention to children's and families' social environment, home visitors develop sensitivities and accompanying skills in recognizing and relating to cultural diversity. They know that things can have different meanings for people of different race, ethnicity, religion, educational status, or socioeconomic class. For example, the home visitor should expect different cultures to have different informal networks—people outside the home with whom the family interacts. Networks can provide information and support, but they can also cause stress.

A first step in education for working with diverse cultures is helping home visitors recognize how their own behaviors, attitudes, and values reflect their own culture. Then, when relating to families of a different culture, home visitors can keep their own biases from blocking communication with a family. Second, staff in-service meetings can assist home visitors in gaining specific knowledge of the cultures they serve. This is another topic in which consultants who represent different cultures can broaden a program's perspective.

Professional development of home visitors working with at-risk families entails additional content and process because the families face an increased number of personal (e.g., family conflict, depression, anxiety) and external problems (e.g., housing, jobs). Given this, it is not unusual for these parents to have difficulty focusing on their young children's needs. Home visitors make more visits to at-risk families and need additional professional guidance. It is not uncommon for home visitors who work with troubled families to see the needs of young children being unmet and become frustrated, angry, discouraged, or overwhelmed. Possible problems include the lack of a quiet place to meet with parents, repeated interruptions during the visit, and angry or hostile parents. Given this work context, staff meetings that focus on patterns of at-risk families and adaptations in working with these families provide an invaluable resource for home visitors.

Family Systems, Family Life Cycle, and Adult Development   A third area of continuing knowledge and skill involves adult development, family systems, and family life cycle. Social scientists have developed theories of adult development to aid in our understanding of differences among adults. Developmental theories describe predictable sequences of growth and adaptation throughout life.[12] Development includes changes in a complex interwoven fabric of interpersonal behavior, moral and ethical behavior, cognitive complexity, and preoccupations. Different periods in life involve different age-related tasks and life issues. For example, parents in their early 20s with very young children often are preoccupied with different issues than parents between 30 and 40 years of age. The young parent may be just beginning a career. In contrast, in our culture, the period between 30 and 40 is often the time of rapid career advancement; thus, career may preoccupy parents at this age. Just as home visitors individualize their approach with families of different cultures, knowledge of adult development can help them relate effectively to individual differences among parents.

Family systems theory helps us understand that the behavior of each family member is dependent on every other family member. Each family member has a role, expectations, and a place in the total family structure. A gifted child may have the role of strengthening his parent's feeling of competence and thus feels compelled to succeed in all tasks. A father may have the role of unquestionable control and power; thus, in his family interactions, he feels obligated to reward and reprimand each family member.

Families also go through a developmental process—a family life cycle—that involves shifts in family organization and functioning. It is helpful for home visitors to learn how a family is organized; this organization will vary in different life cycles of a family, including marriage, childbirth, separating (e.g., entering child care or school, when the second parent begins to work), school age and adolescence, the empty nest, and retirement. Home visitors most often work with families within the same life cycle; however, these families may be intimately related to extended families in different phases of a family life cycle. Thus, an understanding of family life cycles can assist home visitors in their ecological approach to families.

Home visitors may work with families who experience problems associated with divorce, single parenting, or blended families. Professional education can provide an understanding of these increasingly common family patterns. Divorce is a transitional process, not a legal relationship, and children are an integral part of the process.[13] With every divorce comes the challenge of reorganization for both parents and children. Daily routines will change, separation issues will become dominant, and issues of marital responsibility versus parental responsibility will need to be clarified. As parents go through the divorce process, they are redefining themselves. During this process, home visitors can assist parents in helping their young children understand these substantive changes and at the same time feel secure in their parents' love. In some unfortunate cases, of course, the task is to help the child begin what is often a lifelong process of accepting the reality that one of their parents has abandoned them.

Once a separation is finalized and the young child lives with only one parent, patterns of single parenting emerge. It is important for home visitors to acknowledge that one parent can manage the economic, physical, and psychosocial tasks of family life. Home visitors should learn the many strengths of single parenting, such as increased flexibility, children's increased understanding of their parent's work, and increased expectations that every family member contributes to the maintenance of the whole family.[14] Understanding the potential strengths of single parenting assists home visitors in relating to single parents in a respectful, supportive, and affirming manner.

Networking with Community Agencies   A fourth area of knowledge and skill involves networking with community agencies. As discussed in Chapter 2, home visitors should know what they can do and what is beyond their expertise. During visits in a family's home, it is not uncommon for parents to initiate discussion of personal difficulties, such as conflicts with their spouse or parent, or external difficulties, such as child care or housing. As a result, familiarity with community resources becomes knowledge upon which home visitors often rely. When home visitors work with families with multiple problems, networking with community agencies is a recurrent part of their work. Cynthia, Director of an Even Start program, describes some of her experiences.

One of the successes and also frustrations we have had in our work with different community agencies that serve our families is discovering how difficult it can be to get services. For example, I called a rape crisis line at 10 in the morning because a mom had come in and told us she had been raped by her boyfriend and needed to talk to someone. We had never handled this kind of situation before, so we called the rape crisis line. The machine said to call back at 10:30.

Just the phone systems we have now can be problematic for our families. You call a number and are told to press 1 for this, 2 for this, 3 for this, 4 for this. A lot of people get lost and don't know which button to press. And they'll hang up and won't try. Just the way the system is set up sometimes thwarts people's attempts to get help.

Then we have situations where counseling is available with a sliding fee. But again, child care and transportation are not available. And most counseling centers will not do home visits. On the other hand, once we work with our local medical clinics, we often can expedite getting appointments for the kids when we call the clinic and tell them this is one of our families. We have a contact person there. In fact, we have a case now in which the child had been seen at one of the bigger hospitals in town. Because mom missed 2 appointments and had no transportation for a 30-mile round trip, the hospital said they would not work with this family anymore. I called our local clinic who got the family into a different hospital that does provide transportation. And now the child is being served.

Cynthia and her staff know the individuals who work in different community agencies. Given their relationships with these individuals, the staff can gain personalized help for parents who cannot successfully use the agency.

That kind of coordination makes a world of difference. We try to put our people into job training and vocational rehabilitation programs. Through networking, knowing someone who works there and will take our calls, we can get our parents access. The parent doesn't have to deal with number 1, number 2, and so forth. Once you have a person who knows who you are and knows your program, then you are much more likely to get something done.

The other day we had a parent who wants to go the community college and was having difficulty getting a transcript. I called my contact at the community college who went to admissions and was able to troubleshoot for the parent. That's the way things can happen. All too often people get lost in the system and have trouble getting services; they get frustrated and give up.

What we are able to do is walk them through the process and thereby keep their spirits up. "Yes, it's a pain. Yes, it's a bummer. But yes, you can do it. Here's the number. Call now. Here is what you need to say." And the next time our parents will know how to do that, will know how to ask that question.

Cynthia's staff knows individuals in different agencies and knows how the agencies operate. Thus they can help their parents learn how to work within an agency and, when necessary, they can call upon a specific person in an agency to help a parent who is having difficulty using that agency.

Staff meetings can be a setting for joint exploration of community resources: governmental agencies such as public welfare, the Women, Infants, and Children program, Child Protection Services, mental and physical health agencies, and private agencies such as recovery programs, battered women's shelters, or out-of-home child care. This is an area where outside consultants can broaden staff's knowledge. In some situations, home visitors may have the knowledge of available community resources, but lack the ability to help parents access these resources. Skillful approaches can be a staff meeting or individual supervision topic, as discussed later in this chapter.

Education for Effective Skill Building

Knowledge and skill are mutually interdependent. Team meetings can focus specifically on skill building, especially communication and relationship-building skills—the building blocks of home visiting. When staff meet regularly and can discuss their work in small groups, these meetings can become an environment for reflecting together about their hands-on work. The skills discussed in Chapter 2 can be addressed, either by people sharing concretely their experience or by sharing videos of their work. These group discussions involve recurrent themes:

- Forming and maintaining relationships of trust and support
- Learning to take the perspective of the parent
- Expressing strong feelings, negative and positive, and having these feelings reflected back
- Understanding the developmental potential of individual children and individual parents
- Understanding the program's limits of responsibility

Working collaboratively to learn and reflect on practice is a slow process. This process is possible when all staff members are to committed support, affirm, and guide one another's personal and professional growth in a climate of openness and inquiry.

Continued Education in Rural Areas

A large part of our nation is rural; thus some home visiting programs cover large geographical areas. Rural experiences are different from those of urban residents in terms of geography, economics, culture, and social norms.[15] Living in a rural area can also add risk factors. A large number of rural residents live without basic conveniences such as plumbing, running water, heat, telephones, or transportation—public or personal. The most vulnerable groups in rural areas are pregnant women, babies, and young children, given the greater risk of poverty, lack of resources, lack of mental health services, and lack of public transportation. Yet many rural families have deep historical roots and often have large extended families, greater familiarity with one's neighbors, a strong spiritual life, and closer ties to the natural world and the seasons.[16] These rural people have long-established relationships and familial times to be counted on for support as needed. However, other rural families may be very isolated, far from shopping, medical facilities, schools, and community contacts. Still others may be separated from their neighbors by language and culture.

Rural areas typically lack basic infrastructure and are distant from many types of goods and services. Professionals travel long distances along poor roads, which is inconvenient and expensive. A lack of telephones, mobile phones, and Internet connections may cause scheduling and communication issues. Sparse population and economic difficulties in rural areas also mean that there is a lower tax base from which social service agencies can derive funds.[17] In addition, specialized training for rural settings is not readily available; thus, rural agencies must provide training, supervision, and an accessible professional library.

Home visitors must consider the following characteristics of rural areas:

1. A population that is spread sparsely across a large land area
2. Special (and often diverse) geographic and climatic features of the area to be serve
3. Difficulties in recruiting and retaining qualified personnel
4. Unequal distribution of available service providers
5. Scarcity of public transportation
6. Values and rules of rural culture as they relate to individuals with disabilities and to early intervention[18]

Rural children in the United States are more likely than nonrural children to enter kindergarten with lower key early literacy skills and are significantly more likely to receive special education placement.[19] Less stimulating early experiences stem from the fact that rural children are more likely to live in poverty and have mothers without college education. Rural mothers of young children are more likely than nonrural mothers to work full time. Rural mothers also are more likely to suffer from depression.[20] Native American and Alaskan children live primarily in rural areas, are likely to be poor, and are often raised without developmentally and culturally appropriate early childhood education programs. Nearly all aspects of Native American education have been far below the U.S. standards.[21]

Personnel working in rural areas need to be knowledgeable about rural child-rearing practices and family support systems. Because the professional often works in isolation, he or she needs to be a self-directed learner and problem solver.

Professional development systems vary from state to state. The administration's political climate, available funding, and needs of the rural population can determine a state's approach.[22] Cultural distinctiveness of the rural population and the lack of uniformity within the early childhood profession's educational standards can hinder rural professional development.[23]

Many rural agencies make a conscientious effort to recruit and train staff from the local communities. Given the limited resources of rural areas, professionals often fulfill multiple roles for clients. However, boundaries need to be set so that the home visitor does not become everything to everyone.

Innovation sometimes is easier in rural areas. Although there may be a lack of funds, resources, and professional staff in rural areas, new ideas can be easier to initiate and are often met with less resistance, perhaps because one encounters less bureaucracy.

Administrators may initiate unconventional forms of continued professional education. Telephone and mail communication become avenues of collaboration among home visitors and their mentors. Supervision by telephone has the advantage of being easily accessible, relatively low cost, and accessible from a variety of locations. Telephone work is most feasible if the supervisor and supervisee have established a relationship prior to their telephone communication.

Similarly, technology such as faxing, voicemail, e-mail, and instant messaging can offer a means of continual collaboration with both peers and mentors.

Programs can develop a video or DVD library as an integral part of ongoing education; the use of video can further extended into videoconferencing. Videos can illustrate exemplar home visiting, while demonstrating and discussing the use of supervision and mentorship processes. The power of videoconferencing is that the supervisor and supervisee can hear and see each other in real time. Videoconferencing is especially helpful when there are language differences between the supervisor and supervisee. State universities often offer videoconference networks; it can also be done via Internet through several services with minimal equipment (a computer, Internet connection, camera, and phone or microphone).

Web-based staff development, such as the program offered by West Virginia University, uses a variety of formats for education, such as case study chats, practice exercises, discussion groups, and group projects.[24] Networks of professionals formed across large distances also can support and provide opportunities for continued growth. The Foxfire Teacher Networks provide a model of professionals across geographical distances. Foxfire offers summer workshops for educators, which evolve into networks. These support systems allow Foxfire graduates to engage in continued collaboration in the interest of promoting professional development.[25]

Paraprofessionals

Home visiting emerges from several disciplines—most commonly social work, education, and nursing. Some community-based home visiting programs, however, hire visitors without related professional training.[26] Therefore, these paraprofessionals may be challenged by learning processes in which they were not formally educated.

Some family needs may be most appropriately met by paraprofessionals familiar with the culture and economics of that family. Paraprofessionals usually live in or near the communities of the families served by a program. It is crucial that paraprofessionals and professional staff have specific roles and responsibilities, especially if a program serves high-risk families. It also is critically important that paraprofessionals obtain systematic preservice and in-service professional development. This professional development can provide needed child development, parenting, and related information crucial for staff members' knowledge and skill development.

Programs with limited budgets may see the use of paraprofessionals as cost effective, as paraprofessionals generally have lower salaries than those with formal education or may only work part time. However, home visiting programs that primarily use paraprofessionals have not demonstrated strong intervention impacts and have higher participant dropout rates.[27]

Paraprofessionals may encounter their own challenges. Some paraprofessionals may overidentify with a client, project their own situations onto a client, or have low expectations of the client. If the visitor lives in the same community, parents may be reluctant to reveal any personal issues for fear of loss of privacy. Also, without proper training, the paraprofessional visitor may be biased by their own experiences.[28]

SUPERVISION

Education and supervision are both means of learning. This approach to professional development is fundamentally different than many in-service education programs, which offer unconnected workshops or courses of instruction. The supervision discussed in this chapter is not characterized by unequal power. Home visiting supervision involves mutual expectations and shared evaluation, much like the relationship of home visitor and parent. This is very different from the model of supervision adopted in some disciplines that is based on monitoring and evaluation, which is in turn based on a set of standard competencies.

Regular collaborative supervision establishes a relationship to promote continued professional development. Supervision entails clarification about the home visitor's purposes and goals, as well as an ongoing willingness to explore similarities, differences, perceptions, misperceptions, and concerns. When the supervisor is emotionally present, he or she creates a safe setting for home visitors to discuss their experiences (both successes and failures) and gain feedback from an experienced practitioner.

At its best, reflective supervision includes careful listening, observation, and awareness of the supervisee's emotional state. The effective supervisor defines the work in progress as a shared responsibility between the supervisor and the supervisee. These exchanges lead to a cooperative dialogue that promotes an understanding of self and the family. The supervisor does not take over; rather, he or she may suggest approaches or reframe points of view. Through reflective supervision, home visitors gain a greater understanding of their emotions and actions. By sharing stories, home visitors become aware of what they implicitly know and consider the meaning of their work. As they work with their supervisor, they develop a common language and shared vision.

Effective supervision parallels home visitors' relationships with their families because it is also a relationship of respect, support, collaboration, and mutuality. Ideally, the supervisor's expertise includes having been a frontline worker who conducted home visits. Within supervision, home visitors become increasingly skilled in focusing on the nuts and bolts of their experiences, reporting these experiences, and gaining feedback, knowledge, and/or suggestions.

For example, Dan is an outside consultant who provides group supervision for Cynthia's home visiting program. Cynthia describes her early work with Dan.

It was my first year doing home visiting. I was working with two small kids, mom, and dad. I had completed a developmental screen with each child, and was explaining it to their mom and dad. Out of nowhere, when I asked the question, "Is the child learning to help in the house, or imitating helping?" mom commented, "I wish I could get him (the dad) to help," as she looked at her husband. The dad replied, and they began arguing back and forth. Dad walked out of the room angry. Mom sat there and began crying. I just sat there like a bump on the log. I finally said, "Would you like me to leave?" She replied no. And dad was within an ear shot. Everyone felt uncomfortable. I finished explaining the Denver [Developmental Screening Test] and left as soon as I could.

That week when we met with Dan (the team's supervisor), I explained the situation—how I felt ill at ease and didn't know what to do. Through talking it over, Dan helped me understand that I'm not there to be a marriage counselor, or help them talk it through. That's not necessarily what I'm there for. It's obvious they are having marriage difficulty. And they let me see that. Dan's suggestion was when you find yourself in that situation, instead of getting pulled in or doing nothing, you could say, "You both seem to be having difficulty, would you like to talk to someone? Would you like me to recommend someone for you?" Or you can say, "This seems to be a difficult time, would you like me to leave and come back later?" Dan affirmed my response, which was the same as his second suggestion. And when I went back to their home I suggested someone for them to talk to.

In this visit, Cynthia had responded in an appropriate manner to the parents' fighting. Her response was intuitive. As a new home visitor, she had not thought through issues of maintaining boundaries, nor did she have a clear understanding of the options she had in situations like this. Being able to share this experience with the team and the team supervisor provided Cynthia with a deeper understanding of her work and affirmed her response to these parents.

Within supervision, the focus is primarily on process and interaction. Supervision offers a secure setting to reflect on the emotional reactions of one's practice.[29] The setting is safe enough to expose one's insecurities, mistakes, and questions. In turn, the supervisor reflects back the home visitors' thoughts and feelings and offers support. Collaboratively, the home visitor and supervisor interpret and gain understanding both of troublesome aspects of work and the successes. In these experiences, home visitors can gain an improved understanding of their thoughts, feelings, and actions, as well as support, guidance, and encouragement to move forward in their work. Cynthia describes a supervisor who helped her better understand herself and her work experiences.

One of the persons who influenced my work life was Lee Samuels. Lee was my supervisor when I worked for the Head Start program in Oregon. Lee was extremely bright. What Lee did for me was to help me look at myself, and look at my strengths and my weaknesses, and learn to understand myself better.

He was able to do that in a supervisory role. He's probably the only supervisor I ever had who would sit me down on a regular basis and process what was going on in the program, what was happening, why it was happening, and how we could take it somewhere else. Lee helped me look at my own personality traits, where they were effective and where they weren't.

Lee helped me realize I don't have to have all the answers. Performance has been very important in my family; and I've always felt like I have to know everything. He helped me realize I don't—that true power lies in knowing what you don't know, in being able to admit it, and then seeking help.

Lee taught me a lot about being a supervisor, how to help people grow. He was never afraid of his female side. In that respect he taught me something about men too. He would talk to me about being a man; and I never had a man do that. If I'd be upset with my husband or something, Lee would say, "Well, Cynthia, this is the way men look at it." That really helped me too on a personal note. No one had ever done that for me.

For Cynthia, Lee helped her reflect on her personal style and her work experiences. Their relationship had the same kind of mutuality that effective home visitors have with their parents. Just as Cynthia shared her perspectives, Lee also shared his.

When families have multiple problems, supervision becomes more important for the home visitor. Some feelings caused by these families can be problematic, such as futility, vulnerability, and hopelessness. At these times, the home visitor needs to be self-aware. Self-monitoring becomes essential, as does support, affirmation, and guidance from peers and supervisors.

Structural barriers may exist within home visiting programs, such as limited funding for one-on-one staff supervision. Accepting these dilemmas is the first step in moving toward a supervision model—awareness of the need. Once administrators understand supervision, they can work towards lessening or removing structural barriers.

Effective administrators provide clear program philosophy and principles to help guide their home visitors. Because home visitors work in many different home settings, these key principles and philosophy guide their decision making. A conversation with three professionals in the PAT program illustrates one program's overarching principles and philosophy. As Director of Early Education, Margaret has been in charge of her district's home visiting program for 13 years. Janice has been a home visitor for 9 years. Having been a home visitor for 4 years, Cynthia now spends half her time directing the district's Even Start program. Although they were interviewed on different days in different settings, parallel themes emerge in the portrayals of these three professionals.

Margaret: You integrate the principles and philosophy in the totality of your program, coming back to it in a lot of ways, in what you say in all the different contexts of working with the staff. First is empowering the parents. And that's not possible without having rapport with parents and supporting them. And at the core is the home visitor's strong foundation in child development.

Janice: We always are striving to empower parents. In as many subtle ways as possible, I find the strength of the parent and build on that. When I use handouts, I'll say, "You probably are doing this already." If you have a mindset that you'll fix parents, they'll know it. If you go in with the attitude that parents know a lot, and together we'll be working for the benefit of the child, they'll sense the respect you have for them. Respect is essential. And the home visitor must be secure in the basics of child development.

Cynthia: The key is respect of parents, and understanding the notion of reciprocity. You are a partner, not doing something for parents, but everyone is learning together. And you must be knowledgeable about what you are talking about. Basic child development is a must, but so are several other disciplines too, like nutrition and health. And you have to be introspective, for we learn by reflecting on our experience.

PEER MENTORING: A PROGRAM EXAMPLE

The professional development of home visitors focuses both on content and process. Content areas such as child development, parenting practices, risk factors, family systems theory, and community resources provide the knowledge base for home visitors. Many home visiting programs have regular staff meetings in which topics are discussed, often with the help of an outside professional. Reflecting on the process of how the home visitor establishes and maintains a positive, facilitative relationship with parents and their children helps the home visitor assess his or her work. Home visitors can improve the quality of their work when they understand both content and process—what they bring to the parent and how they bring it. The approaches discussed earlier in this chapter are based on the melding of content and process.

In most home visiting programs, professional development takes place through group meetings. Unfortunately, one-on-one reflective supervision is not available in all programs. Peer mentoring and supervision can fill this void.

In a large multicultural district with 30 home visitors, a 5-year project of peer mentoring and supervision was implemented. As in most home visiting programs, no home visitors were formally educated on home visiting, nor did they have any academic training or experience in reflective supervision. The administrator divided the home visitors into teams of five or six individuals, which met twice a month. Team leaders made video recordings of each of their team members at work once a year. The team member reviewed the video, both alone and with the team leader, then chose the segment that he or she wanted to show to the team. During the first meeting of the month, a home visitor shared his or her video and the team discussed it. At the other meeting, each team met with a child and family therapist to talk about their work with high-risk families or difficulties they or their families are experiencing.

The home visitors needed to trust each other for this process to be effective. All but four new home visitors had worked together for several years and knew each other well. They used the staff room to complete their paperwork, when they would often chat informally with each other. Despite this, team members required a level of trust that had not yet developed.

During the first 3 years, the project progressed very slowly. Although being videotaped was part of their job requirement, most home visitors resisted it. Also, most families were not willing to be videotaped during a home visit. The few brave souls who shared their videos made the meetings very successful, with team members providing feedback, suggestions, and alternative approaches. For example, one home visitor's video showed her giving developmental information to the parent, but she did not provide an appropriate interpretation of either a child or parent action that she had observed. When the parent and toddler repeated "mommy" and "Susie" to each other, the home visitor could have told the parent that these alternating repetitions help Susie to understand that taking turns is a component of all conversation. Or, when the toddler walked backward into her mother's lap, the home visitor could have commented that the child's action indicated her increased sense of body in space. The home visitors who shared their recordings found these comments from their peers to be constructive, not negative. Slowly, more and more home visitors volunteered to share their recordings.

Initially, all feedback was positive praise. With time and experience, however, individuals learned new skills in peer mentoring and supervision. They learned to ask open-ended questions regarding the home visitor's intentions and expectations of the visit. The meetings became contexts to discuss difficulties such as working with teen parents, developmentally slow parents, or parents who often miss their visits. By the program's last 2 years, most home visitors had developed an increased ability to be self-reflective. They also developed new home visiting skills such as descriptively affirming parents and children rather than using global evaluative comments such as "good" or "nice." When descriptively affirming a child or parent, the home visitor concretely describes the observed parent or child behavior, thereby helping the parent or child recognize his or her own successes.

[The team leaders met monthly with a psychologist who had experience and knowledge of reflective supervision. In these meetings, team leaders shared what had happened in their individual team meetings, receiving feedback, support, and suggestions for new strategies to be used in forthcoming team meetings. Not surprisingly, different teams with different home visitors had different team processes. However, salient issues emerged across teams, such as strategies to keep team members on task. Sometimes team leaders discussed difficulties such as unnecessary, off-topic chatting during team meetings or excessive negativity from a team member, both of which impede the flow of meetings and inhibit the growth of new home visitors. In all teams, experienced home visitors took responsibility to give suggestions to the new home visitors; in time, the new home visitors began using the meetings to ask specific questions of the experienced visitors. Each team had different strategies in using the effective approaches described earlier. However, team members consistently gained skills in giving descriptive affirmations instead of global evaluative comments. Individual team leaders shared that team meetings were very important, both to develop leadership skills and to give needed structure.]

Ex to Difficulty & Dilema

Home visiting is a daunting task and a better introduction to the job was needed. Therefore, in the project's fourth year, two home visitors were chosen to mentor first- and second-year home visitors. For the first 6 weeks, new home visitors observed their mentors and other experienced home visitors conducting home visits. Observing experienced home visitors gave a new perspective to the important issues in home visits. These first- and second-year home visitors met with their mentors monthly and had weekly phone conversations. Given the close one-on-one relationships between the experienced home visitors and their mentees, meetings often became the time to discuss dilemmas associated with being a new home visitor. For example, new home visitors often had difficulties managing the required paperwork and balancing work time with their own mothering needs. Mid-year, the mentor accompanied the mentee on a home visit, took written notes of this visit, and shared and discussed the notes with the new home visitor. This new aspect of the program revealed that home visitors are initially confused about the job requirements and are so anxious about being knowledgeable that they spent hours preparing for a single home visit. Mentors thus stressed that home visitors should instead focus on the most important skill—developing the relationship with the parents.

After the third and fourth years of the program, a videotape was created to illustrate 16 effective approaches in home visiting. Home visitors found the most salient approaches to be descriptive observation and affirmation, descriptive interpretation, suggestions within context, and active participation of parent. Following these suggestions, a second video was created, which also included common difficulties of providing developmental interpretation of observed child or adult action and promoting active involvement of the parent(s) during the home visit. These videos of exemplar practice were used during the first team meeting of the year and as deemed appropriate.

By the fourth year, the project of peer mentoring and supervision had become a taken-for-granted part of each home visitor's work. During the fourth and fifth program years, team meetings strove to focus on one of the difficult approaches from the video. Home visitors were asked to chose one approach and document their experience with it throughout the program year.

A qualitative formative evaluation was conducted annually by the director, who took verbatim notes on all observed team and team leader meetings. These notes were shared with all observed participants, who had an opportunity to provide written comments on them. Thus, as the program progressed, data were available to evaluate the program and make needed changes.

At the end of the fourth and fifth program years, about 80% of home visitors evaluated their experience in this project as being very helpful. These home visitors not only thought that they had developed new home visiting skills and insights, but they spoke of their increased skill in peer feedback, support, and suggestions, as well as personal development such as increased flexibility, ability to listen, and ability to be self-reflective. Professional development had intertwined with personal development. Negative comments most often centered on the high demands of this half-time position. Each case load included high-risk families, each visit involved paperwork, and the program's new curriculum meant more preparation time.

Before this project began, one coordinator was responsible for all the observations of home visits as well as all mentoring and supervision, but over time the project developed three new tiers of leadership: 1) home visitors developed skills in peer mentoring and supervision; 2) team leaders gained leadership skills in mentoring and supervision; and 3) experienced home visitors gained new skills as they mentored new home visitors.

ASSESSMENT AND EVALUATION

Successful programs have ongoing assessments of home visitors' approaches and their effectiveness. In addition, agencies or government funders usually require this assessment. Any program evaluation should begin by defining the key elements of one's program, which can be an enlightening experience.

Often, professionals are faced with issues of quantity and quality. Program quantity usually includes both intensity/depth and duration of involvement. Intensity and duration include issues of participant dropout and regularity of contact. Keep in mind that *enrolling* and *participating* are not the same things.

The program quality can be far more difficult to measure. Quality assessment is aided if a program has clearly stated (sometimes within a manual) the roles of its professionals, its appropriate services, and the intended outcomes. Identifying the intended outcomes of a complex program may not be a simple matter. For example, a central theme dominating many studies is the relationships between families and the program professionals. The issue is not only the professionals' competence, but their relationships with the families they serve. Parents play a central role in helping professionals understand how their familial and cultural contexts influence their child's development. Thus, assessment can be an educational process for parents as well.

Meisels and Atkins-Burnett[30] identified five elements of early childhood assessments:

1. Target of assessments
2. Context of assessments
3. Methods of assessments
4. Assessment personnel
5. Fusion of assessment and intervention

Assessments should occur within a naturalistic setting that is comfortable and familiar to the child. In contrast to past assessments in formalized environments, today's assessments make use of everyday experiences to help young children demonstrate what they know and can do.[31] Assessment involves multiple sources of information and uses a variety of methods, including the parents' perceptions of the child's abilities; thus parents are active participants in the assessment process. The value of an assessment is tied to its utility—that is, its contributions to everyday decision making about the specific intervention.

Meisels and Atkins-Burnett[32] identified the following principles of assessment:

1. The assessment must be based on an integrated developmental model.

2. The assessment should follow a certain sequence.
3. The assessment involves multiple sources of information and multiple components.
4. The child's relationships and interactions with his or her most trusted caregiver should be the cornerstone of an assessment.
5. An understanding of sequence and timetables in typical development is essential as a framework for the interpretation of developmental differences among infants and toddlers.
6. The assessment should emphasize attention to the child's level and patterns of organizing experiences and to functional capacities, which represent an integration of emotional and cognitive abilities.
7. The assessment should identify the child's current competencies and a continuous growth model of development.
8. The assessment is a collaborative process.
9. The process of assessment should always be viewed as the first step in a potential intervention process.
10. Reassessment of a child's developmental status should occur in the context of day-to-day family and/or early intervention activities.

Factors that determine who conducts the assessment will depend on state licensing issues, the purpose of the assessment, and the nature of the program. Practitioners who are likely to be conducting assessments include psychologists and occupational therapists, licensed clinical social workers, and early childhood educators.[33]

In many programs, external validity matters. External validity is the degree to which a professional can assume that the results of a study are generalized to the population from which the sample was drawn. Most studies that desire external validity have samples including control and experimental groups. An externally valid study can often be generalized to other populations.

Gilliam and Leiter[34] identified three components of assessment research: 1) process studies, 2) outcome-impact studies, 3) and cost–benefit studies. The goal of a process study is to learn exactly what a program did and to document each of the program's processes. An outcome-impact study seeks to demonstrate a causal relationship between participation in the intervention and desired outcomes. The use of control and experimental groups is a scientifically rigorous method of measuring program effects.[35] Programs also sometimes use pretest and posttest comparisons to determine effectiveness.

Gilliam and Leiter[36] identified three steps involved in a cost–benefit analysis. First, the staff documents and totals the costs of running a program—direct, indirect, and administrative costs. Second, they divide the total cost of operating the program by the number of participants served in the program. Third, they calculate a cost–benefit ratio by dividing the cost per participant by the benefit per participant as estimated through the outcome-impact study.

An effective and persuasive report has the following characteristics:

- Contains a table of contents
- Is brief and focused
- Uses simple declarative sentences to provide clarity
- Uses a simple layout to guide readers who scan
- Is visually descriptive

Evaluation writers should be ready to answer questions from funders or key decision makers after submission.

Some programs, especially those that serve children with special needs, may implement assessments of parent–child interaction. These assessments include two components: 1) the behavioral repertoire of both the child and the parent and 2) the reciprocity within the parent–child interaction. Research indicates that the parent and child each contribute unique characteristics to the interaction and their active tendencies determine the quality of the reciprocal relationship. Essential elements of a positive reciprocity include harmony, turn-taking, and rhythmicity.[37] Assessments should be a joint process between the parent and the professional. The parent's ideas and assessment of their relationship with their child are central elements.

Weatherston[38] (2000) identified four basic principles for a successful parent–infant assessment:

1. Infant and parent are assessed together.
2. The assessment occurs in a familiar setting.
3. A thoughtful systematic assessment takes time.
4. Parents must be considered as partners throughout the assessment process.

When the evaluation process is successful, professionals and parents begin to build partnerships that will be helpful to further intervention.

DIFFICULTIES AND DILEMMAS

The professional development discussed in this chapter may seem new and offer challenges to both home visitors and their administrators. Some home visitors may have difficulty with the professional development principles and suggested approaches discussed in this chapter. They may not be introspective or they may not have had prior experiences that promote self-knowledge.

Each person enters a field with a distinct personal and professional biography. Individuals may have a very private personal and professional life, making them reluctant to openly share their home visiting experiences with others. If the home visitor's prior professional experience involved hierarchical communicating and relating, promoting partnerships with parents characterized by mutuality may be frightening. When an individual's biography is very different from the demands of the current position, uncertainty can be expected. By recognizing these obstacles, administrators can provide time and support for home visitors to adapt to change.

Administrators also have professional development needs, but their needs may not be addressed by program policy, structure, and finance. In many programs, administrators work independently and may feel the same kind of isolation as home visitors. Administrators may have been promoted from direct service and may not have the benefit of preservice education directly related to their new role. As a result, administrators often have to create innovative ways of ensuring their own professional growth. Seminars at national conferences such as the ZERO TO THREE Training Institutes[39] can offer a setting for shared learning and gaining new insights for continued education of home visitors.

Administrators within a geographical region can also meet regularly. These meetings can provide the kind of peer supervision and guidance discussed in this chapter. An outside consultant with supervision expertise can assist in facilitating these regional meetings and can help expand members' notions of what is possible. Erikson Institute has taken leadership in offering a nine-session supervision seminar for administrators and supervisors of programs serving infants, toddlers, and their families in the Chicago area.[40]

CONCLUSION

This chapter has discussed how home visitors, as artisans, learn best through practice over time. This learning through practice is possible if home visitors reflect on their practice; in this reflection, they gain new understanding of the meaning and purpose of their practice. These skills can be promoted when a program's staff development is interactive. Team meetings can provide a setting for home visitors to tell stories to each other in a climate of mutual inquiry. They can share successes (a directive mother now engages in spontaneous play), express frustration (repeatedly the family is not home on the scheduled time), discuss dilemmas (conflicting concerns between grandmother and teen mother), and even share failure (a family's withdrawal from the program).

When team meetings are small enough to develop relationships of trust, these home visitors' stories can be the springboard for them to practice reflection, gain support, and provide feedback, encouragement, and new ideas. Learning from each other is the given expectation. Just as the personal relationship between home visitor and parent can strengthen a parent's role, when home visitors work together with shared goals and common bonds, the experience can be similarly strengthening—deepening the home visitor's understanding and enabling them to move forward with renewed commitment.

A solid foundation in child development is the first step in home visitors' continued education. Because home visitors' work cuts across disciplines beyond child development, staff meetings can be the setting for outside consultants to broaden the home visitor's knowledge base. When process is intertwined with content—that is, when home visitors can talk together about how their work relates to this content—then they can apply this new learning to their everyday work.

Regular collaborative supervision allows home visitors to discuss their work and gain feedback and guidance from an experienced practitioner. Supervision offers a safe setting in which to reflect on one's emotional reactions, expose mistakes and insecurities, and ask questions. Together, supervisors and home visitors reflect on and interpret both the difficulties and the successes. Many structural barriers within home visiting programs may make individual supervision impossible. Given this reality, administrators can adapt their program structure to provide features of the supervision model.

Professional development is a lifelong process in which home visitors should actively reflect on their practice, both individually and with peers. Program participants meet together in a climate of inquiry. This mutual, respectful collaboration offsets the individualistic nature of home visitors' everyday work, providing support, encouragement, and guidance for their return to the field.

Promoting Healthy Parent and Child Development

Developing a Sense of Self

The Foundation of Social and Emotional Development

"I do like a mother's love," said Tootles, hitting Nibs with a pillow. "Do you like a mother's love, Nibs?"

"I do just," said Nibs, hitting back.

"You see," Wendy said complacently, "our heroine knew that the mother would always leave the window open for her children to fly back by; so they stayed away for years and had a lovely time."

J.M. Barrie, *Peter Pan* (1911, p. 128)

THE CONCEPT OF "SELF" OR "sense of self" is elusive for adults. A person demonstrates a sense of self by saying, "This jacket looks like me." Or, when adults commit a faux pas, self-awareness makes them embarrassed. But can a baby have a sense of self?

Initially, an infant has no awareness of self,[1] but there are components of sense of self—inner experiences inferable through observed infant behavior. In infant research and theory, therefore, the terms *self* and *sense of self* are used in a different way than with adults.[2] Sense of self is an inclusive concept comprising both social and emotional development. It appears to develop within a paradox because we develop our own individual sense of self only through our interactions with others. Babies and young children develop a sense of self through day-to-day child-rearing interactions that parents often take for granted. These interactions are mutually created—parents shape their infant's actions at the same time that babies are shaping their parents' actions. This sense of self begins at the moment of birth and remains with us throughout our life.

The infant's emerging sense of self is the organization of feelings, actions, and expectations underlying our behavior.[3] The sense of one's self is extremely complex, but it is the core of what it means to be human. Adults can talk about their inner life, but the components of the infant's sense of self are inner experiences inferable only through observed behavior. For example, when a 3-month-old engages in social smiles and coos at others, we can infer an emerging sense of self in relation to others—a social self. Babies experience a sense of self long before they experience self-awareness.[4]

Because sense of self is abstract and unobservable, discussing it is difficult. However, we know that the developing sense of self is the scaffolding, the anchor, and the foundation of development. Emde defined development as the following:

> Development consists of changes within individuals over time. It involves increasingly organized complexity. As such, it involves processes of differentiation (divisions into subsystems), integration (articulation of wholeness), and successive ordering of parts and wholes (hierarchization). Moreover, development necessarily involves dynamic exchanges within the environment.[5]

Since the mid-1980s, infant research has used video of babies and their parents to revolutionize our understanding of the infant's developing sense of self. For example, we now know that babies are born with specific emotions and abilities to relate socially. Changes in sense of self do not happen because of changes in the infant alone. Rather, changes are the result of the infant's physiological and mental capabilities, as well as their experiences with significant others.[6] From birth, the newborn is experiencing both self and others. As Winnicott stated, "There is no such thing as a baby,"[7] meaning there is no such thing as an infant without its parent. The capacity to experience oneself only occurs as the infant relates to another. Therefore, development is a product of continuous interactions of babies and their experiences provided by their families and social context.

Given their drive to explore and master their environment, young children are active participants in their own development. Development is shaped by a dynamic interaction between biology and experience, between nature and nurture. The amount of change in the child's first 3 years has no parallel in the life cycle; this change is most dramatic in the sense of self.

In what context does the sense of self develop? Social-emotional development encompasses developing sense of self and is intertwined with all other developmental areas. For babies and young children, sense of self as well as social-emotional development occurs in developmental leaps.[8]

Emde and Robinson identified the basic motives in early development:

1. Activity: Babies are active, exploring and eager to master their everyday world.
2. Self-regulation: Babies have an inborn propensity to regulate their behavior as well as their bodily processes.
3. Social fittedness: Babies are motivated and programmed to initiate, maintain, and end social interactions.

4. Affective monitoring: Babies guide experience based on what is pleasurable and unpleasurable.
5. Cognitive assimilation: Babies have an impulse to explore the environment and see that which is new.[9]

Every few months, significant changes occur in the baby's and young child's sense of self. Major shifts in the infant's social experiences result from these gains; in turn, these shifts in social experiencing have an impact on the infant's sense of self. This chapter will track these developmental changes, which encompass the behavior of infants, young children, and their parents. The chapter will also explore how home visitors can support, affirm, and promote young parents' understanding and relationships with their infant and young children.[10]

NEUROPHYSIOLOGY

The brain is an interconnected network of billions of cells; its basic unit is the *neuron.* Neurons send information in the form of electrical signals throughout the body. Each neuron is made up of the *cell body, the axon,* and *dendrites,* which are like tree branches that extend from the neuron's cell body. Dendrites receive impulses and axons send impulses. The junctions from one neuron to another through which messages pass are called *synapses.*[11] Building the brain is a complex interaction between genes and the environment.

The term *brain development* refers to neurochemical and structural changes in the brain. Babies' experiences activate neurons and determine the number of dendrites that will form. The process of making connections is most active in a fetus and continues during the first few years of life. During the prenatal period, the brain's structure and functioning are established. By birth, most of the billions of brain cells that form the mature brain are in existence. In the early years, children's brains form twice as many connections as they eventually will need. Connections that are not used repeatedly are eliminated.

The baby's brain will grow more during the first year of life than at any other time. At 6 months of age, the brain is 50% of its adult size; at 3 years of age, the brain is 80% of its adult size. At 10 months of age, the cerebral cortex develops and receptive language emerges. The cerebral cortex plays a critical role in focusing attention, working memory, and other executive functions. Between 10 and 12 months, the baby's prefrontal cortex is growing. The prefrontal cortex is uniquely a part of social-emotional development and makes emotional regulation and focused attention possible.[12] During the first 3 years of life, children learn more than they will learn in any other period in their lives.

The central nervous system controls the complex processes that regulate both signals from within our bodies and signals from the environment. Since the early 1990s, neurobiological research has helped explain the connection between psychosocial and neurological aspects of development. Neuroscientists now are able to use technology to look at the brain and watch it work. Through this neuroimaging, researchers can measure chemical functions within the brain, such as glucose utilization, cerebral blood flow, oxygen utilization, and protein synthesis.[13] This research indicates that emotional development and emotional regulation parallel brain development. Experience is the product of an ongoing, reciprocal interaction between the environment and the brain.[14] Thus, changes in the brain trigger changes in babies' behavior and social-emotional development. In turn, the babies' experiences, especially everyday moment-to-moment caregiving interactions, influence brain structure and chemistry.

Scientists once thought that babies' genes alone determined their intellectual potential and how they behaved. Neuroscientists now know that the combination of genetic and environmental influences ultimately determines babies' social, emotional, and intellectual development.[15] A baby's environment includes such things as the foods and substances their pregnant mother consumes, people and places, toys and books, language, and most important, interactions with their parents. These interactions with their parents actually cause physical changes in the brain.[16] Repeated positive caregiving experiences make a decisive impact on the architecture of the brain, which is unique to each individual. Neglect of a baby's need for love and stimulation can affect brain development and cause lifelong problems. Neuroimaging shows much less density in the brain cells of neglected or traumatized babies; these babies typically have brains 20%–30% smaller than normal.

Cortisol, a hormone that increases in response to stress, contributes to the fight-or-flight reflex that helps babies respond to challenging situations. In moderate doses, cortisol is beneficial because it helps the brain respond to stress. However, when a baby or young child is traumatized, an excess of cortisol is produced, which can lead to prefrontal cortex damage and problems with memory and self-regulation. High levels of cortisol can also damage the hippocampus, which has been associated with memory deficits.[17]

Myelin, a fatty coating covering neurons, helps to strengthen brain processing. A well-balanced diet is important to myelin formation. Nutritional deprivation can therefore have a detrimental effect on brain development.[18] Undernutrition during pregnancy has been linked with prematurity, low birth weight, low brain weight, and smaller head circumference. During infancy and toddlerhood, malnutrition can trigger medical and social problems such as reduced resistance to infection, decreased physical activity, cognitive and emotional difficulties, and motor skill development deficits.

Neuroscientists believe there are sensitive periods of time during brain development when neurons can create connections most easily and efficiently. Each of the brain's system—vision, hearing, language, intellect, motor, social-emotional development—has its own sensitive period. During these sensitive periods, a certain kind of experience can have a profoundly different influence on future behavior than having that same experience at any other time in development. In language, the grammatical processing subsystem is more sensitive to early experience than is the semantic processing subsystem.

When a baby sends out a signal, their brains are receptive to the responses of others to that signal. The responses the baby receives become embedded in the neural maps of the baby's core sense of self. If the parent's responses to the baby are contingent, the baby's neural machinery creates an internal sense of coherence in the connection between the baby's self and the parent.[19] This emotional signaling supports increased neuronal connections in both the cerebellum, which deals with rhythmicity and timing, and the prefrontal cortex, which handles planning and sequencing actions, problem solving, and emotional regulation.[20] The executive functions of the prefrontal cortex in the brain create an innate instinct for autobiographical memory, self-awareness, response flexibility, and self-regulation. The development of the prefrontal cortex also supports symbol formation.

Emotional signaling with caregivers is a process shaped by attachment. Thus, the capacity for self-regulation is not taught; rather it emerges over the first 2 years of life as a result of interaction between the baby's maturing executive functions, such as the neurological capacity for self-regulation, and interactions with the environment.[21] As the baby grows older, an understanding of when to use specific self-regulatory behaviors improves; this new capacity for self-regulation is intentional and adaptive to outcomes.

The ability to detect changes in sensory stimulation and to establish associations between conditions are available before birth. The brain can biologically detect a change in the sensory environment, compare the event to past events, and create a new representation that combines the current event with existing representations.[22] A change in the environment or an event that is different from acquired knowledge recruits the child's attention and makes it likely that a new association will be formed.

Memory is the manner in which the brain responds to experience and forms new brain connections. Memory begins to develop after 6 months of age. Continuing through at least 24 months of age, there is dramatic improvement in imitation.[23] Connections are made in two major ways through two forms of memory: implicit and explicit. The creation of specific circuits of the brain responsible for creating emotions, behavior responses, and perception is implicit memory. Implicit memory is early nonverbal memory that is present at birth and continues throughout life. Interestingly, the child is not even aware that this internal experience is being created from something from the past.[24] Memory capacity changes throughout infancy and preschool in terms of the length of time over which children remember, the robustness of their memories, and the efficacy and productivity of different types of reminders.[25]

Neuroception describes how neural circuits distinguish whether a situation or people are safe, dangerous, or life threatening. Neuroception takes place in primitive parts of the brain without conscious awareness. Faulty neuroception might lie at the root of several psychiatric disorders of young children such as autism, depression, reactive attachment disorder, and anxiety disorders.[26] Neuroception can explain why a baby coos when rocked by her caregiver but cries when a stranger approaches. Young children who have experienced trauma most often have a faulty neuroception of the risk of their environment.

Brain development is a "use it or lose it" process. Research indicates that trauma or substance abuse during fetal development or infancy has a devastating effect on brain development. Through early childhood, parental neglect, stressful living conditions, or lack of appropriate stimulation jeopardize early brain development, possibly resulting in problematic social and emotional development and/or a dramatic reduction in later learning.

Emotions and Intelligence

Greenspan and Shanker defined intelligence as "[t]he ability to generate or create a full range of ideas in the areas of one's human emotional experiences and then reflect on them and organize them into a logical framework."[27] Earlier cognitive theorists omitted the central role of emotional experience through which intelligence develops. We now know that emotions are the architect of the young child's cognitive capacities. Two capacities central to intelligence are the abilities to create and reflect on ideas.

Motivation and communication are two primary functions of emotion. Emotions are essential for both creating and reflecting on ideas. For example, as a 10-month-old attempts to tickle his mother, the baby has an emotional intent—to wish to tickle. This early sense of intentionality stems from the baby's emotional intent. We could review the many games babies play with their parents; central to these games is the emotional joy involved. Repeated emotional communications between the baby and caregiver in everyday child-rearing interactions contribute to the development of individual differences in intensity and temporal patterns of emotional disposition.

Emotional Regulation

Emotional regulation is part of social-emotional development. Babies modify emotional reactions to accomplish their goals and to adapt to environmental demands; adequate adaptation requires both reaction and regulation. Babies often are good at reaction but need help with regulation. Initially, the parent and child accomplish emotional regulation together, but accomplishing this regulation is not always easy. Parents need to be able to read and understand their babies' needs and have the knowledge and resources to respond in helpful ways. When a baby cries, the parent comforts her. When a baby smiles, his mother talks to him. Early regulation is deeply embedded in the baby's relations with others.

The key to emotional regulation is the baby's emotional security. Emotional security emerges from a regular schedule of daily activities, the presence of a parent, the baby's attachment to his or her parent, and the home's emotional climate. Emotional regulation develops as parent and baby engage in a contingent cycle of signals and responses. Parents' sensitivity is closely linked to their baby's developing emotional regulation. Beginning in the third month of life, babies develop effective communication and emotional regulation within the context of their repeated interactions with their parents or significant caregivers. Parents' behavior can stimulate and confirm their baby's emotions and guide the baby's emotional regulation. Babies are quite skilled at tailoring their behavior to fit their caregiving environment and to optimize the likelihood that their parent will remain nearby.[28] For example, if they become overstimulated during an interaction, babies can avert their gaze and thereby lower the intensity of the stimulation.

The prefrontal cortex plays a central role in processing emotion information and regulating emotional regulation. Both the prefrontal cortex and the amygdala are involved in the information processing that leads to emotion and coping responses. Studies suggest intersystem connections between cognitive-language abilities and socioemotional regulatory behaviors, as well as the importance of the early development of emotional understanding and emotion knowledge for emotional regulation and coping strategies. Emotional regulation is basic to normal development; poor emotional regulation is a substantive factor in the beginning of psychopathology. Negative life events may produce experience-based changes in the brain and thereby contribute to under- or over-regulation of emotions and consequent psychopathology.[29]

Babies' emotional regulation may be significantly affected if they have a genetic or emotional conditional such as autism, Down syndrome, anxiety, mood disorders, anger, aggression, or hyperactivity. Similarly, babies with prenatal drug and/alcohol exposure often have emotional regulation difficulty.

DEVELOPING THE BODY SELF: BIRTH TO 6 MONTHS

From birth, the parent–baby relationship has an interpersonal aspect and an intrapsychic aspect (occurring within the mind, psyche, or personality). The everyday parent–baby interaction is the interpersonal aspect. The intrapsychic aspects involves how the mother and father see themselves as parents and how they see their baby. The parent's intrapsychic reality includes their past memories and past influences.[30] The newborn's behavioral states are influenced by physiological profiles created by changes in brain chemistry.[31] Integrated visual, tactile, kinesthetic, and auditory experiences developed by movement and activity make it possible for the baby to make a fundamental distinction between internal experiences and surrounding stimulation from shortly after birth. This perception distinguishes self-initiated action from surrounding activity and, over time, contributes to self-awareness.[32]

Mothers evolve a new psychological organization after giving birth—the motherhood constellation.[33] Stern identified seven main features in the motherhood constellation:

1. Mothers' interest, attention, and curiosity about others shifts with the advent of pregnancy and/or the birth of the child.
2. Mothers become relatively less attentive to and interested in issues of competition, dominance, and sex and more attuned to issues of cooperation and caring.
3. Mothers develop new sensory preferences and sensibilities.
4. Mothers are centrally preoccupied with issues of loving.
5. Mothers fall in love with their new baby.
6. Mothers have a new fear that arises and takes form. There is a hypervigilance and fearful preoccupation to ensure the safety of the baby.[34]
7. New mothers need other, experienced women around them.

Parents' interactions with their newborn primarily center on physiological regulation. As parents hold, caress, rock, and talk to their newborn, they learn to adjust their behavior to their baby's behavior. For example, parents gently rock the baby when it begins to fuss or talk to their baby during feeding. Just as a baby's behavior triggers a response from the parent, the parent's behavior triggers a response from their baby. For example, the baby becomes quiet as the parent rocks or looks intently into the eyes of the talking parent while the baby nurses. This mutual influence will continue in their everyday interactions.

Some babies may have sensory systems that are over- or underreactive; thus, the baby may not readily respond to the parent's efforts or may be fussy. In turn, some parents may themselves have shortcomings in their abilities to be responsive to their babies. We discuss these problems later in the Difficulties and Dilemmas section.

Parents of newborns experience both delight and uneasiness about their new task as a parent. Home visitors can help parents feel more at ease by providing helpful developmental information, including the six states of consciousness: deep sleep, light sleep, semialert, wide awake, fussing, and crying. Newborns typically sleep 16–17 hours each day.[35] During deep sleep, babies can shut out most environmental noise. During light rapid eye movement sleep, babies are more vulnerable to being awakened. When parents know what to expect, they are more in control of their caregiving, as described by Shelly:

I tell people that don't know anything about the program that home visitors will give you ideas of what to look for, what to expect next in the development of the child, and things you can do that can help that development to go along. And I just tell them that we wouldn't be without it... We waited a long time before having children, and not knowing what to do after having the baby, we were like well, you know. I guess I was kinda iffy about some things, and not knowing how to do other things.

Newborns show preferences for familiar sights, sounds, and odors. The human fetus can recognize the mother's voice.[36] Babies may recognize and even prefer their mother's face and voice as early as 2 days of age.[37] They respond differentially to the valence in their mother's vocal contours[38] and prefer listening to melodies sung by their mothers and stories they heard while they were in the womb.[39] Newborns can distinguish changes in the frequency, loudness, and timbre of the human voice and differences between vowel sounds.[40] They can also react to sweet, sour, and bitter tastes. These attention biases allow babies to learn quickly about physical and psychological properties of objects and people. In addition, the preference toward the mother plays an important part in the formation of the mother–child bond.

Emotions are the key to the baby's psychological engagement. The way parents hold their baby influences the baby's sense of security and ability to focus calmly.[41] Home visitors can encourage parents to vary how they hold their baby to learn which position helps the baby to relax most. For most young babies, it is soothing to be swaddled gently but firmly with arms and legs in a blanket that is then wrapped around the body.

Schaefer described of the spiritual elements of infant experience. First, newborns are present because their experience lacks organized memories of previous experiences, expectations, and/or desires. Presence is pure awareness that is free from comparison, judgment, fear, or desire. When babies are about 3 months of age, a developmental leap brings new behaviors that promote sociability and another spiritual element, joy, emerges. At this point, the baby has a strong sense of being open and drawn toward someone in wonder and curiosity, without any fear.[42]

Every parent quickly learns that crying is one behavior their baby does well. By the time the baby is 8–10 weeks of age, the parents can recognize different kinds of crying. Brazelton and Sparrow identified typical patterns of babies' crying:

- Boredom is a fussy, whimpering cry, which usually stops as the parent softly talks to the baby.
- Fatigue occurs at the end of the day and often is rhythmic.
- Hunger is accompanied by rooting and searching for something to suck on.
- Pain has a piercing, unrelenting quality. Often the babies' face will be screwed into a tight knot or they will bring their arms and legs up to their body in a tight ball.[43]

Babies demonstrate interest in their surroundings through facial expressions, body movements, and eye gaze. They have both a physical/cognitive reaction and an emotional reaction to each experience; they experience basic emotions of pleasure, comfort, and distress. Young babies can focus at a distance of about 8–10 inches, which is why the nursing position is ideal for mutual gazing and interaction.[44] Between periods of fussing, sleeping, and eating, babies develop longer periods of quiet alertness when parents can interact with them. These periods of mutual attentiveness and interaction deepen the parent–baby bond.

Newborns are predesigned to seek stimulation, to selectively respond to their environment, and to participate in social interaction. Newborns have some voluntary muscle control. They choose to look at faces, will suck to soothe themselves, and turn away from unpleasant sounds or sights.[45] These behaviors indicate that the newborn is capable of purposeful actions.

The newborn's sense of being is integrated. Different experiences can be joined if they share the same quality of feeling. For example, a mother may comfort her baby in different ways, speaking softly, stroking softly, walking calmly. The baby experiences these different occurrences as the same form of comfort. A sense of organization thus is created.

The young baby's experience is controlled by what is pleasurable and unpleasurable; in other words, emotions are the organizing basis for guiding behavior. Initially, very young babies have little ability to manage their feelings and are dependent upon their parents for this regulation. As they interact with their young baby, parents respond empathetically and help their baby avoid too much excitement or discomfort. In that interaction, babies learn to regulate their own emotions, termed *affect regulation*.[46]

Brazelton and Cramer illustrate affect regulation:

[A] mother will lean over her baby, reach for a flailing extremity, hold the baby by the buttocks, enclose him or her in an envelope made up of her intense gaze and her soft vocalization. Out of this cluster of five behaviors, she will heighten one of them, her voice, to elicit a response. As her voice increases gently, the infant responds with a cluster of behaviors—relaxation of the whole body, softening of facial features, intense looking at her, then a soft "coo." The mother's clustering of behaviors around each vocalization is as important in producing the response as her voice alone. A baby must be "contained" in order to attend to her. The mother also must learn her baby's system of clusters. The capacity of a mother to form a behavioral envelope to contain the baby, to maintain the baby's alert state, and to allow the necessary rhythms of attention—withdrawal becomes critical to her ability to communicate.[47]

Holding, touching, caressing, and rocking are central ways parents regulate their babies' feelings. In these everyday child-rearing interactions, babies experience love and comfort through physical affection, which helps the babies to regulate their emotions and responses.

At 3 months of age, cycles of wakefulness are extended, babies become more focused, eye-to-eye contact is extended, and the infant enjoys frequent spontaneous social vocalizing and smiling. Young babies have excellent motor memories. Memory allows young babies to have a sense of continuity with their previous experiences. For example, babies have memories of past interactions with their parent that provide them with expectations guiding their behavior.[48] These memories are nonverbal, consist of internal experiences, and provide a guide for their present experiences. They include a wide array of social behavior between infant and parent, such as simple interactive games like Peekaboo and Pat-a-cake. Specific emotions emerge; joy becomes differentiated from contentment, while sadness and later anger become differentiated from general distress.[49]

Self-Calming

The newborn's first task is to achieve calmness—to be regulated inside and interested in the surrounding world. One of parents' first areas of guidance is assisting their new baby to self-calm, allowing them to stop crying or fussing without help from anyone else. This is achieved by 8–10 weeks of age through sucking, arm and leg movement, a certain body position, or vision.[50] Self-calming is a mutual achievement of parent and baby learned through their communication. By learning the different meanings of the baby's cries, parents know when they can let their baby self-calm versus when the baby needs to be fed. Babies may show early individual differences in both self-calming and attention, perhaps in response to emotional parts of their environment; these may be linked to later complex tasks. The home visitor should discuss self-calming during the first visit after a baby's birth because many parents are unaware of its importance.

Babies and toddlers prenatally exposed to drugs and/or alcohol are likely to be fussy and have difficulty calming themselves.[51] Some suggestions for the care of these babies are given here:

- Hold the baby to give him or her a sense of security.
- Bright lights, fast movements, or loud noises should be avoided.
- Keep the baby in a position directly facing the parent.
- A gentle foot, ankle, or back massage can help a tense baby to relax.
- The baby may have uncoordinated suck and swallow reflexes, so allow ample time for feeding and be as relaxed as possible.
- Solid foods will need to be introduced gradually in small amounts.
- A bedtime ritual can assist in calming the baby before sleep.
- Parents should gently touch the baby frequently for brief periods.
- Parents should speak frequently, throughout the day, to the baby.[52]

In some cases, nothing will stop the crying of these babies because they experience discomforts that cannot be relieved. In these situations, parents will need a helper to provide them with a break.

Parents' Affect Regulation

Early child development theorists and researchers discuss *affect* and *emotion* interchangeably.[53] In this book, emotional regulation refers to the central role the parent has in helping the young baby regulate; affect regulation designates a parent's empathic response to the baby's signal. At 2 to 3 months of age, newborn reflexes disappear, crying decreases, recognition memory increases, consistent smiling occurs, and the baby has extended play with significant others. Prosocial behavior (e.g., babies' positive behavior and increased attention toward their mothers) and social expectancies (expecting to share emotionally) are increased.[54] Now the baby and adult face each other in close proximity and interact facially, vocally, tactilely, and with behavioral gestures. In this play, babies learn that social interaction is dynamic and always changing. They discover that their responses have effects on the adult's behavior and expect that people will respond to and interact with them.[55] Because this social play is so affective, babies learn about the emotional expressions of people. By $3\frac{1}{2}$ months of age, babies can discriminate the expressions of their mother's different emotions.[56]

A baby's healthy social-emotional development depends on the parents' ability to see meaning in the baby's behavior and respond appropriately. Home visitors can help parents understand the meaning of their baby's gestures and movement. Parents who successfully read their baby's cues and respond appropriately feel confident and enjoy their parenting.

Some parents are not responsive to their baby's signals of distress. This nonresponsiveness should trigger the home visitor's concern. Crittenden identified four reasons for parents' lack of appropriate response:

1. Parents appear to be unaware of their baby's signals.
2. Parents recognize the signals but misinterpret them
3. Parents interpret the signals correctly but do not know how to respond appropriately.
4. Parents understand how to respond but for various reasons, such as being depressed, do not respond appropriately.[57]

Babies whose fathers participate in bathing, feeding, diapering, and dressing are more socially responsive and scored higher on the Bayley Scales of Infant Development than those fathers who did not provide regular care.[58] Fathers interact differently with their babies than do mothers and thus expand the baby's range of potential emotions. In addition, when fathers share in caregiving, they also are providing emotional and physical support for the mother.

Temperament

Home visitors also can help parents understand the wide differences in a baby's responsiveness to people and environment, in the baby's activity level, and in how quickly the baby becomes upset. These differences reflect inborn patterns termed *temperament*.[59] Temperament is a biological bias for specific feelings and actions that first appear during infancy and early childhood and can be adapted by environments into personality traits. Temperamental biases are determined by brain neurochemistry. Temperament is a physiological and psychological process and is influenced in part by genetic factors; however, environmental factors can alter initial temperamental profiles. Expressions of temperament are likely to change over time. Temperament differences are seen in mood, movement, ease of soothing, degree of alertness, adaptability, and distractibility. Babies' temperaments affect the way they respond to their parents.[60]

A child's temperament characteristics are influenced by gender, age, developmental stage, environment, and constraints of the physical setting. Genes are dynamic in nature and change in the quantity and quality of their effects as the organism changes developmentally.[61] Thus, genetic factors can cause change as well as continuity in behavioral development. Ease of arousal to stimulation (reactivity) and the ability to modify that arousal (self-regulation) are two primary temperaments of the first stage of a baby's development.[62]

Temperament influences social learning, with some children more responsive to reward, others to punishment, and some children highly responsive to both. The development of coping strategies is also closely linked to temperament. Some young children experience high distress to strangers, whereas others experience little distress. Young children's tendencies toward approach versus inhibition demonstrate significant stability of long developmental periods, with substantive implications for the children's social development.

Beginning in the first few months of life, temperament differences elicit different reactions from the environment and influence how parents react to their babies and young children. Studies indicate that mothers of difficult babies experience lower self-confidence than do mothers of less difficult babies. Young children's negative emotions predict their parents negative responses.[63]

A parent's responses to a child's activity may change over time as the child becomes older and the parent expects more sustained attention. Parents may tolerate higher activity levels for sons than daughters. Parents in high-risk environments may value their child's hyperactivity and aggression as survival strategies, whereas their child's teacher may define these behaviors as problematic.

Meaningful patterns of relationship exist between temperament and adjustment in young children's development. Many studies show temperament is linked with psychopathology.[64] Mood and anxiety disorders may be related to temperament and personality characteristics in the following ways:

1. A predisposition to the development of disorders (e.g., in response to stressors)
2. A personality that shapes the course of a disorder (e.g., by producing an environment that maintains the disorder)
3. A disorder produces enduring changes in personality (e.g., increased levels of insecurity)
4. The psychopathological condition is an extreme manifestation of the underlying personality trait[65]

Studies indicate that dysregulation traits of temperament are more highly associated with children's problem behaviors when parenting is negative or harsh.[66]

Temperament creates some constitutional differences in a young child's reactivity and self-regulation. Some temperaments are associated with psychological disorders. Young children who are extroverted are at risk of externalizing behaviors and aggression. Behavioral inhibition puts children at risk for anxiety, depression, and other internalizing symptoms. Young children's self-control and attention promote the development of rule-abiding behavior.[67]

Parents can learn to adapt their response to their baby's unique temperament. Karyn's discussion with her home visitor Janice is illustrative.

Karyn: One day he screamed all day. I called the pediatrician, and he said to put him on the dryer and turn it on. I let go, and got angry; and then he said to bring in the baby. He said that Greg was okay and he is going to be a difficult baby.

Janice: He still cries, but now you feel better because you know it is not a health problem. (Karyn nods yes.) There's so much learning that goes on. The baby needs to learn your signals; you need to learn his signals. You don't know each other very well yet. It's really tricky.

Karyn: He's jumpy. Like, when the nipple on his bottle makes a sound, he jumps. Even when he's sleeping, he's jumpy.

Janice: Swaddling—wrapping him snuggly in his blanket and cuddling him, often helps, keeping him closed in. Have you tried massages?

Karyn: No.

Janice: Try rubbing his shoulders. Babies carry tension in their shoulders, like we do. And put him on his back, stretch and bend his legs one at a time, and massage them, and rub his tummy.

Janice comments that the pediatrician's suggestion of calming Greg by using the hum and vibration of the dryer is the physician's way of telling Karyn, in everyday language, that her baby's temperament is "difficult"—that Greg is difficult to soothe and comfort. As she rephrases Karyn's description, Janice lets Karyn know that she has heard her feelings. She provides a suggestion directly related to Karyn's concerns. In this conversation, no doubt Karyn feels understood and affirmed.

A parent's behavior can change a baby's temperament.[68] Extreme irritability, however, can remain on some degree throughout the baby's first year. Some, but not all, irritable babies develop a reserved, timid, and fearful style in the preschool years caused by extreme sensory sensitivity, which is typical of babies and young children suffering from regulation disorder.[69] The Difficulties and Dilemmas section of this chapter discusses regulation disorder.

Bonding and Attachment

Young babies develop their sense of self within everyday child-rearing relationships. Infant theorists use the terms *bonding* and *attachment* to explain this relationship.[70] Attachment can be defined as an enduring emotional tie that unites one person to another over time and across space.[71] By the end of the first year, the baby's attachment to significant others is fully developed.[72] Most mothers and fathers form a strong initial bond with their infant at birth or in the hours and days immediately following. However, home visitors must understand that not all parents feel positive after their infant's birth and some parents may not quickly bond to their infant. When parents do not feel bonded immediately, they may think that something is wrong with them and may feel guilty. Home visitors can assist these parents in recognizing that this new infant brings a giant change to the parent's life, their ambivalent feelings are a normal part of being a parent, and it may take time to learn how to feel comfortable in their new role as parent. Further, some parents experience difficulty bonding with their second child, feelings that surprise and trouble them. Again, the home visitor can assist the parent to understand that these feelings are normal.

Home visitors can help parents recognize early forms of communication and how responsiveness fosters the baby's sense of connectedness and security, as Janice does.

Janice puts Jene (3 months) on an infant blanket and gives her a three-ringed rattle. Jene begins to fuss once again. Her mother, Natalie, picks her up and softly bounces her as she softly, rubs her back. Janice uses the baby's voice to affirm Natalie's responsiveness, "I know how to communicate with my mommy, and she understands me."

Natalie prepares a bottle for Jene and holds her in her lap as she continues to chat with Janice. Jene falls asleep.

Janice says, "It's important to pay attention to a baby's signals. We could have continued on the floor, but we followed Jene's signals. She became fussy. Kids at all ages need to know that adults respect their feelings. It's time for Mommy to pick me up."

Janice supports and affirms Natalie's responsiveness to her infant's signals. She helps this young mother understand that her responsiveness is communicating respect to even such a small infant.

Both the baby's temperament and maternal behavior contribute to the developing attachment relationship, but not all babies have a single attachment figure. Babies may show strong attachments to both parents or to parents and another caregiver, such as their out-of-home child care teacher. Emotional availability, nurturance, warmth, and provision of comfort are the most salient parent behaviors that promote attachment. The securely attached baby will gain emotional regulation and seek comfort for distress with the attachment figure.[73]

Parents and their babies develop a natural pattern of attachment behaviors. Babies signal their needs by crying or smiling, their parent responds, so the dance begins.[74] This mutuality is essential for the development of a healthy attachment.[75] As home visitors observe attachment behaviors, they can help parents recognize the significance of these behaviors. Tracy's home visitor, Janice illustrates.

Mia has awakened from her nap and her mother, Tracy, has just brought her into the living room. Mia smiles as Janice softly says, "I'm so glad to see you."
Mia then begins crying as she nestles her head in her mother's shoulder.
Janice says, "It's so typical of babies this age—to switch emotions. Two things are happening: first, they can be happy then sad, and vice versa so quickly, and more importantly, Mia knows the difference between Mom and other people."
Janice continues, "You're so wise to comfort her when she feelings that way. She knows mom is here." (Mia now is smiling at Janice.) "And with mom here, it's okay to smile at others. It's also nice to be having people in your own home. There is security here and a gradual way for Mia to deal with a couple of new people."

Janice's observations of Mia's behavior and her mother's appropriate response supports and affirms Tracy. As she observes, Janice interprets the developmental significance of Mia's behavior and gives Tracy a simple suggestion.

Specific attachment patterns result from the interaction of characteristics of the young child, capacities of the child's parent, and the broader context of their relationship. It may be difficult for some parents to provide sensitive care to their children. When a parent can maintain a high degree of sensitivity, psychological availability, and responsiveness, even temperamentally difficult babies can develop secure attachments. However, a parent's depression or stress from economic difficulty or marital conflict can interfere with the sensitive and responsive caregiving needed for secure attachment.

Babies may form a type of attachment with one parent that is different than the attachment formed with another parent. For example, a baby may have a secure attachment with her mother but an insecure attachment with her out-of-home caregiver. The secure attachment with mother may temper the baby's insecure attachment with the out-of-home caregiver. In some cases, an outside figure may provide the security the baby does not get from either parent. However, spending time in child care usually does not undermine young children's relationships with their parents. As a result of the consistent high turnover in child care providers in the United States, young children are more often insecurely than securely attached to these providers.[76]

Securely attached babies feel connected and trust that their parent will be available, responsive, and loving. In addition, by responding quickly and appropriately to a baby's signals, the attachment figure strengthens the baby's sense of competence and efficacy. A secure attachment helps to structure the baby's brain so that the baby can handle stress better and to relate positively to other people. The outcomes of attachment influence social and personality development, including the development of social skills, social expectations, emotion regulation, behavioral self-control, relational schemas, self-confidence, trust in others, conscience development, and the enhancement or deterioration of emotional well-being.[77]

Thompson spoke of how attachment is an important influence beyond infancy.

> Secure or insecure attachment is important not only as an indicator of the early parent–child relationship, but it is believed to influence emergent self-representation, social skills and dispositions, personality development, and self-regulation. The influences of attachment security increasingly characterize the child, not just the relationship with the parent.[78]

With repeated everyday child-rearing interactions, babies develop an attachment and an internal working model of their relationship with their parents. Babies' internal working models are a cognitive representation or a memory of their interactions with parents. Internal working models permit babies to form expectations, attention, interpretations, and memories, which in turn guide behavior.[79] These models are flexible and dynamic; they serve as a guide for future emotions, perceptions, and behaviors across the life span.

Babies are thought to internalize conceptions of themselves for their early relational experience and incorporate them into their developing internal working model, which forms a lens for experiences that affect their self-concept. In reality, socioemotional development is representational, integrative, affectively oriented, and relationship based.[80] Internally organized attachment operates at an unconscious level.[81] When most of babies' interactions consist of experiences of comfort, warmth, and pleasure, babies develop an inner understanding that close relationships are trustworthy and nurturing.[82] As a young child changes and the environment changes, working models will be updated.

Babies and young children draw social maps of their everyday world. Attachment is the baby's first social map and encompasses how the baby understands his or her everyday social environment. When babies are poorly attached, the babies are termed "psychologically homeless; and the social map begins to emerge without appropriate boundaries, allies, and orientation to emotional north, south, east and west."[83] Studies indicate that securely attached children are more competent in emotion understanding among peers[84] because of their mother's elaborate talk about emotion.

Within these attachment relationships, babies begin to develop an inner sense of themselves. Loved babies see themselves as lovable and worthy of attention. As significant adults respond to them, babies develop a sense of compe-

tence and confidence. Longitudinal studies confirm the long-term consequences of early attachment.[85] When babies' cries are ignored or met with
harshness, these babies develop a sense of self as unworthy.[86] Two different
worlds are created for those babies who are securely attached and those who are
insecurely attached.

Greenspan and Lewis identified ways in which a baby around 5 months of
age participates in a loving relationship:

- Responds to caregiver's smile with a smile
- Initiates interactions with loving looks and smiles
- Makes sounds and/or moves mouth, arms, legs, or body in rhythm to
  caregiver
- Relaxes or acts comforted when held or rocked
- Coos when held, touched, looked at, or spoken to
- Looks at caregiver's face with rapt interest
- Anticipates the caregiver's face or voice with curiosity and excitement
- Looks uneasy or sad when the caregiver withdraws from play
- Becomes angry (furrowed brow or piercing cry) when frustrated by
  caregiver
- Recovers from distress within 15 minutes with caregiver's help[87]

A baby's emotional interactions with significant others is the source of intelligence, morality, and self-esteem. Joyful parent–baby interactions spark brain
growth in areas that focus on emotional expression, which in turn helps the
baby's ability to interact lovingly. Daily positive child-rearing interactions are
babies' first lessons in understanding that they can make something happen.[88]

The personalities of young children and the quality of their early relationships are complexly intertwined.[89] Anger proneness at 7 months of age is related to the child's cooperation at 15 months of age. Children with unresponsive parents and anger proneness are generally unwilling to cooperate. In
contrast, children with anger proneness but maternal responsiveness in infancy
are quite cooperative.

Current research also demonstrates intergenerational influences in attachment. There is significant agreement between mothers' and their babies' patterns of attachment, as well as between the mothers' and their own mother's attachment patterns.[90]

Insecure Attachment

Withdrawal and aversion are normal adaptive coping strategies for babies. All babies occasionally look away and turn their heads and bodies away from their caregivers, usually to regulate arousal down to a comfortable level. On the other hand,
some babies experience maternal overstimulation, intrusion, or other mother–baby
difficulties, such as a mother's consistently loud voice or rough handling. These
maternal patterns may lead to extreme forms of baby aversion and withdrawal.

Babies whose cries often are ignored learn that parents are unreliable. When babies have psychologically unavailable parents, they develop models of relationships as empty and unfulfilling. These negative internal relationship models shape both the expectations and behaviors of the babies. At age 3 years, children from disorganized attachment show a higher level of externalizing and internalizing problems than securely attached children.[91] In addition, boys are more likely to have insecure attachments at age 12 months than girls.[92] These differences in security attachments are the outcome of variations in maternal sensitivity during a baby's first year.[93]

Secure or insecure attachments may change during the early years of life. For example, a baby who begins with an insecure relationship may later develop a secure attachment to the same parent as the parent becomes more comfortable reading the baby's signals. The birth of another baby or a period of high family stress may alter a young child's attachment.[94] Risk factors associated with insecure attachment include poverty, child maltreatment, maternal illness, and maternal drug and alcohol abuse.[95]

Insecure attachment increases the risk for future psychological disorder.[96] Studies indicate that insecurely attached children score significantly higher on measures of disruptive behavior.[97] Aspects of the parent–child relationship also can contribute to the level of attachment. Managing a child who is having difficulties, a large number of children in the family, and conflictual parent–child relationships contribute to insecure attachments.[98]

Social Development

Unlike adults, babies do not think symbolically. However, they do experience presymbolic representation, such as motor representations, of their interaction patterns. Moment to moment, babies anticipate sequences between their own behavior and those of their caregiver: both in time (rhythm, pausing, tempo) and in space (intrusion, approach/avoid). Babies understand predictable relationships between their own movements and those of their caregiver.[99] They even can predict that certain actions will be followed by certain consequences in the environment, leading to a primitive sense of causality.[100]

During their first year of life, babies carefully observe peers, which indicates a clear sign of babies' social interest. Babies are also responsive to other babies' emotional signals. Around 6 months of age, babies sometimes respond to another baby's cry by crying. Around 8 months of age, babies begin object sharing.[101] They also often respond to their play partner's behaviors. However, much of their play is side by side without interaction, termed *parallel play*.

Much of what happens in social relationships is the process of one person's emotions interacting with the emotions of another person. Each person feels empathic emotional communication. As early as 2 months of age, babies are interested in others. Beginning with the parent and baby gazing intently at each other, simple playful interactions develop. As the 3-month-old smiles, the parent smiles and talks softly; with time, babies become familiar with the emotional language of their significant others and the emotional messages conveyed by the tone of voice and body movements. In another month or so, the baby laughs and soon will enjoy Peekaboo. Very young babies also enjoy the companionship of other babies and toddlers; around 6 months of age, they will stare at or try to get the attention of another baby by a smile or babble.

THE AUTONOMOUS SELF: 7–18 MONTHS

The transition between 7 and 12 months is marked by a growth spurt in the prefrontal cortex.[102] Babies between 7 and 9 months of age have a history (memory) of relating with their parents and increased experiences in communicating by facial expression, body movements, and posture.[103] Infant specialist Robert Emde speaks of the developmental leap in this period as "the onset of focused attachment."[104] A new form of experiencing connectedness emerges: two-way communication. Babies can initiate and respond to social gestures. They enjoy simple interactive games such as Pat-a-cake and Peekaboo, providing evidence of shared joint attention. Schaefer speaks of the third element of infant spiritualization emerging, which is awareness of other's awareness.[105] Now babies realize that they are not alone and their parent is aware as they are.

After 7 months of age, babies can remember past events that are not in the perceptual field and hold them in their memory. Babies now begin pointing and can follow their parent's pointing. By 9 months, babies will make requests by pointing for a bottle or to go outdoors. When babies are hungry, they no longer have to cry; they can instead go to their mother and point to what they want. When the baby wants her mother to read her a book, she can go to the bookshelf and remove the book she wants her mother to read.

The prefrontal cortex helps the baby sequence and plan actions. The baby offers her father a toy. As her father reaches, the baby withdraws the toy and turns away. Babies understand humor or incongruity. For example, they see incongruity when the parent tries to drink from a book instead of from a sippy cup. They demonstrate their humor by funny gestures, positions, sounds, or behavior that is unexpected or inconsistent. For example, they place a bowl on their head, put their head between their legs, purposely mispronounce a word, pull their parent's ear or squeeze their nose, or use their fingers to eat applesauce.

Developmentalists say the baby is giving evidence of shared intention.[106] Babies have both a physical/cognitive reaction and an emotional reaction to each experience.[107] By 9 months, many babies are crawling about to explore their surroundings. In order to resolve uncertainty, babies will pause and look from their desired goal to their parent; this is to gain assurance from their parent, thus giving evidence that the baby can understand the parent's expression of feeling. This reliance on attachment figures for a sense of security is termed *social referencing*.[108] These new skills allow the baby to begin to understand that their inner experiences are shareable with someone else.[109] They can carry an image of mommy or daddy inside their head, even when mommy and daddy are out of sight. These social skills are the first steps in a process that helps toddlers learn to become more cooperative.

Individual differences in babies' social experiences cause differences in their early social understanding. Babies' experiences in face-to-face interaction with significant others affect their more generalized influences on social expectations. In other words, differences in early parental sensitivity may be important for how young children begin to comprehend the nature of others' intentions.[110]

Around 12–18 months of age, babies react to others' negative emotions. They sometimes react to another's distress with concerned attention and prosocial behavior such as verbal reassurance. Prosocial behaviors are associated with indices of cognitive development.[111] Both emotion and intelligence are parts of the same pattern of growth.[112] Now toddlers can exhibit pleasure, disgust, anger, annoyance, and surprise. Two-way communication helps the child become empathic and eventually distinguish right from wrong. Also at this age, babies can retain a mental image of an object, termed *object permanence*. During their second year, toddlers develop visual self-recognition (in a mirror) and verbal self-reference ("Rosie big").

The baby can now activate a representation for a past event and relate that representation to features in the current situation, a process called *working memory*. In the first half of the second year of life, toddlers become problem solvers. Now that they are moving, they can get what they want; they also know that they can enlist their parents to help them get what they want. The toddler is starting to understand how the physical world works (e.g., doors open and close and are to go in and out; if I can't see something, I can climb on furniture to see). In the toddler's second year, the toddler can infer selected mental and emotional states in others, can represent actions that are prohibited, and is consciously aware of some of the self's feelings and intentions.[113]

Parents' Responsiveness

In their interactions with their babies, parents often understand the feelings behind their baby's behavior and respond in a way that matches their baby's feeling. Parents' behavior is not a strict behavioral imitation. Often, the match is an expression by a different sensory expression, such as when the baby's stretching movement is matched by the parent's stretching voice tone and tempo. As parents reflect back their babies' feelings, the babies feel connected, gain understanding of their own feelings, and thus understand their own sense of self. Daniel Stern illustrates how babies and their parent share feelings:

A 9-month-old girl becomes very excited about a toy and reaches for it. As she grabs it, she lets out an exuberant "aaaah!" and looks at her mother. Her mother looks back, squinches up her shoulders, and performs a terrific shimmy of her upper body—like a go-go dancer. The shimmy lasts only about as long as her daughter's "aaaah!" but is equally excited, joyful, and intense.[114]

Parents experience the feeling qualities of their baby's experience. Parents' behavior often mimes the baby's feeling, such as when the baby says "aaaaah" and the parent raises her hands high or the baby taps a spoon on the high chair and the parent claps. When parents' behavior reflects the same quality of feeling, young babies experience their parents' empathic responsiveness and communication.[115] When parents label and discuss emotional experience, they help their toddlers to give meaning to their emotional experience. When parents frequently discuss emotions (e.g., "Do you miss Sissy, now that she's gone to school?"), their young children will have a clearer understanding of emotion. Parents may coach their toddlers to develop strategies to take turns, deal with a frustrating task, or comfort a friend.

Trust

As babies become mobile, they actively explore the world around them. When they are securely attached, babies use their parents as a safe base from which to explore. Erikson speaks of babies' first developmental task as achieving basic trust as opposed to mistrust.[116] Babies learn to trust others to meet their needs; in turn, they trust themselves to make things happen. A trusting baby sees the world as a good, stable place to be. Trust emerges when babies have their needs met: the physical needs of nourishment, sleep, and warmth, as well as the psychological needs of cuddling, talk, and play. When babies experience consistency in having their needs met, they are self-confident that they can give cues to let someone know what they need and that they can influence others. Home visitors can help parents recognize what their baby is learning when they respond to their baby.

Greg (9 months) begins to cry. His mother, Karyn, picks him up, and his crying ends.
    Karyn's home visitor, Janice, speaks as if she is in Greg's voice to affirm Karyn's responsiveness, "That's so reassuring to me. Mom really understands what I mean, and she is helping me."

As Karyn spontaneously interacts with Greg, Janice helps her understand how important her actions are for her young baby's understanding of self and the world around him. As Karyn consistently responds to her son's behavior, her son develops an understanding that he influences another; through these experiences, he develops a sense of *personal control*.[117]

When home visitors sense that a parent is not responding to his or her baby, they can model spontaneous gestural and verbal responses to the baby as an example for the parent. In these interactions with the baby, the home visitor can help the parent see the baby's pleasure in the interaction and understand the developmental importance of this process. Some home visitors may be working with parents whose own problems prevent them from tuning into their baby. We discuss this problem later in the Difficulties and Dilemmas section

Loveys

An object connected to their parents' warmth and love can provide security for young babies and toddlers, especially during transition times, such as from waking to sleeping.[118] Such objects, sometimes called *loveys,* allow young children to comfort themselves in the same manner as thumb sucking. A single beloved object taken to bed may become part of a young toddler's self-comforting routine. Mia's "aw" is illustrative.

Mia (17 months) asks her mother, Tracy, "Where is aw?" Tracy explains to Janice that "aw" is Mia's name for her special pillow. Tracy explains that the pillow was a fancy pillow that she had received as a shower present. She and her husband would say "aw" as they would put Mia to bed. And one night she asked for her "aw," and ever since, it has been her special pillow.

Loveys are a normal part of development. Home visitors can help parents understand how loveys play an important role for young children who are learning to comfort themselves.

Stranger Anxiety

A sign of strong attachment occurs around 8 months of age when babies protest being separated from their parents and show fear of strangers and strange places. The intensity of these fearful reactions varies widely from one baby to another. This pattern often is referred to as *stranger anxiety.* There seems to be no clear basis for this typical fearful pattern. It seems to occur as babies become more aware of new places and of new people. After about a month or so, most babies learn how to handle new experiences.

Because stranger anxiety is quite predictable around 8 months, home visitors can give parents needed information so that parents can expect this first sign of fear in their infant and know that their infant's behavior is normal. When visiting babies during this phase, home visitors can respect the baby's fear and help the family feel at ease.

Home visitor Janice arrives at Tracy's home. Maggie (8 months) is crawling about the living room. When Janice begins to speak, Maggie stops crawling and begins to cry. Her mother picks her up as Janice comments, "Someone strange is in my house."

Janice then sits on the rug, several feet from Maggie and her mother, and says, "I'll stay away and won't rush her. When Janice and Carol come, Maggie is not sure yet. We are not Mia (her sister), Mommy, or Daddy. She knows she loves Mia, Mommy and Daddy. She's not sure of these new people, and needs some time to get used to them."

As Janice speaks, Tracy returns Maggie to the floor. However, Maggie begins crying again. As soon as Tracy picks her up and holds her, Maggie stops crying. Janice comments, "That's so wonderful, the way you just pick her up and love her when she is unhappy. She can feel secure knowing you are there." Maggie coos as she nestles in her mother's arms.

In a prior visit, Janice had discussed stranger anxiety with Tracy. As Maggie expressed fear of Janice, Janice respected Maggie's discomfort and moved away from her. As she observes Maggie, Janice interprets to Tracy the meaning of Maggie's fear response.

Independence and Autonomy

Developing independence and autonomy is an integral part of the healthy development of sense of self and begins in toddlerhood A newborn gives evidence of purposeful action when she sucks her fist and calms herself.[119] We have discussed how this self-calming is the newborn's first achievement of independence. At 5–6 months of age, babies begin and turn away from interaction with their parent—another sign of autonomy. By 8 or 9 months, babies can sequence at least two movements as they go after something they desire. This new skill is called *motor planning* or *motor sequencing.*

Toddlers want to be in charge and make things happen. Now they begin to connect their arm and hand movements with the sounds and sights that follow, as they are beginning to understand cause and effect. Similarly, they know that they can elicit a smile, hug, or kiss by their own smile. Once they become mobile, this mobility sparks new explorations and feelings of independence and autonomy, accompanied by feelings of ambivalence. As they play, toddlers occasionally "check in" with their parent by making eye contact or saying something to them, often from a distance. At this age, psychological rather than physical contact can provide the needed security. Toddlers are learning to regulate their own arousal levels, another strand of emotional regulation.

Around 12 months of age, babies begin to say words and to engage in pretend play—skills that indicate the beginning of symbolic thinking. Several psychological competencies begin in the second year of life:

1. Initial comprehension and expression of meaningful speech

2. A capacity to infer selected mental and feeling states in others' representations of actions that are prohibited and encouraged by adults, together with an early understanding of "right," "wrong," "good," and "bad"

3. The conscious awareness of some of their own feelings and intentions[120]

These toddlers are testing new feelings of separateness yet continue to be pulled toward their parent. Dependence and independence are a part of toddlers' daily explorations. Within a few moments, the toddler may both push away mommy and cling to her. As toddlers test both their parents' limits and their own growing independent actions, this negativism is a natural phase of the developing sense of self.

Not only are toddlers more mobile, but their plane of vision has changed so that they can view things from a new vantage point, which provides pleasures, challenges, and frustrations. With supportive parents, toddlers now can learn to remain organized in the face of frustration. Toddlers' ability to stay emotionally organized long enough to solve frustrations or problems (e.g., to rebuild a block tower that has fallen) enhances their sense of self-worth and competence.

Competent parents understand that their toddler needs simple, clear limits. Limits help toddlers organize their behavior and feel in control. Even when parents firmly set limits, toddlers sometimes protest in tantrum, as they yell and their limbs swing out in rage. Tantrums are a normal part of toddlerhood. Home visitors can encourage parents to allow their toddlers to try to master new challenges and frustrations. They can explain about changing behaviors the parents can expect in the coming weeks and months. When they understand that their toddler's sudden refusal to cooperate in dressing is a normal developmental phase, parents can develop accepting responses and at the same time set clear boundaries. During her visit with Karyn and Don, Janice discussed changes they can expect in their son's behavior.

This is about the age that it will seem as if Greg (14 months) is saying, "Oh yeah, I'll show off my autonomy." He'll test your creativity. Fourteen to 24 months is one of the most difficult times with little guys.

Another challenge. He's not going to want to do something you want him to do. This is something that is going on inside him, not like walking. He's testing, not in a nasty way, it is legitimate testing. It'll be important to prioritize what you never are going to let him do. He'll find all kinds of ways to say no before he can say the word. It's called negativism.

Home visitors have the opportunity to normalize toddler's negativism and strivings for independence, as well as to help parents see these behaviors as central to the developing sense of self.

Emotional Regulation

Emotional regulation is the foundation of early childhood development.[121] It entails expressing emotions effectively in relationships in many different settings. By around 8 months of age, the frontal cortex has increased metabolic activity.[122] The baby's generalized distress now changes to expressions of anger, fear, and disgust[123] and babies experience different emotions in different contexts. When toddlers are uncertain, they search for the facial expression of their significant other to resolve uncertainty and regulate their behavior accordingly. This action is termed *social referencing.*

By the middle of the second year, toddlers can make efforts to avoid emotionally arousing situations, can engage in self-reassuring talk, or can change goals that have been frustrated.[124] With appropriate caregiving, toddlers are more able to experience a wide range of emotions. They can learn to tolerate more intense feelings without falling apart and are able to recover from strong emotions. They learn to seek help when needed.

Between 15 and 18 months of age, toddlers express embarrassment, shame, guilt, and pride. These emotions may result from the child's growing appreciation of the meaning of communication by others.[125] The child should have a sense of responsibility in the elicitation of emotions such as anger or sadness in others.[126] The growth in emotional development that children sow over time is deeply tied to their cognitive development as well.[127]

Young children who learn to regulate their emotions have an easier time with frustrations and a happier time relating to others. Not surprisingly, positive relationships with peers are closely related to positive emotional regulation. How a child responds emotionally to an event sometimes is governed by how the event is construed. As toddlers' cognitive and language skills develop, parents' verbal interpretations, especially of distressing situations, are very important. The parents provide toddlers with tools with which they can learn to reframe situations for themselves. For example, a toddler begins to cry when a very large dog barks loudly. The toddler's mother responds, "Oh, the dog's scared you. But he's just barking loudly because he saw that cat climb up the tree over there."

Parents can help toddlers regulate their emotions when they select and control the toddler's environment. For example, parents can avoid placing their children in stressful situations, such as a very crowded room, or intensely arousing situations, such as playing very loud music. Often, toddlers experience stressful separation from their parents. Sensitive parents try to ease their child's distress by letting the child take a favorite toy or familiarizing the child with the new environment.

Some child development experts now use the term *emotional competence* to group together emotion-related skills. Emotional competence is self-efficacy in emotion-eliciting social transactions. Studies indicate that at 2 or 3 years of age, children spontaneously talk about their own feelings as well as about others' feelings.[128] Young children's understanding about their own emotional experience includes the past, present, and future; it is most reliably sparked in familiar interpersonal contexts. Emotional development includes learning to regulate emotional expression as well as regulating the emotions themselves. It is important for parents to always strive to let young children know that their feelings are valued and they can express their emotions openly. At the same time, some expressions may be off limits, such as yelling or screaming when upset. The more parents talk about young children's feelings, the quicker children will learn to self-reflect that they are angry, sad, and so forth. Self-reflection enhances the skill of regulating emotional expression.

Parent–Child Play

As babies grow older, parents' focus on their babies' physiological regulation decreases. Now that their baby can experience new forms of shared experiences, parents' engagement in interactive games enhances their baby's developing sense of self.[129] From the beginning, parents and their babies may engage in playful games, making faces, changing voice tone, playing chase, tickling, or rolling balls. As their baby matures, these games are extended from gestures to simple play sequences. In these games, babies experience warmth, shared attention, shared feelings, pleasure, and connectedness—a sense of being understood and valued. They also learn turn-taking, which is the essence of conversation.

During their visits, home visitors can affirm parents' playful interactions with their young children.

Janice has just arrived at Karyn and Don's home. As Janice, Karyn, and Don chat, Greg (13 months) walks about the room with a small car in hand. He then goes to his father, who hugs him warmly, and asks him, "Where is your nose?" Don and Greg then play a brief game of Greg identifying and then touching his own and his father's nose and eyes. Greg goes to his mother, who says, "Teeth." Greg replies "Teeth," as he touches his mother's teeth, then chuckles. He then returns to his father, who hugs and kisses him.

Janice quietly comments, "You are giving your daddy lots of love. And he's going to soak it up too." When hearing Janice, Greg walks toward her for a moment then, chuckling, returns to his father, then mother as he babbles with sentence intonation.

Since Greg's birth, Don has been very engrossed in parenting. Unless on vacation, Don usually is at work during Janice's home visits. However, Karyn often discusses with Janice her husband's evening play experiences and sometimes has specific questions from Don, such as suggestions for new play activities. Home visitors have innumerable opportunities to reinforce to parents the importance of showing love through physical intimacy like holding, hugging, kissing, massaging, or rocking.

As toddlers spend endless hours playing, they are learning to see patterns: I build a tower and I know how to knock it down; If I push the car fast, it will roll across the room. As parents engage in Hide and Seek games and other search games with their toddlers, they are strengthening their toddlers' visual-spatial processing ability. Visual-spatial processing is essential for feeling secure in space and becomes vital for later math and science skills. In their play with their toddler, parents can show them how to rock the dolly and pat the kitty gently. Through these extended interactions, toddlers learn about caring and develop a moral sense of right and wrong. When toddlers become angry or aggressive, the way in which parents respond teaches them how the family views anger and aggression. Young children can learn acceptable angry feelings as well as how to express anger acceptably.

During their visits, home visitors can initiate simple play sequences with babies and toddlers, inviting parents to enter into this play. As they engage in interactive games, home visitors model healthy baby–adult interactions. As parents play with their child, the visitor can help parents understand the developmental significance of these experiences.

THE SOCIAL SELF: 19 MONTHS TO 3 YEARS

Five cognitive abilities occur after the second year of life:

1. Reliable integration of past with present
2. Anticipation of the future
3. Appreciation of causality
4. Enhanced reliance on semantic categories
5. Detection of shared relations between events and categories[130]

At about 18–24 months, toddlers can speak in two-word sentences such as "Baby cry" and "Me up." Now toddlers have the ability to refer to themselves as external, objective people (e.g., using verbal labels to refer to themselves, recognizing themselves in the mirror). Increased language means increased shared experience and a sense of togetherness between toddlers and their parents.[131] Independence, autonomy, and negativism continue. If autonomy is not achieved, shame and doubt emerge and may be themes for the rest of the child's life.[132] Memory grows and pretend play sequences expand, such as washing the doll's hair and then feeding her. With multiple word statements, extended pretend play, and declarations of autonomy, toddlers have reached another developmental leap.

Emotions entail thinking as well as feeling. Young children are able to infer what other people are thinking, intending, believing, or feeling. Even 2-year-olds can understand that people have inner experiences of feeling and desiring and other people will feel good if kissed and hugged.[133] Young children can develop a rich inner life only if they have a rich experience of relationships from which they can derive their inner images. These experiences include images of warmth, security, dependence, love, anger, and protest. Young children's emotional and cognitive development are intertwined and support each other. From 18 to 30 months of age, toddlers increase in their ability to gain self-control. Cheerful toddlers may have developed an emotion regulation style that provides positive emotions in engaging others and in coping with challenging experiences.[134] Positive emotions may buffer the intensity of distress felt by a child. This cheerful disposition stems from both genetic and environmental factors.

As toddlers take initiative, parents have many opportunities to encourage their child. As toddlers try to put on their own shoes and socks, strive to open the door, or climb into their car seat, parents can positively acknowledge their child's effort (e.g., "You put on your shoes all by yourself!"). Encouragement helps the child recognize his or her accomplishments and know that they are valued. Encouragement requires specific feedback, describing the child's specific action. Home visitors can assist parents in recognizing that encouragement helps their child recognize success, feel a sense of mastery, know that they are valued, and motivates them to continue to take initiative.

During a home visit, Cynthia helps Sally understand how her responses to her son, Willy, can support and encourage his play. This is important for Sally to learn, for she often tells Cynthia that Willy seems to always be running about and getting in trouble.

Willy (19 months) has dumped out the small colored wooden blocks onto the rug. Willy hands two blocks to his mother, Sally, as Cynthia says to Sally, "He's inviting you to play."

Sally says, "I guess so." She then taps the two blocks together, as does Willy; and they both chuckle.

Cynthia says, "You brought him right around. He also likes when you imitate him too. It lets him know you like what he is doing." As Cynthia speaks, Sally softly hugs her son.

As the adults chat, Willy begins stacking the blocks.

Cynthia says, "You put them on top of each other. Yeah!" Sally repeats, "Yeah."

Sally evens the blocks on her son's tower as she says to Cynthia, "He gets so discouraged when they fall."

Cynthia says, "And you're helping him so that he doesn't get discouraged."

Sally then rolls a block, and her son imitates her.

Cynthia says, "When I imitate his actions, I am telling Willy that what he does is wonderful."

Cynthia understands that Sally is concrete learner. Cynthia describes what Willy is doing; in this way, she encourages him and models for Sally. In addition, she describes to Sally what she is doing and how her actions are encouraging her son's involvement.

Sex-Role Identity

Children move through a series of stages in understanding gender identity. By age 3 years, children learn to identify their own and others' sex. Between 3 and 5 years, children learn that gender remains stable over time.[135] Sex segregation in play also emerges early, by 27 months for girls and 36 months for boys.[136]

Toddlers also are developing sex-role identity, which is somewhat different than gender identity. Sex roles are socially defined behaviors, attitudes, rights, and duties associated with being male or female.[137] As more mothers of very young children work outside the home and as more fathers share in household and childrearing tasks, sex-role expectations have changed. Nevertheless, remnants of sex-role stereotyping continue. For example, thinking of men as independent, aggressive, logical, and assertive, and women as dependent, gentle, emotional, and dependent is sex-role stereotyping.

With societal changes (e.g., both parents working outside the home), young children can develop the behaviors, attitudes, and values that allow them to be active participants both in the workplace and within the home. Boys can learn to express their feelings and develop caregiving skills; girls can develop assertive and problem-solving skills. For children to develop to their fullest potential and take advantage of the full range of available options to them, it is essential for them to know that men and women perform a wide variety of jobs and that each gender is able to express a full range of abilities and emotions.

Parents are their children's primary models for learning what it is to be male or female. When young children's fathers cook and change diapers or mothers fix computer problems and put oil in the car, these actions counterbalance traditional sex-role stereotypes. Parents also send messages to their children about sex roles by the toys they purchase for their children and the kind of behavior they allow, encourage, and/or punish. Parents can provide a range of experiences for both their sons and daughters. Boys can help with household tasks such as cooking or folding laundry and girls can assist in raking the lawn or assembling toys.

Most parents do not think about sex-role stereotyping as part of their child's everyday experiences. However, television programs for children and commercials frequently reflect sex-role stereotyping. Males outnumber females. Women tend to be portrayed in submissive, passive roles. Like television, children's books often reflect sex-role stereotypes; for example, main characters usually are active boys and girls are onlookers. Recently, more nonsexist picture books and toys have become available.[138] Home visitors can help parents recognize this sex-role stereotyping and sensitively discuss the issues.

Topics such as sex-role behaviors are value laden and become sensitive in times of societal change. Home visitors always must be respectful of parents' values and must recognize that some parents value sex-role stereotyping. There are times when a home visitor's information violates explicit values parents hold; as guests, home visitors may choose to refrain from sharing information in respect for parents' values.

Body Image

Toddlers love their body and its parts. They like to run around naked. They often are proud of what their body produces—feces, urine, mucus, and gas, all of which are their accomplishments. As toddlers move and explore their everyday environment, they are developing new understandings of their body image. Young children's emerging interest in their body strengthens their sense of self. Toddlers love to play games identifying parts of their body, "dance" to music, scoot about on four-wheeled toddler toys, play chase, and catch and throw balls. As they move, they gain an understanding of their bodies in space and movement. This knowledge of movement is termed *kinesthetic understanding*.

Knowledge of one's body begins at birth. Parents are central to their toddler's growing sense of body image because they provide the indoor and outdoor space for movement, toys, and games and participate as play partners.

Sexual Learning and Desire

Closely related to body image is sexual learning. Babies learn about sexuality each time their parents bathe, dress, and diaper them. In these everyday interactions, parents communicate to their child their own attitudes toward their baby's body. For babies and toddlers to feel positive about their body and sexuality, it is important for bath time, dressing and undressing, diapering, and toileting to be pleasurable times.

During the first and second years, babies' experiences such as rubbing their genitals and taking pleasure in skin contact with others are similar to later sensual pleasure. Greenspan observes, "The capacity for intimacy and the interest and pleasure derived from the company of others are the earliest phenomena that indicate real desire."[139] The desire for closeness with others is a normal want throughout life. Babies and toddlers are very curious; thus, they want to explore each part of their body from all angles. However, some parents may not realize that the feeling the children have in their genitals is not the same as the intensely excited feeling adults experience in sexual stimulation. The child's masturbation may therefore frighten the parent or evoke a strong negative response that the child is doing something wrong. Home visitors can help parents understand that masturbation is normal and will pass with time.

Home visitors can help parents understand their children's sexuality and sexual exploration. Parents cannot prevent these explorations. Parents are most effective when they adopt a relaxed attitude and accept the fact that their toddler will outgrow these explorations. If they are uncomfortable with their child's genital play, parents can distract their child with another activity. When parents criticize, punish, frown, or pull their toddler's hand away from genitals, their child learns that their genitalia and feelings coming from them are bad and wrong.

Play

From birth, babies explore their everyday world and create new meaning from their experiences. From early infancy, the child participates in shared imaginative family games, musical interactions, and stories. During the second year, toddlers enjoy imaginative pretend play, alone and with parents. A child's pretend play initially develops through imitation. In pretend play, they try out new roles (mommy) and create scenarios (going to work). They act out simple everyday experiences such as washing their doll's hair, feeding and putting their doll to bed, or giving their parents a cup of coffee. In this play, toddlers express their feelings, "think" about their experiences, and try out behaviors that they have seen others exhibit. In this acting out, toddlers are in control and gain mastery over their feelings. As they pretend to be mommy or daddy, they explore a wide range of themes and feelings. When parents join in this pretend play, they can affirm their toddlers, share in their enjoyment, and have opportunities to extend the play. Home visitors can help parents understand the importance of pretend play, how it develops, and how important it is for them to join their young child in pretend play.

Greenspan and Lewis identified common themes of toddler's pretend play:

- Closeness or dependence
- Pleasure and fun
- Assertiveness and exploration
- Cautious or fearful behavior
- Anger
- Limit setting
- Recovering from distress[140]

Children as young as 3 years can reason and draw causal inferences from their pretend narrative. For example, a 3-year-old can explain that her doll's hands are dirty because she was playing in the mud. As young children engage in pretend play, they are eager to explore and understand their social world. Children's pretend play is like when adults go to the theatre—it is emotionally absorbing.

When parents are play partners with their child, the child can take the lead—a role that the child rarely can take. In playing with their child, parents enter into the emotional tone of their child. Playing together is a time of extended conversation. Often parents can clarify and extend the child's play. As they play, the child feels a deep sense of connectedness and affirmation.

Social Development

One of the major developmental tasks of early childhood is establishing relationships with other children. The structure of play environments influences how well toddlers play together. For example, if toys invite collaborative play (e.g., blocks rather than puzzles), toddlers are more likely to get along. As they relate to peers, children evaluate their self-worth and competence. Patterns of peer interaction in early childhood predict whether children are competent or deviant in the tasks of middle childhood and adolescence.[141] For example, a toddler who is repetitively aggressive, hyperactive, and impulsive may be identified as conduct disordered at age 10 years.

Getting along with peers is one of the core developmental tasks of young children. Secure attachments with parents in infancy promote social competence. Experiences during a child's second and third year of life seem to be pivotal for the child's developing abilities to be cooperative and considerate toward others.[142] As toddlers develop motor and language skills, they enjoy playing with other young children; in this play, important social skills emerge.[143] These social skills include

1. The ability to coordinate behavior with that of the play partner
2. Imitation of the peer's activity and an awareness of being imitated
3. Turn taking based on observed peer responses
4. The demonstration of helping and sharing behaviors
5. The ability to respond appropriately to the peer partner's characteristics[144]

These social skills are significant new aspects of the young child's sense of self and promote a positive affective quality to peer interaction. As they play, toddlers learn from other children's action and get feedback on their own action.

Toddlers are more likely to initiate play with toddlers with whom they are familiar.[145] Toddlers develop reciprocal relationships, but only through positive overturns and agonistic interaction.[146] Some pairs of children, before they are 2 years old, seek out each other as companions, comfort each other in distress, are happy when together and are unhappy when separated, and can engage in reciprocity.[147] These same patterns often are observed among siblings, who can be intimately attached. Friends who play together engage in more cooperative, imaginative pretend play earlier than their peers.[148]

Friendship is the dynamic in which moral sensibility is formed. In caring about their friends, children think about their needs and rights in a different way than when asked about hypothetical situations or when their siblings are involved. The power politics of parent–child and sibling relationships are different from those of friendships: friends are usually closer in status and dominance. Friendship also marks the beginning of the young child's new independence from parents.[149]

When children are toddlers, many parents form playgroups for their children. In addition, many community organizations have programs for parents and their toddlers to come together for play (e.g., churches, community centers, libraries, and some public schools). Home visitors can assist parents in thinking through possible ways of providing peer play for their young child. Often, parents will seek their home visitor's advice regarding this issue. Shelley's conversation with Janice is illustrative.

Shelley: Is it important for Erin (24 months) to be with children her own age, or is it okay for her to be with older children, like her cousins?

Janice: Erin could handle preschool, but it's not essential. The way you get a child ready for being 3 [years old] is by giving her what she needs at age 2. Whenever Erin goes to school, she will be fine because she is securely attached to you and to Rob. Some children need preschool, either because they don't have exposure with other children, or because their parents are not teaching.

Erin plays frequently with her older cousins and Janice reassures Shelley that this play is wonderful. When families live in areas containing neither neighborhood children nor relatives with young children, Janice informs the parents of the school district's weekly playtime for parents and their 2-year-olds.

Achievement Motivation

Young children's self-evaluations have three stages of development:

1. Children younger than 22 months are neither concerned with others' evaluation of their performance nor self-reflective in their evaluations. However, they do show positive emotional reactions when they accomplish a task and negative emotions when they do not.

2. Two-year-olds react more to others' evaluations by seeking approval when they do well and turning away when they do poorly.

3. After age 3, children are able to evaluate their own performance, without needing to seek how adults react to that performance, and engage in more autonomous self-evaluation. Children age 3 and older also react more strongly to winning and losing than younger children.[150]

During the preschool years and into kindergarten, young children do not have a clear sense of their ability even though they do respond to success and failure.[151] Conceptions of goodness and badness are primary at this time. Parents' perceptions of their child's competencies and likely success also influence their child's self-beliefs.[152]

Moral Identity

Moral identity encompasses self-awareness, a sense of self-integration, stability of time, and an attachment to one's moral goals;[153] it involves both personal and contextual factors. Moral identity is a dimension of individual differences; that is, persons who define themselves in moral terms may do so in different ways. The basis of self-control, integrity and moral desires is deeply relational. Social influence brings on moral development and provides a context for review of one's capabilities, guidance on how best to express one's capabilities, and strategies needed to accomplish it.[154]

THE NARRATIVE SELF: 3–5 YEARS

Young children experience another developmental leap around 3 years of age when they begin telling stories.[155] Usually these stories are autobiographical or family centered. Now children can replay experiences for themselves that occurred in the past. With their new verbal skills and their new mental abilities of representation, young children see connections of time (what I'm doing now, what I did before lunch) and space (what is next to me, what is in my yard). With this new ability, young children are gaining skills in self-reflection and a new form of shared experience with their parents. Because of their young age, they do not always take the viewpoint of the listener, thus stories may have significant omissions.[156]

At this age, the past, present, and future are starting to make sense. The child also is understanding near and far spaces. Children can now create connections between their ideas and the ideas of another person. They have learned to answer and ask *who, what, where, when, how,* and *why* questions. However, they learn to answer *who, what,* and *where* questions before *why* and *how;* the latter questions are more difficult because they require the child to examine the roots of their own feelings or wishes. The child can logically link ideas by using "if," "but," or "because." Their emotional thinking is expanding as well. Now they can go beyond actions to express their feelings in words, such as pleasure, excitement, anger, assertiveness, fear, closeness, dependency, and surprise.[157]

At this age, children can link two ideas together. For example, they can think, "If I pick up my toys, mommy will be happy." They can anticipate events in the future, such as going to the ice cream store after a nap or going to the circus on the weekend. The child is also beginning to get a sense of his or her own unique features or skills.

Home visitors can help parents recognize these many changes in their preschoolers. They can encourage parents to be play partners and to have lengthy conversations with their child. When parents understand the meaning of their role as a play partner or a conversational partner with their child, they are more likely find time to engage in these experiences with their child.

Once parents and children have developed a personal relationship with their home visitor, both children and parents love to report family experiences. These reports are good opportunities for young children to "practice" their skill in telling stories. Shelly and her daughter, Erin, are illustrative.

Erin (37 months) tells Janice, "My daddy comes home, but he has to work at the firehouse now."

Janice asks, "What does he do at the firehouse?"

Erin says, "He goes out on fire calls. Sometimes he has some parties—when it's dark out." Shelly then suggests to her daughter that she tell Janice what happened last night when the fire officers were done with their fire.

Erin replies, "Honk-honk-honk." Shelly explains that, before returning to the firehouse, the three fire trucks had passed by their house. All three stopped and honked for Erin and Shelly, who were standing at the window. As Shelly is talking, Erin runs into the bedroom and returns with a small walkie-talkie, called a scanner. Erin tells Janice, "That's where my daddy talks."

Shelley and her daughter regularly report family happenings to Janice. Erin's comments contain omissions, for she is not always skilled in taking the listener's perspective. As Shelley tells her story, both her mother and Janice ask questions to assist her ability to add details. As she tells these stories, Erin experiences self-reflection, shared reflection, and enjoyment; her language and thinking skills are also strengthened. These stories are a vivid example of the social creation of a sense of self; in her telling, Erin gains an increased sense of connectedness.

Young children sometimes are egocentric (i.e., unable to take another person's perspective), but at other times they can be sociocentric (i.e., able to take another person's perspective).[158] For example, children often adjust their conversations when speaking to children younger than themselves, such as when a 3-year-old uses shorter and simpler phrases when speaking to an 18-month-old sibling. In other words, they are taking the younger sibling's perspective.

Social Development and Play

At 3 years of age, children's relationships begin to expand beyond their immediate family. Preschool children's social skills expand dramatically. Important to their developing sense of self are opportunities to play with peers. Up until this point, young children primarily have been relating to parents and siblings. Peer play, as noted earlier, was parallel play. Playing with same-age playmates is a 3- and 4-year-old child's first relationship with equals. In this play, young children experience a variety of roles—leading as well as following. They receive feedback, model other children's actions, try out aggression, experience conflict, problem solve, and learn giving and taking among equals.

Because peer play is a new experience, difficulties inevitably emerge; parents need to teach their young child to negotiate—to use words instead of hitting, to take turns, and so forth. Home visitors can help parents understand this developing process.

As Erin (37 months) completes a puzzle, Shelly softly tells Janice that recently when Erin's friend Kathy aggravated Erin, Erin pushed Kathy. Shelly states that she's surprised to see her daughter be aggressive.

Janice responds, "You can help Erin learn how to deal with problems by herself. You can suggest that she use words such as 'stop that.' When children this age get together, they are going to have problems. Frame it in a positive way. Tell Erin that if there is trouble, make sure that you talk about it. However, children this young are not good about negotiating. She also needs to know it's okay to ask for help from you."

Until she was 3 years old, Erin played only with her older cousins. Now Shelly has begun to provide same-age playmates for her daughter, who is her first and only child. Janice helps Shelly understand that Erin's difficulties are normal and that Shelly can assist her daughter in learning basic social skills.

During the preschool years, children learn to differentiate between their internal emotional state and their external expressive behavior. Over time, children acquire knowledge about when, where, with whom, and how to express behaviorally their emotional responses. Children who enjoy substantial family support and moderate structure have a large repertoire of coping strategies and can adapt to a wide variety of emotion-provoking situations.[159] At 3–5 years of age, children express their curiosity about body differences and functions in their exploratory sex play with peers. Such questions or play may raise parents' anxiety. Sex play most often includes examining one another's bodies and occurs as children engage in simple role-play themes of family or doctor. Usually parents can redirect their child's sex play if they think it is inappropriate. When sex play seems to stem from children's unanswered questions about body differences, then parents simply can discuss these differences or read an appropriate book about the human body to their child.

Many preschoolers develop special friends. Preschoolers often choose peers who are similar to them. Their play with friends is distinct from their behavior with other children who are familiar but not friends; it is more sustained and complex. Children of this age also display more prosocial mutual activity with friends than with nonfriends. By the age of 4 years, children can identify best friends as well as peers they like and dislike. Some children develop imaginary friends, which is normal. The ability to make friends is associated with social-cognitive and emotional maturity. Friends, as compared with nonfriends, use negotiation and disengagement in resolving conflicts.[160]

The quality of young children's friendships varies significantly. Some children flourish in solitude. Others are companions in rough-and-tumble play but not in more sedentary activities. Children also differ in the extensiveness of their friends. Some have several close friends, whereas others have only one or two. Children with friends have more empathy and are more altruistic than those without friends.[161]

We know that friends can be very important as supports in very stressful situations. When a young child experiences divorce, a sick parent, or the birth of a sibling, a close friend can reduce stress. Often, young children do not discuss family difficulties; nevertheless, their friend can offer comfort or distraction. Pretend play and conversation can be strong distractions for a young child experiencing stress.

Children this age have new opportunities in prosocial behaviors, which include sharing, helping, and cooperative behaviors. These behaviors expand young children's understanding of self in relation to others. Cognitive, affective, and behavioral components of caring develop with age. As a child's perspective-taking skills increase, their skills in empathy, sympathy, other prosocial behaviors increase. In addition, girls score higher than boys on all elements of caring, although the differences are not dramatic.[162]

Young boys and girls have different fantasy play, different aggressive behavior, and different ways of insulting each other. Beginning around 3 years of age, children begin to choose to play in groups with same-sex partners. These choices increase with age.[163]

As young children play with each other, much of their play offers opportunities of developing skills in sharing and cooperation. As more mothers of young children are employed outside of their home, larger numbers of children experience social interaction with peers in out-of-home child care. Observations of young children in out-of-home child care provide vivid examples of spontaneous groups of children engaged in prosocial behavior. Several of the author's out-of-home child care observations of 3- to 5-year-olds are illustrative.

Lucretia, Demetrius, and Jerry (all 4 years of age) have covered most of the rug area in the block center with train tracks that they have snapped together. Over the tracks, they build bridges with blocks. The three children then each push a train car about their track. Twice they knock down the blocks structures and rebuild them.

These children have used train tracks and blocks to cooperatively build structures for moving their vehicles about. Their play includes give-and-take decision making and shared enjoyment.

Four girls, each with a hula hoop, have formed a circle. Emma seems to be the leader, for she counts, "1, 2, 3, 4, 5. Go," and then the children twirl their hoops. Emma gives the children directives as to their spatial location, such as "Lea, you may go over there, No, Cherise, over there."

Five girls (3 and 4 years old) are sitting in a circle outdoors. The children are playing "Doggie, doggie, where is your bone? Somebody stole it, run back home." Josie is the leader, for she tells individuals, "Now lay in the middle" for a turn to be the dog. After about 6 minutes, Suzy suggests, "Let's play Duck Duck Goose," and everyone does so, with Josie again leading.

Jerome beats a rhythm with the palm of his hand of the bottom of a cylindrical container as four children clap and stomp their feet. Occasionally Jerome calls out "stop," and the children do in fact stop. Then, when Jerome says okay, the children again begin clapping and stomping to his rhythm.

In these vignettes, the children spontaneously begin a play sequence together. Emma, Josie, and Jerome are developing leadership skills. All of the children share in an activity in which they experience feelings of connectedness and delight. Social dominance, developed naturally, is an important feature of the children's peer group.

Perhaps the most complex form of group interactive activity during these preschool years is sociodramatic play. By the third year of life, children are able to share symbolic meaning through sociodramatic play. Now young children can take on complementary roles in a rule-governed context. These children's ability to share meaning during pretend play is a form of intersubjectivity, and increasing sophistication of their "theory of mind." There are three essential developmental functions of sociodramatic play:

1. It creates a context for mastering the communication of meaning.

2. It provides opportunities for children to learn to control and compromise, which arise during discussions and negotiations centering on pretend roles and scripts.

3. Social pretense allows for a "safe" context in which children can explore and discuss issues of intimacy and trust.[164]

Sociodramatic play represents a substantive milestone in the social lives of young children.

Preschoolers bring the narrative self into their pretend play.[165] They use their imagination in pretend play and act out imaginative characters, super-heroes, or other characters they have not experienced. They substitute symbols for real objects as they role play. With their peers, they cooperate and learn about how their peers view the world and how their peers judge their actions. Their pretend play includes joint decision making (e.g., who will play which role), co-operative activities (e.g., cooking and setting the table), potential disputes (e.g., deciding what specifically to role play), and lots of shared enjoyment. Increasingly, the child develops a sense of self-in-relation—a social self. When parents join their child in pretend play, the child feels a deep sense of connect-edness.[166] Often the parent may clarify the play sequence or extend it. The parent enters into the emotional tone of the child so that the child feels affirmed. Home visitors can share this information and thereby enhance parenting.

Parents can provide opportunities for their young child to assist in family tasks. Through this, the child experiences being a valued and responsible mem-ber of the family. Young children can assist in household tasks such as cooking, setting and clearing tables, folding laundry, raking leaves, washing cars, and dusting. As the family eats a meal in which a young child assisted, the child feels a sense of pride and accomplishment. Family tasks help a young child develop a sense of social responsibility—an ability to respond to others.

Gender Identity

During the preschool years, preschoolers increasingly prefer same-gender type toys and activities. Studies indicate that there are more gender-typed prefer-ences for boys than for girls.[167] Children vary their preferences by the activity; the size of gender difference also varies by activity.

Gender differences in physical and motor skills relate to girls' earlier neu-rological development and better fine motor skills and boys' greater muscle strength.[168] Boys' play is marked by rough-and-tumble play, whereas girls' play usually is cooperative.[169] By preschool, children spend little time with peers of the opposite sex. Although single parents have a less gender-specific role than parents in two-parent families, studies show very small effects of paternal ab-sence on gender development.[170]

Executive Functions

Executive functions such as paying attention, planning, and sequencing actions are grounded in the child's emotional interactions with significant others. When a preschooler can carry out several action steps in a row (i.e., plan and sequence actions), they are engaging in executive functions. In these cases, they are competent in independent goal-directed activities and task persistence, such as completing a 48-piece floor puzzle.

When very young, children depend on parents to provide information and assistance to support their child's immature attention, memory, and language. Vygotsky referred to this support as *scaffolding*.[171] This scaffolding is critical for a young child's developing executive functions.[172] Attention and motor planning problems may be caused by a child's lack of reciprocal emotional interactions with significant adults. One study found that mothers' verbal input to their 3- and 4-year-olds affected the children's executive abilities at age 6 years.[173]

The Development of Self

As they advance in self-awareness, young children grow in social interaction and gain greater insight into others. We have learned that the development of self begins at birth, as the newborn interacts with significant others and gains feedback. In the third year of life, children perceive themselves as the objects of attention and thought of others. At age 4 years, self-awareness that evokes expectations from past events, recalls specific past experiences, or anticipates future events demonstrates that young children can perceive themselves in a temporal context.[174]

Self-Esteem

Central to a young child's sense of self is judgment of self-worth, often termed *self-esteem*. Self-esteem is the evaluative part of the child's sense of self. Feelings of competence and self-esteem develop when young children experience repeated success in their activities.[175] There also seems to be a close relationship between children's cooperative interaction, prosocial behavior, and positive feelings about self.

Two classes of behaviors are characteristic of high self-esteem in young children:

1. The child actively displays confidence, curiosity, initiative, and independence, as well as trusts in own ideas, approaches challenges, initiates activities confidently, takes initiative, sets goals independently, is curious, explores and questions, is eager to try doing new things, describes self in positive terms, and shows pride in his or her work.

2. The child adaptively reacts to change or stress, as well as is able to adjust to changes, is comfortable with transitions, tolerates frustration and perseveres, and is able to handle criticism and teasing.[176]

A sense of self-confidence does not seem to be dependent upon competence. Socializing agents play an important role in a young child's developing self-esteem. In fact, some young children's self-representations may be unrealistic.

Home visitors can encourage parents to provide a wide variety of play activities in which their child can experience mastery and success. Parents' everyday child-rearing interactions also communicate messages to their child that the child is valued and of worth. Parental encouragement through positive descriptions of the child's behavior and achievements helps the child recognize success, feel self-esteem, and continue to take initiative (e.g., "You carried your milk so carefully none spilled" or "You used so many colors in your painting, it looks like a happy picture!").

The Secure Child

Greenspan says the secure child has "the ability to engage in and rely on vital relationships with mother, father, and siblings, as well as other adults."[177] By communicating through facial expressions and gestures, young children negotiate safety, danger, acceptance, and approval, which are essential for feeling secure. As the young child acts successfully on the significant people around her, she gains inner security. As she relates to others to get what she wants, she gains confidence. This same ability helps children negotiate their peer relationships. Since preschoolers are just learning how to express their feelings verbally, parents use their child's gesturing as a primary way to understand and comfort their children when they are confused or stressed.

Preschoolers who have learned to figure out how to get what they want—to solve problems—will feel secure. During these years, children learn to verbally explain what they need. With ideas, preschoolers can label feelings, tell others how they feel, and discuss why they feel that way. Preschoolers also learn to reason and think about their feelings and their social world.

Parental Attunement

Parent–child interaction is mutual and resembles a dance. It is within these everyday "dances" that the child develops a sense of self. Sometimes problems of either parent, child, or surrounding environment can impair healthy development of these mutual interaction patterns and accompanying difficulties in development of self. If home visitors are keen observers, they can recognize when difficulties are emerging.

Beyond simply conversing with the parents, home visitors should also interact with the child and observe parent–child interaction. Some parents may be able to appropriately talk with the home visitor, yet have serious shortcomings as they interact with their child. If a home visitor observes repeated lack in parental attunement and responsiveness to the child, they could be observing serious parenting problems, which lead to children defending themselves by becoming apathetic and nonresponsive.

When people become parents, they sometimes bring with them dilemmas from their own childhood that can influence the way they parent. Childhood experiences that are not fully processed may create leftover issues that can affect how parents react to their children. It is as if one's child evokes these unresolved (and often unremembered) conflicts—what Fraiberg terms *ghosts in the nursery*.[178] Signs of this problem include a child who does not respond to the home visitor's attempts to engage or a child with little emotional expression, such as smiling and frowning. When parent–child interactions indicate potential "ghosts in the nursery," home visitors need to assist the family in seeking therapeutic resources in the community.

DIFFICULTIES AND DILEMMAS

Home visitors need to be alert to biologically based problems within the baby—termed *regulation disorders*.[179] Some babies' sensory systems are over- or underreactive—sensitivities in vision, touch, sight, hearing, or kinesthetic (movement) sensitivities. Some babies have motor tone problems; for example, they feel very loose and have difficulty holding up their head. Motor tone is the balance between flexor and extensor muscles. If a young baby's motor tone is low, holding her head up may require too much work. Babies with high or low motor tone may have difficulty sequencing their actions. Babies with regulatory disorders are characterized by having difficulty in behavioral and physiological, sensory, attentional, motor or affective processes, and thereby difficulty in maintaining a calm, alert, or affectively positive state. Parents will need to provide tactile stimulation and muscle exercise for underreactive babies.

Babies with these regulation disorders may be very fussy. In turn, parents have difficulties soothing their baby and may feel failure. Problematic baby–parent exchanges escalates the baby's difficulties. Often, parents need assistance in adjusting their interaction style to meet their baby's learning style and sensitivities, such as varying their voice pitch for an auditory underreactive baby. Evaluation by an occupational therapist may identify specific regulation difficulties. Sensory integration often is a treatment for these difficulties.

The study of regulation disorders is fairly recent, so many practitioners are not aware of these subtle difficulties in infancy. If home visitors can strive to be sensitive to babies' sensory reactions and motor tone, then they can screen these difficulties at a very young age. Young children who are unable to relate to other people, maintain eye contact, and/or communicate verbally may have symptoms of autism. Autism is likely caused by a unspecified neurobiological factor and occurs on a spectrum; the least amount of disability is termed *Asperger syndrome* or *pervasive developmental delay*. Children with pervasive developmental delay have some of the patterns of autism but not all. Children with Asperger syndrome are not as withdrawn as children with autism, have excellent speech and good intellectual skills, but have a paucity of nonverbal communication, poor empathy, and nontypical communication patterns.

Young children with autism have stereotyped behaviors such as hand flapping or toe walking; they seem to prefer activities involving objects rather than those involving social interaction. As a result, young children with autism tend to be significantly more delayed in social skills and social behavior than children without autism. Approximately 75%–80% of children with autism have intellectual disabilities. As profiled in psychological testing, children with autism have significant deficits in abstract reasoning, verbal concept formation, and skills requiring social understanding. In contrast, they may be skilled in rote learning, memory skills, and visual-spatial problem solving.[180] Children with autism do not have a "theory of mind" and thus lack reciprocity in communication and empathy. Most children with autism have substantive regulation disorder, especially high sensitivity to touch.

Children with autism need special education that is highly structured and oriented around the individual needs of each child. Their education should include speech and language therapy, as well as occupational therapy. In families with an autistic child, home visitors can provide support and helpful guidance. They might help a parent find respite care or help a family connect with community resources.

CONCLUSION

Beginning at birth, newborns are capable of purposeful action, expressing feelings, and relating to their parents. These behaviors point to the newborn's sense of self—the inner organization underlying observable behavior. This sense of self develops only within babies' interactions with their parents; these interactions are mutually created, with each partner influencing the other's behavior. With age, emerging patterns of behavior point to the developing sense of self. As the baby develops new behaviors, the parents develop new understanding and new strategies of parenting their child. Table 4.1 portrays this progression, showing the baby's developing sense of self and parenting behavior that promotes this development. Parents' responsiveness (see Table 4.1) and physical affection given to a very young baby continue to be necessary parenting strategies throughout the young child's development.

Babies are embedded within and dependent on their caregiving contexts. We have tried to show how the relationship between child and parent is the foundation of this developing sense of self. In a similar manner, the home visitor's relationship with parents is at the core of her ability to assist the parents she visits. Home visitors' interactions with parents affirm and support parents, as well as provide observation and interpretation of child and parent actions. In the same sense that the parent–child relationship is formed by everyday childrearing interactions, the home visitor's interactions—supporting, affirming, and guiding—are the core of the home visitor–parent relationship.

Table 4.1.   The child's developing sense of self and the parenting behavior that promotes development

Infants' and young children's developing sense of self	Parenting: Understanding and behavior
Birth–6 months	
Cycle of six states of consciousness	Mutuality in infant–parent interaction
Self-calming	Predictable expectations regarding
Individual differences—temperament	development
Qualities of sense of self	Physiological regulation
Capable of purposeful action	Assisting infant to self-calm
Experiencing unity	Adapting to infant's temperament
Experiencing feelings	Regulation of feelings
Memory and expectations	Empathic responsiveness
Attachment behavior	Physical affection
	Bonding and attachment
7–18 months	
Intersubjective relatedness	Respect and responsiveness to stranger
Shared attention	anxiety
Shared intention	Accepting child's lovey
Shared feeling states	Expanding child's language
Trust	Boundaries of acceptable behavior
Sense of personal control	Engagement in interactive games
Loveys	Play with child
Stranger anxiety	
Emergence of words	
Independence, autonomy, negativism	
Emergence of pretend play	
19 months–3 years	
Multiple-word sentences	Behavioral expectations and limit setting
Extended pretend play	Verbalization of child's feelings
Experiencing mastery and competence	Encouragement
Gender identity	Modeling and provisioning for sex-role
Sex-role identity	understanding and identity
Body image	Assisting in child's sexual learning
Sexual learning	Provisions of play
Play with other children	Play with child
Emergence of social skills	
3–5 years	
Telling stories	Providing for peer play
Egocentrism and sociocentrism	Extending conversations
Peer relationships	Providing family responsibilities
Prosocial behaviors	Play with child
Self-esteem	

Given the explosion of new scientific knowledge, effective home visitors need to be active learners; they should read and attend seminars to be knowledgeable about the latest findings in neurobiology, child development, cultural diversity, and early intervention. Young children thrive in a context of nurturing, responsive, and secure caregiving interactions. Home visitors have the opportunity to actively promote these caregiving interactions and thereby substantively promote the development of both child and parent.

Guidance and Discipline

The widow she cried over me, and called me a poor lost lamb, and she called me a lot of other names, too, but she never meant no harm by it. She put me in them new clothes again, and I couldn't do nothing but sweat and sweat, and feel all cramped up. Well, then, the old thing commenced again. The widow rung a bell for supper, and you had to come to time. When you got to the table you couldn't go right to eating, but you had to wait for the widow to tuck down her head and grumble a little over the victuals, though there wasn't really anything the matter with them. That is, nothing only everything was cooked by itself… .Pretty soon I wanted to smoke, and asked the widow to let me. But she wouldn't. She said it was a mean practice and wasn't clean, and I must try to not do it any more.

Mark Twain, *The Adventures of Huckleberry Finn* (1855/1947, p. 2)

DISCIPLINE TOPICS ARE THE FOCUS OF more parent meetings than any other child-rearing topic in most programs for young families. With the changing nature of American society, parents' ambivalence in directing and setting limits for their children is understandable. Parents often are uncertain about religious values and gender roles. They may have neighbors with different cultural ideas about discipline. Many parents are not sure if they share the same values and attitudes that their children are taught at school. In addition, many new parents live far from their extended families and the support they provide. In single-parent families and families in which both parents work outside the home, parents have little time to develop informal social support systems to draw on for assistance. As they experience these societal changes, parents often feel uncertain when guiding, teaching, and setting boundaries for their young children.

Everyday guidance and discipline of children has crucial significance. Physiological traits alone do not define a baby's potential. Research since the late 1980s has shown that a baby's inclination toward boldness or timidity stems from a complex interplay of biological and environmental factors.[1] What children experience from moment to moment, especially in their early years, is just as important as their genetic heritage with relation to behavior.[2] Patterns established by the caregiver can alter children's innate tendencies. A soft-spoken caregiver who minimizes auditory and tactile stimulation, for example, can lessen a baby's irritability that is caused by her sensitivity to sound and touch.

Brazelton and Sparrow identified young children's accomplishments acquired through their parents' discipline:

- Self-control and recognizing one's own impulses
- Recognizing one's own feelings and their origins
- Recognizing and considering the feelings of others
- Developing a sense of fairness and the motivation to behave fairly
- Becoming altruistic and discovering the joy of giving[3]

Without discipline, children may not be able to accomplish any of these skills.

Social interaction also affects the physiology of the brain. The quality of everyday caregiver interaction shapes and strengthens babies' and young children's growing experience of both inner and outer reality. Nature and nurture—biology and experience—are continuously interacting. As Greenspan explained, "Consciousness develops from this continuous interaction in which biology organizes experience and experience organizes biology."[4]

Parents may have good intentions about discipline, but may not have all of the information, skills, and support that they need to be successful. For example, they may be strongly motivated to parent differently from their own parents, but may still choose inappropriate parenting methods because they do not understand developmental principles. A young father whose own father was unavailable may strive to be his son's best pal and thus avoid setting limits. A mother whose own mother was harsh and critical may worry that she will harm her daughter's self-esteem if she is firm and gives consequences for misbehavior.

Anger and violence also lead to ambivalence about discipline. Violence is deeply embedded in our culture and is the dominant theme in children's television cartoons, political rhetoric about crime and foreign policy, and the everyday lives of many families. Anger and violence lead to parents' ambivalence in two ways. First, parents do not know how to react and sometimes are frightened when their children are angry and violent. Second, parents do not know how to handle their own anger and violence, especially when they engage in impulsive physical punishment. Although parents hear about nonpunitive rational means of disciplining their children, many have no experience with this sort of discipline from their own childhood. Parents may need the home visitor's help in dealing with their confusion about discipline.

This chapter interweaves three themes in the discussion of a young child's development:

1. Parental discipline: Teaching appropriate cultural and familial norms and setting limits

2. Parental guidance: Providing experience and assistance to enable development of understanding and abilities

3. Child development: Young children's development of autonomy, self-confidence, competence, and control

Child development is the goal of parental guidance and discipline.

GUIDANCE AND DISCIPLINE

Discipline is a form of teaching that is defined as "training that corrects, models, or perfects the mental faculties or moral character" and "a control gained by enforcing obedience or order."[5] Early education literature on obedience and discipline often has emphasized that the goal is to help young children develop self-control. In other words, young children adopt their parents' and caregivers' rules of behavior as their own.

This book proposes an additional goal of discipline: teaching the child emotional self-regulation. Emotional self-regulation is the ability to respond emotionally and to adapt one's emotional experience to moment-to-moment situational demands. Each stage and age makes its own demands, builds on earlier achievements, and requires new adaptive behaviors to respond to the environment appropriately. Strategies of emotional self-regulation originate in the young baby's simple efforts to cope with distress through self-soothing. They quickly become integrated into a network of behavioral strategies by which children (and adults) seek to maintain personal well-being, manage their relationships with others, and manage self-presentation to the social world.

Structuring and limiting young children's everyday experiences is essential in helping them control feelings such as anger, greed, and envy, which are as basic to being human as empathy, love, and compassion. If young children are cared for in a loving and consistent fashion, they can learn to care for others. A primary task of parenting is to teach appropriate behaviors, attitudes, and values that will allow the child to manage self-control and relate well to other people. Two primary purposes of discipline are readily apparent: to stop children from doing something dangerous, hurtful, or annoying to themselves and to others (to control children) and to impart values (to teach children).[6]

Effective parents have both short- and long-term goals as they discipline their children. Obedience is the short-term goal and self-control is the long-term goal. Initially, the young child obeys. Over time, this obedience becomes internalized; that is, parents' rules become part of the child's conscience and their natural way of interacting with others.[7]

Brazelton described three stages of self-control or self-discipline:

1. Trying out the limits by exploration

2. Teasing to evoke from others a clear sense of what is okay and what is not

3. Internalizing these previously unknown boundaries[8]

For example, a crawling baby is fascinated by the many electrical cords and goes to the electrical outlet. Her parent reacts strongly and negatively to impress upon her that electrical outlets are off limits. Then, once the baby knows her parents will react, she will look to make certain her parent is watching before she reaches to touch the outlet. She is eager to hear her parent forbid her to touch and thereby is reassured. Finally, after several months, when she comes to the outlet, she'll shout "No!" to herself. Now, the limit is a part of herself—she has internalized it.

Guidance is closely related to discipline. To guide is "to assist [a person] to travel through, to reach a destination in, an area in which he does not know the way, as by accompanying him or giving him directions."[9] Babies, toddlers, and preschoolers are new to this Earth, with a very small amount of experience and much to learn. Parental guidance is essential.[10] Whether the activity is feeding, dressing, playing, or disciplining, guidance is embedded in parents' everyday interactions with their young children.

A DEVELOPMENTAL APPROACH

This chapter follows a developmental approach to guidance and discipline. This developmental approach assumes that as new developmental accomplishments are achieved, babies and young children need new strategies of parental guidance and discipline to nurture their development. For example, helping a baby to learn how to self-calm is one of the earliest responsibilities of parenting.[11] Once the baby begins to crawl, setting limits becomes a priority. As the young child develops symbolic skills in thinking and speaking, problem-solving skills are a major component of guidance and discipline. Although the need for a specific parenting strategy may emerge at a specific developmental phase, parents need to continue using these strategies as their children develop. For example, children of all ages require assistance in self-calming (although the skill may be termed *frustration tolerance* once the child is a preschooler). Similarly, both children and adolescents need clear, consistent limits and problem-solving skills—limits so they know the boundaries of safe and acceptable behavior, and problem-solving skills to resolve their difficulties with other people.

EARLY INFANCY: BIRTH TO 8 MONTHS

The important events that help or hurt development are the split-second, ordinary, daily, repetitive, nonverbal events that occur between baby and caregiver. Stern called these interactions *microevents,* or "relatively small and short-lived events, such as what the mother does with her eyes and face at the moment when the baby's smile at her increases in amplitude."[12]

During the first few months of a baby's life, much of what goes on between baby and caregiver includes helping the baby achieve physiological and emotional regulation. Sleeping and eating are two primary tasks of the baby. During the babies' first 3–4 months, the brain has not matured enough to allow for regularity in sleep. By age 3–4 months, however, babies may take two to three regular naps throughout the day. By 6 months, most babies need a morning and afternoon nap for a total of 2–4 hours.[13] Research has shown that sleep, emotion, and attention are all linked.[14] Naps are very important for optimal learning when babies are awake because babies who are good sleepers are able to maintain focus and learn. Colicky babies often have irregular sleep patterns and can cry inconsolably. Like adults, babies who are not getting enough sleep tend to be quite irritable.

Beginning at the birth of a baby, a positive climate within the home sets the stage for positive parental guidance and discipline. Routines and schedules are central components of a positive home environment. Babies thrive on safe, predictable routines: periods of cuddling prior to sleeping, parents' soft talking during feeding and diaper changing, and parents' responses to crying. During a baby's first 6–8 weeks, the baby's patterns of sleeping and feeding are not very predictable. After the first 6–8 weeks, parents can begin to adapt their baby's waking and bedtime feeding to their desired schedule.

Balancing the Needs of Babies and Parents

Parents of very young babies find they need to structure their own lives to ensure enough sleep, healthy food, time off, and time with friends and family that is not centered on their child. Then, they will be able to interact with their baby with patience and understanding. When home visitors work with parents of very young babies, they can ensure that parents are taking care of themselves. Janice's first home visit after Greg's birth is illustrative. Janice initially inquired about Greg's delivery and his mother Karyn's social support during the first few weeks. In her conversation with Karyn, Janice ensures that Karyn also is caring for herself. This is especially important because Greg (age 5 weeks) has been very colicky.

Janice: My third son was colicky. Even when it's the third baby, it's tough.

Karyn: I did get out for 45 minutes to go shopping last night.

Janice: You need to do that for yourself. It's normal. Also, you are having changes in your hormones.

Karyn: It's a more difficult adjustment—not working. It's hard, not getting that feedback that I got when working.

Janice: And your husband wants attention.

Karyn: I told him, "At least you get feedback at work."

Janice: Nobody says, "You're doing a good job." I can tell—you are doing a good job. Have you talked with your sister-in-law?

Karyn: Yes, a little, but it's different for her. She has a good baby, and she is
          breastfeeding.

Janice then tells Karyn about a forthcoming group meeting for mothers
and their new babies. She suggests that the group meeting can help Karyn meet
people with common experience who can support each other.

Janice: When you have a baby who cries, no one knows what you're feeling. I
          know that's how I felt with my third one. I remember calling the doc-
          tor and asking if I was doing something wrong. He was wonderful,
          told me to call him back in a week, and he offered to give me some-
          thing to help me with my hormones. The information helped me to
          settle down. Yet, I still didn't want to hear [my baby] cry anymore.

In this first visit after Greg's birth, Janice listened empathetically to
Karyn's comments regarding Greg's colic and her missing feedback. Not only
does Janice listen to Karyn, but she addresses Karyn's need for support. With
some parents, home visitors can suggest the parents visit their physician for additional help. Janice also shares her own parenting experiencing with a colicky
newborn. In this sharing, Janice strives to build a sense of connectedness with
parents. Just as they share the intimacies of their life, she lets them know that
she is a person with similar thoughts and feelings. Chapter 2 discusses this pattern of sharing by parent educators more fully.

Temperament

Temperament is the inborn ways a baby reacts to others and the environment,
including activity rate, rhythmicity, adaptability to new experiences, response
intensity, and general mood. Babies' temperaments not only affect the way they
respond but also the way others respond to them. Babies express three distinctive temperaments: easy, difficult, and slow to warm up.[15]

Different baby temperaments call for different parent responses. A need
exists for a "goodness of fit" between a baby's temperament and his or her parents in order for healthy baby and child development to occur. Goodness of fit
"exists when the demands and expectations of the parents and other people important to the child's life are compatible with the child's temperament, abilities,
and other characteristics."[16] Parenting a difficult baby can be very challenging.
Difficult babies may be slow to develop regular sleeping and eating cycles, may
respond vigorously and negatively to new things, and may cry more often.
Temperament patterns can persist through preschool years and occasionally
through adulthood. At the same time, temperament is not fixed, but can be
adapted by the child's relationships and experiences.

How parents react to their difficult baby depends on their own characteristics, expectations, and history of childhood parenting. Parents who are easy-
going can adapt to a difficult baby more readily than parents who are intense

and somewhat inflexible. Different styles between parents and babies do not automatically lead to problems. When problems do persist, developmental guidance can assist parents. For example, home visitors can clarify innate temperament differences for parents. This clarification assists parents in understanding their new baby and in helping them have appropriate expectations.

A baby's first anger outburst may happen before she is even 4 months old.[17] Anger is a signal that a baby's sense of well-being appears to be threatened. Angry feelings are an internal signal that warns of a threat from without or within. The baby recognizes her own basic needs and communicates them effectively in anger. As babies repeatedly express their needs and are responded to, their belief in their ability to affect their world is enhanced. If a baby's protests are repeatedly ignored, the baby will stop protesting and her facial expression will become bland. Unfortunately, some parents and out-of-home caregivers may see these shut-down babies as "good" babies.

Essential to parental guidance is availability—not only physical but especially emotional availability. A mother may be in the same room as her baby, but she may be watching television and oblivious to the baby. When parents are emotionally available, they can respond empathetically to their baby; thus, an ebb and flow of interactions involving mutual feedback develops. Brazelton and Cramer explained:

> In periods of attention, infants can begin to signal their mothers with smiles or frowns, with vocalizations, with motor displays such as leaning forward, reaching, arching the head coyly, and so on. Mothers respond contingently when they can read the messages conveyed in these signals. As a mother responds, she learns from the success or failure of each of her own responses, as measured by the baby's behavior. In this way, she refines the contingency of her responses and develops a repertoire of "what works" and "what doesn't."[18]

Along with emotional availability is the need for parents to respond to their babies' cues. That is, babies' behaviors such as vocalizations, smiles, and frowns signal their parents to respond. In turn, parents' responses to their babies invite further baby forms of communication; then, mutual communication and shared enjoyment takes place.

Beginning in their first visit, home visitors should keenly observe how the parent and baby interact. Does the parent respond to the baby's vocalization (e.g., grimace, smile) and is the response a good match to the feeling being expressed (e.g., pleasure, curiosity, discomfort)? The match does not have to be a mirror of the baby's behavior; rather, the match needs to speak to the baby's feeling. When the parent coos or cuddles the baby, does the baby respond with a similar emotional expression? Home visitors can model for the parent's responsiveness and reciprocal communication. In this way, they can promote parents' skill. This responsiveness and mutuality is the foundation for healthy attachment that gives babies a sense of trust, both in having their needs met and in their ability to signal their parents' responsiveness.

LATE INFANCY: 8–17 MONTHS

As babies begin to move, new challenges emerge as parents find their child's behavior less predictable. Babies' mobility allows them to leave their parents and discover their own independence. This new independence may cause the baby to feel overwhelmed and to seek renewed dependence. Babies need to trust that their parents are nearby; this availability provides the security for the child to leave the parent. By 9 months, babies expect to learn about any situation by looking at their caregiver's face. At around 10 months, when confronting something new or uncertain, babies first look at their parents' faces to the expression, indicating whether this new situation or object is fearful or pleasant. Psychologists call this *social referencing*.[19] The parent provides security for the baby to continue to explore.

The child's mobility means consistent discipline becomes a necessary part of parents' love of their child. This is the time that home visitors need to help parents understand their child's need for learning limits. Such learning is dependent on parental discipline and guidance. Between 8 and 17 months of age, children do not have the developmental skills to learn self-control; thus, parents' external control and the child's increasing obedience become very important.

In later phases of baby and toddler development, issues of control surface and often dominate parent–child interaction. Home visitors can assist parents in learning how to distract their toddlers, which is an effective guidance strategy for children this age. Providing a substitute or alternative activity can refocus the toddler's attention and prevent angry outbursts. Instead of saying, "Don't grab your brother's block," the parent can hand the toddler another toy.

This developmental period often includes a tug and pull between parents and their toddlers. Daily tasks such as diapering, feeding, and dressing can become times of struggle (e.g., the baby's constant movement during diapering and dressing). Central to learning independence is the inevitable "no" response to parental requests. When they start walking, toddlers want to explore their newly discovered "walking world" nonstop, with no understanding of the danger of electrical cords, hot stoves, stairs, heights, and so forth. They initially resist their parents' limits. When toddlers begin to use words, they use them to make demands. These new strides entail ambivalence, which the child expresses in sending contradictory messages.

Between 6 and 12 months of age, children are able to maintain a regular eating and sleeping schedule. Once babies have learned new motor skills like crawling and climbing, however, the surge in development may disrupt their nap schedule and they may be more resistant to being put in their crib. During these times of developmental growth, a calming activity such as reading or singing can assist babies in settling down. Most important is regularity and firmness. It helps to always remember that learning to fall asleep is an important skill for babies to master.

When children can eat together with the family or with other babies in child care, mealtime becomes a dual activity—mealtime plus social time. Babies are now able to eat solid food and, as soon as they develop their pincer grasp (around age 8–10 months), they can feed themselves with their hands. Exploring food can become as important as eating it. Eating is an activity in which babies can begin to exercise autonomy. Learning to use a cup themselves is exciting for babies. Once caregivers realize this, they can allow time for babies to explore their new skills and avoid making mealtimes into a battleground. By 12 months of age, children should be able to eat finger foods (e.g., cheese and bread cut into small pieces, sausages, fruit, or vegetables) on their own; by 16 months, they should be able to master a small spoon or fork. Feeding oneself is a sign of growing independence. Admittedly, eating becomes more messy and make the parents' clean-up task more demanding, but parents can learn to accept the increased mess if they recognize that their child is learning self-help skills.

As the child becomes mobile, discussion of safety becomes part of home visiting. Observation and supervision by parents are preconditions of safety. When observing, parents can anticipate potential safety hazards and redirect their children's action. The following interaction between Jean and her 17-month-old son is illustrative.

Jean is folding laundry on the couch as Ricky rides his wooden horse about the living room. Ricky gets off his horse and climbs on its back to stand.

Jean asks, "Ricky, is that safe?" Ricky does not say anything or get off his toy horse. Jean says, "You better get down, Ricky. The horsey might fall over, and you would bump your head on the chair."

Ricky gets off the horse and knocks the toy over so that it is lying on its side. Jean asks, "Is the horsey okay? Did the horsey get hurt?"

Ricky says, "Check and see."

Jean responds, "Check and see if he's okay."

Ricky says, "Horsey ouch."

Jean says, "The horsey has an ouchy. Maybe you'll need to get the doctor's kit."

Toddlers like Ricky constantly explore and experiment; however, they do not have the capacity to judge potentially dangerous situations. By being a careful observer, Jean was able to anticipate potential problems, an important guidance skill. When Ricky stood on his horse, Jean positively redirected his potentially dangerous action with an explanation that he could understand. Jean then used Ricky's action (i.e., knocking over his horse) to initiate an alternative activity—role-playing that the horse was injured. Once babies begin moving, childproofing the house becomes very important. Table 5.1 provides a checklist for home safety that can be helpful for parents.

Another normal part of a toddler's exploration that emerges at around age 1 year is biting, hair pulling, scratching, and hitting. The toddler initially does not understand that these actions hurt the other person. Parents should respond calmly but firmly, telling their toddler that they may not do that and stopping them until the toddlers can stop themselves. If a parent becomes horrified and overreacts, this overreaction sets the pattern rather than removes it. Biting is especially frightening for parents. Home visitors can help parents recognize that they need to help their toddler understand that under no circumstances do they allow biting. Substitutions such as dolls or teething toys can be given for the child to bite when needing to release feelings of anger and frustration. When biting, toddlers do not mean to hurt and are frightened afterward—especially if the victim is another small child who now is screaming. Parental response should include a firm limit, reassurance that they will help their child overcome the incident, and reassurance that they love the child. Janice discussed biting.

Parents need to understand that kids bite because it works. Biting is done out of frustration. Usually, biting is to get someone's attention, or a way to get a toy. Children bite because they don't have other tools to get what they want. Biting needs to be approached in stages. A baby explores with her mouth through biting. A toddler bites to get what he wants, for he can't talk very well. When an older child bites, the biting often represents a larger problem.

Table 5.1.   Home safety checklist for parents

Is your home poison-proof? (This includes house plants.)
Is the bathroom safety-proofed? (Keep bathroom door closed.)
Are all sharp objects (e.g., knives, pins, scissors) out of the baby's reach?
Are all small objects (e.g., buttons, beads, hairpins)out of the baby's reach?
Are electrical plugs covered?
Are your child's crib and room area safe?
Have you removed easily overturned lamps and tables, electrical cords, and sharp-edged furniture?
Are stairways gated at the top and gated two or three steps from the bottom?
Are plastic bags and soft pillows kept out of your child's reach?
Are long cords out of the child's reach and away from the crib?
Are there guards in front of open heaters, fireplaces, furnaces, and so forth?
Are hot liquids, curling irons, toasters, coffee pots out of the baby's reach?
Are the baby's toys safe?
Are all kitchen cabinets (within the baby's reach) free from harmful items or safety locked?
When in an automobile, does your child always ride in the back seat in a child safety seat?
Are guests' purses (which may contain medications)always put out of the child's reach?
Is there any chipping or flaking paint in a home built before 1978?

From Parents as Teachers National Center. (1999). *Born to Learn Curriculum Prenatal to 3 Years* (p. 363). St. Louis, MO: Author; adapted by permission.

As babies become mobile, a primary task of the home visitor is to help parents recognize that they must set limits (see Table 5.2) and then help their children follow them. Safety is parents' first guide and distraction is their most effective strategy. As mobility increases, accompanied by independence and determination, setting limits becomes much more difficult; at this time, home visitors can give parents needed support and guidance.

Clear limits help young children know what is expected of them. When very young children are tired, very hungry, or overwhelmed with stimulation, they are most likely to lose control and need parental limit setting. Parents can offer an alternative activity and divert children of this age. Some parents have difficulty being consistent in their limit setting. Open discussions with home visitors can give these parents the courage to persist, even when they feel unsure of themselves.

TODDLERHOOD: 18 MONTHS TO 3 YEARS

Throughout their waking hours, toddlers continue to relate to the world by exploring it. The toddler wavers between bold demands of independence and autonomy and intense periods of clinging and dependency. Toddlers insist on doing tasks without help, such as dressing or getting in the car seat, even when they do not have the necessary skills to do them alone. As toddlers struggle with independence, they frequently respond to their parents with intense negativism. It is as if they are testing both their parents and their own newly discovered independence.

In the second year of life, the child is able to understand another's feelings. For example, a toddler will pat a crying baby. Between their second and third year, children begin to think about their thoughts, memories, feelings, beliefs, and interests. Soon thereafter, they recognize about other people's thoughts and feelings.[20] Parents can foster this empathic ability by identifying their own feelings or other people's behavior and feelings to the toddler.

Table 5.2.   Positive guidelines for setting limits for toddlers

Choose the most important issues, and limit the number of rules so they can be enforced consistently.

Rules should be reasonable for the child's age and developmental level of understanding.

Tell the toddler in a positive manner what you want him or her to do. Rather than stating rules in the negative (e.g., no running), offer a positive alternative (e.g., please walk).

All adults need to consistently enforce the rules at all times and in all places.

State rules in a simple, brief, specific manner, and be sure the toddler understands.

Focus on the behavior. Avoid labeling the child negatively (e.g., "bad," "naughty," "dumb"). Instead say, "It hurts him when you bite."

Talk in a calm but firm manner. Avoid shouting.

As toddlers explore their everyday home environment from their new vertical, mobile perspective, it is natural for them to be absorbed with feelings of independence and autonomy. Toddlers explore without stopping to remember limits. An adult blocking and thereby frustrating a toddler's exploration most likely will lead to an angry, aggressive outburst from the toddler. Home visitors can help parents understand that negativism is a normal phase of development and should be expected as their toddler navigates between striving for independence, parental obstacles, feelings of dependency, and fears of separation. If parents overreact to their toddler's exploratory or negative behavior, they may be reinforcing this behavior because negative attention is better than no attention at all. Negative behavior that at first is merely exploratory (e.g., testing new limits) can become energized to continue if parents overreact. Often, a toddler's "no" does not even signal a negative intention; rather, it is voiced as a declaration of independence and can often be ignored. Sally's response to Jeff (age 27 months), for whom she provides child care, is illustrative.

Jeff and Suzy (age 4 years) have just finished eating breakfast. As the children get up from their chairs, Sally says to them, "Let's brush our teeth before we go outdoors."

Jeff replies emphatically, "No, no, no, no!"

Sally replies in a singing voice, "No, no, no, no."

They enter the bathroom, and Jeff sits on Sally's lap as he watches Suzy brush her teeth.

Sally says, "Let's watch Suzy. While we wait, let's squeeze a little [toothpaste] on your brush." Jeff initially is restless, but as Sally continues speaking softly, he calms down.

Sally continues, "Now let's get it wet." Then, Jeff takes the toothbrush and puts it in his mouth. Suzy finishes and leaves the bathroom. Jeff immediately goes to the stool in front of the sink and begins brushing his teeth.

Sally consistently expects Jeff to brush his teeth after eating and merely ignores Jeff's negativism. Jeff seems rebellious because he frequently says "no" as he tests Sally's limits and asserts his independence. Understanding toddlers' struggle for independence and their frustration with limits, Sally maintains her consistent expectations. Jeff follows through without resistance. Unlike Jeff, some toddlers do not obey; instead, they may have a temper tantrum.

Temper Tantrums

In this period of ambivalent struggle for independence, a toddler's inner turmoil sometimes erupts into a temper tantrum. Frustrated from not being able to do or get what they want, toddlers may roll on the floor, kicking and screaming. When having a tantrum, toddlers are out of control, which can be very frightening for them. Tantrums also frighten parents and are often difficult for them to understand and tolerate. Home visitors can help parents understand that tantrums are another normal part of development and that, even when he or she is having a tantrum, their toddler must accept their limits. Parents need to respond to their child's feelings and explain the reason for the tantrum. For example, parents should give their child the words to name how he or she is feeling and at the same time let the child know that they understand what their child wants, but that now is not the time (e.g., "I know you are angry because you want to go outdoors, but you must take a nap before we go outdoors").

Different children respond differently to parents' assistance in calming down. Some children need a time alone in a quiet room. Others need a parent's soft cuddling. All children need to understand that their parents recognize how awful they feel, but that a tantrum is not the way to get what the child wants. Once a tantrum has ended, parents can reassure the toddler of their love with a warm hug. Even though the parent has ignored the tantrum, the parent wants the toddler to know their love and acceptance of them.

As toddlers approach 3 years of age, if their parents have given them consistent limits, they most likely have achieved inner controls and tantrums have disappeared. Parents may be embarrassed when their child has tantrums, especially in public or in front of the home visitor. Parents may think something is wrong with their child or their parenting ability, so they may respond to the tantrum with their own anger and violence. Home visitors can normalize tantrums and help parents understand ways to handle them. Janice explained her approach.

If you say, "Does Joey have temper tantrums?" often parents will be defensive because they might be embarrassed about tantrums. But I still want to talk about tantrums at the appropriate age. Rather, I say, "How is Joey handling his temper?" I want parents to view it as normal and as temporary, and I want them to realize the importance of dealing with the emotion. For example, the child really does feel crazy, and parents need to be supportive: "I know you are mad." And that is different than giving in on the issue: "I'll give you a cookie so you stop crying." I want them to know they can support the child and still maintain their firm limits.

Learning Rules

Young children learn rules and expectations unconsciously in the course of their everyday lives with family members. These rules are learned in the same manner that toddlers learn rules of grammar, termed *practicing knowledge.*[21] Each child has a unique temperament; thus, young children respond to a parent's rules and expectations in their own way. Similarly, parents need to adjust their expectations to the uniqueness of each child.

A toddler learns to comply with rules between 12 and 18 months of age. However, complying with parents' rules is not a simple task for the young child. Home visitors can remind parents that it is easier for the toddler to comply with a "do" command than a "don't" command.

When parents take time to have extended play with their toddlers, this play gives the toddler a web of important meanings.[22] The toddler feels affirmed and connected, especially when a parent enters into the toddler's emotional tone of play. When toddlers have lengthy interactions with caring, nurturing adults, they not only learn how to regulate their own behavior, but also they begin to do so in terms of the perceived needs of others. Parents communicate moral concepts about caring and compassion each time they show their toddler how to pet a dog, rock their doll, or pat their baby sibling.

Toddlers learn how to care by the way that their parents respond to them, such as when they fall or are sad. Over time, this will be reflected in how toddlers respond to their parents, such as by giving them spontaneous hugs. Toddlers are quick to learn the "shush" gesture. Around 18 months of age, toddlers are able to be empathic and express altruistic behavior, such as patting the head of a crying baby sibling.

Misbehavior

Sometimes, no matter what strategy a parent uses, the child refuses to cooperate. Struggles with toddlers can be very difficult for their parents. With growth in mobility and more mature cognitive functioning, toddlers begin to see themselves as separate from their parents. Ambivalence and conflict emerge when toddlers desire both to be separate from their parents yet want them to satisfy their wishes. At the same time, the toddler is a central part of his or her parent's own identity; therefore, as the toddler struggles with independence, the parents are struggling with their own identification and separation from the child.[23]

When toddlers misbehave, parents can use time-out to allow both their child and themselves to calm down. Time-out can be an effective way to help an out-of-control child become calm. In time-out, parents remove their child from all attention for a short period until the child feels he or she can manage. Time-out need not be a punishment; rather, it is a strategy to help the child become calm. Tracy's response to Mia provides an example of using time-out.

Mia (age 34 months) begins moving her doll's bed across the living room floor. Her sister, Maggie (age 18 months), tries to assist, but Mia pushes her away. Finally, Mia pushes Maggie so hard that she tumbles down. Tracy then tells Mia that she needs to go to her room if she can't manage her behavior.

Mia shouts, "No."

Tracy then carries Mia, who cries loudly, into her bedroom. When Tracy returns, she tells Janice, "She goes crazy in her room, and then suddenly she comes out when she's all done crying. I tell her to stay in there until she's done crying."

Janice replies, "It's good that you have followed through. You handled that situation so well. I hope that everyone could do it that well." Mia then returns to the room and sits on her mother's lap. Tracy comments that usually she might have left Mia in her bedroom a while longer.

Janice says, "The amount of time isn't the important thing. She just needs to have time-out so that she can gain control. You let her come out when she's feeling better; then, you can explain to her what's happened. Sometimes when she is screaming, she can't even hear you. She has to first get it all out. Once it is all out, then she'll be fine. It's important that she knows you understand how she feels, but she still cannot push her sister."

Once the child has calmed down, the parent can talk about feelings to the child. When a child misbehaves but is not out of control, time-out is not an appropriate parental response. Instead, parents can give consequences that relate to the child's misbehavior. For example, if a child refuses to eat any dinner, the parent can inform the child that there will be no more food until breakfast. Children's misbehavior thus can be a learning situation. In some situations with young children, it often is enough for parents to stop the inappropriate behavior and offer an alternative behavior. For example, a parent can suggest to her 3-year-old son that he give his 2-year-old sister a toy to trade, rather than grabbing his sister's toy. What many parents find difficult is their need to be consistent and follow through once they address their child's misbehavior. For example, if a parent warns his 3-year-old that she must stay in the grocery cart or they will leave, the parent must leave when his daughter gets out of the cart, even when this decision is very inconvenient for the parent. Home visitors can help parents think ahead about how consequences affect the parent as well as the child and devise consequences that do not punish the parent more than they punish the child.

Toddlers gain security in knowing that their parents control them. When rules are broken, toddlers need to know there will be a consequence—a parental response. Consequences can be natural or a logical follow-up of the misbehavior. When playing at dinner, Suzy spills her milk. Suzy then is responsible for cleaning up her milk—a natural consequence. Suzy whines throughout her friend's birthday party. Because Suzy cannot manage her behavior, her mother takes her home from the party—a logical consequence. Often, there is no appropriate natural consequence for misbehavior. For example, if a toddler bites, it is not appropriate for his parent to bite the toddler in return. In these situations, parents need to acknowledge their child's angry feelings but let their child know that the behavior is not allowed. Parents should provide an alternative (e.g., vigorously punching playdough).

A calm home atmosphere with predictable routines, uninterrupted periods for play, and time for parent–child shared experiences nurtures a young child's development of self-control. As home visitors help parents understand what to expect of their toddlers and how to positively nurture their development, they can emphasize preventive discipline, which is parenting that prevents the occurrence of misbehavior and prevents parent–child battles. Giving clear behavioral expectations assists young children in controlling their behavior and prevents misbehavior. When changes will occur in routines, children can be told in advance so that they can be ready for these changes. Anticipating potential problems and providing alternatives can avoid struggles. For example, when a mother knows that her son will become overstimulated if she takes him grocery shopping with her, she can choose to take him on errands that do not invite overstimulation, such as to the gas station or cleaners. When single parents do not have a ready support system, completing errands without their child may demand careful planning, such as doing an errand before picking up their child from child care or swapping child care with a friend so that each can shop alone.

Providing limited choices respects the child's emerging abilities and encourages independence and autonomy. In the following example, as Mia (age 26 months) and Maggie (age 8 months) are playing, Tracy and Janice discuss preventive discipline strategies.

Mia has just tossed a wooden square across the floor. Her mother tells her, "Don't throw; it may hurt Maggie."

Mia then returns to the shape-sorter truck and places a green triangular shape in the appropriate space. As Mia is playing, Janice comments to Tracy, "When Mia gets ready to throw, it is good to head her off at the pass. That is, tell her what she can do—before she gets herself into trouble."

A few moments later, Tracy gives Mia a cracker to eat. As Mia sits on her mother's lap, eating her cracker, Tracy says to her, "Crackers all over. We'll need to vacuum."

Mia says, "I'll help."

Janice responds, "It's important for children to realize consequences of what they do—not punishment. If I spill something, I'll help clean it up."

Tracy says, "She's driving me nuts—getting her dressed in the morning. I give her choices, but she'll want something else."

"You need to choose your battles—what matters," Janice explains. "Possibly you could take turns. Yesterday, it was your turn [to choose the clothing]. Two-year-olds are beginning to understand taking turns. I'm not saying it'll be a lot easier, but it also can help her understand turns."

"She wants to do everything herself," Tracy adds.

"And it's frustrating for you," Janice acknowledges. "You are wise to give her limited choices, even if she chooses a third. Limited choices, instead of, for example, 'What do you want for breakfast?' It's important if a choice is offered, you can let her have what she chooses. When we give children choices, we are nurturing their decision-making process. Psychologists talk about it as autonomy. There is an underlying developmental issue in giving choices. Just remember, it's not part of her personality but part of her development!"

In this conversation, Janice achieves a healthy balance as she affirms Tracy's parenting actions, interprets the developmental meaning of the 2-year-old's actions, and gives suggestions related to Tracy's ongoing parenting dilemmas.

When young children misbehave and are in conflict with their caregivers, caregivers can help them learn how to manage experiences of disagreement and provide a foundation for the growth of empathy. For example, when caregivers discuss their child's feelings (e.g., "I know you are mad that you cannot have that cookie you took"), young children learn to recognize their own feelings and understand their caregivers care about them.[24] When caregivers give explanations for rules, young children can more readily make them their own, a part of their conscience formation. Having disagreements often involves experience in negotiation (e.g., "No, now is not the time for cookies, but I promise you may have them after lunch"). Toddlerhood is the time that children's cognitive skills are developing so that they can understand their caregivers' rules, apply them to their own behavior, and with time, internalize them.

Fears

Fear is an emotional response activated when threats or signals of upcoming danger are present; its function appears to be a defensive one.[25] When a fear occurs, a young child's motor activity is inhibited as the developing child's response system gears up for coping mechanisms such as fleeing, fighting, or hiding.[26] As the developing child's sense of self and sense of outside world expand, fears of such things as strange places, loud noises, Halloween masks, or specific animals may develop. Young children sometimes act out their fears in play and in art. The child may make imaginary fires, tumbling towers, or physician's shots. Across the pages of children's artwork, images of frightening things and situations may be portrayed. In blocks, young children may crash towers and buildings. When a young child is frightened, parents should convey that they can keep the child safe. Parents can foster persistence and perseverance as they share great stories in which a figure overcomes adversity, such as *The Little Engine That Could* and *Where the Wild Things Are.* When a child plays with a new and unpredictable friend or relates to an unfamiliar pet, they give evidence of being mindful despite fear. When adults repeatedly comfort a fearful child, they enable the child to learn to manage fear on their own.

Highly inhibited, fearful, and nonadaptive young children are at greater risk for developing anxiety problems, whereas unusually fearless children are at greater risk of developing conduct problems.[27] Positive parent–child relationships affect the self-control of relatively fearless children. It seems that fearless children can be motivated to acquire social rules by positive and enjoyable aspects of the parent–child relationship. Beyond young children's normal fears, some children have fears of traumatic events, present or past. Chapter 11 discusses these fears.

Home visitors can help parents understand that all young children are sometimes fearful. Janice's response to Shelly's concern about her daughter's fear illustrates how a home visitor can assist parents in this area.

As Erin (age 30 months) plays, her mother Shelly softly tells Janice, "Erin seems to be afraid of men. At the grocery, an elderly man talked to Erin, took her arm, and playfully said, 'Why don't you come home with me?' I thought he was being playful, but Erin seemed frightened."

Janice says, "Fears are quite typical for children Erin's age."

Shelly continues, "I told Erin, 'Did he scare you? He didn't mean to.' And I left it at that. Later, I told her that if a stranger touches you, you need to get me. But then my brother-in-law, who Erin knows real well, walked into our home, and Erin cried."

Janice explains, "This is very typical. Don't try to talk her out of it. Tell her to come to you, just as you did. Let her know that you'll keep her safe. Don't discount her feelings. She really is afraid. It's her age, and it's a piece of development. It's very important never to belittle her feelings."

"I have a tendency to say, `Don't be wimpy,"' Shelly admits.

Janice says, "Her fears are very real, and at this age, fantasy and reality are not separate."

As Shelly describes her daughter's fears, Janice helps Shelly understand that fears are a normal part of development that parents need to respect. Within the context of a parent's concern, Janice is able to provide developmental information (i.e., "Fears are real at this age") and suggestions (i.e., "Let her know you'll keep her safe").

Parents cannot eliminate their young children's fears, but they can help them learn how to deal with their fears. For example, parents can respect their child's fear of monsters by explaining that monsters are imaginary, by reminding the child that mom and dad are in a nearby room, and by adding a nightlight to the child's bedroom. It is helpful for parents to know that fears are a normal phase, which will pass if the parents do not overreact. Overreaction can validate and reinforce young children's fears.

As a child's world expands, he or she experiences new fears (e.g., loud noise of fire engines, unpredictability of a neighbor's dog). When parents recognize what their young child fears, they often can prepare their child and let their child know that they are present to protect the child. Similarly, parents can limit television viewing and be with their child during potentially scary programs. Young children sometimes have nightmares, which are frightening but also a normal phase of development. Home visitors can help parents understand that they can calmly and quietly awaken their child and offer comfort, which usually allows the child to return to sleep.

LATE TODDLERHOOD: 3–5 YEARS

Negativism, tantrums, and recurrent parent–child struggles diminish as the child turns 3 and the calmness of early infancy reappears. Given their verbal and intellectual ability, 3-year-olds enjoy in shared experiences with others. Dinners with 3-year-olds can be satisfying shared family experiences. Children can carry on internal dialogues, plan their play, use words as substitutes for objects or people in role-play, and begin to control their own behavior. Three-year-olds can tell a story with a dramatic story line;[28] these stories are usually autobiographical.

Beginning at age 3 years, preschoolers have expanded experiences with others their own age. In these experiences, they learn new patterns of behavior from their peers and try out their own actions. Conflict and emerging aggression is common, especially when the preschooler is frustrated by peers. At the same time, preschoolers develop skills in sharing, turn taking, and cooperative play.

Some children hold back from social experience or even from letting themselves fully experience their world. In children ages 4–7 years, reticence was found to be associated with indices of anxiety, social maladjustment, and peer rejections. In addition, reticence and solitary-passive withdrawal were negatively related to peer acceptance at both 4 and 7 years of age.[29] Home visitors can discuss a child's reticence with parents and develop strategies to assist the child, such as having playdates with a friend from school, having cousins over for dinner, or extending the parent playtime with the child.

Simple Explanations and Alternative Action

With the child's increased verbal skills and beginning reasoning skills, parents can give simple explanations with suggested alternative actions as they redirect their child (e.g., "Throwing your ball in the house will break the lamps. Let's go outdoors to throw"). In other words, effective parents should give reasons for their limits. Reasons help children develop standards of right and wrong.

Parents can also verbalize children's feelings and thereby help their child recognize the feeling, a first step in controlling one's emotions. When a child grabs her sister's doll, the mother can say, "I know you're angry because you want the doll." Parents also can help their child know that they will help solve the problem: "When Lucretia is finished, I'll make sure you get the doll." Now that children can think about ideas and understand consequences of their behavior (e.g., "If I kick my brother, Daddy will catch me and punish me"), they are developing a true moral consciousness. With time, children learn to think about the consequences in terms of how another person will feel (e.g., "If I hit Sammy, he'll be mad at me").

Now that young children have a sense of causality, they sometimes want to be nice to others so that others will be nice to them (e.g., "I think I'll climb on Mommy's lap and give her a big hug").[30] The child knows that Mommy then will give a return hug and kiss. The child's sense of right and wrong no longer focuses on not doing bad things. Doing nice things leads to simple rewards.

Increased Aggression and Misbehavior

Parenting 4- and 5-year-olds entails some new challenges. As the sense of self and sense of outside world expand, curiosity and increased aggression emerge. Four- and 5-year-olds are fascinated by aggressive television superheroes, ghosts, and monsters. Because there is so much violence on children's television programming, preschoolers benefit from having their television viewing limited and monitored by their parents. Home visitors experience a dilemma when approaching this topic with parents who have their television on all the time and whose children often watch television alone. In these situations, home visitors need to remember that it is not their role to change family patterns but to support families and provide developmental information.

Whining, stuttering, lying, stealing, and swearing emerge at 4 and 5 years of age. These behaviors often are exploratory and temporary; however, when parents overreact, their child's behavior may become habitual. Children of this age have some skills in cooperative play, but possessiveness, conflict, lack of sharing, and name calling also characterize their peer play.

As children get older, parents begin to rely more on explanations, compromise, or other nonassertive negotiating strategies. Preschoolers tend to follow behavioral standards more readily, but they also can be quick to assert their own opinion. For example, they may think any food that is mixed together is "yucky" and therefore will not eat stew or spaghetti. In healthy, positive parent–child relationships, preschoolers' cooperation is not a matter of compliance but rather a combination of the child's ability to understand, accept, and want to cooperate.[31]

By the time a child is 5 years of age, dawdling as she gets dressed, brushes her teeth, or eats becomes common. When a child dawdles, parents can build in plenty of extra time to avoid battles. Sulking and pouting often occur. If parents ignore this sulking and pouting, children soon learn that the behavior has no value. When frustrated, a child may turn against her parent (e.g., "I hate you, mommy!"). These strong negative feelings are a surprise to both child and parent. When parents understand such behavior, they won't take it personally and will realize that it will soon pass.

Teasing and tattling also may emerge at this age. As a child notices differences in people, he or she may feel insecure; this insecurity may provoke teasing to feel powerful. Parents can ask about the teased child's feelings (e.g., "How would you feel?"). If parents consistently address their child's tattling concerns, the child will think that tattling is being rewarded and probably will continue the behavior. Often parents can merely say, "Your responsibility is to take care of yourself."

In the 1990s, early educators across America reported an increasing number of hyperactive, impulsive, and aggressive young children in their classrooms.[32] Aggressive behavior can be defined as behavior directed toward another person with the intent to hurt or frighten. In infancy, physical discomfort and the need for attention are elicitors of aggression, whereas peer conflicts and conflicts over material possessions become the elicitors in the third through fifth years of life.[33]

Overactive, negative, and/or unpredictable children often have mothers who tend to be more aggressive, less nurturing, and less responsive than mothers of even-tempered children. A conflictual parent–child interactional pattern, over time, contributes to a child's aggression. This interaction pattern often is associated with high-risk factors such as poverty, mother's mental illness, and violence. It leaves young children with limited skills to regulate their behavior. During the second year, with the toddler's increased mobility, parents' discipline is heightened. Mothers who were unresponsive or inconsistent had young children with heightened aggression. A clear bidirectionality exists in the parent–child relationship.[34]

The use of force against one's peers ebbs and flows between 1 and 3 years of age. In the toddler's second and third year, the child becomes increasingly aware of other people's feelings and possible action. The toddler's growing understanding of their peers' desires and intentions probably affects the circumstances in which the toddler chooses to use force.

High rates of aggression during the preschool years are due to several factors. Genetic components, temperamental qualities, punitive and inconsistent parental discipline, learning from siblings, exposure to media violence, and poor quality child care may relate to aggression.[35] Large gender differences in aggression have been found in children as young as 17 months, with boys having as much as twice the amount of aggression as girls.[36] The gender difference for verbal aggression is somewhat smaller than for physical aggression, but in the same direction. Aggressive disorders can begin before age 3 years.[37] In fact, studies indicate that the frequency of anger outburst and aggression increases rapidly from the 1 year to approximately 3 years of age, then the frequency seems to decrease.[38]

The biggest "cause" of physical aggression among young children is competition for desirable objects or space. Children younger than 3 years of age have limited ability to understand the impact of their aggressive behavior. Longitudinal research indicates that aggression that begins in early childhood shows moderate to strong continuity over time.

During the same time that aggression surfaces (between 2 and 5 years of age), the executive functions of the prefrontal cortex—such as self-regulation of thought, action, and emotion—develop. As these executive functions develop, we see a decline in young children's aggression. By 3 years of age, most children can effectively use a rule to control their behavior. Children with attention-deficit/hyperactivity disorder (ADHD) or children with high levels of aggression tend to have poor executive function.[39]

Aggression also has been associated with low language proficiency, as early as the child's second year of life.[40] Interestingly, the development of aggression shares some milestones with language development. Among normally developing children, as aggression diminishes around three years, language abilities grow at a staggering rate. For some children, however, language does not progress as anticipated and physical aggression continues to attract concern, particularly with boys.[41]

Factors influencing young children's aggression include maternal unresponsiveness and poor attachment, marital conflict, and multiple familial stressors. Studies indicate that when fathers are in residence but engage in high levels of antisocial behavior, their children have increased conduct problems.[42] These behaviors can also be triggered by anxiety found in young children who are experiencing consistent violence, maltreatment, or domestic violence; who are given no behavioral limits or consequences; or who have minimal shared time with their parents. Inconsistent limits and lack of routines or consequences can generate a great deal of anxiety in children; this anxiety most often is expressed in aggression, impulsivity, and hyperactivity. There is some evidence of familial transmission of aggression; however, most dominant is the shared at-risk environment of young children and their parents.[43] Research has extensively documented the link between aggressive behaviors and peer relationships among young children.[44]

Extreme Aggression   Inconsistent, punitive, and coercive discipline as well as insecure attachment and child maltreatment are linked to antisocial and aggressive behavior in young children.[45] These social-behavioral deficits are common across psychiatric disorders, including ADHD.[46] Aggressive behaviors may indicate serious problems if they occur very frequently, are quite extreme (e.g., hitting another child's face), the child shows no remorse, or the aggressive behavior persists and/or increases. In these cases, a competent mental health professional can be helpful.

Studies indicate consistent predictors of extreme aggression. Aggressive acts are usually situationally and contextually determined. Stable patterns of aggression can be predicted by individual differences such as heredity and dispositions. Life experiences such as physical abuse contribute to aggression. In addition, factors such as socioeconomic status, large family size, single parenting, teenage parenting, and low education are related to aggression. Harsh parenting may also lead to aggression.[47]

Children with ADHD may exhibit similar behavioral problems:

- Lack of planning and thinking before action
- Inability to select what is important from what is not important
- Easy distractibility
- Inability to maintain attention
- Difficulty in self-monitoring[48]

The "Impossible" Child   Some children, termed *impossible* by Garbarino and Bedard,[49] become explosively angry when they cannot handle their environment. These children seem to be delayed in developing skills critical to tolerating frustration and becoming flexible. Some parents are better equipped to help these children get along with others. Without early intervention, however, these children are likely to have serious problems as they get older and their behavior becomes more and more problematic. Some children refuse to listen to parents or teachers, others do not pay attention at school, and others turn to chronic aggression.

Young children can be impossible for many reasons. They may have genetic abnormalities or a temperament that is quick to become angry. Although some young children are more biologically vulnerable than others, this predisposition depends to a large degree on the young child's experiences. Impossible children may have been emotionally or physically hurt at an early age, neglected, or abused. They may live in an environment with unhealthy habits of interaction and little response to the children's needs.

This phenomenon seems more prevalent now than in past years for several reasons. First, a greater number of seriously premature infants survive today than in the past; some of these babies face the added complication of maternal cocaine or alcohol abuse. Second, more and more children live in single-parent families in which one adult is responsible for child rearing. This parent often does not have the social supports that promote effective parenting. Third, the fast pace of modern life does not allow the time that child rearing takes. The less time a caregiver spends with a child, the less likely it is that the child will respond to the caregiver's requests. Parents then have to seek outside assistance in dealing with their children. Finally, parents face multiple demands and child rearing may not be their priority. They may leave the task of child rearing to other people or it may be neglected altogether.[50]

If an impossible child lives in a violent environment, anger will become a dominant theme. Fortunately, if the child's caregivers teach him or her socially acceptable behavior and communication skills, the anger may become immersed in healthy emotions.

Conscience

It is well known that behavioral difficulties often emerge as a part of normal, age-specific challenges. Caregivers who consistently give clear explanations as well as talk about feelings and intentions, especially in disputes, are promoting healthy conscience development. Children learn the predictable consequences of their misbehavior, and these consequences help them remember the rules. They learn why some actions are not appropriate, how some actions can be harmful, and how some of their actions affect other people.

Conscience can develop in situations other than misbehavior. When parents and their young children talk often about what they are doing or have been doing, these conversations often contain implicit moral lessons. For example, at dinner, a father described how his coworker needed to leave work early each day to relieve her sister and take care of her elderly mother who is very ill. His young daughter learned that he was sympathetic to his coworker's personal life.

Once preschoolers understand consequences and internalize rules, they develop a moral consciousness or conscience. They have learned to anticipate the consequences of their actions: "If I hit my brother, he'll cry, and I'll be sent to my room." At first, consequences are concrete: specific behaviors lead to specific consequences. As they get older, children also learn that consequences include how another person will feel after a given behavior. Preschoolers who live in emotionally healthy families expect pleasant consequences when they do nice things and will do nice things in order to receive positive reactions. They have learned to anticipate their parents' warm hugs or nodding smiles; parents' warnings or warm expressions are experienced as the child's own inner voice.[51] Greenspan and Lewis explained that this inner voice has two components: "the inner presence that guides you in a positive way, eventually with ideals and values, and another presence that can be critical or make you feel guilty or bad."[52]

Children at this age have triangular thinking, which helps them set their own limits. A girl may stop hitting a playmate because she now can consider how the other child or her father might feel about the action. She knows that her playmate would get upset if hit and her father would disapprove. Once the child has internalized her parent's approval, she may stop hitting playmates. A preschooler who receives lots of nurturance and lots of love from parents can learn to tolerate disappointment without misbehaving.

Anger

Anger is a feeling that people experience when a goal is blocked and they become frustrated. A key function of anger is to provide the energy and motivation to eliminate barriers that block intention. Anger is critical to survival because of its self-regulatory and social communication functions. It makes ready the body physiologically and psychologically to initiate self-protective and instrumental activity.[53] Typical stresses of preschoolers that lead to anger include conflict over possessions; physical assault or verbal exchanges by an adult or child, such as teasing or taunting; rejection; and issues of compliance.[54]

Young children can learn to express their anger in a way that helps them either to reevaluate the intention that is blocked or to find constructive ways of eliminating the block. Home visitors can help parents realize that they can play a pivotal role in helping their children recognize their anger. Talking about feelings helps young children recognize and understand their feelings. When parents see an angry child, they can talk about the child's feelings (e.g., "I see that you are very angry because you cannot go outside now"). Expressing the child's emotion in words is an important first step toward enabling the child to recognize and understand the emotion. Once parents have helped their child recognize his or her anger, they can encourage the child to label it verbally (e.g., "I'm mad that you took my truck"). In situations with peers or siblings, parents and children can discuss what makes them mad and how they can express anger. Then, they can find a solution that allows everyone to get what they want without blocking what another person wants.

Around 4 or 5 years of age, children begin to struggle with issues of "right" and "wrong" and fairness. Anger is not only to protect one's self-interests. Now the child may be upset because of injustices suffered by others. Feelings of right and wrong, although developing new dimensions, will persist throughout the child's life.[55]

In handling anger, the parents' first concern should be to ensure safety. Setting clear limits reassures children that parents will not allow anyone to become hurt. As parents soothe their child, they can talk about angry feelings and the feelings of the person who was hurt. In addition, anger can be the basis for problem solving: What was the cause of the child's anger? How can the child deal with this anger?

When a child seems angry most of the time, when his anger reactions are out of proportion to the causes of his anger, or when anger interferes with family, friends, and/or important activities, then the child's anger may be a symptom of a more serious underlying problem. Parents then should seek professional help.

Home visitors can suggest to parents that reading children's books about anger also assists young children in understanding this feeling, such as *I Was So Mad*[56] and *That Bothered Kat.*[57] The home visitor may help the parents better manage their own anger in the process of teaching their child.

Methods of Discipline

Parents most often raise their children in the manner in which they were parented as young children. Some parents view spanking as the appropriate response to misbehavior. When home visitors work with parents who believe that spanking is their right and the most appropriate form of discipline, the home visitor is confronted with a challenging task: "How can I empower these parents and at the same time inform them of alternative methods of discipline?" Many parents do not know any strategies other than spanking. Home visitors can suggest that parents can leave the grocery story rather than hit their misbehaving child. Parents can calmly tell their child that he will go to school in his pajamas if he won't get dressed because his dad cannot be late for work.

The home visitor must remember that parents are the ultimate decision makers and the home visitor merely shares new information. As they chat with parents, home visitors can share some of the negative results of physical punishment. The home visitor must also find specific parenting strategies that can be affirmed (see Table 5.3).

Rewards

Home visitors often are challenged by those parents who rely on rewards to guide their young child. Rewards can undermine a child's motivation. Children learn to act to gain a reward, rather than gain pleasure from activities and accomplishments in and of themselves. When a young child repeatedly receives rewards, the absence of reward can feel like punishment. For a reward to be an effective way to control children's behavior, children must be unable to acquire the reward on their own; in other words, they must remain dependent on their

Table 5.3. Potential problems in the use of physical punishment

Children learn by observation. Parents are modeling aggression and violence as they physically punish their child.

When they are spanked, children can experience strong underlying messages such as rejection.

Physical punishment does not guide young children toward behavior their parent considers right.

Physical punishment works only as long as the parent is present.

The memory of being hit is remembered more than the misbehavior that triggered the physical punishment.

Physical punishment is no longer an effective control method once the child is an adolescent.

A child who behaves only in response to spanking is being set up for problems in school because many schools do not allow teachers to spank.

parents. In reality, as children grow older, they become increasingly able get their own rewards (e.g., earning their own money to go to the movies). As with the topic of punishment, visitors can inform parents of the negative consequences of excessive use of rewards. They can emphasize that rewarding a child inhibits self-direction.

Praise

General evaluative praise responses can have similar negative effects on a young child. Repeated slogans such as "good boy," "good job," and "nice girl" communicate to young children that they are pleasing the adult; thus, they may foster short-term obedience. These comments tell children nothing about themselves, except that they are pleasing the adult. These general praise statements do not contribute to a young child's self-reliance, self-direction, or self-control.[58]

One long-term goal is for children to recognize their accomplishments and be pleased with themselves. Home visitors can help parents learn how their specific, positive descriptions of their child's actions are not only rewarding but also are helping their child recognize his or her own accomplishments and feelings of self-worth. Such comments offer encouragement (e.g., "You can put on your shoes and socks without any help! I'm proud of you"). Young children often thrive on their parents' recognition of good behavior. It is a challenging task for home visitors to emphasize both the importance of parents' positive responses to their child's good behavior and at the same time help parents learn ways to be positive without using external rewards or global praise.

Problem Solving

The ability to solve problems is a powerful skill in maintaining self-regulation and can be a guiding principle of discipline for preschoolers. Preschoolers have the verbal and cognitive skills needed to participate in solving misbehavior problems. When parents include their child in this process, they show that they respect and value their child's perspective. Children can be encouraged to think of alternative solutions to grabbing, hitting, racing in the house, and so forth. Home visitors can assist parents in understanding that, when solving problems, their children can develop a sense of responsibility for their actions. Young children may need their parents' assistance to think of alternatives.

Just as parents strive toward nurturing problem-solving skills in their young children, home visitors can strive to approach parents' discipline questions as opportunities to solve problems jointly with them. If a parent's question about discipline can be solved jointly, then the parent can own the solution. Janice uses this approach when LeToya, the mother of Suzy (age 38 months), expresses a concern.

LeToya: We've had problems with Suzy sleeping in her bed, going to sleep. Last night, she lay in her bed and screamed for an hour.

Janice: Do you have a routine?

LeToya: We read a story and get a drink of water before bed. She wants a light on.

Janice: Was there anything different yesterday? What about her food?

LeToya: We had roast, potatoes, and carrots, and she loves roast. Last night, we ate later than usual—8 o'clock.

Janice: When do you usually eat?

LeToya: About 6:00, but last night we ran errands before dinner.

Janice: Children this age have no sense of clock time, rather a sense of event time. It sounds like you've figured it out—having such an unusually late dinner. She probably knows that after dinner, she gets to play. Maybe not having playtime had something to do with it. Small children are hooked on routines. I would encourage you to stick to routines of having the same thing happen in the same order every night. Then, she'll know that falling asleep is the last step in what is supposed to happen.

Janice strives to support and empower parents while offering developmentally appropriate strategies. She asks parents what they have tried and does not hesitate to probe the situation so that she can understand what is going on in the family. Janice explained:

You want to get all the alternatives on the table. And in the discussion, you can intersperse your own ideas, but you want the parent to come up with the solution. I try not to make many suggestions. Rather, I try to point out strong points of the parent and build on that. They are more likely to use these comments of mine than a suggestion. If I were to give a lot of suggestions, I doubt if they would be remembered. But also, our primary task is empowerment. I have learned that parents respond much better if an idea is coming from them rather than from me. For example, when figuring out a problem, I search for a way to say, "That's probably it; you figured it out." I might highlight something on a handout, or I might frame a suggestion as "Some parents have found it helps if… "

Beyond discussions with parents, home visitors can model effective guidance and discipline as they engage in activities with young children. In her interactions, Janice is a skillful model. She frequently anticipates problems and redirects children with alternative actions. If a child does misbehave, she positively redirects the child with a simple explanation. When a child is frustrated or angry, Janice verbalizes the child's feelings and thereby helps the child recognize and accept his or her feelings. Throughout her interactions, she frequently describes the child's actions and thereby affirms the child.

DIFFICULTIES AND DILEMMAS

Some young parents, with little parenting experience, feel insecure and stressed when their own parents or spouse disagree with their method of parenting. These disagreements often emerge as the parent adapts nonreward or nonphysical punishment methods of discipline as suggested by her home visitor. Home visitors can assist these parents through support and discussion. The visitor can remind a parent that she can discipline according to her values when alone and not discuss this with her spouse or parent. Parents also need to know that their child will be fine even if they disagree about the methods, as long as one parent does not demean the other.

Sometimes a child's incessant aggression can distort a family's everyday relations with each other. When a young family has a child who is persistently out of control, the home visitor may advise the parent to seek professional assistance. Psychiatrists, social workers, counselors, and psychologists can assist these families.

CONCLUSION

This chapter began by describing how many parents are ambivalent in directing, redirecting, and setting limits for their young children. Of all possible child-rearing topics, home visitors can be certain that parents will be eager to discuss guidance and discipline. At the same time, home visitors need to recognize that this is an area where parents feel vulnerable. Possibly, parents are disciplining in the manner in which they were parented as a young child. If so, a critique of their methods is a critique of their family heritage. If a child's behavior is out of control, the parent may see this misbehavior as a reflection of his or her own incompetence and thus will be very sensitive. Home visitors need to approach this topic with sensitivity and respect because if parents do not feel respected, they cannot hear and integrate the home visitor's information and guidance.

Home visitors need to be knowledgeable of the different guidance and discipline strategies required for different periods of the baby's and young child's development. Table 5.4 shows the progression of infant development and the accompanying parental guidance and discipline needed to promote this development. It is important to recognize that parenting behaviors continue to be

Table 5.4. Progression of child development and accompanying parental guidance and discipline

Developmental patterns	Guidance and discipline strategies
Birth–8 months	
Crying as response to discomfort	Positive home climate
Vocalizations, gestures, and body movements	Helping infant self-calm
	Emotional availability
Expressing different temperaments	Observation
	Contingent responsiveness
	Reciprocal communication
	Adapting own behavior to infant's temperament
9–17 months	
Mobility	Home safety precautions
Independence and autonomy	Anticipation of potential problems
Social referencing	Distraction; alternative suggestions
Exploration	Limit setting: Clear behavior expectations
Dependence	Consistency
Biting, hitting, hair pulling	
18–36 months	
Independence and autonomy; clinging dependency	Verbalization of child's feelings and intentions
Exploration	Time-out
Negativism	Giving limited choices
Temper tantrums	Natural and logical consequences
Simple role play	Assigning family responsibilities
Fear	Ignoring minor misbehavior
	Respecting and valuing child's perspective
3–5 years	
Verbal skills	Simple explanations accompanying limits
Cognitive skills	Assisting child in problem solving
Extended role-play	Providing experiences with peers
Aggression	Assisting child in conflict resolution
Whining, lying, swearing, stealing	
Problem solving	

needed as the baby develops. These parenting behaviors remain important strategies in promoting toddlers' and young children's development.

The home visitor's task is indeed complex. First, he or she needs an understanding of the development of babies, toddlers, and young children. Second, the home visitor needs knowledge of appropriate guidance and discipline strategies to promote this development. Finally, the home visitor needs to be able to develop an accepting, nurturing relationship through which the home visitor can support, affirm, and guide young parents.

Communication and Language

I noticed that people would name some object and then turn towards whatever it was that they had named. I watched them and understood that the sound they made when they wanted to indicate that particular thing was the name which they gave to it, and their actions clearly showed what they meant, for there is a kind of universal language, consisting of expressions of the face and eyes, gestures and tones of voice, which can show whether a person means to ask for something and get it, or refuse it and have nothing to do with it.

Saint Augustine (c. 396–397 A.D./1961, p. 29)

THE DEVELOPMENTAL PROCESS FOLLOWS A CONTINUUM. Beginning at birth, babies communicate nonverbally with their caregivers; then as toddlers, they develop language; as preschoolers, they tell stories. Very young babies can communicate effectively with their parents, but true mutuality, in which complex thoughts and ideas are exchanged, awaits developmental changes during the first 3 years. For typically developing children, language emerges spontaneously in social settings as a means of communicating[1] and originates from everyday interaction.[2] Gesture has accompanied vocal communication for most of the last 2 million years.[3] This chapter gives a brief developmental overview of communication and language and discusses how home visitors can address these developmental areas in their work with young children and their parents.

COMMUNICATION AND LANGUAGE

Communication is people sending messages to each other. We communicate when we let people know what we want and what we are thinking. Communication can be expressed in many ways: a baby's cry or smile, a parent's encouragement, a singer's style, or a couple's dancing. Beginning at birth, babies learn to communicate when their parents feed, bathe, diaper, dress, and play with them. The baby's emotional signaling develops into communication and language skills.

Language is a specific form of communication: a shared, rule-governed social system that is capable of symbolically representing thoughts. Language makes it possible for people to express and understand a wide variety of messages.

Three major initial conditions exist for the development of language:

1. Children must be able to organize sensory information.

2. Speech occurs as a continuous sound wave. Children therefore must subsequently segment it, categorize it, and organize its variations according to semantic value.

3. Children must recognize that the adult speech they hear is motivated by an intention to produce meaningful sounds.[4]

Children need both expressive and receptive abilities to communicate well. Expressive ability is the ability to produce vocalizations, gestures, and/or speech, whereas receptive ability is the ability to receive and comprehend the communication signals of another. Emerging literacy is the young child's understanding of the meaning of written words and increasing ability to use written words to understand and communicate with others.

Communication, language, and literacy focus on meaning. Young children experience meaning through social interaction, as illustrated by Tracy and Mia.

Mia (age 26 months) is placing shapes on a formboard. As she places a triangle onto the formboard, Mia says, "There we go."

Mia's mother, Tracy, repeats, "There we go."

Janice comments, "It's so good you repeat."

Tracy says, "I do it so much that Mia will continue repeating until I do, or she'll say, `Mommy, do it.'"

Janice replies, "It gives her two pieces of feedback: She knows that she is being understood, and she is hearing the way the words are supposed to be pronounced without being corrected."

This chapter follows the progression of phases of language, communication, and early literacy from birth to 5 years of age.

PRESPEECH: BIRTH TO 10 MONTHS

In the prelinguistic phase of language development, birth to 10 months, baby–caregiver interaction is the setting in which babies learn to express their needs, wants, and intentions. The child's learning of speech depends on maturation and reorganization of the relevant organs.[5]

Birth to 3 Months

The newborn is wired for interaction; that is, newborns have strong inborn preferences and behavioral tendencies to interact with others. Babies communicate from the first moments of life by giving positive and negative signals. From the beginning, newborns and parents repetitively interact. These interactions only take a second or two. The mother moves her eyes and mouth as her baby looks at her or cries. These repetitive communication patterns are the building blocks of regulation of babies' emotion and behavior.[6]

Babies can see at birth but not in detail; they lack depth perception and the ability to focus both eyes on a single object. Newborns, however, can turn toward a light and recognize contrast. They like circular shapes and prefer looking at the human face. Newborns see best when objects are 8–15 inches away; they can recognize contrasts and see brightness, color, and motion. At age 2 months, babies can track horizontally, follow a moving person, and smile in response to a smiling face.[7] Newborns often stare at the mouth of an adult, especially when the adult is talking, but eyes most retain babies' attention. Eye contact is therefore a key aspect of nonverbal communication. At age 3 months, babies enjoy looking at their own hands and can reach for, grasp, and mouth objects. They also can recognize their parents and everyday caregivers.[8]

At birth, hearing acuity is greater than visual discrimination. Babies are born with a remarkable ability to hear differences between speech sounds. Newborns have the capacity for discriminating speech sounds used in all the world's languages, even those they have never heard. They are capable of distinguishing a broad range of consonant and vowel contrasts and very quickly can recognize similarity of sounds belonging to a single phonetic category. Babies are particularly attentive to speech. They can distinguish voices and show a preference for their mother's voice.[9]

Babies use nonverbal behavior or movements to produce their first stories or prenarratives. Establishing eye contact is an effective first step. Jervay-Pendergrass and Brown illustrate how a 6-week-old tells the story of a jammed bottle.

> Six-week-old Erin Nicole lay in her mother's arm drinking… from a bottle. Her bright eyes conveyed delight. Suddenly, however, her facial expression changed; she stopped sucking; and her darkening gaze went first toward her bottle, then away. Something happened! Erin Nicole's mother, momentarily puzzled, took the bottle, and then turned it upside down to make sure that the liquid was flowing. It was not.[10]

Erin Nicole's eye gaze and facial expressions communicated a narrative to her mother, who was able to learn what the difficulty was. Some parents are not quick to read their babies behavioral cues. In these cases, home visitors can help parents learn to read their babies' facial gestures and movements so that they can communicate effectively with them.

Babies' ability to hear sounds and voices is a central part of their language learning. Babies are born with the ability to begin to categorize different speech sounds. Even newborns are able to discriminate utterances in one language from those of another. Research of babies in bilingual homes indicates that very young babies can discriminate utterances from two languages.[11]

Babies develop several different cries to represent different kinds of discomfort. Parents intuitively follow cue signals accompanying their baby's vocal or nonvocal behaviors. Movement, sound, and rhythm entail the common experiences that the baby and parent bring to their interaction. Bateson describes these reciprocal interactions as "characterized by a sort of delighted, ritualized courtesy and more or less sustained attention and mutual gaze."[12] Intuitively, parents strongly tend to imitate their baby's facial and vocal expressions. Starting at about 2–3 months, babies show pleasure by cooing; by 3 months, they play with speech sounds, especially as they participate in vocal play with their parents. Playing and having fun are key ingredients in baby and parent social interaction.[13] This playful interaction often involves imitation within routines such as dressing. It is the setting in which babies learn what to expect from their parents and in which the parents learn what to expect from their babies.[14] Within these first months, babies learn to read cues from their parents' facial expressions and speech. Similarly, parents learn to read their babies' cues from vocalizations, body movement, and facial expressions.[15] Parents learn that different cries have different sounds and meaning: a soft cry for attention, a steady rhythmic cry for hunger, and a loud shrieking cry for pain. These prelinguistic interactions are parallel to adult conversation.

From the first days of their life, babies imitate. By 2 months, babies can detect equivalences between touch and sight.[16] For example, they can visually recognize the ball that previous they had held in their hand. At this age, babies communicate via facial gestures, cries, gestures of the hands and body, and pantomime. Around 3 months of age, turn taking appears. Now mother and baby respond to each other by taking turns vocalizing. Babies' capacity for timing and rhythmicity gives rise to their motor planning and sequencing, higher-level planning, and sequencing capacities, such as taking the mother's hand to show her the desired toy. These higher-level planning and sequencing capacities ultimately involve complex reflective thought and verbal communication and influence cognitive and academic abilities.[17]

Beginning with their first visit, even a few weeks after the child's birth, home visitors can help parents to understand the meaning of their babies' vocalizations. As parents and the home visitor discuss the baby's sounds, the home visitor can encourage parents to respond to their child's vocalizations, thus promoting the parent–baby vocal play that is crucial for the baby's development of language and communication. The following conversation between Janice and Karyn about Karyn's 6-week-old son, Greg, is illustrative.

Karyn: [Greg] makes moaning noises. Is that normal?

Janice: Yes. You'll enjoy listening to how his sounds change, changing into vowel sounds and then adding consonants. And he'll get responsive. That's something to watch for. You can make sounds, and he'll respond. He's not using words, but he'll understand taking turns. "I can say something, and she'll respond. She'll say something, and I'll respond." And smiling—waiting for you to respond—all that is reciprocal. Babies look for that... Have you tried sticking out your tongue?

Karyn: Yes, and he does that.

Janice: That shows how responsive he is to you.

Janice responds to Karyn's question while providing both developmental information and suggestions to foster Greg's optimal development. Janice's statements are simple and clearly stated within the context of a mother's concern. In these answers, Janice has begun to talk about the most important underpinning of communication and language—namely, the significance of spontaneous baby–parent exchanges.

4–10 Months of Age

Between 4 and 6 months, babies connect vowel and consonant sounds together in a string of sounds called babbling.[18] Babies are so delighted with listening to themselves babble that they practice these vocalizations without an audience. On Janice's visit when Greg was 4 months old, Karyn told Janice that now Greg could say *uh, moo, boo*, but mostly *oh*. Within the context of this mother's spontaneous sharing, Janice affirmed Karyn and provided developmental information and suggestions.

Janice: He's now stringing vowels and consonants together. [To Greg] You're used to having someone talk to you. I can tell. [To Karyn] It's good to imitate his sounds. It's interesting about language development. Babies babble in their own language. You can hear the difference between babies in Japan and America: The sounds coming out are the sounds of their own language.

Karyn: Really!

Janice: He's working on the sounds he needs for English. [To Greg] You are a good talker, and that's the best news!

Janice explains to Karyn that babies change their sounds to sound like their parents' language. This pattern illustrates that hearing and discrimination come before making sounds.

During each visit, Janice and Karyn discuss the progress of Greg's language. When Greg was age 5½ months, Karyn told Janice that Greg now said "ma," but she knew it did not mean anything. Janice then explained, "You'll change that for him. As you respond differently to different sounds, he'll learn that some of his sounds do mean something." In the winter, Greg had a series of ear infections. Janice explained to Karyn that it's important to keep close track of Greg's hearing because this will have a major impact on his language. When Greg was age 7 months, Karyn reported to Janice:

Karyn: He doesn't say a lot, primarily "da, da, da."

Janice: That's a change from last time, and he is repeating syllables—that is a big step.

Karyn: Every once in a while he'll say "ba."

Janice: When you think about it, it makes sense, sounds in the front of his mouth: *da, ba, ma*. And now he is getting to the age when it is appropriate to begin saying what he is doing.

When Karyn reports Greg's pattern of making sounds, Janice provides developmental information to help Karyn understand her son's progress. Karyn started the conversation about language. Seeing Karyn's interest, Janice is able to give a simple suggestion that Karyn can begin describing what Greg is doing. When visiting babies and their parents, Janice helps parents to understand how they stimulate their babies' growing skill in language and communication.

Janice's comments to another mother of a 7-month-old illustrate how home visitors can help promote their child's language development.

Jene (age 7 months) begins babbling, and her mother, Natalie, imitates her sounds. Janice comments, "It's important to imitate her sounds like you just did. That is as rewarding to her as it is to you. What fun to get a response, and to feel connectedness."

Janice's comments affirm Natalie's spontaneous approach to her baby; at the same time, Janice provides an interpretation of the developmental importance of her interaction to Jene's babbling. When imitating, parents follow their baby's lead as they match their baby's behavioral style and tempo. This type of engagement is common with the roles of imitation and play in cognitive development. This parental response often encourages the baby to respond and turn-taking sequences begin. Turn-taking promotes the baby's developing communication skills.[19]

Natalie picks up Jene, who smiles at her. Natalie softly chuckles in response. Janice helps Natalie understand how important these brief spontaneous interactions are for the development of babbling. She says, "Mommy laughs right with you. It's important that you laugh with her. `I smile. What is Mommy's reaction? I am hurt. What is mommy's reaction to this?"'

Once again, Janice helps this mother recognize how her responsiveness is developmentally very important to her baby.

During the first year of life, babies make remarkable progress toward understanding the sound structure of the language of their social experience. Studies indicate that babies 6–8 months old can discriminate nonnative words, whereas babies 10–12 months old lack this ability.[20] These results indicate that the listening experience brings about the baby's change in nonnative consonant perception within the first year of life.[21] Phoneme sensitivities existing in the baby will be maintained only if these phonemes are present in the baby's language experience.

At age 6 months, babies have 20/60 vision and may not acquire 20/20 vision until they are 7–9 months old. Most of the babies' visual skills now are nearly equal to those of an adult. By 7 months, babies can retrieve a partially hidden object; by 8 months, they can find and retrieve hidden objects. Eight-month-olds can play Pat-a-cake with assistance; by age 9 months, they can play with no assistance.[22] When home visitors talk to parents about how their baby's vision is developing, they can help parents learn how, when, and what to provide for visual stimulation. They also can talk about signs of possible vision problems so that parents can obtain the earliest possible treatment. Most home visiting programs conduct an annual screening that includes the baby's vision.

A very large change takes place between 6 and 10 months. By 5–6 months, babies can make consonant sounds. Between 6 and 10 months, consonant–vowel sequences produce a kind of syllable, often repeated over and over.[23] This rhythmic babbling often has a sentence-like flow. Now babies often sound like they are making a statement or even asking a question. Studies indicate that by $7\frac{1}{2}$ months, babies can segment words from fluent speech.[24] Babies this age also remember the sound patterns of familiar words.

Between 8 and 10 months, substantive changes occur, which are characterized by speech perception and production, memory and categorization, imitation, joint reference and intentional communication, and word comprehension.[25] At this age, babies can recognize and understand spoken words. Because comprehension precedes the ability to produce words, babies can understand individual words before they can say them. This ability to understand is called *receptive language* and lays the foundation for early speech. Babies can recognize that some of the sounds that they hear are always associated with the same experience, person, or object. They may recognize their names and turn toward the speaker. They can understand and respond to "no" when their parents use it forcefully. They can copy nonspeech sounds such as tongue clicking or lip smacking.

By age 9 months, babies' vocalizations and gestures show that their actions are purposeful. Now the babies' sounds are no longer random; rather, their sounds are those of the baby's specific culture. Using gestures or combinations of gestures and sounds, they begin demanding or asking for things. In addition, babies play gesture games with parents, such as Pat-a-cake, and copycat games in which the baby imitates the parent's motor movement, such as the game So Big. The baby's linguistic creativity arises from the continuous flow of back-and-forth emotional signaling that provides new emotions to stir the next sequence of communication. Coregulated, emotional interactions between significant others and babies are essential for developing language and communication. One of the most important results of babies' development of communication abilities is the effect these abilities have on the emotions that babies can experience and express, as well as the impact this has on their cognitive development.[26]

Home visitors' conversations with parents help them to understand their child's development and their own pivotal role in this development. During the baby's first months, home visitors discuss how different cries signal different kinds of discomfort and how cooing signifies pleasure. Parents are encouraged to play sound and gesture games with their babies, to talk to their babies about the things they and their babies are doing, to read simple stories, and to recite rhymes as they hold their babies close to them. As the infant becomes older, home visitors point out the baby's rising and falling intonation, which is similar to the intonation of sentences and is a sign that babies are paying attention to the speech around them. Home visitors also call attention to the baby's frequent use of pointing to ask for things (e.g., pointing to a desired cookie, pointing to the arm of a doll to show the parent it is broken). When babies are about 10 months old, home visitors make certain that babies can understand simple directions.

Janice's dialogue with Tracy illustrates how home visitors can help parents understand their child's developing language.

Maggie (age 10 months) makes repetitive sounds in a rhythmic manner as she crawls about the room. Janice asks Tracy, "Does she like to repeat sounds like that often?"

Tracy says, "Yes, it's one of her favorite activities."

As she makes rhythmic sounds, Maggie puts her hand to her mouth. Her mother begins singing softly, "One little, two little, three little Indians... ," and Janice sings with her.

Janice comments, "Rhythmic babbling is good for language development, for the muscles in the mouth. The occupational therapist who works with our staff says it's really beneficial to help develop those little muscles they need for talking. Your singing is a wonderful way of encouraging Maggie's exploring with sounds."

In her conversation with Tracy, Janice interprets the significance of Maggie's rhythmic babbling and Tracy's singing and, in so doing, she assists Tracy in understanding her baby's language development.

EMERGENCE OF FIRST
WORDS AND JARGON: 10–15 MONTHS

Around age 10–12 months, babies make giant strides in all developmental realms—movement, cognition, language, and social-emotional development.[27] Now babies can understand many regularly used words, phrases, and simple directions, such as "Get the ball" and "Don't touch." Understanding language becomes an important underpinning for babies' emerging speech. Babies learn to wave bye-bye and can appropriately clap and roll their hands in Pat-a-cake. They can vocalize along with music and acquire exclamatory speech such as "ouch," "pop," and "uh-oh." To resolve uncertainty, when moving toward a new desired goal, babies look back and forth from their desired goals to their parents and, in this way, gain encouragement from their parents. These gestures, called *social referencing,* indicate significant emotional development.[28]

Very young children form categories based on reality well before learning the linguistic signals that correspond to these categories. By age 12 months, infants acquire new skills in the ability to think symbolically, with accompanying gains in communication and language. Toddlers' early words are shaped by their social environments—by the objects and social interactions in their daily activities with important people in their lives.[29] Many first-learned nouns are given broad meanings. For example, the word "dog" is applied to all four-legged animals. Until about age 2, children often are unclear about the differences among animals and plants, such as the difference between a dog and fox. Toddlers differ in the way they develop their first vocabulary. Some toddlers use an expressive style; their early words are linked to social relationships, such as "hi," "want," and "me." Other toddlers use a referential style; their early words refer to objects, such as "keys," "ball," and "Mommy."[30] Once babies reach the first-word milestone, vocabulary growth proceeds slowly. It usually takes 3–4 months for the toddler to add the next 10 words. The baby uses single words for many purposes: labeling people and objects (e.g., "Daddy," "ball"), requesting objects (e.g., "key"), requesting action (e.g., "go"), protesting (e.g., "no"), greetings (e.g., "hi"), and attention seeking (e.g., "see"). Toddlers usually take 5–6 months to have a vocabulary of about 50 words.[31]

Several critical factors exist for a young child's language to emerge from coregulated, affective interactions:

- Motor capacities, including increasingly complex vocalizations, facial expressions, affect intonations, postural changes, and problem-solving actions.

- Increasingly complex social interactions that enable groups to move beyond communicating simply to meet concrete needs, such as food and shelter, and use communication for social goals.

- The use of communication for communication itself rather than only for meeting concrete needs.[32]

Parents delight in sharing with their home visitor their baby's gain in new words.

Karyn: Can you believe that Greg [age 14 months] already can say about 12 words!

Janice: Wonderful!

Karyn: And our favorite word is "trash." We took him to the botanical gardens, and he pointed out each of the trash cans for us. He also loves fans, but the sound he uses for fan isn't an English word, so we don't count that.

Janice: But it is a word if it's spontaneous, consistently used, and you know what it means.

As Karyn shares her son's growth in vocabulary, Janice shares in her delight. Janice also provides developmental information to help Karyn understand her son's developing language.

When beginning to learn words, toddlers continue to use gestures or their body to communicate, especially when they are frustrated. Janice explained this to Karyn.

Karyn says, "Greg does a little head banging. The doctor said to ignore it."

"He wants to communicate," Janice explains, "but he sometimes can't and gets frustrated."

Karyn then describes how, during his bath, Greg became frustrated and began banging his head against the tub. She figured out he wanted to hold the shampoo bottle. Once she gave it to him, he was fine.

Janice says, "Your analysis is right on target. Babies this age are going to use their bodies when they don't have the words. When he learns to use his arms better, then he'll not use his head. It's like the developmental patterns we talked about when he was a very young baby—development progresses top-down and center-out."

Head banging can be very worrisome to new parents. Janice helps Karyn understand why her toddler might bang his head. Her explanation sparks Karyn's sharing of a recent example of Greg's head banging and her response. Janice not only affirms Karyn's response to her baby, but also provides developmental information so that Karyn can better understand Greg's behavior.

Between 13 and 15 months, toddlers frequently string sounds together as if they are carrying on a conversation. Child developmentalists call this *gibberish* or *jargon talk*. Home visitors can encourage parents to take advantage of their child's jargon talk by responding to whatever they think their baby might be saying, for example, "I know you like the way Mommy is washing your back." This turn-taking in pretend conversation helps toddlers learn the basics of conversation. Some children, especially those who begin to talk very early, skip this jargon phase. Others continue using jargon along with real words. Jargon usually disappears by age $2\frac{1}{2}$ years.

Another parenting strategy that home visitors can promote is called *parallel talk*. Parallel talk refers to adults describing what the young child or caregiver is doing as the young child acts, as illustrated by Janice.

Janice places on the rug a cylinder filled with small film canisters. The cylinder's top has a hole in the center. She places film canisters on the rug next to the cylinder. Greg (age 14 months) puts a canister into the hole.

Janice says about the small canisters that Greg is manipulating, "In it goes… turning it around." Greg shakes the cylinder. Janice helps him remove the lid, and he dumps out all of the film canisters. Janice says, "Now it is empty, all gone." She then puts the top on the cylinder, and Greg again begins putting the small film canisters into the hole. Janice remarks, "In it goes. Into the can." As he puts the canisters into the can, Greg looks at his father and babbles, and Janice explains, "Telling Daddy all about it." Greg empties the cylinder once again. Janice repeats, "Now it's empty, all gone."

Janice then begins talking to Greg's mother and father, Karyn and Don. "When Greg is playing, just describe what he is doing. That helps him know you are interested in what he is doing. As you describe for him what he is doing, that is the way he learns words to think. It builds language, connected with experience. Sometimes it might seem kind of boring to you, but developmentally it is very helpful. I also was helping Greg build the concept 'empty' and linking it with 'all gone,' which he knows—building his vocabulary."

Janice is helping Karyn and Don understand that they can foster their child's understanding of language if they describe specifically what Greg is doing as he acts. Janice's comments are made as Greg plays and are stated as both developmental information and suggestion.

WORD COMBINATIONS: 16 MONTHS TO 2 YEARS

For ages 16–24 months, toddlers' understanding of new words and simple directions continues to expand. They rely less on gestures and more on words to understand meaning. The meaning of verbal sounds that toddlers master are grounded in the coregulated emotional interactions that underpin the growth of the baby and toddler's mind. They absorb new meanings as they experience new words in everyday conversational interactions. Now they can understand simple and short sentences. They continue to understand many more words than they can say. By 18 months, they can understand much of what is said to them even though they may only speak a few words. Toddlers now understand and enjoy rhymes and songs. They love picture books, can turn the pages, and begin labeling the pictures. They can recognize and point to several body parts.

Vocabulary growth is sensitive to the interaction of genetic and environmental factors and is predictive of multiple aspects of later development.[33] Children learn new words in many contexts. Sometimes parents read rare words along with the rest of the text in story reading. Sometimes parents introduce new words as they play with their child, identifying toys such as dinosaur names. As the toddler plays, the new word is embedded in the context as part of the ongoing activity. As families engage in mealtime discussion, new words again can be introduced in context.

Studies have indicated a link between a child's temperament and parental behavior, as well as a link between temperament and linguistic and cognitive development. Thus, individual characteristics of a young child that affect parent–child interactions also have important consequences for development.[34]

At around 18 months, there is a rapid increase in vocabulary, which continues through the preschool years. The toddler's and young preschooler's language development follows a predictable sequence. Toddlers combine a word and a gesture, termed a *holophrase*, such as saying "cookie" while grabbing mother's hand. Then, between 18 and 24 months, they begin using two-word sentences to express an idea, called *telegraphic speech*. Toddlers use this telegraphic speech for many purposes: requests (e.g., "stop it"), responses to requests (e.g., "doll mine"), and commenting (e.g., "Daddy hat"). By 24 months, toddlers typically produce 200–500 words.[35]

Interestingly, not only do babies use gestures in their early stages of language development, but toddlers also use gestures with their two-word utterances.[36] Two major categories of gestures are deictic and representational. Deictic gestures include request, show, and point gestures. Representational gestures include both gestures related to actions performed and conventional gestures such as shaking the head for "no."

During this rapid expansion in vocabulary acquisition, toddlers also make substantive gains in their receptive language abilities. A longitudinal study on the receptive language abilities of toddlers (age range from $14\frac{1}{2}$ months to 25 months) found that the children responded spontaneously to a familiar spoken word by rapidly looking at the visual referent that matches the word they hear. Also, 24-month-olds could shift their gaze to the correct picture before the end of the spoken word.[37] Neuropsychological research on babies' responses to spoken words during this period revealed a major shift in cerebral organization that is closely linked to language knowledge.[38]

Parents have innumerable opportunities to reinforce and extend their toddler's telegraphic speech, as illustrated by Erin.

Janice has just arrived at the home of Shelly and her daughter, Erin (age 22 months). Erin says to Shelly, "Daddy, firehouse." Shelly affirms, "Yes, Daddy is working at the firehouse today." As Erin and Shelly complete the puzzle they had been doing before our arrival, Erin tells Janice, "Daddy cut lawn. Erin swing. Mommy push." Shelly says, "Yes, last night Daddy cut the lawn while Mommy pushed you in the swing."

Shelly has learned from Janice that when she extends Erin's speech she is both affirming Erin and promoting her language development. These expansions often remake Erin's sentences with correct grammar. Shelly's response tells Erin she is interested and encourages Erin to continue talking. During this home visit, Shelly describes to Janice a recent errand she and her daughter have taken.

Shelly describes how Erin noticed and named the many items alongside the road as they were driving. She comments, "It's not often that we are in the car that we are not talking. I remember last year, you said how important it is to talk about what we are doing."

Shelly has integrated Janice's information and now uses it in her everyday interactions with Erin.

Initially, young children's first ideas emerge as discrete items of thought without relation between the thoughts. The 2-year-old may say "bottle," "go outdoors," and so forth. Not until the third and fourth year does the child form bridges among his or her ideas and thoughts. Connections between a child's ideas depend on the caregiver's ability to understand and respond to the child's ideas.[39]

The ability to combine words occurs around 20 months. Toddlers recognize grammatical categories and word order early. Children create their own grammatical systems by harnessing an array of domain-general linguistic, communicative, perceptual, and cognitive skills.[40] Toddlers between 19 and 24 months love to label objects and begin to form categories of objects in their mind, such as "truck" for all large vehicles and "dog" for all small four-legged animals. Now, the child can understand simple phrases when visual cues are not present, such as "Let's go get Daddy" or "Let's go in the kitchen to eat lunch." By the age of 24 months, toddlers are beginning to speak in sentences and know the essential elements of grammar before they are taught. When parents read to their child, the child can follow the sequences within simple stories. Home visitors can help parents learn to tell stories with their toddlers. Kaon's help in telling Justin's story is illustrative:

Justin says, "Zoo."
    Kaon responds, "Daddy took you to the zoo yesterday, didn't he?" Justin nods his head. "And what did you and Daddy ride?"
    Justin says, "Train."
    "You and Daddy rode the train," Kaon says. "And did you see the tigers?" Justin nods yes. "And what did the tiger say?" Justin roars and chuckles in delight.

Parents can tell stories about experiences they have had with their toddlers and in this manner promote their toddlers' thinking and language development. Similarly, they can ask questions. Research on conversations between mothers and toddlers indicates that when mothers ask questions and always respond to their children's speech, their children's language development is promoted. When the adult and the child focus on something together, both the adult and child talk more often and engage in longer conversations. Stories are central to the growth of young children's thought processes and language. Given the intertwining of language and cognitive development, storytelling strengthens young children's cognition.[41]

Parents often may not notice their young child's developmental gains in language. As home visitors interact with a child and parent, they have many opportunities to call attention to the child's growth in language and thinking.

When Mia (age 25 months) asks her mother for another drink, Janice comments, "Mia continues to express new concepts, doesn't she, like 'another.'" When, at age 30 months, Erin tells her mother that she can't find a toy, Janice tells Erin's mother, "Using the contraction 'I can't' is complex language use for a 2-year-old." As Erin and Mia talk to themselves as they play, Janice discusses with their mothers that as the children describe to themselves what they are doing or give themselves instructions, they are using their own language to guide their behavior.

Parents' increased understanding of their children's progress inspires their understanding, appreciation, and motivation to stimulate their child's development further.

From the beginning, children's language is meant to communicate. At the same time, young children learn to use language in private monologues to make sense of their everyday world and to help them attend to the task they are performing. In other words, young children's private speech is a tool for guiding and regulating self and problem solving.[42] Research indicates that these monologues are vastly different from dialogues. The book, *Narratives from the Crib*, reported the results of a 2-year study of the monologues of Emily and her dialogues with parents before bed.[43] These monologues and dialogues were recorded for 15 months, between ages 21 and 36 months. Most striking was the contrast between monologue and dialogue speech. Emily's monologues were much richer and more varied than were her dialogues with her parents. In her monologues, Emily told stories of daily events that had happened or that she had been told were going to happen. She also recreated stories and created imaginary happenings. Some of her monologues were problem solving, sorting out her everyday world, or often organized around daily events such as eating, sleeping, and dressing. Emily's monologues primarily served "the evident purpose of representing and sorting out her experience, using language to make sense."[44]

The amount of time mothers and child care providers talk to their young children is strongly related to the children's vocabulary growth.[45] Early differences in vocabulary growth seem to be quite stable to school entry. Most adults speak in simpler sentences and simpler vocabulary to children than they do to other adults. This pattern has been termed *motherese*.[46] Typical characteristics of motherese include short and grammatically simple wording, concrete vocabulary, and repeated phrases. As home visitors observe how parents' child-rearing interactions are promoting their child's language, they help the parents recognize these patterns.

Tracy: Mia [age 23 months] started talking at such an early age.

Janice: So many words and sentences. Tracy, I really believe that one of the reasons her language is so good is that there is a pay off for her. When she asks, you respond. You are the best motivation. That's wonderful.

Mia: [As the adults chat, Mia goes to her mother] Tap, Mom?

Tracy: Hammer.

Mia: Go find it.

Tracy: I don't know where it is.

Janice: That is a perfect example. You don't correct her, but merely say the right word, "hammer."

Tracy: Yeah, she knows it goes tap, tap.

Janice explains that Tracy's comment is dependent on what her child says: "When she asks, you respond. You are the best motivation." Tracy's response stimulates her daughter to talk more. In her interpretation of this mother's actions, Janice helps Tracy understand how important she is in Mia's developing language.

Differences in timing of language development is normal.[47] Young children's speech contains immaturities typical of their age (e.g., errors in pronunciation), which may be worrisome to parents. Parents frequently share these concerns with their home visitors. They may express a concern about what they call stuttering, but this is often normal dysfluency that occurs in almost half of all preschoolers. Home visitors can help parents understand that their young child may sound as if he or she is stuttering because motor skills have not caught up with thinking skills. Parents can give their child time and try to ignore the stuttering until their child outgrows this normal dysfluency. As parents question and express concern about their young child's immature speech, Janice provides information and suggestions.

Shelly: I try to get Erin [age 29 months] to say words the right way. Is that stressful for her?

Janice: Immature articulation is typical of children Erin's age. Let her go. At this age, your goal is communication. If she gets hung up on how words are said, communication won't flow as easily.

Shelly: Rob's [Erin's father's] family goes crazy and are always correcting her.

Janice: If someone is hung up about that, try and get her to say it for Erin without correcting, without making her repeat. You don't want to slow her down.

In these conversations, parents learn what they can expect in typical child development and feel reassured that they are promoting their child's language. Home visitors can help parents pay attention to what their child is saying, not how they are saying it. Children learn to talk naturally, not from instruction.

TELLING STORIES: 2–5 YEARS

As toddlers approach 2 years, their ability to understand speech increases significantly. They can understand 200–300 words, as well as simple directions with prepositions, such as "Put the cookie on the table."[48] Young children can understand and respond to simple questions, such as "Where is your ball?" If they do not want to do something, they refuse by using "no." New words take on meaning only when attached to emotion and intentionality.

The toddler uses several levels of expression:

- Ideas or words and actions are used together. Ideas are acted out, but words are also used to signify the action.
- Action words are used instead of actions, and these action words convey intent (e.g., "Hit you!").
- Feelings are conveyed through words, but are treated as real rather than as signals (e.g., "I'm mad," "I'm hungry," "I need a hug").
- Words are used to convey bodily feeling states ("My muscles are exploding," "My head is aching").

- Words convey feelings, but they are mostly global feeling states ("I feel awful," "I feel okay").
- Words begin to convey more differentiated feelings ("I feel sad" or "I feel angry") and therefore are beginning to more fully represent a specific feeling that is not tied to action.[49]

In the second or third year, the young child can deal not only with behavior but with ideas.

She begins to grasp that one thing can stand for another, that an image of something can represent the thing itself. This realization allows her to create an inner picture of her world. Moreover, these symbols can represent not only for her own intentions, wishes, and feelings but those of other people as well.[50]

Now, the young child has gone from an action mode to the symbolic mode. Children can make this transition because of changes in neurology as well as the richness of their affective experiences in relationships with significant adults. This shift requires a long-term involvement of parents who promote interaction, who join the child in conversation and pretend play, and who give the child sheer pleasure in being acknowledged.[51] Whereas younger babies communicate to get something, children at this age enjoy communication for communication's sake.

Parents can help the young child learn to reflect. If a child says she wants to go out in the rain, the caregiver can ask why and help the child understand what will happen if she goes outdoors in the rain. The ability to make connections among emotions and ideas evolves into the capacity to step back from an experience and reflect on one's own feelings.

Listening is an important skill in language learning. Good listening does not just emerge. As in talking, listening skills are learned gradually through everyday interactions with parents. Home visitors can help parents develop skills so that their energetic 2-year-old maintains attention when listening. Respectful ways for parents to help their child learn to listen include the following:

- Keep your facial expression interesting.
- Vary your voice tone.
- Be sure to have your child's eye contact before speaking.
- Squat down to your child's eye level so your child can easily look at you as you speak.
- When necessary, distract your child to gain attention; for example, suddenly whisper or sing a chant.

The children's neurological development continues toward more and more complexity. The increased complexity allows the young child to mentally recreate complex events observed. The child now has a memory that includes not only patterns of action, but also emotions, intentions, and desires. Children at this age are developing a rich inner life from their experiences of warmth, dependency, exploration, assertiveness, curiosity, love, empathy, anger, and protest.

The young child can organize knowledge of familiar and reliably structured events, such as having meals. Even categories such as mealtimes have two types of hierarchies. First, events are organized hierarchically in that they may contain small event units (e.g., "eating dinner" may include subevents such as preparation, eating, and clearing). Second, two more events can be combined into a general category (e.g., dinner is within the meal category). Although preschoolers construct categories, their hierarchical inclusion structures of categories are not well established until their early school years.[52]

The organization of time varies culturally and linguistically. Time is a central dimension of a child's action, activity, and events. Usually time is described in terms of sequence and duration, both being basic to a child's experience. Events may be sequenced in relation to each other, such as having a nap after lunch, or in terms of duration, such as finishing dinner. Young children learn that there are specific times during the day when certain events take place, such as the regularity of lunch, dinner, and bedtime.

During their third year, children learn to understand most adult sentences. They can recognize and name themselves and other familiar people. They can understand and respond correctly to two related directions given at one time, such as "Pick up your shoes and put them in your room." They can understand descriptive words such as "big," "heavy," and "fast."

At this age, children can engage in extended simple conversations. By the time they are 2½ years old, they talk in three- and four-word sentences. They make simple requests, such as "Open the door." They love singing songs such as "Jingle Bells" or "Happy Birthday." Children now have a speaking vocabulary of 300 or more words. As they explore their everyday world, their developing language supports their thinking about this world. Language not only reflects what the child is thinking, but it also makes thinking possible.

Young children's simple sentences are creative, but these sentences also follow rules. Children begin using plurals, past tenses, and prepositions in a fairly predictable sequence. Similarly, the initial use of questions and negatives follows a predictable progression: using "wh" words at the beginning of the sentence without the auxiliary verb, such as "When mommy come home," and omitting the auxiliary verb with a negative, such as "I no go." In addition, children express different meanings with the same sentence form. The young child may say "Daddy hat" to connote "This is Daddy's hat," which she has picked up off the floor. On another occasion, "Daddy hat" means "Daddy is putting my hat on me." Throughout the preschool years, vocabulary continues to increase and more complex sentence forms are learned.

In conversation, children as young as 2 years change the form of their language according to the person with whom they are talking. A toddler will say

"Gimme" as he grabs another toddler's cookie; to his mother, however, he may say "More juice." Research on children's conversations with younger children demonstrates that 3- to 5-year-olds are quite skilled at using simpler language when talking to younger children.[53] These changes give clear evidence that very young children can adapt to another person's level and recognize that other viewpoints exist.[54]

Once young children begin forming sentences, parents can incorporate spontaneous, incidental conversations into daily routines, such as eating meals together, getting ready for bed, or riding in the car. Mealtime conversation allows young children to learn a lot from listening, watching, and participating in conversations. During mealtimes, young children hear and participate in stories about everyday life. Telling stories during mealtime help young children learn what kind of information goes into making a good story and how to organize a set of events in a specific sequence so that the story is clear. Conversation includes joint attention and joint activity. In conversation, young children learn both speaker and listener roles. Conversation also involves taking turns. Just as babies engage in emotional interactions, young children are involved in emotional gestures, such as tone of voice and facial gestures, as they engage in conversations. Just as in earlier emotional interactions, emotional signaling, timing, and rhythmicity are central components to young children's conversation.

Home visitors can assist parents in understanding the value of conversation for promoting language, thinking, communication, and emerging literacy. They can help parents understand that because conversation symbolizes ideas, thoughts, and feelings—which in turn are grounded in experience—conversation promotes young children's thinking and reading readiness. Furthermore, as young children engage in conversation, they experience feelings of connectedness and shared enjoyment with their parents.

Between 2 and 3 years of age, children have the underlying cognitive ability to order events and tell stories. They tell stories that are based on their creative play. For example, they may make up a story about a building that they constructed with blocks. Stories also often are about the children's everyday experience. Home visitors can encourage parents to tell stories with their children about shared experiences. Narratives of a 3-year-old reflect one very basic characteristic: the sequencing of events through time. Temporal organization is basic to narrative. Very young children are extremely accurate in remembering temporal sequence, especially sequences with causal components. Narratives are important in cognitive organization, for understanding the actions and intentionality of other people, and for reflections on the self. Much of a young child's psychological development during these early years occurs as children tell, retell, transform, and reconstruct their stories for themselves and for others.[55]

Interestingly, the language young children use in stories often is more complex and more advanced than language used in other settings. For example, they show an understanding of hypothetical relationships such as "if, then" or "when x, then y." Bruner states that through stories we create and re-create self-hood. He argues that self-making is a product of self-telling.[56] As young children tell stories about past experiences, they begin to understand the continuity of past and present time. Their ability to view interpersonal situations from multiple perspectives increases, including those of their potential selves and of others. When young children hear and share stories, they learn important characteristics of language, such as rhythm, sounds, sequencing, and vocabulary. Children not only hear stories read from books, but also watch narrations on television and construct narratives in dramatic play.

Even young toddlers narrate particularly striking, surprising, or perplexing events. This narration of unexpected events lets us know that toddlers have some degree of awareness of what is normative and expected in their everyday life. As young children narrate their personal experience, they can voice and reflect upon the temporal and causal ordering of everyday events in their lives. These narratives clarify basic routines that are important to the young child. Over time, children initiate personal narratives more often. Toddlers demonstrate precocity in narrative sequencing (e.g., after my nap, when daddy comes home).[57] However, young children often have difficulty creating coherent narratives. Sometimes a series of actions are temporally disconnected. Beginning a story and getting another's attention may be particularly challenging for a young child. Some children have learned to use prefaces such as "You know what?" or "Guess what?"

Three levels of preschooler's narratives have been identified:

- Narratives that communicate mental representations of experience, as well as the role of self and others in that experience

- Narratives that have organized plots or points; typically a plot involves a problem or tension followed by some kind of resolution

- Narratives that are spoken discourse, located in a specific conversation with another person[58]

Not all parents know how to have conversations with very young children. Home visitors have many opportunities to model and discuss how to have extended conversations. On Janice's first home visit after Christmas, Erin's (age 33 months) new kitchen set was in the living room.

Janice says to Erin, "This must be your most special Christmas present."
Erin affirms, "Yes." She then picks up a frying pan and brings it to Janice. "A pan."
Janice repeats, "A frying pan."
"And I have toy pots," Erin adds.
Janice asks, "You have new toy pots?" Erin nods yes and then goes to Janice with her toy potholder glove on her hand. "Does that protect your hand?"
Erin says, "No, it keeps my hand from getting hurt."
Janice replies, "That's what we mean when we say `protect.'"

As Erin speaks, Janice carefully listens. She asks Erin questions to encourage her to think and continue talking. Janice has visited Erin and her parents since Erin's birth. Erin looks forward to Janice's visit; usually upon Janice's arrival, she is eager to tell Janice stories. In turn, Janice replies in a manner to extend Erin's comments. Over the months and years, Janice has had many opportunities to share with Shelly the value of talking with her child. In turn, Shelly often shares with Janice her conversations with Erin and her delight in Erin's creative verbal constructions.

When parents engage in pretend play with their young children, it provides wonderful opportunities for promoting young children's language, as Cynthia demonstrates.

Cynthia puts toy pots and pans, dishes, and plastic food on the rug as she asks Willy's (age 21 months) mother, Sally, and grandmother, Donna, "Have you seen any pretend play?"

Sally responds, "Not really."

Donna clarifies, "He pretends to read and to talk on the phone."

Cynthia says, "Both are part of the beginning of pretend play. Pretend play would be a wonderful activity for you to do with Willy. Let's do a little today."

As Cynthia gives herself and Sally a cup, she hands Willy a pitcher as she says to him, "Please pour some coffee for Mom and me." As Willy pretends to pour, Cynthia says to Sally, "See, he is pretending. You will see that he imitates what you are doing." Cynthia and Willy pretend to cook eggs for breakfast. She asks him for some juice and holds out her plastic glass, which Willy pretends to fill. She asks him, "Would you like some juice?"

Willy replies, "Like juice." Cynthia pretends to pour juice for Willy.

Donna adds, "We used to think pretend play was harmful to children."

Cynthia responds, "It is important to use imagination. Pretending helps with Willy's language development. Pretend play also helps with Willy's thinking and planning. He'll begin to pretend experiences from his everyday life."

In this home visit, Cynthia uses a pretend-play activity to show Willy's mother and grandmother how they can promote his language through playing with him. Sally thinks very concretely, so Cynthia provides developmental information directly related to the experiences that Sally is observing. On a subsequent visit, Sally described how she and Willy have enjoyed pretending to go to the grocery store and cook together.

Preschool children are also active questioners. Questioning is an important way for young children to explore the world. When children ask questions based on what they see and wonder about, they have some control over their learning. They actively search for what they want to know. As they ask questions, they are creating connections among different parts of the symbolic self that has emerged. Through children's questions, adults can capture the inventiveness of children's thinking and explorations (e.g., "Why do clouds move?" and "Why do churches have steeples?"). Home visitors can encourage parents to be active listeners and respectful responders to their child's questions. Home visitors can model this active listening and can use a young child's question as an opportunity to extend their thinking, such as "Why do *you* think the clouds move?"

Research from the Home-School Study of Language and Literacy Development indicated that the ways mothers talked to children, the level of vocabulary that mothers used with their children, and the types of activities in which mothers and other family members participated were related to how children did on kindergarten tests. Preschool children who demonstrated higher-levels skills had experienced interesting talk with their family members, with lots of new words and literacy activities such as frequent book reading with different family members.[59]

EMERGING LITERACY

Just as communication and language learning is a social activity, emerging literacy occurs within a social context—the everyday activities and interactions of parents and their babies and young children. This section uses the term *emerging literacy* to refer to the young child's awareness of print and its functions.

Writing is used to express meaning and the function of reading is to understand meaning. Studies indicate that reading is a process in which the reader draws on previously acquired learning to gain meaning from print.[60] Young children become ready for reading by experiencing print in books and on signs and by writing and drawing. Through these processes, they learn that written marks have meaning. Literacy development is gradual and is a part of the total communication process that includes listening, speaking, reading, and writing.[61]

The emotionally satisfying process of reading or reciting rhymes to babies while holding them close is the beginning of their emerging literacy. As babies develop, storybook reading remains a powerful influence on the language development of young children. In addition, the very young child can learn that books are a source of enjoyment.

Young children have an easier time learning to read and write when they have experienced meaningful use of written language in their everyday lives. Early and frequent reading to young children can be one of the most important foundations in the growth of reading readiness. Emerging literacy includes listening to stories, reciting stories by memory, asking and answering questions about stories, scribbling, and using other forms of drawing and writing.

When a story is read, children learn the following:

- There is a sequence and a cycle to every story.
- Symbols and words put together convey meaning.
- Stories follow a predictable sequencing of events.
- Everything has a name (a word); different words mean different things; and sometimes, words have different meanings in how they are linked.[62]

Recent research shows the importance of parent–child interactions on literacy. Children with greater home support for literacy demonstrated higher scores on early literacy measures.[63] Also, young children who have extended discourse in pretend talk during the preschool years had better language and literacy skills in kindergarten.[64] Parent–child book reading was associated with children's language comprehension skills in another study, but only among parents whose discipline had relatively high levels of nondirective reasoning. A negative association between physical punishment and children's language comprehensions skills was found.[65] In addition, a very strong positive relationship between mealtime narrative and explanatory talk during the preschool years and higher scores on vocabulary, definitions, and listening comprehension measures in kindergarten has been demonstrated.[66]

When babies are a few months old, home visitors can integrate story reading with picture books into each visit. With parents who have low literacy, Cynthia's home visits have a central focus on story reading.

Cynthia gives Willy (age 22 months) a picture book of farm animals as she says to him, "Willy, I have a really neat book here." Willy immediately takes the book and sits next to Cynthia, with the book open between his legs. Cynthia shows Willy how their fingers fit through the holes in each picture in the book.

Willy's grandmother, Donna asks him, "How does the cow go?"

He replies, "Moo."

Willy then goes to Cynthia's bag as Cynthia asks him, "Do you think I have more books in here?"

Willy affirmatively replies, "Uh-huh." Cynthia gives him a second book, and he sits down and turns the pages to look at the pictures.

Cynthia says to Sally, "He's changed his approach. Remember how he used to take the book and back into your lap? Now he turns the pages alone. See what he has learned about books?"

Willy says, "Orange."

Cynthia remarks, "Did he say `orange'?"

Sally explains, "He knows the color orange. He'll sit over there for the longest time." Sally points to the shelf filled with picture books in the next room. As the adults chat, Willy continues to look at his book. As he turns a page, Sally says, "Pumpkin," which he repeats.

Cynthia says, "When you say it, he repeats it back."

Willy says to Cynthia, "More."

Cynthia responds, "You give me your book, and I'll give you another." Willy gives Cynthia his book, and she gives him one that has pictures of trains. "See how he listens," Cynthia says to Sally. "I tell him to bring me a book, and he brings it to me. He understands."

Donna then tells Cynthia that the local store had a sale of children's books, and she bought six for Willy and three for his best friend. Cynthia responds, "You bought a good variety, with good concepts to work on. Willy is using his language a lot more. And he's trying to respond to all my questions. It's good to ask him questions and then wait for his response. I can tell you both talk to him and read to him a lot."

Given Cynthia's consistent pattern of modeling and encouraging conversation and story reading, early literacy is a central part of Willy's everyday life. Babies and young children love daily story-reading rituals. Young toddlers like Willy often enjoy looking at books themselves and love hearing the same story over and over. Soon, they can repeat it themselves. Parents often express surprise at how quickly their toddlers learn the stories and enjoy pretending to read as they tell the stories to themselves while looking at a book. These activities help the children learn the importance of written symbols. One of the parents with whom Janice works described this process.

Evan loves the book you gave him. I read it over and over to him. His daddy reads it to him, and when nobody will read it to him, he just reads it himself—oh just the pictures, but he knows every animal!

Many preschoolers spontaneously learn to read environmental print, such as advertisement logos, cereal boxes, and tee shirts. When writing and drawing, young children experiment and developmentally proceed through exploratory motorial scribbling, which is purposeful scribbling that follows conventional writing patterns, mock writing, representational letters, inventive spelling, and finally, conventional spelling and writing forms. The process of learning to write is an early phase in learning to read.

Home visitors assist parents in understanding that their young child also needs numerous opportunities and time to draw and write, as well as a caring adult with whom to talk about these written expressions. Parents learn that having a variety of printed materials available, along with a variety of paper and drawing and writing tools, stimulates their young child's interest in reading and writing. Similarly, their child's understanding of the meaning of writing is enhanced if the everyday environment contains a great deal of written language, such as notes, recipes, grocery lists, newspapers, magazines, books, and so forth, as well as if the child sees his or her parents frequently reading and writing. Keep in mind that community libraries usually have a wide variety of high-quality children's books. These libraries can be a great resource for parents who have low incomes.

Often, parents of preschoolers ask home visitors questions about stimulating their child's skill with the alphabet.

Shelly: I have another question about reciting the ABCs. Is Erin [age 34 months] too young to get her to write them? She already knows how to write her name.

Janice: Follow her lead on that. Don't push hard. She's now doing wonderful pictures. Creativity has to be expressed. When you tell her how to make letters, you are telling her how to do things correctly....Let her write her scribbles, and then you can ask her what it says and write down what she tells you. If she is strictly confined to making letters, it doesn't give her the chance to write on her own and then say what it says, which is a significant step in her learning about the meaning of words. That is valuable creativity. She will do much more of it and is still getting her fine motor control.

As Janice works with Shelly, she helps Shelly understand developmentally appropriate writing and drawing activities and the importance of writing down what Erin says about her drawings.

Home visitors can help parents understand how they can promote emerging literacy throughout each day. Beyond reading stories to young children, families' everyday activities also can provide young children with meaningful experiences with written language. Young children see their parents write grocery lists and can suggest items to be included. As children make pictures and tell their parents about them, parents can write these dictations on their children's drawings. When another adult or older sibling reads these dictations on a child's drawings, the child experiences a powerful example of how meaningful letters are.

Home visitors can explain to parents that when they provide play experiences for their children, this play often fosters language, communication, and emerging literacy. For example, as children use words to substitute for objects, talk about what they are doing, and decide what roles they will play, this fosters their language development. As the 3-year-old uses a long scarf tied around her waist to represent a skirt or uses a block for a telephone, she is using symbols—one thing is representing another. These early symbolic experiences help young children understand the symbolic nature of writing. Visitors also can encourage parents to provide toys that can refine children's small muscle and eye–hand coordination, such as puzzles, snap-together toys, crayons, and pencils. Developing this coordination assists the child's later ability to discriminate letters and words.

DIFFICULTIES AND DILEMMAS

Young children are at risk for communication and language difficulties because of biological conditions such as Down syndrome, low birth weight, anoxia, or otitis media, as well as environmental conditions such as poverty, caregiver–child interaction disturbances, or child maltreatment.[67] Prelinguistic communication often can indicate strengths and problems in later language acquisition. Intervention before age 3 years can prevent later problems. There is a significant relationship between preschool communication and language disorders and later learning difficulties.[68]

Research indicates strong relationships between communication and emotional and behavioral disorders. One study compared a group of children with expressive language delays to typically developing children of the same age on measures of development and behavioral difficulties.[69] Scores on social and cognitive development measures for children with language delays were significantly lower than scores for typically developing children. Children with language delays exhibited more symptoms of anxiety and depression, withdrawal, sleep problems, and other behavior disturbances.

The United States is a multicultural society. Therefore, home visitors work with a wide variety of families with different ethnicities, family interaction patterns, and accompanying language usage. In their work with families, home visitors often need to adapt their process to address unique family patterns. For example, home visitors working in Hispanic cultures must be skilled in communicating in Spanish.

Another dilemma for home visitors can be working in homes in which parents do not spontaneously speak with their babies and young children and who themselves have minimal literacy. Home visitors can learn to adapt their approach to address these patterns. Incorporating high-interest story reading into each visit provides parents with opportunities to see their young child's delight in this activity.

During the visit, home visitors can encourage parents to use picture books with their child and can leave several high-interest books for the parents to use between visits. Cynthia often uses books in home visits. Marquisha, one of the mothers Cynthia visits, has six children between ages 3 and 21 years. Marquisha described how her work with Cynthia has changed her parenting.

I think working with Cynthia has made a lot of difference in the way I'm parenting my kids. Now I read to them. I used to read to them just every now and then. If they didn't seem interested, I would just go ahead and put the book down. Working with Cynthia, she helped me to get them interested, to wanting to sit them on my lap and do it the fun way. I'll stop and let them try to read, you know, because they be wanting to read, too. So I stop and let them read a little. They don't know what they be reading, but they know the pictures real good. They learn the pictures, and it helps them learn the story.

Now I read to them at least once a week. Before, I read to them probably once a year.

Marquisha's oldest three children are between 18 and 21 years old. She described how her work with Cynthia has helped her relationship with her older children.

I can deal with my two older sons better now than what I could. I used to tell Cynthia all the time, "I cannot deal with my sons the way I can with my older daughter because she listens to me more." I just couldn't deal with my boys the way I wanted to.

Talking made the difference in helping me relate to the boys over the last 4 years. I used to talk to them, but mostly discipline talk, and listening to Cynthia talk to my oldest ones helped me understand what I was doing wrong. Now I just sit down and talk to them, or joke with them, something like that. I was doing that with my daughter, but I didn't realize that they needed it, too.

Marquisha was the fourth of nine children growing up in a single-parent family with a low income. Previously, she had three brief experiences in general equivalency diploma (GED) programs. Her oldest brother is her only sibling with a high school diploma, which he received when in the military service. She is very proud that her two oldest children have their GED certificates and the third is working on it.

Table 6.1.   Developmental progression of language, communication and emerging literacy and accompanying parenting practices to promote this developmental progression

Developmental patterns	Parenting practices
Birth–3 months	
Watches parents' facial expressions change	Changes facial expressions and voice during interactions with infant
Hears differences in sound and speech	Imitates infant's facial gestures and sounds
Has several different cries	
Makes eye contact with parent when parent is talking	Begins and responds to give-and-take vocal play with infant
Shows pleasure by smiling and cooing	Sings and talks softly during routine activities
4–10 months	
Uses vowels and consonants to babble	Repeats infant's sounds
Laughs and smiles in response to familiar persons	Describes what infant and self are doing during routine caregiving
Babbles rhythmically with sentence-like flow	Plays simple gesture games with infant (e.g., hide and seek with towel)
Playfully imitates nonspeech sounds (e.g., lip smacking, tongue licking)	Reads simple picture books to infant
Understands regularly used individual words	Sings simple rhymes and songs to infant
Recognizes name and turns toward speaker	Encourages infant to respond to his or her name
Plays gesture games such as Pat-a-cake	
Uses gesturing to ask for things	
Understands and responds to "no"	
Enjoys simple picture books	
11–15 months	
Understands simple and short sentences	Continues give-and-take vocal play with infant
Understands simple directions	
Enjoys picture books and simple story books	Identifies infant's body parts, and encourages infant to point to them
Imitates gestures like Peekaboo	Sings simple rhymes, fingerplays, and stories
Waves bye-bye	
Says first words	Reads simple storybooks
Checks to see if parent is looking before exploring on own	Talks about what infant and self are doing
Strings sounds together in gibberish (jargon talk)	Responds to infant's jargon talk as if infant is speaking words
16–24 months	
Has increased understanding of words, simple sentences, and simple directions	Plays simple interactive games like "chase me" and telephone talk
Follows simple directions	Has simple give-and-take conversations with toddler during routine care
Enjoys and understands simple songs, rhymes, and fingerplays	Extends toddler's speech
Uses "no" to protest	Sings simple rhymes, fingerplays, and songs
Uses "hi" and "bye" greetings	Reads familiar storybooks

Developmental patterns	Parenting practices
16–24 months	
Uses jargon speech with state, command, and questioning inflections	Has toddler's eye contact before speaking
Refers to self by name	Actively listens and responds to toddler's talk
Names pictures, objects, body parts	Encourages and participates in pretend-play with toddler
Says two-word sentences	
Makes simple verbal request (e.g., "More milk")	
2–5 years	
Understands and responds to questions	Has extended daily conversations with child
Asks questions, especially about what child sees and experiences	Actively listens and responds to child's talk
Has large increase in vocabulary	Responds to child's questions and invites child to continue talking
Speaks in full sentences	Asks child open-ended questions
Tells simple stories of immediate experiences	Encourages and participates in pretend-play with child
Enjoys songs, fingerplays, and storybooks	Sings songs and fingerplays with child
Enjoys using language in pretend-play alone and with others	Reads storybooks with child
Has extended give-and-take conversation	Provides a variety of writing implementations and paper for the child to use for drawing and writing
Enjoys drawing and writing	
Recognizes frequently seen words such as fast-food advertising	

My dream for Tarina [my 3-year-old daughter] is to see her walk across the stage, which I have never gotten a chance to see. I want to see Tarina walk across the stage, do the things my oldest daughter or I didn't do. But most of all I would like to see her be able to make up her mind to want to do the… educational, everything… on her own. You know, because in case if I'm not here, I would like to know that my daughter, that I left enough in her mind to motivate her to want to do everything that she want to do, you know, to succeed in life.

CONCLUSION

In their work together, parents and home visitors can interweave communication and language development into their discussions and activities. Parents enjoy sharing their young child's gains in language and appreciate having a friend with whom to share concerns. As home visitors observe and interact with child and parent, they can listen, affirm, support, and reassure parents. They can provide suggestions, information, and interpretations within the context of their observations, their activities, or parent concerns. As parents become more aware of what to expect from their children, they also become more observant of their children's emerging communication and language. With knowledge and understanding, they can promote their young child's communication and language through their child rearing and provision of developmentally appropriate activities and experiences. Table 6.1 summarizes the developmental progression of language, communication, and emerging literacy and accompanying parenting strategies that can promote this developmental progression.

Play, Learning, and Development

Child, how happy you are sitting in the dust, playing with a broken twig all the morning!

I smile at your play with that little bit of a broken twig.

I am busy with my accounts, adding up figures by the hour.

Perhaps you glance at me and think, "What a stupid game to spoil your morning with!"

Child, I have forgotten the art of being absorbed in sticks and mud-pies.

I seek out costly playthings, and gather lumps of gold and silver.

With whatever you find you create your glad games. I spend both my time and my strength over things I can never obtain.

In my frail canoe I struggle to cross the sea of desire, and forget that I too am playing a game.

Rabindranath Tagore (1958, p. 48)

PLAY IS A CHILD'S PRIMARY TASK and the main way children learn and develop. Babies and young children love to play because play is intrinsically motivating; that is, children play for the enjoyment and satisfaction of the activity itself. Through play, babies and young children understand and gain mastery of their bodies and their experiences in the everyday world. Unlike adults, who leave their everyday work so they can play for relaxation, young children's primary way of learning is through play; play is children's work.[1]

Babies and young children are curious by nature. In their play, they explore spontaneously. First, they explore their own bodies and then the surrounding world, people, and things. As they play, children create and make something entirely new. After she described the many steps a young child needs to understand how the telephone works, Margaret Mead observed, "This is the creative moment. The child, like Alexander Graham Bell, has just created the telephone—suddenly, from all the little bits and pieces of slowly understood meanings, the idea of telephone has come up."[2] To explore, to understand, to master, to create—these are some of the central meanings and purposes of play. Young children gain knowledge and understanding through their actions.[3]

Play has had a venerable history throughout historic and modern thought. The ancient Greeks, such as Plato, Socrates, and Aristotle, explored the meaning of play as they sought to understand human thought. Theorists during the Enlightenment and the Romantic Period also expressed thoughts on play. Locke noted that children are players by nature, pursuing their imagination for sheer pleasure. Kant thought that imagination is the context in which adult knowledge and reason operate. Froebel thought that by means of play, children encounter forms of nature, knowledge, and beauty. In Froebel's kindergarten, objects (termed *gifts*) and experiences (termed *occupations*) nourished the young child's development. At the turn of the 20th century, Dewey spoke of how play helps the young child to make ideas and experiences his or her own.[4] Today's children are being taught to play differently than in the past.[5] Toys are now available in a wide variety of places, including fast-food restaurants and physician's offices. In addition, television and video can diminish the quality of play when young children imitate characters rather than use their imaginations.

There are four types of play:

1. Solitary play: The child plays alone (e.g., watching the mobile over the crib or zooming miniature trucks along the floor).

2. Parallel play: Two children play side-by-side, occasionally glancing at each other.

3. Associative play: Children play side by side but imitate each other and incorporate components of their counterpart's play.

4. Cooperative play: Children join together to create a happening or produce a product.[6]

This chapter discusses the role of the parent, additional meanings and purposes of play, the developmental progression of play, and the home visitor's role in promoting optimal child and parent development. In addition, the essential features of play, including exploration, imitation, repetition, and sensory experiences with a variety of materials and experiences, are discussed and illustrated with vignettes.

BIRTH TO 12 MONTHS

From birth, babies use their senses to engage in play. As their parents playfully interact with them, babies experience approval, connectedness, and shared delight. These interactions often are very brief; for example, a mother moves her eyes and mouth when her baby smiles or responds with sounds when her baby coos.[7] These exchanges are the beginning of everyday patterns of playful parent–baby exchanges. Even when they do not interact directly with their baby, parents are a stabilizing presence, giving their baby a sense of security. As babies develop, effective parents need to continue being active play partners who are tuned into their child's interests, ideas, and feelings. Communication is often achieved through gestures, such as when a parent quickly lifts the baby's arms up to indicate surprise.

Social Interaction

Babies are born with biological readiness for social interaction. From birth, babies are able to begin and end social interactions with others. Affect—the term for feeling and emotion in developmental literature—is central to the babies' experiences of relating to others. From their earliest moments, babies' experiences are governed by what is pleasurable and not pleasurable. Newborns can begin and end interactions with others; for example, a newborn can focus on mother's face as she speaks or turn away from mother.

Between 1 and 4 months of age, babies' play involves watching and practicing body movements.[8] Young infants playfully explore their bodies, beginning with their mouth and hand, and their parents' bodies. During tasks such as dressing, bathing, feeding, and diapering, skilled parents take time to talk, smile, and cuddle with their baby. As they care for their baby, they can play with him or her by touching, holding, imitating, and playing simple Peekaboo games.[9] A variety of parental behavior seems to be instinctive.[10] For example, parents in virtually all cultures give exaggerated hellos and imitate their baby's facial and vocal expressions.

Newborns prefer to look at people's faces. By age 8 weeks, they smile, give more direct eye contact, vocalize socially, are more responsive, and experience longer periods of wakefulness.[11] Active interest in toys and people increases with accompanying learning and development. For example, when a father approaches his 3-month-old daughter lying in her crib, she smiles, kicks her legs, and moves her arms excitedly. Mutual involvement and attention between baby and parent are essential for the baby's healthy development. These shared interactions provide shared pleasure and a sense of connectedness. Parents and babies communicate by facial and vocal expressions, as well as the quality of movement, such as how the parent picks up, cuddles, or soothes the baby. Parents and their babies develop patterns of interaction that become highly ritualized; that is, parents approach their baby, respond to their baby's awakening, and smile and coo in a similar manner each day.[12]

These playful routines are the same for every parent and baby, yet the particular interactions are unique. In time, parents learn how much activity and which forms of sensation and communication their baby enjoys most, whether sound, touch, sight, or movement.

Exploratory Play

During the first year, babies' play is primarily exploratory as they investigate their bodies, objects in their everyday environment, and other people. Babies first learn to bring objects to their mouth and explore them with their lips and tongue; shortly after that, they bring objects before their eyes to examine. With increased motor coordination, they turn small objects around, bang them, and continue to put them into their mouth. Moving, touching, and making sounds are basic components of these play activities. Parents' responses are crucial to the development of these exploratory actions. Parents have the opportunity to encourage babies' play through positive responses; for example, parents can imitate their baby's facial expression or body movements.

Not all new parents understand that beginning at birth, their baby is capable of actively relating to them and that their interactions with their baby are essential for the baby's optimal development. It therefore helps when home visitors share this developmental information and make certain that parents understand the developmental significance of their active involvement with their baby. Home visitors can model, praise, and encourage these daily patterns of interaction, as Janice did.

Karyn holds her son, Greg (age 4 months), as Janice softly speaks to him. "You're looking right at me. You have very good eye contact." Greg begins cooing and Janice repeats the same sounds. Janice continues, "You're used to having someone talk to you. I can tell. You are a good talker, and that's the best news! I'd never get any work done if I were your mommy."

This is Janice's second home visit since Greg's birth, and she can observe that this mother and baby interact frequently. As she relates to Greg, Janice both models imitation of Greg's vocalizations and affirms Karyn's talking with her son. Karyn asks Janice what would be good toys to buy for Greg.

Janice replies, "Small things that he can get a hold of—the kinds of things I see you have. Bright things, things he can get a grasp of, things that make different kinds of sounds—a variety of different kinds of stimulation to explore. Small kitchen items such as measuring spoons are as good as toys." Janice then moves the ring rattle out of Greg's view, but Greg does not follow it. She says, "Notice how out-of-sight still is out-of-mind." She then puts a rattle in Greg's hand and he puts it in his mouth. Janice tells Karyn, "That's babies' primary way of exploring. It makes sense, for feeding is so important, and the mouth is the first body part that really works for them."

Janice stresses that exploration is the primary way young babies play. Within the context of Karyn's questions and Greg's actions, Janice gives developmental information.

Karyn tells Janice that each night Greg's daddy has extended play with him for a few hours; much of this play involves moving him about and pretend wrestling.

Janice says, "For Greg, that's real learning, playing together with Dad, and it's great that dads have different play patterns than moms have."

Janice returns to Karyn's home when Greg is 5, 7, and 9 months old. Each time, she brings a tub of small assorted kitchen items and toys. As the months progress, Greg continues to make developmental strides. As she and Karyn observe Greg's play, Janice identifies new areas of learning and development. Within the context of Greg's play, she chats with Karyn and gives her developmental information, suggestions, and interpretations of the meaning of Greg's actions.

Greg (age $5\frac{1}{2}$ months) is seated on the rug while supported by his mother. Janice puts a tub of baby toys next to Greg, who looks into the tub.

Janice: It's important for you to watch to see how he reacts to containers. As he gets older and has eye–hand coordination, he'll immediately dump [the tub].

Karyn: He used just to look at his toys; now he grabs.

Janice: Isn't that neat! It's hard for him to reach in [the tub]. I'm allowing a little bit of frustration, for frustration now helps him deal with frustration later. [Janice gives Greg a rattle, and he puts it in his mouth.] Straight to my mouth. Greg, that's what we want to see. It doesn't mean he's hungry, but exploring.

Karyn: His favorite toys are the small ones.

Janice: Developmentally, it's very predictable what kinds of toys a baby likes. He likes small things because he can hold them and can get them to his mouth.

Janice spontaneously expresses delight in Greg's actions and helps Karyn see meaning in her son's play. Janice explains that Greg's eye–hand coordination will soon allow him to dump things. As she and Karyn watch Greg's approach to the tub of toys, Janice helps Karyn anticipate steps in her son's development and understand the important role of motor development in her son's play. As she observed when Greg was 4 months, Janice again calls attention to how Greg is learning by exploring objects with his mouth. After she leaves Karyn and Greg, Janice writes down what Greg did with these toys so that she can identify changes during the next visit.

Six weeks later, Janice returns to visit Karyn and Greg. She helps Karyn recognize and understand her son's new gains in motor development and she affirms Karyn's keen observation of her son.

Janice gives Greg (age 7 months) a tub of toys, and he reaches in the tub and pulls out a toy. She says, "Last time, he didn't get anything from the tub; now he's getting his hand right in there. That's really good." Greg tips the tub and all of the small baby toys fall out. Janice says, "He's much more secure in the sitting position."

Karyn affirms, "The last week or so."

"Your mommy watches close and knows when you've changed," Janice tells Greg. "He handles that toy very well," she tells Karyn. "Notice he takes it in both hands and has lots more freedom with his fingers. He turns it over and turns it back." Greg drops a toy, which rolls to his side, and he turns to find it. Janice says, "You lost it! And he remembered where it was. That's very significant. He dropped and looked for it. This is something to watch for." Greg rolls over on his stomach and reaches for a toy. "You can see how motor development and curiosity are hooked together."

As Greg explores the small objects in the tub, Janice helps his mother see how his actions point to gains in his fine motor skill. Janice links curiosity with motor development to help Karyn understand the manner in which her baby learns through play.

Janice returns when Greg is 9 months old and once again gives him a tub of toys. As Greg plays with the toys, Janice again comments on Greg's actions and how these actions point to Greg's developmental progress.

Karyn: [Greg's] Dad has asked me to ask you what can he do with Greg besides playing and reading books.

Janice: That is really the way a baby learns, in all areas of development. For Greg, that's real learning-playing together. Suggest [to Greg's dad] that he mimic what Greg is doing. Mimicking extends his attention span, affirms his play, and invites him to continue [the play].

Karyn: He plays with Greg about 3 hours each night.

Janice's first home visit with Karyn and her husband, Joe, was during Karyn's third trimester of pregnancy. Joe clearly is very immersed in parenting. Joe also wants to use this home visit program to assist in his parenting. In turn, Janice acknowledges that Joe is a central player in his son's development and gives a helpful suggestion.

In play, babies actively explore the effect they have on objects in their environment. Around 5 months, the baby bangs, drops, and throws objects; this cause-and-effect play makes and organizes the many connections between neurons in the baby's brain. Repetition helps babies learn in an organized way because the same connected nerve pathways in the brain are used over and over.[13] The baby's repeated actions become permanent brain cell connections in the baby's brain and always are available for use.[14]

Beginning at around age 6 months, parents and their babies enjoy playing motion sequence games, such as Pat-a-cake and Peekaboo. Parents often invent new games as their baby gets older. For example, when a baby hits two blocks together, the parent makes a popping sound as she claps and the sequence is repeated. Beyond the shared enjoyment and connectedness the baby feels in these experiences, these patterned games anticipate the young child's learning to take turns.

Babies usually begin to creep and crawl around 8–10 months of age. Movement offers new ways to explore and suddenly the baby is cruising or crawling in every possible direction. Travel offers babies new perspectives and new discoveries within their everyday world. They can explore all sides of the living room couch and, with practice, can learn to pull themselves to an upright position. This is the time for home visitors to remind parents that they need to make certain they have childproofed their home (e.g., put gates on open stairways, put safety latches on low kitchen cupboards that contain cleaning supplies, put plugs on electrical outlets).

12–30 MONTHS

The most striking characteristics of toddlers are their interest in movement, their curiosity, and their strong attempts to be independent. At first, simply walking and climbing are totally absorbing. With movement, toddlers realize they can be independent of their parents. Yet, toddlers have strong security needs of attachment and accompanying feelings of dependence. As they explore their newly found skills in movement and their newly found upright world, toddlers struggle with the ambivalent feelings of independence and dependence. Much of toddlers' play centers around this ambivalence because it is at the core of striving to form their own identity. When toddlers begin games of give-and-take with their parents, it is as if toddlers are exploring what is "yours" and what is "mine." As they become more surefooted and begin to run, toddlers explore whether the parent knows where they are in hide-and-seek games.

Nancy (age 24 months) and Ricky (age 22 months) have been playing in the sandbox and Ricky's mother, Jean, is seated with them. The children leave the sandbox and run into the garage to hide from Jean. Jean goes to a large tree near the sandbox and calls out, "Where are you? Nancy and Ricky, where are you?" The children laugh gleefully and look out at Jean.

Jean tells the children, "You can't find me?" Jean then walks behind the tree, and the children run toward her. As the children come to the tree, Jean walks around the tree so they can't catch her, as she says playfully, "Where's Nancy and Ricky? Where are you?" The children giggle as they run around the tree with Jean. When they catch her, they race to the garage as they say, "We hide!"

In their spirited hide-and-seek play with Jean, these toddlers are experimenting with their strong feelings of separation and independence. In these games, toddlers also learn turn taking and cooperation.

Pretend Play and Continued Exploration

Playing alone, toddlers enjoy dumping and filling containers repeatedly or piling blocks and knocking them down. These seemingly endless play sequences give the toddler practice in fine motor skill development and eye–hand coordination. In this exploratory play, they are learning about cause and effect: how their own actions have an effect on objects. As they initiate play with toddlers, home visitors provide everyday play experiences and use these experiences to assist parents in understanding the meaning of their toddler's play.

As she shakes the cans, Cynthia places two cans, each containing plastic poker chips, on the rug next to Cassandra (age 14 months). As she gives the cans to Cassandra, Cynthia says to Cassandra's mother, Samantha, "Let's see how she plays with these toys."

Cassandra throws a chip, and Cynthia says, "She found a new way to play with this."

Samantha puts a chip into the can as she says to her daughter, "Can you do that?"

Cynthia asks, "Mommy made a different sound, didn't she?" Samantha then helps her daughter by supporting one can as Cassandra dumps the chips from one can into the other. Cynthia says, "That's neat, the way you put your hand under hers, and allow her to do it, but help her a little bit." Cassandra puts her hand in the can and shakes the chips. Cynthia says, "Now we're making some new noises."

As she dumps out the chips, Samantha says to her daughter, "Let's try it again." Cassandra puts the chips into the can and looks up to her mother, who nods affirmatively. Cassandra continues the task.

Cynthia says, "Just with a look, you gave her encouragement to do it. You gave her that go-ahead to do it, and she did. See how this finger is coming together with that?" Cynthia demonstrates the pincer grasp with her hand. "That is called the pincer grasp," she says. "The pincer grasp is developing and is really important because you have to have the pincer to be able to write. Another thing, this is good for using her eyes with her hands. In order to pick them up and put them back in the can, she is building eye–hand coordination, which is another skill needed in writing."

As Cynthia talks to Samantha, Cassandra dumps and fills the cans with chips. Cynthia explains, "Lots of times we think this is fun, and we don't recognize it's learning too."

As she watches Samantha assist Cassandra in this new task, Cynthia tells Samantha the importance of what her toddler is doing. She also helps this mother understand how this play fosters Cassandra's pincer grasping and basic eye–hand coordination skills needed for writing.

At age 12 or 13 months, toddlers typically begin to say their first words. As they gain increased skill in speaking and understanding language, toddlers love naming games. Just as they love to explore their hands and feet as young babies, toddlers love to name the parts of their bodies, pictures in books, and objects in the world about them. During this period, toddlers love spontaneous, impromptu games with adults, especially when their bodies are involved.

Jeff (age 18 months) brings the basket of plastic Easter eggs to Molly, his family child care provider. Jeff puts a half-egg on Molly's nose as he says, "Nose."

Molly responds, "On my nose! I'm going to put a purple egg on Jeff's nose."

As Molly holds the egg over Jeff's nose, he laughs gleefully. Molly then says to Jeff, "And I can make it a hat," as she puts her half-egg on top of her head. Molly puts two more half-eggs on her head as she says, "Three hats." The hats fall off and Jeff laughs.

Jeff then puts a half egg on his head as he says, "Hat."

Jeff has initiated a simple pretend game and Molly is skilled at entering into his play as a play partner. Molly imitates Jeff, who in turn imitates Molly, a common play pattern among young toddlers and adults. Molly encourages and extends Jeff's language ("on my nose") and takes the play one step further as she puts the egg on her head. In his play, Jeff practices his language and experiences shared enjoyment and connectedness.

Often, an adult can support and extend a toddler's play without being a full participant, such as when Jean, a child care provider, is folding clothes in the room where three toddlers, Nancy, Ricky, and Jason, play.

Nancy (age 19 months) pretends she's getting on a school bus and rides past Jean as she says, "Beep, beep."

Jean asks her, "Where is your horn?" Nancy then makes the sound of the school bus horn. Jean adds, "Picking up the kids from school? Got any kids?"

Nancy says, "Pick up."

Jean affirms, "Picking up the kids." Jean reaches down to the floor, picks up a play person, and hands it to Nancy as she says, "Here is one."

Jason (age 28 months) then sees another play person across the room and gives it to Nancy as he says, "Here's another people. I find one."

Nancy then rides off as she says, "Go school."

Jean skillfully provides guidance to these young children's play. Nancy has taken the lead, but Jean enters into the play and extends it. Like Molly, Jean promotes Nancy's language as she repeats and extends Nancy's spontaneous comments.

In their work with parents, home visitors can help parents understand that play is the means by which their toddler is learning and that they can significantly influence their toddlers' play, learning, and development. When parents understand the meaning of their toddlers' playful explorations, independent actions, and negative responses, they will not see these actions as mere signs of the so-called "terrible twos." Instead, they can strive to provide an environment that encourages developmental progress within clear limits. Shelly and Rob, who have had a home visitor since Shelly's third trimester, illustrate this type of learning.

Shelly: It helps to know that these things are going to occur, and what Erin [age 26 months] is doing now is good. This is good that she wants to play with the knobs on the stereo. You know, most people would just say "No" and slap their children's hands, but we knew that was just a way for Erin to investigate things. Instead of correcting her for something that wasn't really going to hurt, we let her do it, and she doesn't play with anybody's knobs when we go to their house. We didn't have to stand there and yell "NO" at her because we knew that these things were going to pass and that this was good for her to investigate things. Just those little things that we knew ahead of time, I think, helped us prepare for each step.

Rob: Yes, knowing what's coming up when you see her do something. Knowing, "Hey, this is a stage that this child is going through." And you should pick up on it and work with it rather than put her on a leash!

Toddlers seem to spend most of their day experimenting. They climb into cupboards, twirl to music, scatter their food about their highchair tray, and splash vigorously in the bathtub. Objects in their everyday world become toys and their approach to experiences is playful during dressing, eating, and bathing, as well during "legitimate" playtime. Home visitors can assist parents in understanding that their toddler's exploration, experimentation, and testing is their way of knowing and learning. To assist parents in seeing and understanding this dominant approach of their toddlers, Janice often brings a "curiosity bag" filled with "beautiful junk" for the toddler to explore.

Janice puts a cloth toy bag on the floor as she says to Mia (age 24 months), "Here is a whole bag for you to explore." Mia sits down and begins to pull items out of the bag as Janice comments to Tracy, "This is basically a bag of junk. It's important to continue to give Mia opportunity to explore and to be creative."

Tracy replies, "When Mia is downstairs with me as I am doing laundry, she is always finding things—anything that is new and different—and she's always asking me, 'What's this, Mommy?'"

Mia has pulled a toy plastic milk bottle out of the bag and begins to shake it. Janice helps Mia begin to open the lid, and Mia finishes opening it and dumps a play person on the floor. She then goes into the bag and removes a car as she says, "Ooooh, car." She puts the play person in the car as Janice comments, "Sure, he can ride in the car."

Mia replies, "I too big."

Tracy affirms, "You are too big to ride in that car."

In each of her visits, Janice emphasizes that Mia is learning as she actively explores her everyday environment. Bringing a bag of everyday "beautiful junk" for Mia to explore helps Tracy observe how her toddler is learning, as well as how to take the toddler's point of view toward objects in her home. As Mia investigates the items, Janice assists Mia and her actions are powerful models for Mia's mother.

As Mia looks through the bag, Janice comments to Tracy, "Children all have their own style with this bag. Mia is so precise—looking and deciding what she wants. When you think about how her exploring has changed—initially everything went right into her mouth. Now, she explores things with her hands and eyes."

Mia takes a small cosmetic bag but has difficulty unzipping it. Her mother says, "Bring it here, and I'll hold it so that you can unzip it." Mia does as her mother has directed. Janice comments, "It is good that you structure the job so that she could do it herself." Mia unzips the bag and removes a small play figure that she identifies as Cookie Monster.

As Tracy assists her daughter, Janice affirms the manner in which Tracy enables Mia to succeed at a task. With this bag of beautiful junk, Janice models encouragement and uses Mia's play to help Tracy understand how her toddler's curiosity, exploration, and learning are progressing.

Quality of the Home Environment

The home visitor can also help parents understand that the quality of their home environment makes a difference in their child's play. Home environments that promote play include a relaxed atmosphere with minimal adult directives, adequate and safe space, and a variety of objects and toys that promote active participation and creative construction.

When the home visitor brings everyday objects and simple toys to use during visits, he or she can help parents to understand the values of play activities that invite construction, foster eye–hand and fine motor coordination, and encourage imagination and self-expression. Some toys encourage early role play, such as dishes, pots, pans, dolls, blocks, and toy trucks.

Pretend Role Play

Toddlers not only begin to speak in words but also begin pretend role play. These two actions give evidence that toddlers can think symbolically; that is, they can represent actions, objects, and people in their minds. As they pretend, young children learn to communicate through the use of language, gestures, and symbolic objects. In pretend play, toddlers begin to use meanings other than those usually attached to objects or actions. For example, they pretend to feed a toy dog with a cup or pretend a stick is a horse to ride. Usually, the role play centers on simple themes of everyday home experiences.[15] Two-year-olds often take the role of parent. In their play, caretaking may involve tasks such as cooking, feeding, giving baths, putting children to bed, or cleaning. In these role-play sequences, toddlers replay their familial activities, explore their related feelings and reactions to those experiences, and gain mastery of these feelings. For example, as they rigorously wash their doll's hair, they are gaining control of their own feelings when their hair is being washed.

Home visitors can help parents understand the value of this role playing. During their home visits, they can initiate role-play activities with the toddler and encourage parents to join in the play.

Home visitor Winneta has placed a checkered tablecloth and assorted plastic dishes, utensils, and plastic food on the tablecloth. She suggests to Jayla (age 25 months) that they have a picnic.

Jayla brings a plastic hamburger in a bun to Winneta, who says, "Let me have a bite. Mmmmm… real good." Jayla then brings her mother, Sheryll, a hamburger and sits next to her as she pretends to eat a hot dog and potato chips. Sheryll tells Winneta that just as Jayla is pretending to eat her plastic hot dog without a bun, she also eats real hot dogs without a bun.

Winneta explains, "She brings her real world into her pretend play. That's very important. Pretend play helps understanding of her real world."

"My husband plays this with Jayla in her kitchen in her bedroom," Sheryll adds.

Winneta exclaims, "Super!"

Sheryll describes how, the previous night, Jayla took the dustpan and broom and pretended to sweep and then put everything away.

Winneta says, "I encourage you to let her continue to role play. By acting out her experiences, she better understands her feelings about these experiences."

During this extended role-play sequence, Winneta helps Sheryll understand that role playing is an important way for Jayla to understand her everyday experiences. Jayla's dad works a split-shift work schedule and often is part of Winneta's home visit. In fact, he came home at the end of this visit and read a story to his daughter. Winneta explains her commitment to involving both parents in her home visits:

I feel each [parent] has their own style. And they both bring equally important techniques. Maybe Dad might be real interactive and playful and like to do motor things, whereas Mom might like to do more calming things, reading things. I try to tell parents they are both equally important, and their roles are very important even though they are different.

Encouraging Parent–Child Play

An important goal in home visiting is to encourage parents to be partners in play with their young child. As parents enter into their child's play, their child feels affirmed, has a sense of connectedness, and has an invitation to express himself or herself imaginatively and constructively in play.[16] Many home visitors can play skillfully with a very young child and have constructive conversations with the parents about the child's development and their parenting. Commitment and ability to stimulate parents as play partners is a skill that home visitors develop with experience and professional guidance. The following home visit illustrates this process.

During her home visit, Janice places a box of about 50 small, colored wooden blocks on the floor next to Erin (age 30 months). Once the blocks are on the rug, Erin immediately begins to build a simple structure. Janice then makes the same structure as she says to Erin's mother, Shelly, "One thing I really like to do with blocks is to follow the child's lead."

Shelly asks, "You mean imitate?" Janice nods yes.

Erin then lines up several blocks and puts a second row on top of the first. Janice duplicates the pattern as she says to Erin, "That's a neat building you're making. Is mine like yours?"

Erin smiles and says, "Yeah."

Janice then suggests, "Let's let Mommy build. You build, and Mommy can copy." As Erin begins a new block structure, her mother duplicates it while saying, "Look at mine! It's just like yours." Erin smiles and claps enthusiastically. As Erin and her mother continue building, Janice comments, "One of the nice things with blocks [is] it gives you the opportunity to follow her lead. Children need to be the leader."

Shelly reflects, "I never thought about that. I don't imitate her, even when we color together."

After this home visit, Janice talked about her rationale for involving parents in play activities with their toddler.

It's a goal for almost every visit, to involve the parent and child together in a play activity. And I definitely involve the parent more when the child is a little older than when there is a baby. I ordinarily initiate the activity with the child, so that I have the opportunity for modeling, because I think modeling is an important aspect of what we do. But then I always like to say, "Give Mom a turn," or "Let's let Mom do it now," or, "We can all do it together." The easy ones are the blocks where the parent mirrors what the child has built. It's also pretty easy to do with dishes. Playdough is really easy. If you have an activity built around the child exploring something, then you have the parent back off. But even then, I will try to reserve time for a book for Mom and her child to read together.

When parents learn to be active participants in their child's play, home visitors can talk about the specific meaning and purpose of this type of parental involvement for their child's development. For example, a parent's active involvement as a play partner gives the child a sense of connectedness and self-worth. The parent is promoting the child's ability to maintain focus, which is an essential readiness skill for school success.

30 MONTHS TO 5 YEARS

During the preschool years, children achieve mastery in play, especially in imaginative constructions and dramatic role play. Play often stimulates problem solving; for example, "How can I prevent the wall of my block building from falling down?"[17] In role play, children ages 30 months to 5 years can represent real and imagined experiences (e.g., pretending to build an apartment building, to be a Halloween witch, or to put out a fire). In this way, children express themselves creatively and feel a sense of power because they are in control of their play. These experiences help children to develop an increased sense of competence and self-worth. As home visitors provide these types of play activities for young children, they can help parents understand the developmental meaning and purpose of these experiences.

Pretend Play

As young children act out roles, their play is process oriented; that is, the activity is pleasurable in and of itself and no product is needed. For children 30 months to 4 years old, play themes remain mostly about family situations; however, role-play sequences become more elaborate and extended. Pretend roles are fluid and shifting; for example, in one minute, the child is a sister, whereas in the next she is a mother. These young children have not firmly separated reality and pretend; thus, they dislike being the baby. Because a major task for young children is still separation and identity formation, it is not surprising they most often choose to be the mother.

When preschoolers play together, their play varies depending on the child's sex and the sex of the child's play partners. Young children show clear preferences for same-sex play. Studies indicate that boys' same-sex play is more active, forceful, and stereotyped than girls' play.[18] Boys are more likely to play in same-sex groups, whereas girls are more likely to be involved in same-sex dyadic play. Play in larger groups is more likely to produce more conflict.

Most noticeable in preschoolers' play is their delight and complete absorption in role-play sequences. For example, Amos, who just had his third birthday and started a child care program, engaged in a brief role-play sequence with his teacher, Dana.

Amos sets the table and calls to Dana, who is seated at the nearby puzzle table, "Dana, I'll give you some coffee and lunch."

Dana comes to the table as she says, "Good, I like that a lot," and she pretends to eat.

Amos tells Dana, "Now I'll make you a birthday cake." He takes a plate to Dana, and they sing "Happy Birthday." Then, Amos hands Dana a physician's kit as he says, "Now this is your present."

Clapping her hands, Dana replies, "Oh, I love it. Thank you. But now I have to go home. Thanks for the party."

Amos turns to Dana as he tells her, "Now it's closing time."

He takes Dana's hand as Dana asks him, "Now where are we going?"

Amos replies, "We're going home."

Dana questions, "Are you my daddy?"

Amos replies, very seriously, "Yes, and we need to use the seat belts so it won't be dangerous." Amos and Dana leave the housekeeping area hand in hand.

Dana is a full participant in Amos's play. This role gives Amos respect and a feeling of connectedness. As the leader of the play sequence, Amos is able to act out his everyday world at home and have it affirmed by Dana. Within the play, Amos is able to be creative and enters into conversation that is grounded in his reality. During this, his first week away in child care, Amos is able to experience that this is an environment where adults understand and value him.

As they acquire more control of finger movement, preschoolers become proficient in using small materials, such as working with puzzles; cutting with scissors; using brushes, pencils, pens, and markers; manipulating snap-together toys such as Lego; and using modeling clay. Organized sports such as T-ball, soccer, and gymnastics are also very popular. Because an increasing number of preschool children spend much of their day in group settings, they experience more directed motor skill activity. In addition, young children spend time in free play on a playground where they engage in multiple kinds of motor activity.

Development of Abstract Thinking

An essential feature of young children's play is their ability to have appropriately playful exchanges with peers that involve a mutual understanding of what is real and what is not. In this play, the child experiences a sense of belonging and sharing the trust of others. Young children love to replay events, especially birthdays, holidays, and outings. Role play of 4- and 5-year-olds no longer centers on family themes. At this age, children have a firmer sense of self, can better separate fantasy and reality, and thus know they are pretending. Because children can now use one object to represent another in pretend play, this representation indicates that the child's thinking is moving from the concrete to the abstract.[19] As their representation and language skills develop, a child's need for realistic objects to communicate symbolic meaning is lessened. With age and pretend-play experience, children learn to represent imagined objects without using anything concrete. Children in the playground of their child care center illustrate this point.

Four boys are pretending that the large horizontal concrete pipe is a haunted house. Dan sits on top of the west opening and J.T. sits on the opposite side. Rob pretends to be a bat and continually makes bat movements with his arms as he runs from one end of the pipe to the other. Chris whispers the magic word to J.T. before he enters the pipe. Chris is a ghost who makes "whoooo" sounds as he moves about the pipe.

Another role-play sequence in the same playground further demonstrates this behavior.

Jana and Treeva have just entered the playground and run to the day care sign, which they pretend is a restaurant sign.
 Jana asks, "What do you want?"
 Treeva replies, "An ice cream cone."
 Jana pretends to give one to Treeva, who leaves the area as she pretends to lick the cone. Annie comes to the area, and Jana asks, "What do you want?"
 Annie answers, "Cherry pie."
 Jana responds, "We have only chocolate pie. Do you want some?" Annie nods yes and Jana pretends to give her some.
 As Annie leaves, Jana says to herself, "All the children are gone now." Before leaving the area, she calls out loudly, "Anybody want food or drinks?"

To engage in social role play, young children use their emerging social interaction skills and engage in shared meaning; the development of shared meaning is a pathway to young children's early literacy. Children often collaboratively construct a pretend world. This role play involves an implicit script, negotiation, and differentiated roles. Young children who are good pretenders tend to be good at making friends. In addition, the pretend play of close friends often is more complex than that of their peers.

Pretending is a form of thinking and learning; in fact, it is an intellectually demanding activity. As children grow older, they engage in thematic play of a familiar or imaginary theme. Older children's pretend play is less repetitive than that of toddlers and is sustained by language. Sometimes, children imagine unpleasant or scary events, during which they are able to master their fears. They also enjoy the feeling of power as they act out superheroes or bossy parents.

Studies indicate that pretend play helps children form their personalities and develop social skills, including prosocial skills.[20] Pretend play provides a mental rehearsal for social development as children experiment with new roles. Play stimulates language as it fosters communication, expression, and reasoning.

As young children transform an object into another object, this symbolic play is an important form of early literacy. Language development is a central feature of sociodramatic play. In fact, preschool children in pretend play make use of more future and past tense verbs as well as probabilistic terms in their speech, more so than in their spontaneous conversation.[21] As young children use everyday objects in novel ways, they are decentering; that is, they are able to use a pretend setting in multiple ways. This decentering is a representational skill that children will employ in domains such as reading and writing.[22]

As older preschoolers gain greater understanding of both happenings at home and in their community, adults can provide props for children to role-play sequences beyond their homes. Family child care provider, Jean, has structured a post office for her son, Ricky (age 4 years, 1 month), and another child, Nancy (age 4 years, 3 months).

Jean has made a mailbox from a cardboard box and she has small envelopes for the children to use for their letters. She suggests to Ricky and Nancy that they each get a crayon or a pen and paper and write a letter.

As she puts the envelopes on the table in front of the mailbox, Jean says, "Here's our envelopes. Whenever you get your letter done, you can get an envelope. You need to get a big storybook to write on." Jean gives the children small pieces of paper to write on as she says, "I'm not the one who will write. I am the post officer. I have some stamps [stickers]. Who are you going to write to?"

Ricky replies, "To George Washington."

Nancy replies, "To my mommy [who is in the hospital]."

Ricky brings his mother his paper and asks her to write "George Washington" on it, which she does. Nancy then asks her to write her mother's name, which Jean does. Both children then make pictures on their papers, fold them carefully, get envelopes, and carefully put their papers into the envelopes. Ricky tells his mother, "I'm folding mine good." Jean nods yes. Both Ricky and Nancy then get stamps and put them on their envelopes, and then they place the envelopes inside the box.

Jean has sequenced the tasks clearly for these young children. Each child writes three letters; as they make pictures, they tell Jean about the pictures and to whom they are writing. The children remain focused on the task for approximately 30 minutes. This simple role-play activity offers opportunities for fine motor and eye–hand coordination, creativity, and oral communication. Together, Nancy and Ricky experience shared enjoyment in the task.

Children's dramatic role play with other children helps them learn to communicate and take the perspective of others.[23] Role play demands joint decision making, such as choosing which child will play which role and what the action will be. In this play, children experience how other children act out being a mother, father, or sibling.

In a home visiting program for families with young children, home visitors need to initiate brief play sequences during each of their visits. Janice explained how she tries to help parents understand the meaning of learning and play.

One way I think our program is important is pointing out to parents that play is important, that when the child is young and trying to do a puzzle or shape sorter, I can talk about that as a way of learning and problem solving for the young child, and I compare a task to how things are going to be different when she gets a little older. Yes, we look at it as maybe just play, but it is very serious problem solving for the child, and I try and help the parent to appreciate that when a child is experimenting and exploring, when they are trying a multitude of the things that they do, when they are pretending, doing private talk, it isn't just silly little play activities. It is something that is very valuable in the total scope of preparing them for the different kind of learning that will happen when they get to the first or sixth grade, and they are sitting at a desk in the classroom. It is all learning, and it just is a different method. It is both serious and necessary for the young child.

Play sequences in Janice's home visits illustrate how she stimulates children's learning through play. As the children play, Janice helps parents understand that, in their play, these young children are learning about relationships. When Erin is 33 months old, Janice provides a matching game for her.

Janice places an assortment of vehicles and play people on the rug. Then, she makes a long line, about 4 feet long, with red yarn on the living room rug. She suggests to Erin, "Let's see if we can make a parade." She puts a fire truck with a toy fire officer on the front end of the yarn as she asks, "Can you find another fire truck?"

Erin searches and exclaims gleefully, "I found one!"

There is a play fire officer in the truck, and Janice says, "Can you find a [fire officer] to match?"

Erin finds the fire officer as she says, "I found one!" Erin then picks up a racecar driver doll, and puts it into the car. Following Janice's suggestions, she finds the second racecar, puts it behind the first, and puts a driver in each seat.

Janice asks, "Which car will go next?"

Erin picks up the police car and puts it behind the racecars. "How about this one?" she asks.

Janice says, "A police car. How about a driver for it?"

Erin replies, "I can't find one."

"I think she's behind the horse," Janice says. Erin finds it.

Janice tells Erin's parents, Rob and Shelly, "That's a great way to reinforce prepositions, such as 'behind,' as she is playing."

Erin continues making the parade for several more minutes. As Erin plays, she and Janice talk about "next to," "in front of," and other spatial relationships. Janice explains to Rob and Shelly that matching is an important premath relationship skill.

When Erin's toy parade is completed, Janice initiates a second matching game. This game uses pictures of Sesame Street characters. As they play, Janice explains to Rob and Shelly that first young children learn with concrete objects, then with objects and pictures, and then with pictures alone. The fourth step is letters and numbers.

After this visit, Janice described her intent in introducing these games.

My goal is to help parents see that their child is able to pick out things that are alike, to see similarities and differences, and most young children do it spontaneously as they explore. I want parents to be aware of that. It helps me talk about the young child's intellectual development. And I guess what's fun about it is that a child does it spontaneously, and the parent begins to notice what they are doing... and the second game gives me a chance to help parents see the difference between using objects, touching and manipulating them, to see things that are alike as opposed to using pictures that are alike. I don't get to this progression with every child, but Erin is very quick. It depends on how they handle the objects in the first game as to whether I pull out the cards.

Pretending is not only a form of play, but also a form of thinking and learning. Pretending is a critical step in passing from the sensory-motor intelligence of infancy to the symbolic thinking of adulthood.[24]

Rough-and-Tumble Play

In rough-and-tumble play (R&T), children alternate roles, such as chaser and chasee. R&T tends to occur in spacious areas such as outdoors, is physically vigorous, and usually involves running, falling, and wrestling. R&T and aggression are not significantly intercorrelated in studies.[25] Mostly males engage in R&T, which may explain some of the gender separation in play. Often R&T establishes and maintains dominance among boys. Some children do not engage in R&T but develop into well-functioning social children.[26]

Toys and Materials to Promote Creative Self-Expression

When parents provide pencils, pens, crayons, felt markers, paint, chalk, playdough, and clay, they invite young children to explore and express themselves creatively.[27] Before age 3 years, children's drawings primarily consist of scribbling. The activity initially is a motor activity. As children begin to think symbolically and develop motor control and eye–hand coordination, they make representative drawings. When children draw and make something uniquely their own, they feel good about themselves and feel a sense of competency. These tools also provide enjoyable releasing experiences.

Jasmine (5 years) and her brother, Dillon (3 years), usually go to their art table after they finish breakfast, before they go to school. Jasmine loves stories of princesses and fairies; thus many of her pictures depict princes, princesses, castles, and fairies. Dillon continues to scribble, but many of his pictures are of dinosaurs, trucks, and horses, all of which he loves. On the table are markers, crayons, and colored pencils. The cupboard next to their table includes assorted paper, scissors, and glue. Jasmine also loves to make books. She and Dillon created a museum for their grandparents. Jasmine made an "Rt Bok" (Art Book). In her book, she has a rectangular depiction of paper, a crayon on the next page, then crayon on paper, then a picture of a cat's face. The book continued in this manner to illustrate cutting hearts and snowflakes.

These children's creativity probably will continue in their language and other forms of behavior as they develop.

Construction toys such as blocks and snap-together toys invite another rich medium for imaginative construction. During the preschool years, these constructions become representational (e.g., building a house, a train, or a school). Whether the activity includes creative art or manipulative toys, the child experiences initiative and mastery. There are no rules to follow. In this play, children also learn about spatial relations, such as size, shape, and form.

ELECTRONIC PLAY

Computers, video games, and electronic toys are virtual playgrounds for young children. Young children need a great deal of practice to gain mastery in these contexts. These play avenues allow children to engage in the "as-if" quality of fantasy. Critical issues include how and to what extent children should use electronic play.

Developmentally appropriate software should

- Contain simple and spoken directions
- Allow independent exploration and discovery
- Be open-ended and allow children to maintain control
- Provide many opportunities for problem solving
- Allow children to impact the program through a variety of responses
- Emphasize the process of discovery
- Teach cause-and-effect relationships[28]

DIFFICULTIES AND DILEMMAS

Some family patterns trigger difficulties for the home visitor. One of the most common activities of family life—television viewing—can be one of the most problematic for the home visitor. Other challenging family patterns that a home visitor comes into contact with include parents who did not themselves learn how to play as children, whose primary focus is assisting their young child's academic learning, or whose style is very directive.

Television Viewing Habits

Increasingly, television and video viewing is replacing active learning through play. It is important for home visitors to be knowledgeable about the impact of television and video on children's play. Dilemmas include both the excessive amount of television watching and the content of children's commercial television programming. Children 3–6 years of age watch an average of 4–6 hours of television each day; for children from low-income families, the hours increased by 50%.[29]

Mass media is omnipresent in homes with young children. The average family has two or three televisions. In many homes, the television is on during all waking hours. Even when the young child does not pay consistent attention to the television, young children are exposed to "background media."[30] There are four possible impacts of background media on the amount and quality of young children's play and interaction:

1. Background media may distract the child and disrupt the child's ongoing play.

2. Very young children often talk to themselves as they play. Researches see this private verbalization as the foundation for the development of verbal thought and internalized self-control. Background language from a television or radio may interfere with this private verbalization during play.

3. Background media can enhance the child's attention during play. It may be possible for children to learn to selectively focus their attention on their ongoing play and not be open to other stimulation.

4. Background media for the very young child may be the foreground for the child's parents, and the parents' focus on television may hinder parent–child interaction.[31]

The deregulation of children's television programs in 1984 allowed television shows and toys to be marketed together.[32] The dominant theme of television programming, video, and these related toys is violence. Within 3 years of deregulation, the profits from war toys (e.g., Power Rangers) were enormous.[33] By the 1990s, the American Psychological Association (APA) had gathered numerous studies and had concluded that there was a direct link between the aggression in young children and the violence viewed on television.[34] The APA concluded that television and videotape violence could account for 10% of children's aggressive behavior.[35] Preschool teachers report that, in much of their play, children imitate television characters, resulting in marked increases in violence and aggression and changes in peer interaction.[36] A longitudinal study examined the relationship between television violence viewed at ages 6–10 years and adult aggressive behavior 15 years later in life. The study concluded that childhood exposure to media violence predicted young adult aggressive behavior for both males and females; these results persisted across socioeconomic status and intellectual ability. Thus far, we know little about the impact of media on the development of babies and toddlers.[37]

Young children always have played war games, but in the past, children chose the content of the war play and used their imagination as they invented pretend heroes and enemies. Currently, children's war games most often are imitations of television programming and videos. When watching television dominates how children play, creatively acting out one's everyday experience and gaining mastery over these experiences often is no longer the dominant theme in children's play.

Home visitors have many opportunities to talk about the impact of television in their conversations with parents. They can help parents understand the meaning and purpose of active learning through play, and the distinction between imitating television characters and creatively role playing. They can suggest that parents watch television with their children. As they watch, parents can discuss with their children what is being viewed or can choose to monitor the programming as being developmentally inappropriate. Unfortunately, parents frequently use television and videos as babysitters, allowing the parents to do something else in a different part of their home.

The Internet is also a concern for children because it allows unsupervised access to many inappropriate aspects of American culture, such as graphic news reports and pornography. In addition, video games for both the computer and television, which are often violent, are particularly popular with boys.[38] Studies confirmed that boys who played violent video games showed more aggressive thoughts and behavior than boys who did not.[39] Parents now are faced with the challenge of not only monitoring television but also the computer.

Home visitors need to be respectful of family patterns while responsibly providing developmental information on the impact of television on young children's development. For example, as a child engages in role play with her home visitor, the home visitor can explain to the child's parents that this type of role-play decreases as the time that young children spend watching violent cartoons on television increases. Use of television remains the parents' decision; however, the home visitor can provide appropriate information regarding its developmental impact.

Parents Who Have Difficulty Playing with Their Children

A further challenge that home visitors may face involves parents who do not enjoy or know how to play with their baby or young child. When home visitors are working with parents of very young children, it is important for the home visitors to see whether those parents enjoy playing with their baby or toddler. A parent who does not enjoy playing probably does not know how to play. Parents who were reared in a troubled family may not have extensive joyful childhood play to draw on in their relations with their baby. Spontaneity and having fun is not a given among all parents. Janice spoke with me about this issue.

Some mothers really don't know how to play with their baby. They know how to do something for their baby, like change her diapers. They may know how to make their baby laugh. They know how to ask their baby questions, but they just don't seem to catch on as to how to play. It's as if they need to be taught. Once a parent is able to enjoy observing her baby and home visitor play together, then the home visitor can go a step further and invite the parent to join in the play.

This one mom I'm thinking about—I'd invite her on the floor. She'd come down sometimes, but not all the time. We'd do something, and then she'd be back up on her chair, just being apart from, instead of a part of, the activity. That is something that for me as a home visitor has evolved over time, in that I'm better at encouraging parents now than I used to be. But there are just some parents that just won't do it.

I think there's a certain amount of distance that some parents always may have with their children, and they see their role as a directive role and a caretaker, as opposed to a playmate. Getting them to even see themselves as a playmate and then to act that out is real difficult. It's as if they fear they are losing ground in maintaining the respect they want. They fear the authority and response will somehow get muffled.

For these parents, home visitors first have to engage in play with the baby or young child and help the parent see and understand the meaning of this play. Once a trusting relationship between home visitor and parent is firmly established, then the home visitor can encourage the parent to enter into the play. It is through concrete experiences in play with their child that parents can begin to enjoy and value these experiences and then provide them for their child on their own.

Parents Who Do Not Appreciate the Learning Value of Play

In addition to not enjoying play with their children, many young parents may not value play as the primary way that their young child learns. Rather, many are eager for their child to excel in more structured learning. One parent remarked that she was more interested that her child "learn his 1-2-3s and ABCs." In fact, 2- to 4-year-olds can learn to recognize numbers and letters; however, this is rote learning without understanding of the meaning of the symbols. For example, many 3-year-olds can count to 10 and recognize numerals, but they often do not grasp the concept of what 3 actually means or the concepts of more than and less than.

At first, parents may see their home visitor as their child's teacher. Their expectations are for this person to focus on helping their child's academic learning. One of the home visitors' first challenges is to help these parents to understand the developmental importance of play as their child's primary means of learning. Once home visitors have established a trusting relationship with parents, they can encourage the parents to enter into play with their child. It is important to have open-ended materials such as a tub of birdseed, beans, or play-dough for sensory play. These activities have no rules. The parent can experience the child's delight while the home visitor explains the developmental value of the play.

Directive Parents

Some parents are very directive in their interactions with their young child. These parents often are anxious that their child perform in the right manner. Given this concern, it is very difficult for these parents to allow their babies or young children to first explore a toy in their own way. When a home visitor recognizes that a parent has such parenting patterns, he or she needs to concretely explain the meaning and purpose of exploration. As the baby or young child does explore, the home visitor can tell the parent specifically what the child is learning. Janice discussed how she has learned to relate to directive parents during home visits.

When I first began doing home visits, I had a low-functioning mother. Each visit, she would take over the toy and play with it herself. Then, she would show her child every step of what she was supposed to do. I didn't feel secure enough to jump in and say anything.

Then, I physically got in the mom's way. And then, I would put the toy far away from the mom, and then engage her in conversation so that her baby first could explore. With experience I got better with that—better with talking with the mom who could not let her child explore. When I saw that a mom was overly directive, I started my chatter immediately. I would put a toy down and say, "Let's watch and see what she does with this."

Janice described how she blocked this mother's intrusion into her baby's play. Her blocking is successful only because she is skilled in establishing a relationship with this mother—a relationship that allows, over time, the mother to hear and integrate new developmental information and parenting strategies.

Directive moms get real embarrassed when their child turns a toy upside down. They are quick to say to the child, "No, that's not the way you're supposed to play with it." Again, I'll be quick to add, "Isn't it wonderful that she wants to explore it from every angle?" I'll also make comments that babies could teach manufacturers many ways that toys could be used.

Janice ties her comments to the baby's actions. Her comments both affirm the baby and parent and inform the parent. The parent's learning is experiential; it is grounded in his or her baby's actions, which Janice observes and interprets.

I'll tell moms another reason why it is helpful for a child to explore a toy is that it'll extend the time a child plays with a toy, and moms always need time. And finally, I'll suggest that in exploring, the child will get more mileage out of the toy. Then, when a directive mom will let her baby explore, even for half a minute, I'll say, "It's so great the way you let Joey explore!" If an older sibling is part of the visit, I'll talk to the mom through the sibling, as I tell him to let his sister first explore.

Janice does not specifically address parents' directive style. Rather, in each visit, she provides play experiences in which she can affirm the baby's exploratory learning, interpret the developmental purpose of this learning, and affirm both baby and parent. Janice is secure in the knowledge that once she has established a trusting relationship with a parent, over time, the parent will learn experientially to value his or her baby's manner of learning.

Strategies suggested previously can assist home visitors when they work with difficult family situations. At the same time, there are situations in which a family rejects all of the home visitor's approaches. In some situations, with some families, home visiting just does not work. Given these potential difficulties, home visiting programs need to provide visitors with a working climate of support and guidance from peers, mentors, and administrators.

CONCLUSION

From infancy through early childhood, play remains the primary method of learning and development. Parents of babies and young children can provide a relaxed atmosphere, space, and interactions that promote and encourage play, learning, and development. In turn, home visitors can help parents develop understanding and skill to promote their baby's and young child's learning and development through play.

This chapter described how babies and young children by nature are curious and spontaneously explore and experiment as they relate to people and to objects. The activity of exploring and experimenting is pleasurable in and of itself; it is intrinsically motivating. As babies and young children explore and experiment, they are playing, which is their primary way of learning. In their play with objects and with people, they often are creative and express themselves imaginatively.

This chapter illustrated and discussed the many ways that home visitors can promote parents' understanding and skill in promoting their child's play. They provide developmental information so that parents can understand the meaning and purposes of their child's play and can anticipate future developmental gains. It is natural that parents may take for granted routine activities such as diapering, dressing, and feeding. Thus, home visitors can be very helpful in discussing how these routine activities are a wonderful environment for playful parent–child interactions. When home visitors observe playful, spontaneous parent–child interactions, they can affirm the parents' actions and describe the meaning of what they are seeing in terms of the young child's learning and development. When they bring small objects and toys with which babies and young children can play, home visitors can help parents see how their child is developing new understanding and skills through their play. They can provide play activities in which they can encourage parents to be active participants and, in this participation, learn how being a play partner benefits their child.

Everyday Rituals and Celebrations

Wee Willie Winkie runs through the town,

Upstairs and downstairs in his night-gown,

Rapping at the window, crying through the lock, "Are the children in their beds, for it's now eight o'clock?"

William Miller (1841)

THIS CHAPTER FOCUSES PRIMARILY ON TWO ASPECTS of family life: everyday family ritual and special family celebrations and traditions. The term *ritual* as used in the chapter refers to the patterns of everyday routines that make up the shared lives of parents and their children. These include mundane practices such as eating, sleeping, bathing, or changing a diaper. It may seem odd to call such everyday happenings *rituals* because they usually are not explicitly recognized or thought out by parents. However, the safe and predictable space that a child finds in these everyday patterns is very much like the familiar space created for adults in traditional rituals, such as religious services, holidays, or birthday celebrations. These rituals help young children to internalize basic processes of morality and emotional regulation and to learn the attitudes, beliefs, and values of their families and cultures.[1] Traditional rituals also play an important role in a child's life and deserve discussion. This chapter calls the more formal or self-conscious traditions *celebrations* to distinguish them from everyday ritual.

Rituals and celebrations are varied and function in the development of the parent–child relationship in a number of different ways.[2] The elements that go into making a ritual include

- Coordinated practices of family members' interaction patterns
- Predictable, repeated patterns of experience over time
- A means of organizing daily life
- A means of regulating behavior

- An expression of a family's shared beliefs and values
- A means of giving each family member a sense of belonging
- A central element of each family member's sense of identity[3]

Not every ritual or celebration has each of these elements, but the whole structure of ritual and celebration in which a young child lives serves these functions.

Expectations and patterns of the larger culture and a family's ethnicity influence a family's ritual. For example, the sleep patterns of families in the United States where young children and parents sleep in their own beds is different from many cultures where young children sleep with their parents. Some extended family members may put pressure on young parents to continue their sleep tradition.

Rituals capture and express family members' relationships with one another and express what members mean to each other. They help children and their families make meaning from familiar family happenings. Daily rituals help to shape family relationships because they tell family members who they are to one another. Some familiar celebrations are like anchor points during transitions, such as birthday cakes and decorating the Christmas tree. Healthy families have other regular and everyday rituals, such as bedtime stories or family dinner. Imber-Black and Roberts wrote about the meaning of rituals:

> They are a lens through which we can see our emotional connections to our parents, siblings, spouse, children and dear friends....They connect us with our past, define our present life, and show us a path to our future as we pass on ceremonies, traditions, objects, symbols, and ways of being with each other.[4]

Three dimensions of ritual have been identified: communication, commitment, and continuity.[5] Everyday rituals such as breakfast and dinner communicate to young children what needs to be done. Because rituals occur during the same time each day, they reflect family members' commitment to each other. As they repeat each day, rituals involve continuity in behavior or the development of family habits.

An evening meal together is a ritual in many families. For example, in many families, everyone has their own place at the dinner table. Family dinner contains both symbols and symbolic actions. Food is one symbol that is different with each family. Food may symbolize nurturance or the family's connection to a specific ethnic tradition. In addition to food, families may have other symbols of dinnertime, such as special china, candlesticks, or silverware. When families eat dinner together each day, parents are implementing their deep desire to have shared time together. During dinner, children feel a sense of belonging, connectedness, and predictability.

However, many families no longer eat regular dinners together. Older children's team sport events, dance lessons, and other activities mean that families are not even home during dinnertime. Some parents may not get home from work until well past dinnertime. In other families, rather than chatting together and learning what each family member did that day, family members watch television as they eat. Many American families eat fast food many nights of the week; in some families, each family member eats whenever he or she wants. Given these patterns, young children miss the feelings of belongingness and security that accompany daily family dinners.

Fiese conducted a longitudinal study examining stability and change in rituals of children from preschool to early school years and found that when dinnertime rituals remained stable, children experienced higher levels of academic success.[6] Fiese also found that when family rituals, such as dinnertime, were disrupted, young children became more vulnerable to developing academic or behavior problems.

Bedtime rituals every night are another time for parents and young children to intimately share. Repetitive bedtime rituals define the parent–child relationship as one of security, comfort, reliability, and safety.[7] As children grow older, they no longer will need to be read to, but they can give their parents a ritual kiss as they say good-night. Some families have weekly rituals, such as a large family breakfast on Sunday mornings, a pizza dinner on Friday evenings, or a particular evening when the children cook for the family.

Many families have rituals to say good-bye to each other before they leave their home or greet each other when they return at the end of the day. Parents of very young children often add hugs and kisses to their good-byes and swing their child when they return. These daily rituals mark a boundary between a family and the family's outside world. In these daily rituals, children discover their roles and responsibilities as a family member. As they grow up, they will sense that ritualistic family processes are bigger than themselves.

When families experience separation or divorce, they often create new rituals. Visits with the nonresidential parent are most meaningful if ritual is embedded in the transition. During separation or divorce, parents may need to give special attention to a young child's bedtime ritual. When a child returns home to her mother after visiting her father, the mother can regularly have special ice cream for a treat. Rituals such as this create a bridge that helps the child feel secure.

When young children's family life is embedded in predictability, simplicity, gentleness, and time to share in the ordinary, they may more readily know and experience spirituality. Rituals, even everyday rituals, are full of symbols and include sensory memory—smells, textures, and sounds. Symbols provide meaning without words. For example, if a family always has music playing softly during their evening meal, the music signifies that the family dinner is a special and sacred time. Some families create new symbols and new rituals, which often signify new meaning or new relationship possibilities. Parents may invent new rituals (e.g., playing with the child every day before work) while continuing a ritual from their childhood (e.g., eating dinner by candlelight).

Gender roles can often be embedded in the preparation and enactment of rituals. With both parents or caretakers employed full-time, some families find it helpful to alternate days when one person focuses on household tasks while the other performs young children's bedtime ritual. Imber-Black and Roberts discussed the function that rituals have in an individual's development:

> They... enable relating, changing, healing, believing, and celebrating, which are, in fact, major themes in all human existence. Any given ritual, whether it be a daily ritual, a special tradition, a holiday celebration, or a life-cycle ritual, naturally may contain one or more of these elements.[8]

Another ritual for some children is attending religious education or language classes, which introduce children to memorable stories from their religious and cultural traditions. In some families, a special time is set aside to recount stories about an extended family member (e.g., a war hero), a religious figure, or a cultural hero. These stories develop a sense of connection to something beyond the family and encourage a feeling of spirituality. Through this type of ritual, children realize that they live in a world governed by love, compassion, and something greater than themselves. Investing in family rituals helps young children understand a deeper meaning to life than the unavoidable and mundane. Although there has been a decline in attendance at formal religious services, more people seem to be seeking spirituality. Garbarino and Bedard noted:

> It is the decline of the sacred that is most important because with it comes an almost inevitable decline in the structure of adult authority....An important part of the social order derives from recognizing the sacred: to set limits, to de-fine what is done and not done, to give a higher purpose.... The issues of sacredness and authority are connected....It is the manifest love rather than the fear of the "wrath of God" that makes a difference— a focus on being a Christlike person rather than a Christian, a Buddha rather than a Buddhist, for example....Spiritual authority is the deepest and strongest authority there is.[9]

Principles of development, parenting, and home visiting approaches are relatively similar throughout everyday rituals. This chapter examines three exemplary routines: 1) sleeping, 2) feeding and eating, and 3) toileting. Following the discussion on everyday rituals is a brief look at the role of more formal celebrations in family life. It concludes with a discussion of some of the dilemmas and difficulties that home visitors experience with regard to everyday rituals and family celebrations.

PATTERNS OF MUTUALITY

Patterns of development and parenting arise across everyday routines of feeding and eating, sleeping, and toilet training. In each area that involves child and parent working together, there is mutuality. For these patterns of mutuality to occur, parents need to learn to read the language of their child's behavior; for example, they need to recognize the meaning of different cries, when to stand back, and when to nudge their child forward.

Each of these areas involves the child's accomplishment: it is the child's task to learn to fall asleep, to decide how much to eat, and to use the toilet. As young children learn to feed themselves, put themselves to sleep, and use the toilet, they are developing increased independence. This process of becoming independent is not always even. Development often occurs in bursts, such as the emergence of new motor or language skills. A burst in one area may lead to unevenness in another; for example, new motor skills may lead to overexcitement and accompanying difficulty in calming down to fall asleep.

As their child grows, parents learn that the different areas of their child's development are intertwined. As motor skills develop, babies can chew and swallow and begin to feed themselves. As their social-emotional and language skills develop, eating times can be pleasurable times of companionship. With increased language and cognitive skill, toddlers can understand and follow directions in eating, sleeping, and toilet-training activities. Because of the emotional bond with his or her parent, the young child is responsive and eager to please. Successes in these everyday rituals are major developmental accomplishments and become a part of the child's identity.

Predictability is central to each of these everyday rituals. Falling asleep becomes a natural part of everyday routine when there is a calm bedtime ritual. When family members regularly come together to eat, eating is enjoyable and the child feels a sense of connectedness. Regular reminders to use the potty become a part of the child's everyday routine until children can recognize their bodily signals for toileting. In time, the preschooler experiences a predictable rhythm—eating when hungry, sleeping when tired, and toileting according to bodily signals.

It is not uncommon for everyday rituals to trigger parents' worry, anxiety, and insecurity. New parents may feel like a failure when their new baby is colicky or when they think their child is not eating enough. Often, parents love the process of putting their child to sleep, but then experience the frustration of nighttime awakenings with seemingly endless crying. Within these experiences, new parents can feel their sense of parenting competence eroding.

Home visitors can provide important support, affirmation, developmental information, and suggestions to help young parents in their important and challenging parenting tasks within these daily rituals. When home visitors prepare parents with information regarding what to expect from their growing baby and young child, parents can develop both confidence in their child's development and confidence in their ability to foster this development. As they observe parent and child behavior, home visitors have the opportunity to interpret the developmental meaning of these actions and to support and affirm the parent. When a parent is feeling insecure or perplexed, home visitors' support and information may assist parents' understanding of both the child and self, and thereby offer needed assistance.[10]

In their many conversations with parents, home visitors can explore the family's rituals and the meaning and beliefs expressed in their rituals. What values are parents passing on to their children when they engage in rituals together? Rituals can help young children assume new roles such as setting or clearing the table. Rituals can also help the family change interaction patterns, such as beginning to have daily dinner together in which each family member is listened to and respected. If a home visitor learns that a family has few rituals, he or she might suggest possible rituals a family might develop, such as eating dinner together or reading stories before a child's bedtime. The visitor can also help parents understand how these rituals promote the child's development. Sleeping and eating are among the most basic of rituals.

Sleeping

Sleep disruptions among babies and young children are a very common concern of parents.[11] Sleep includes rapid eye movement (REM) sleep and non-REM sleep, each characterized by different types of brain waves. During REM sleep, the brain is active while the body is quiet and still. The sleeper's eyes move rapidly in bursts under closed lids, while heart rate and breathing patterns are rapid. Non-REM sleep is the restorative part of sleep when the brain is inactive but the body may be active. Heart rate and respiratory patterns are slow and regular. The pattern of alternating sleep stages repeats five to six times during the night.[12]

Sleep and waking become organized during the first 6 months of life.[13] Adequate sleep is very important for the baby's brain to have restorative opportunities necessary for optimal development. A baby's sleep is mostly regulated by parent–baby interaction but also is affected by the baby's cognitive, emotional, and social experiences. Sleep disruptions among babies and young children are a very common concern discussed by parents. Nighttime awakenings are the most frequently reported problem. However, many children are self soothers and can put themselves back to sleep on awakening.

Feeding and Eating

Parents of newborns must decide whether their baby will be breast fed or formula fed. Breast feeding benefits both baby and mother. First, breast milk is designed to meet the complete nutritional needs of babies. Breast feeding also helps prevent allergies by coating the intestinal lining, which prevents the passage of germs and allergens that could cause allergies. Breast milk has high concentrations of white blood cells, which circulate inside the baby's intestine to combat harmful bacterial. It also contains immunoglobins, which are infection-fighting proteins.[14] Because young babies have weak immune systems, the immunoglobins and antibodies are very important for the baby's health. Studies indicate that breast-fed babies show significant benefits in cognitive and neurological function when compared to formula-fed babies.[15] However, today's formulas are adapted to babies' needs. Whether breast or bottle fed, a baby will need to be burped after each feeding.

Newborns usually lose weight during their first few days, which they regain around 8–10 days of age at a rate of about an ounce per day. Young babies are adequately fed if they urinate with each feeding. Babies who cry or spit up after feeding might be allergic to the proteins in milk.[16] When this happens, mothers should call their child's pediatrician.

Principles of parenting are similar for both eating and sleeping times. As the baby grows up, parents and children develop a predictable feeding ritual. Just as it is the task of the baby and toddler to fall asleep, it is also the child's task to eat. The parent is responsible for what food is offered to the baby, but the baby is responsible for how much is eaten. As the child grows, a continuous push and pull develops between dependence (e.g., being fed) and independence (e.g., feeding oneself). The long-term goal is for young children to feed themselves, to enjoy eating, and for mealtimes to be a social occasion for the family. The family mealtime routine becomes a ritual involving communication, connectedness, a shared identity, and values.

Age Birth to 3 Months

Sleep   Newborn babies have a sleep–wake rhythm that was established in utero.[17] Newborns often sleep 15–18 hours each day, in 3- to 4-hour stretches. Because the baby's central nervous system is immature, activities like feeding and sleeping occur at unpredictable times.[18] Newborns have about seven sleeping and waking periods during a 24-hour period.[19] During their first month, babies will arouse every 3–4 hours during the night.[20] How these cycles change into different patterns is partially dependent on the individual baby's home environment. As parents learn their baby's different states of consciousness, they can begin to prolong their baby's alert states and encourage prolonged sleep states. In a responsive home environment, sleep–wake cycles more quickly become predictable.

In reality, the total amount of daily sleep babies experience is regulated by the environment. Bottle-fed babies have significantly different sleep profiles than breast-fed babies. More than half of all American mothers breast feed their children for 3–6 months or longer.[21] With breast feeding, the likelihood that mothers sleep with their babies increases. Babies who share a bed with their mothers breast feed almost twice as often as babies who sleep in a separate room.[22]

At about 1 month of age, babies naturally become fussy in the late afternoon and early evening; this behavior usually persists until about 3 months of age. An early bath and massage can address this fussiness and ease the evening sleep ritual. Until babies can turn themselves over, pediatricians now recommend that babies sleep on their back to lower the risk of sudden infant death syndrome.

The baby's temperament also affects his or her sleep patterns. Very active babies, or babies who are very aware of sensations, are prone to waking during the night. In night sleep, periods of deep sleep (30–50 minutes) are followed by periods of light sleep (i.e., REM sleep). In deep sleep, newborns can shut out noises around them. During REM sleep, breathing is irregular, babies move about, and they are likely to cry out. Between these two cycles, babies often wake up.[23]

Home visitors can help parents learn that when their baby wakes in the middle of the night, it is normal. Usually at around 3 months of age, babies can learn ways to quiet themselves and return to a deeper sleep. Different babies have different ways of self-comforting, such as finding their thumbs, moving into a new position, or scooting to the corner of their cribs. Babies' ability to soothe themselves—to self-calm—is an important first step in developing independence, which is an essential goal of development.[24] Home visitors can help parents understand the importance of their baby learning to self-calm.

As Janice speaks with Marta, Marta's 3-month-old infant, Brianna, lies on her back, sucking her thumb. Janice comments, "It's good that Brianna is able to put her thumb in her mouth. Anything she'll do for herself, let her do it. Then, in the middle of the night she won't need you. You can help her do for herself. When she awakens in the night, give her a couple of minutes to calm herself first—to get in the right position and find her thumb."

Janice observes Brianna's ability to suck her thumb and thereby calm herself. She then helps Marta understand the importance of this self-calming skill and how she can help Brianna develop this ability.

Encouraging a baby to sleep through the night requires agreed-on commitment by everyone in the family, both parents and older siblings. To parents, especially those who want to hold and comfort their baby, these night awakenings can be very troubling. Home visitors can help new parents understand that it is their responsibility to calm their babies and put them to bed; however, it is the baby's task to fall asleep. When parents put their baby to sleep by rocking or breast feeding, babies then will need their parents to help them to fall asleep when they awaken during the night. Janice assisted a young mother in mastering this ability to let her baby learn to fall asleep.

Janice: How is Jene [age 3 months] sleeping?

Natalie: She doesn't sleep much during the day. At night, I rock her to sleep, and then she sleeps well, much better than Dvonne [Jene's 3-year-old

brother] did as a baby. Dvonne didn't sleep through the night until he
was 2½. He would cry whenever his pacifier fell out of his mouth.

Janice: This is the age to concentrate on Jene putting herself to sleep. Think
about yourself. If I would fall asleep in my bed and awaken in the
kitchen, I would not fall back to sleep. If she falls asleep in your arms
and awakens in the bed, she'll expect you to rock her again.

Natalie: I probably cause more problems. I love to hold my babies when they
go to sleep. I know it would be easier in the long run. With Dvonne,
the minute he would cry, I would go in.

Janice: You can rock her—get her comfortable—but before she is asleep, put
her in her bed. When she awakens and cries, let her go for 5 minutes
for starters. I know it's harder with Dvonne in the room. Space the
time: 5 minutes, then 10 minutes, and 15 minutes. It'll be hard to listen to her cry. Don't talk to her. She needs to realize this is not a social time. It will be helpful to you if she can go to sleep by herself and
begin to develop independence.

When Janice visits families with very young babies, she asks parents questions about sleeping and eating. These questions allow Janice to track the baby's
developing skills at the same time that she learns if parents need helpful information for implementing these routines. Natalie had rocked her first child
asleep for his first 18 months. Janice affirms Natalie's desire to rock Jene each
evening but stresses that Jene needs to be put in bed prior to falling asleep. Jene
needs to learn that her night routine is sleeping in her own bed. Most adults
have had the experience of waking up and not being sure of where they are or
having trouble going to sleep in a bed that is not their own. Janice helps Natalie
understand this experience as she speaks of what it would be like for an adult
to wake up in the kitchen. On her home visiting record, Janice makes a note to
herself to remember to initiate discussion with Natalie during her following visits. Janice understands that this will be a major parenting change for Natalie
and she will need her support in the coming months.

During the first 3 months, babies have cycles of eating and sleeping
throughout the day and night. By 8 months, 60%–70% of babies are able to
self-soothe and return to sleep after a nighttime awakening.[25] Many parents believe that giving their baby food or a bottle will assist in their ability to sleep;
however, Ferber warned, "If your child becomes accustomed to being fed at
night, her system begins to regard nighttime sleep periods as only naps between
feedings."[26] Babies sleep best when their digestive systems are shut down for the
night. At the same time, many breast-fed babies feed once during the night
until about 12–15 months of age.

Some babies have colic during their first 3 months. Colicky babies cry and
cannot be soothed, especially in the late afternoon and evening. When a home
visitor works with parents of a colicky baby, first the home visitor makes certain that the parents and physician have checked to see if there may be a phys-

ical reason for crying, such as a food allergy or obstructed bowel. Then, he or she works to reassure the parent. Fussy crying periods can be a real threat to new parents, who may feel helpless and may blame themselves when not able to soothe their fussy baby. Colic usually ends by the age of 3 months.

Feeding   During the first few weeks, the newborn sets the feeding schedule. Newborns need support from their parents to master eating. At first, parents need to adjust their feeding to their baby's rhythm; gradually, they learn which cries mean hunger and which mean something else. By the time their baby is 6 weeks of age, parents can begin to work toward a regular feeding schedule, which usually is every 3–4 hours. As the baby grows, the number of feedings decreases until age 20 weeks, when four feedings a day are adequate. Serious undernutrition during early infancy causes adverse effects on brain development that are permanent and irreversible.

Feeding a very young baby is about intimacy. The most important part of eating for the baby, other than nutrition, is to experience loving communication during feeding periods. Home visitors can encourage parents to sing, rock, and hug their baby during feeding so that feeding is pleasurable. During feeding, the baby–parent interactions are like a dance, with the baby and parent responding to and influencing each other. Babies indicate they are hungry and their parents respond. The feeding process is babies' first experience in active engagement with their parents. These frequent exchanges are the beginning foundation of the development of attachment.

Feeding can be one of the first challenges for new parents, who may feel very insecure, especially if their baby is colicky. In these situations, home visitors can offer support and guidance that both affirms the parents and provides appropriate suggestions.

Karyn's 5-week-old has been colicky, so Janice assists Karyn. Karyn tells Janice that Greg's pediatrician has given him formula with iron; however, she thinks it is the iron that is causing the colic. The pediatrician explained that recent studies indicate that some developmental problems may stem from iron deficiency.

Janice responds, "This is one of the tricky things. In my position, visiting many families with babies, I hear so much different advice coming from pediatricians." Karyn then tells Janice that her sister-in-law's pediatrician had given her different information. Janice says, "That is one of the reasons you need confidence in yourself. 'I have chosen this pediatrician, and I feel most comfortable with him.' We add one qualification. You are your baby's mom. If the pediatrician says, 'Don't worry,' and you think differently, keep pushing with your pediatrician. How often does [Greg] eat?"

"Every 2 hours," Karyn says, "but it can vary. At night, sometimes 8 hours and last night, two 4-hour stretches."

"These are helpful stretches for you," Janice says.

Karyn adds, "The pediatrician said no solid food for 4 months, but he seems to be never satisfied."

"The reason is, his stomach is not ready," Janice explains "And it might make him gassy. His digestive system is not very developed. See if the no-iron makes a difference. Push your pediatrician on it. Ask him what is the critical period for the iron. Unless he has had a baby in his own home that is crying all the time, he may not understand."

As a new mother, Karyn is ambivalent about the pediatrician's advice regarding iron. Janice supports Karyn and urges her to respect her own judgment—to recognize that she is the expert when it comes to knowing her son. Janice encourages Karyn to be assertive with the pediatrician and to know that his voice is merely one of many. As with sleep, Janice tracks Greg's feeding pattern. She gives Karyn developmental information so that Karyn can understand the basis for the pediatrician's directive regarding solid food. In the next few home visits, Janice continues to support Karyn. Her first topic of conversation with Karyn is feeding and Greg's colic. Karyn also knows that if she is feeling especially stressed, she can call Janice.

Age 4–8 Months

Sleep   By 4 months of age, babies are able to sleep 8 hours without a feeding. Between ages 4 and 8 months, babies will continue to need a morning and afternoon nap. Most babies this age easily accept naps. Home visitors can assist parents in understanding that providing a calm before-nap activity, such as rocking, cuddling, or soft lullabies, assists their child's ability to nap. The brief naps babies have when they are being held or they are riding in a car are not as restorative as napping in their cribs.[27] Babies who do not get enough sleep become overstimulated and irritable. Paradoxically, a shortage of naps also seems to make going to sleep at night more difficult. The more tired a baby is, the harder it is for the baby to fall asleep and stay asleep.

At this age, it is good to help babies to associate falling asleep with being in their own bed. Earlier, Janice helped Natalie to understand how she could help her 3-month-old, Jene, fall asleep in her own bed. When Janice returned again, Jene was 5 months old, and her mother reported the following.

Natalie: When it's time to go to bed, I lay her down, and she'll go to sleep.

Janice: That's great!

Natalie: Sometimes she'll cry for a second, and when she wakes up during the night, she begins talking to herself.

Janice: It's great that you have the patience to let her go back to sleep by herself.

Whereas Natalie nightly had rocked her first child to sleep during his first 18 months, now, with help from her home visitor, she allows her daughter to learn to put herself to sleep and calm herself when she awakened during the night. In response to the news, Janice expressed delight in Jene's new skills and affirmed Natalie's ability to nurture this skill.

By age 4 months, babies' nervous systems are mature enough to allow them to sleep 8–12 hours at night. Some babies need a calming routine so they can relax enough to put themselves to sleep. Home visitors can help parents develop a regular bedtime routine (e.g., singing, reading stories) that is calming and nurturing. It is not too early for parents to begin reading simple stories. The body contact and even tempo of voice tones during story reading provides one of the best calming and nurturing bedtime activities as well as preparing the way for later, when the child will start to develop skills that will lead to reading.

With their burst in learning around 4 months of age, babies can become unpredictable and disorganized.[28] Their rhythmic sleep-wake pattern might suffer and they begin to wake more easily again. As they rouse from deep sleep every few hours, they may no longer be interested in getting themselves back to sleep. Parents can rely on the "wait-and-see" approach; after about a week, babies likely will fall asleep as they did before. If the baby awakens after 6 or more hours, parents may feed them again. By 6 months of age, babies often are sleeping for 10 hours each night.

At around 7–8 months of age, babies' motor development makes significant leaps. Babies can sit up and creep or crawl as they explore toys and other objects with their hands and mouths. With this burst of new skills and the accompanying exploration, babies may suddenly have difficulty calming down for naps and night sleeping. Home visitors can explain to parents how their baby's burst of motor skills is interfering with prior sleep patterns. They can encourage parents to be consistent and firm, with a predictable calming routine before sleep, such as reading stories. Parents may pat or hum to their baby during the night, but they need to make certain that night awakenings do not become social occasions; rather, it is their baby's task to put him- or herself back to sleep.

A small proportion of babies enjoy head banging, head rolling (moving their head from side to side as they lie on their back), or body rocking. These actions are soothing rhythmic patterns of behavior to help themselves fall asleep. These methods of self-calming are normal when they develop prior to 18 months and disappear by around age 3 or 4 years.[29]

Feeding   By 4 months, most babies have a predictable schedule of feeding every 3–4 hours. Just as it is the task of babies and young children to fall asleep, it is also their task to control how much milk they will drink. Parents are responsible for appropriate calm feeding times and for appropriate food, but it is the baby who regulates the amount taken. Home visitors can help parents understand these important divisions of responsibility. When feeding is a calm, predictable, positive, shared time between parent and baby, the foundation for healthy eating patterns is established.

The American Academy of Pediatrics recommends introducing solid food at 6 months of age in the form of cereal with milk.[30] Home visitors can help parents understand that the addition of solid food is a real transition for young babies. It can be problematic for young babies to learn to swallow solid food, eat with a spoon, and tolerate different textures. Babies are beginning to have increased eye–hand coordination and they enjoy exploring with their hands. Thus, they enjoy pushing their bottles, batting the spoon away, or putting their hands in their mouth to help suck their food down. Home visitors can describe these common behaviors that are typical of this transition so that new parents can know what to expect and thus feel comfortable with these gradual changes within feeding patterns. When parents are confident, feeding times can be rituals with happy communication between parent and baby. Home visitors can encourage parents to introduce one solid at a time so that they can learn if their baby has any allergies to certain foods. They also can tell parents to initially expect to see the new food in their baby's stool.

During these months, many babies begin teething. Teething may bother babies because of the swelling around the budding tooth, which feels like a foreign substance in their mouth. It can cause discomfort and fussiness and may lessen the baby's appetite. To help soothe their baby's discomfort, parents can wipe their baby's gums with a wet cloth after the baby eats. This wiping cleans the plaque off the gums in the same way that brushing teeth does. Such suggestions from home visitors can be reassuring and helpful to young parents.

Karyn: Everything goes in his mouth.

Janice: Are his gums swollen? [Karyn nods yes.] Do his gums seem to hurt him?

Karyn: I think so.

Janice: Dentists recommend washing babies' gums after they eat and drink to get off the plaque. This helps the teething process and feels good—to have a soft, damp terry cloth on one's gums... Everything in his mouth, that's so good. He's so curious. And there is a connection between mouthing toys and eating later on.

Karyn introduces two topics: teething and exploration through mouthing. Janice uses the topics Karyn introduced to provide helpful developmental and parenting information. Because Karyn has introduced the topics, she is more likely to hear Janice's information and decide to use it. Janice not only addresses ongoing issues, such as teething, but she helps Karyn have a long-range developmental perspective. Putting items in the mouth is not only the way a curious baby learns; it is also the foundation for tolerating changing textures of food in the coming months and years. This information can help Karyn be at ease and understand the meaning and purpose of Greg's behavior patterns.

With increasing age, feedings become a playful exploration time for babies. With their increased eye–hand coordination, they explore new activities, such as smearing food across their faces and wanting to hold the spoon. Parents need to allow additional time and have more patience while their babies eat. When parents are in a rush, this food play can be stressful. If parents can take their time and play with the baby, such as by making the spoon of food an airplane, mealtime can be a time to solidify attachment and playful interaction patterns.

By the time babies are age 7–8 months, they can grasp items and enjoy playing with their cups. When a home visitor interprets the meaning of these new baby behaviors, he or she can assist parents in understanding that learning through exploration is as important to their baby as feeding and eating. These interpretations are especially important for very young or needy parents, who may see these exploratory actions as the baby's intentional attempts to upset the parent. When a parent understands that playful exploration during feeding is the normal way babies learn, the parent can allow more time for feeding and know that patience is necessary.

By 8 months of age, babies need a snack in the morning and one in the afternoon because their stomachs are small. As they crawl, their increased activity also makes them hungry more often. Milk continues to be the baby's most important food. Around 10 months of age, babies begin to have food preferences. Parents often can offer their babies foods of different textures and different tastes, but babies may not try them the first few times. Eggs are among the foods most likely to set off allergies; thus, parents should save eggs for this age or later.

Age 9–24 Months

Sleep   During this period, most children will continue to nap. One-year-olds typically take two naps of approximately 2 hours each. The 1-year-old continues to sleep approximately 16 hours in the 24-hour period. By age 18–24 months, one nap is usually sufficient. With each new leap in development, sleep can become a challenge. Developmental leaps occur at 12 months and again at 18 months. At around 12 months of age, babies learn to walk and begin saying their first words. The excitement and the frustration of learning these new skills spill over into the child's sleeping patterns. Now, the baby can stand; holding the crib rails while cruising around the crib seems much more fun than sleeping. Changes in routine or a stressful experience, such as immunization shots, also can lead to the baby awakening during the night. Home visitors often can help parents see that these sleep changes are related to their young child's surges in development. Parents need to be firm with themselves and their baby to make certain that sleep remains the child's task, although bedtime rituals can ease the child's transition to sleep. Some parents find it helpful to extend the length of bedtime routines, provide a "lovey," sit by the baby, or pat the baby's back. But, once again, parents must make certain that night awakenings do not become playtimes.

Again at age 18 months, the toddler becomes truly mobile, can speak in two- or three-word sentences, and can begin to enjoy pretend play. It is easy for toddlers to get overexcited and therefore have difficulty settling into sleep. Once again, parents may need to be firm or extend the bedtime routine to calm their toddler. Often, stories after bath time are a calm period of shared enjoyment that assists children in settling down for bedtime.

During the child's first 3 years of life, sleep and wake patterns develop largely through transactions between the child's biological propensities and the caregiving environment. A baby's experience, including their sleep patterns, is largely created through the relationships with primary caregivers. Each time babies experience a transition between sleeping and waking, parents and babies learn how to manage separations at sleep onset and reunions upon awakening. These naturally recurring transitions promote a baby's sense of security and are constituents of the baby's development attachment relationship. When parents are insensitive or inconsistent, the baby's sleep–wake rhythm is uneven and sleep problems may emerge.

During the child's first 2 years, sleep difficulties may occur. Some children experience sleep difficulties because they have fears, especially of separation. Others may have difficulties caused by a schedule that is either too active, too inactive, or too unpredictable. During the first 18 months, children may awaken several times during the night.[31] Parents may be overly responsive and may not allow their child to transition during sleep cycles. Some babies and toddlers always are rocked to sleep and never learn to put themselves to sleep. If these children wake up during the night, even when 3–5 years of age, they will expect a parent to sleep with them.

Feeding   As motor skills develop, so too does the child's interest in eating independently. If parents provide their child with a variety of finger foods and a toddler cup as a part of each meal, they encourage self-feeding. Often, babies and young toddlers allow their parents to feed them while they also are feeding themselves with their hands. Feeding oneself is another independence skill to be mastered. Babies also may want to hold and tap their spoon, although they generally cannot use it properly until age 2 years.

Children with different temperaments will approach feeding and eating differently. An active child may be more interested in the sights, sounds, and other people than food. A quiet child may want to play with the food rather than eat it. Brazelton and Sparrow have given parents advice in assisting their children during meals:

1. Keep mealtimes a sacred time for the family to be together.

2. When the child loses interest in sitting at the table, let the child know the meal is over. No more food until the next meal.

3. Make meals a fun time to be together.

4. No television or promises of dessert to get the child to sit and eat.

5. Let the child feed him- or herself.

6. Let the child help with meals.

7. Have the child's pediatrician check her weight and growth. Ask for supplements if necessary.

8. Don't set meals up as a struggle or the high chair as a prison.[32]

As babies approach age 12 months, they can feed themselves chopped or mashed food and can begin to drink from a cup. Weaning can be a gradual process of replacing nipple feeding with other ways of eating and drinking. Weaning begins as soon as parents introduce solid foods and drinking from a cup. Children will be so involved in these new experiences that they usually do not miss nipple feeding during meals. Breast or bottle often can be reserved for early morning or late at night. As home visitors chat with parents, it remains important for them to track how feeding and eating are developing. When Greg is 9 months old, Janice asks his mother about eating.

Janice: He continues to like to eat and feed himself?

Karyn: Yes! Anything, even though he doesn't have but two teeth. He loves solid food.

Janice: It's important to pay attention to the baby's signals. It'll pay off in the coming months. It's not the teeth that help him chew. It's the jaw. He gets a lot of power from his gums.

Janice continues to initiate conversation about everyday rituals in parenting a baby. In this brief exchange, Janice gives Karyn important developmental information so that Karyn can understand her baby's actions and tune into the meaning of his actions.

Brazelton emphasized that "a rounded diet cannot be the goal for the second year."[33] This is the time during which independence and autonomy are dominant issues; toddlers become sensitive to adult demands about eating. Brazelton suggested that a minimal daily diet during the second and third year should include the following:

*   One pint (16 ounces) of milk or its equivalent in cheese, yogurt, or ice cream
*   Two ounces of protein (e.g., meat, an egg) or cereals fortified with iron
*   One ounce of orange juice or other fresh fruit
*   One multivitamin, which [can] cover for uneaten vegetables[34]

Because autonomy and negativism are normal parts of babies' development, eating times are the setting for toddlers to test newly discovered independence. Parents can expect toddlers to refuse to eat, spit food out, smash their food, or engage in other exploratory or testing behaviors during mealtimes. Home visitors can help parents understand that these new behaviors are normal parts of development and that parents need to be firm. They can assist parents in understanding that when toddlers lose interest in eating, parents should allow their toddlers to leave the table. Parents can tell their child that the meal is over until the next meal and that there are no snacks. Once toddlers learn that there will be no food once they have left the table in the middle of a meal, they will learn appropriate eating behaviors.

Toilet Training   Just as it is the child's task to fall asleep and to decide how much to eat, toilet training is also the child's accomplishment. Like sleeping and eating, the learning process initially involves parent and child working together. Likewise, learning independence is a central part of the toileting process.

Unfortunately, many parents feel pressure to train their toddler early. Grandparents may expect the child to train as early as the parent did and some preschools will not accept 2-year-olds unless they are toilet trained. Sometimes, parents think of their child's early toilet training as a sign of their parental competence. There is no correct age for toilet training; however, most children are not ready until after their second birthday.[35]

Because many parents feel pressure and lack confidence in training their toddler, home visitors can assist by helping parents recognize when their child is really ready for toilet training. Experts agree that there are clear signs of readiness for toilet training. Signs of readiness include when the child

- Is aware of the "need to go" and shows it by facial expression or by telling the parent
- Can express and understand one-word statements, such as "wet," "dry," "potty," and "go"
- Demonstrates imitative behavior
- Dislikes wet or dirty diapers
- Is able to stay dry for at least 2 hours or wakes up dry in the morning or after a nap
- Is able to pull pants up and down
- Is anxious to please the parent
- Has a sense of social "appropriateness"
- Tells the parent he or she is about to urinate
- Asks to use the potty chair or toilet[36]

A child is not ready for toilet training if he or she

- Stands at the toilet but then urinates on the floor
- Doesn't want the diaper taken off at all, screaming and struggling when a parent tries
- Takes off the diaper and then has a bowel movement on the floor
- Struts around with a broad gait and then sits down with a mushy stool in her diaper, appearing not uncomfortable but blissful

- Says "no" if a parent comments that he or she seems ready for a bowel movement
- Shows any resistance whatsoever to using the toilet[37]

Home visitors have an important role in helping parents understand that maturity of the child's gastrointestinal tract and central nervous system is necessary for a young child to be ready for toilet training. This maturity allows the child to know the sensations that come before a bowel movement or urination. Girls often are ready before boys and children with older siblings may learn from them. Any time before age 4 is normal. Children most often gain bowel control before they have bladder control.

All young children need their parents' guidance in toilet training and often home visitors can provide helpful suggestions. Parents need to understand that toilet training takes a long time and accidents are common. One aspect of toilet training is learning a new vocabulary. Home visitors can encourage parents to use whatever words are comfortable to them when they talk to their toddler about body parts and elimination. Portable potties allow young children to have their feet on the floor; also, with a potty, the child does not have to deal with a big, noisy toilet that makes things disappear. It helps young children to see others using the toilet. When they begin the toilet training process, parents can comment in a matter-of-fact manner when they see their child having a bowel movement. Parents can remind their child to use the potty, but it is the child's decision to use it. When the child does produce something, parents can enthusiastically praise their child and can leave it in the potty for their child to take pride in the accomplishment. Home visitors can encourage parents to avoid shaming or pressuring their child. Most young children cooperate because they find pleasure in pleasing their parents and in growing up.

Just as home visitor–parent discussions of feeding and sleeping behavior are important, toilet training is an important recurrent topic of discussion during toddlerhood. Janice and Shelly discussed toileting during Janice's visits when Erin was between 18 and 34 months of age. These discussions illustrate how home visitors can support, affirm, and guide young parents.

Janice and Erin (age 18 months) are rolling Erin's beach ball as Shelly says to Janice, "Erin is interested in the potty, especially since her older cousin is being toilet trained."

Erin says, "Potty" and begins to pull down her pants.

Shelly looks at Janice as she says, "Should I?"

Janice responds, "Sure, if she is interested."

Erin and Shelly go to the bathroom. In the bathroom, Erin says, "Mamma?"

Shelly replies, "Mamma sit down, too."

In a couple moments, Shelly and Erin return to the living room. Erin has her diaper and jeans off, and Shelly is carrying the potty, which she puts on the rug. With a small wad of paper in her hand, Erin sits on the potty.

Shelly tells Janice, "Rob and others say I should train her. I tell them she is not ready."

Janice replies, "Good, but you are potty training because your child is interested. This is all a part of it."

Erin quickly loses interest in the potty and gets up. Shelly puts Erin's diaper and jeans on, and Erin and Janice return to playing ball.

Janice does not introduce the toilet-training topic until the child is 2 years old, the age that Janice thinks is appropriate for beginning the process.

By the time the child is 2 years old, parents have learned that I prepare them for each step. If I bring it up earlier, they'll think it's time to start.

When Shelly initiates the topic, Janice supports her because it is Erin who first had interest in the task.

Janice has just arrived and Erin (age 23 months) has wheeled her doll carriage into the living room and begins showing Janice her dolls. Shelly suggests, "Tell Janice what we have been doing."

Shelly then whispers to Erin, who says, "Potty. I tinkle in the potty." Erin then bends over and puts her hand between her legs to pantomime as she says to Janice, "Wipe and then put it in the potty. Flush. It go—yeah!" Erin claps, and then continues, "Poo-poo, too—baby one and big one, too."

Shelly tells Janice that every single day for a week Erin has used the toilet completely on her own initiative. Shelly states that she had no intention of starting toilet training this early and had not even bought any books about the topic. Recently, Erin was no longer going to the toilet every single day.

Janice responds, "It's great that you are so relaxed about it. Though children need our help, it is the child's decision to use the toilet."

Janice has three visits between Erin's 18th and 23rd months; however, Shelly does not initiate conversation about toilet training. When she does, Janice affirms Shelly's relaxed manner. Just as Janice encourages Shelly to maintain a relaxed manner and take her cues from her daughter, Janice also takes her cues from Shelly when discussing the topic. If Shelly was not relaxed or was pressuring Erin, Janice would initiate the topic. During Janice's next two visits, Shelly briefly talks about toileting.

As Janice picks up her items, she asks Shelly, "Do you have any questions?"

Shelly says, "With regard to potty training, I'm not sure what to do—if it's okay for me to put diapers on Erin or would that be bad to be inconsistent?"

Janice replies, "Consistency is always best, but you need to follow Erin's lead. If she begins wetting, it's appropriate to return to the diapers."

Once again, Janice reminds Shelly that it is her daughter who decides when she will use the potty. When Janice visits the next month (Erin is age 25 months), Erin's father, Rob, also is part of the visit.

Rob: [to Shelly] Did you tell Janice that Erin is almost potty trained?

Shelly: I can't keep track of how often she is dry, and if she does have an acci-
           dent, it's is usually my fault—forgetting before we go out. Most of the
           time, she says it herself.

Janice: That's wonderful.

Shelly: I find we're reusing and reusing diapers. We use diapers when we
           leave the house. Like you suggested, I have been real relaxed.

The previous conversation took place during the last visit before Janice's
3-month summer vacation. When Janice returns in the fall, Shelly gives her an
update on Erin's toilet training.

Shelly: If I would put her on the potty, she would just whine. She has very few
           accidents. I said to Rob, when she wants to go, she'll go. I put a calen-
           dar on the wall in the kitchen. Now, I put up a star when she goes
           potty. I ask her if she wants a star, and she'll say, "Yes," and go to the
           bathroom.

Janice: You're really smart. The decision must be Erin's.

Three months later, Shelly gives Janice another report.

Shelly: Erin [age 34 months] seems to deal well with spontaneity, like if we
           walk into the bathroom and she needs to go potty, it's fine. It works
           much better than when I suggest that we go to the bathroom.

Janice: You are really tuning into her cues. This is another part of her growing
           autonomy, and you know what works, and you use it. You have
           learned what causes confrontations.

Just like the child's learning to walk or talk, toilet training progresses with
stops and starts. Erin is dry for a few days, then she begins having accidents.
Throughout these 7 months, Shelly keeps Janice informed on her daughter's
toilet training. Janice supports and affirms Shelly's approach. Repeatedly, and
in different ways, Janice maintains the theme that toilet training is the child's
task and parents need to remain relaxed. When toddlers experience pressure in
toilet training, they may begin to hold onto their bowel movements. Holding
back can lead to constipation. Any big event, such as a new baby or a family vacation, can bring a regression in toilet training.

Toilet training is another area in which young children need to become
independent at their own speed, and the process can be difficult for parents,
who may think of toilet training as their responsibility. Children often are reluctant to follow their parents' timetable and parents may feel this resistance
points to a failure in their parenting ability. Young children's reluctance may
stem from parental pressure or immaturity of their intestinal tract or central
nervous system. Home visitors can assist parents in this potentially problematic
area by providing developmental information so parents can know what to expect from their child, as well as suggestions, support, and affirmation.

Accidents happen. Accidents occur when a child is under stress, faced with a new demand, or when the child gets so excited in play that he or she fails to notice the bladder's signals. Parents should help the child understand why the accident occurred and reassure the child. If accidents happen frequently in a child who has been toilet trained for some time, there might be a medical cause for the accidents; the parents need to consult the child's pediatrician.

The most difficult aspect of toilet training is staying dry at night. Up to 20% of 5-year-olds and 8% of 6-year-olds are not able to stay dry all night.[38] When a child begins to be evasive or ashamed about his bedwetting, it is time for parents to seek medical help. Only about 10% of children who wet their beds after age 5 years have a medical reason for their bedwetting. Bedwetting is rarely caused by psychological factors; there seems to be a genetic influence. Juvenile diabetes and nocturnal enuresis are also causes for bedwetting.

Some children respond to the pressure to be toilet trained with constipation. The longer a young child goes without having a bowel movement, the larger and harder the stool becomes. As the stool become larger with retention, the child's intestine is stretched and is less able to push it out the bowel. The child's fear is likely to cause further tightening of his anal sphincter, making it even more difficult. Pediatricians can give stool softeners to help a child empty her rectum. At least 10% of young children go through periods of constipation.[39] Increasing fluids, fibrous fruits, vegetables, grains, and activity can help.

Diarrhea can be caused by an infection, such as viral infection. This type of diarrhea lasts a few days and then disappears. Antibiotics, diet, and food allergies also can cause diarrhea. When loose stools continue for a long period, they could be a symptom of a food allergy. When a child has diarrhea, parents need to increase fluids to avoid dehydration and change diapers frequently to avoid skin breakdown.[40]

Age 2–5 Years

Sleep   Two-year-olds usually need one afternoon nap. When parents arrange for their child's nap to end by 2:30 P.M. or 3:00 P.M., the child can be ready for bedtime in the early evening. At this age, many children talk themselves to sleep. Their talk is often a rehearsal of what they have done during the day.[41] Just as many adults go over their day's events in their mind before they fall asleep, many toddlers do the same.

Night fears are common for children 2–4 years of age. Parents should respect their child's fears. Strategies such as leaving the child's bedroom door open, putting a light in the child's bedroom, and extending the bedtime ritual by adding a quiet snack or story often can be helpful. Home visitors can help parents learn that these night fears are normal and that they, as parents, can make sure their child knows they are available for support. Children vary as to when they no longer need naps. Even though a 4- or 5-year-old does not sleep during the afternoon, it can be very helpful if the child has a brief period of rest in the afternoon, such as looking at books or quietly playing with toys on their beds. Most children this age need about 12 hours of sleep every night.[42] The more tired young children are, the more disorganized they are likely to be and the harder they will fight to stay awake.

A soothing bedtime ritual can help the child fall asleep. As preschoolers get older and develop self-care skills, it can be tempting for parents to omit bedtime rituals; however, attention to bedtime rituals remains very important. Preschoolers increasingly encounter new experiences and new people every day; thus they thrive on the predictability and comfort of their special bedtime moments with their parents. Evening story time during preschool also strengthens the child's emerging literacy. Now that bedtime is a little later, parents can add a healthy snack or brief parent–child playtime to the child's bedtime routine. These routines become rituals; ritual continuity provides the young child with a sense of predictability, emotional security, belonging, and shared identity.

Middlemiss investigated severe sleeping problems as waking three or more times a night, waking for more than 20 minutes during the night, taking longer than 20 minutes to settle down for sleep, or going into the parent's bed. Preschoolers' disrupted sleep patterns were found to predict poor adjustment in preschool, even after taking into consideration the role of family stress and inappropriate parenting practices.[43] Regularity of sleep is more important than the amount of sleep. Normal sleep, as well as sleep disorders, can be influenced by the baby's temperament, quality of attachment to parents, physiological state, parental presence during the bedtime routine, and shared sleep arrangements. The United States is one of the few countries that encourages babies to sleep alone, a pattern that was not normative until the 20th century. Benefits associated with shared sleep arrangements include synchronicity of breathing patterns and sleep cycles, increased ease of breastfeeding, and more constant supervision of babies during sleep.[44] At the same time, babies who sleep alone are more likely to learn to self-soothe when they wake up at night.

In families where both parents work and/or when a mother is way from her young baby for extended times during the day, parents may feel that an early-evening bedtime deprives them of "quality time" with their baby. Parents can be reassured that true quality time is when they are changing their baby, bathing, feeding, or playtimes; these interactions are sufficient to meet their baby's needs for socialization. Babies are at their highest level of alertness during morning hours, so parents may want to wake up early enough to have extended time with their baby before they go to work.

Feeding   By age 24 months, most toddlers can use a spoon and a fork, although they occasionally prefer using their fingers. Toddlers usually continue to be messy when eating. Some young children are more sensitive to taste and smell and may react to foods more strongly than others do. Home visitors can reassure parents that it is common for preschoolers to be picky eaters; for example, they may not like things mixed together, such as spaghetti with sauce. Young children are more sensitive to the textures and smells of food than are adults, but they outgrow this sensitivity. If a toddler rejects mixed foods, the parent can substitute something nutritious such as crackers and cheese. Parents' attitudes can make a difference. If parents themselves enjoy cooking and eating and provide a relaxed mealtime, their young children probably will adopt this attitude toward eating. Mealtime then can be a special family time of shared enjoyment—a time in which children know their parents are eager to chat with them and with each other. The predictable ritual of these daily meals nourishes children's emotional security and sense of belonging.

Even if parents are enthusiastic about eating, they may find it difficult to accept their young child's emerging independence and negativism. Some parents believe that they will foster malnutrition if their young child misses a meal. Home visitors can give parents important information regarding their child's need for food. Often, parents need reassurance that if their child ordinarily has a well-balanced diet, missing a meal will not matter. Janice's conversation with Tracy is illustrative.

Janice has just arrived and she and Tracy are chatting. Mia (age 28 months) begins fussing and her mother asks her, "What do you want? Juice?"

Mia says, "I don't want juice!" Tracy and Mia go to the kitchen and return with a small bowl of raisins and cereal.

Janice tells Tracy, "It's good that you give her nutritious snacks. At this age, children often are picky."

"She ate a good breakfast today," Tracy says, "but last night she would not eat dinner."

"How did you feel about it?" Janice asks.

Tracy answers, "I was frustrated. I tried to feed her, but she just didn't want any. So I just let it go. I tried everything."

"Good," Janice says. "It is important to pay attention to the child's natural appetite—knowing on the one hand her behavior, and on the other she is not hungry. If we push, we are denying her own limits. The child should determine how much she eats.

In this discussion, Janice affirms Tracy's parenting. In addition, she gives Tracy developmental information to help her learn the significance of her decision so that she can continue ignoring Mia's pickiness and know that her child will be fine if she misses a meal.

At 4 and 5 years of age, children learn table manners by modeling their elders. It is important for children to develop the rhythm of eating meals when they are hungry, to stop eating when they are full, and to enjoy eating. Home visitors can help parents understand that there are liabilities when they use food for punishment or reward. When food is used as a reward for good behavior, young children learn to connect food with prizes rather than with hunger. When parents withdraw dessert as punishment, they unwittingly teach their child that there is good food and bad food.[45]

Preschoolers enjoy helping their parents prepare meals. When children help cook food, they are sometimes more likely to eat it. When young children help set and clear the table and assist in simple cooking tasks, they are contributing members of the family. In these activities, they get a sense of belonging and pride in their new skills.

Some parents carry *ghosts from the nursery* into their interactions with their children regarding eating.[46] For example, a mother whose own mother always pushed her to eat might do the same for her toddler. Therefore, it is important for parents to reevaluate their own experience as a young child when they get upset about their child's eating behavior. When a parent complains to a home visitor about how stressful mealtime with her child is, the home visitor might discuss this phenomenon.

Our society has an ever-increasing number of working single parents and two-parent working families for whom time is at a premium. With the accessibility of numerous fast-food restaurants, microwaveable dinners, and prepackaged foods, traditional food preparation and leisurely mealtimes may not be a given part of family life. For example, Rolanda and Carl each have high-powered professional jobs. Carl takes their $3\frac{1}{2}$-year-old son, Ben, to his child care at 7:30 A.M. and Rolanda picks Ben up at 5:30 P.M. Ben was 36 months old the first time the family's home visitor, Nina, visited them. Nina initiated a conversation about mealtimes.

Rolanda: Well, in truth, we don't eat together as a family. Carl gets home an hour after Ben and I do, and he uses a couple hours to unwind—reading the paper, exercising on the treadmill, that kind of thing, so Ben and I eat simple meals together shortly after we arrive home. It's a pattern that just developed. We've never discussed it much.

Carl: You know, when we first got married 8 years ago, I used to talk with Rolanda about how special it would be to have family dinners. My own father never returned home from his law office until after 8:00 in the evening, so I grew up without experiencing daily dinners with everyone.

Nina: It sounds like beginning a new pattern of eating together might be worth exploring together. Today, many young working parents are developing a repertoire of simple meals, such as pasta, that they can manage to prepare after a long day at work. And, increasingly, grocery stories have prepared meats, such as rotisserie chicken, at reasonable prices. But, the issue is not the type of food; rather, what is important is that children and their parents daily have time together. Every evening, dinners together can provide this shared time.

Rolanda: Now that I think of it, Carl and I hardly ever eat together. Dinners together would be important for our relationship, too.

Given their high-pressure work, Carl and Rolanda developed a daily pattern that excluded family dinners and never thought much about it. When Nina introduced the topic, they quickly recognized what they and their son were missing. One month later, when Nina returned to visit, Rolanda told Nina that her mother now picks up Ben from his child care on Wednesday and cares for him for several hours. Then, she and Carl can take time to go out to dinner together, a pattern they had maintained for 5 years prior to Ben's birth. Rolanda also explained that she and Carl plan to begin regular dinners with Ben, but this shift is going to take time. Together, Nina and Rolanda brainstormed possible easy meals and ways of preparing some meals during the weekend.

When they talk about eating and mealtimes, home visitors like Nina can help parents understand the developmental significance of good eating habits and family mealtimes. They can talk about how family dinner rituals give each family member a sense of belonging and security. Nina and Rolanda did some problem solving as they discussed possibilities of weekend cooking for weekday dinners and munching on nutritious finger food like carrot sticks and celery with peanut butter instead of making time-consuming salads.

Different people and different families have their own eating habits. For adults, eating often is a social occasion—for example, coffee breaks at work and going out to lunch. Home visitors can assist parents in making family meals social occasions that include their very young children.

FAMILY CELEBRATIONS AND TRADITIONS

Family traditions are regularly occurring events. Some are unique to the family, such as summer vacations and visits with extended families, but others are part of larger religious or national occasions, such as events scheduled for Independence Day, Passover, or Martin Luther King, Jr.'s birthday. Celebrations include rites of passage, such as baptism, bar or bat mitzvahs, weddings, graduations, and religious holidays. They are connected to both the culture and the family's ethnic and religious roots.[47] Celebrations often involve symbols that will be important for the rest of the child's life.

Like everyday rituals, family celebrations and traditions involve predictable, repeated patterns of family interactions. They give family members a sense of shared identity; through celebrations and traditions, family members link past, present, and future. Participating in traditions and celebrations provides connectedness and continuity. Family members feel affirmed and comforted when parts of a holiday celebration are passed on to the next generation. Examples include reading *The Night Before Christmas* on Christmas Eve or attending a block party on Independence Day. Although families differ in the extent to which their traditions and celebrations are child centered or involve people beyond the immediate family, all celebrations and traditions maintain the family's shared beliefs and values.

Some celebrations, such as birthdays and religious holidays, become markers of continuity in a family's life cycle as multiple generations gather together (e.g., great-grandmother attends the baby's first birthday party). Families develop their own style of practicing celebrations. Birthdays can have many important meanings: honoring the aging process, honoring the person who is celebrating his or her birthday, remembering the birth parents, affirming life, or just having fun. Some families go to special restaurants on a birthday or have a treasure hunt for the birthday member to find his or her gifts. Many families remember the birthdays of people who have died or left the family.

Often, giving and receiving are an integral part of rituals. In some families, all gifts are homemade. In other families, all gifts must be wrapped, each member of a family must receive the same number of presents, or a gift must always be a surprise. Rituals of celebration may not be complete without traditional food and drink, music, gifts, or dress.

As children grow and families change over time, birthday celebrations change. Children may become too old for yearly parties with friends. Most family rituals are flexible so that they can adapt to the increasing age and maturity of the children. As home visitors discuss with parents their family's rituals, some parents may discover that they need to think about how they want to keep or change rituals now that their family includes children.

Yearly family vacations are sometimes rituals for families. Families may leave their homes before dawn for long driving trips. Children and parents may play the same games, such as identifying license plates or counting cows. With the increase of both parents working outside the home, vacations often become a special protected time and space for parents and their children. Family members have an increased amount of shared time—playing on the beach together, cooking together, exploring new restaurants together, or playing games together in the evening in a leisurely way—something they may not feel they have time for in their complex lives at home.

In their relationships with parents, home visitors have the opportunity to respect and honor each family's traditions and forms of celebration. Frequently, visits occur close to holiday seasons. Janice's visit during December illustrates this.

Janice arrives at Natalie's home 1 week before Christmas. Dvonne (age 3½ years) greets her at the door and immediately shows her the Christmas tree. His mother, Natalie, suggests that Dvonne tell Janice where they cut down the tree and he tells her they cut it down at a tree farm. Natalie places Jene, Dvonne's little sister, on the rug in front of her. Dvonne excitedly tells Janice what he has asked Santa to bring him for Christmas.

Janice tells him, "We ask Santa for what we think we want, but Santa has surprises, too. Santa also likes to have ideas."

As Janice speaks, Dvonne touches the ornaments and gestures for her to look at them.

Janice says, "You are being very careful with the ornaments, and the needles of the tree still feel sharp, so they can hurt your fingers."

Dvonne affirms, "They feel sharp!"

Janice joins in Dvonne's excitement regarding the forthcoming holiday and engages in an extended conversation with him about his ornaments. By the time this exchange is completed, one-fourth of the home visit time is consumed, but Janice understands that she must address the excitement of holidays before Dvonne can settle down and let her also relate to his mother and baby sister. As Janice relates to Dvonne, she also models extended conversation for Natalie, who smiles as she observes and listens.

Holidays can be stressful for mothers of very young children. Mary is a young mother of two boys: Gary (age 4 years) and Paul (age 17 months). Mary's home visitor, Linnette, has worked with her since her older son was 6 months old, so Linnette understands that Mary tends to become anxious during holidays. When Linnette visits in late November, she tries to assist Mary.

Linnette: It's getting into the Christmas season, a season that can be stressful for kids and for parents. Before decorating or shopping, it might be helpful for you and Stanley to sit down and see if you can make plans to lessen the stress. Other moms have tried things. One mom, she said that decorating the tree is a family thing. She doesn't have a formal meal that night, but puts out healthy finger foods that the kids like. The kids put ornaments on the low branches. Some moms involve the kids in baking cookies. Small kids love to play with cookie dough.

Mary: Our problem is we have 100 things to do. I took the kids to the mall to see Santa. We waited for an hour for him to show up, and then we waited for the picture taking. By the time she flashed, Gary was not smiling and Paul was crying. [By the time Mary had finished her story, she was chuckling.]

Linnette: Lots of time, we put stress upon ourselves. Afterwards, we can laugh about it. It's important to plan.

Mary: Like wrapping. I do it after they are in bed, and I find it a relaxing activity.

Knowing that Mary can let holidays become stressful, Linnette begins a discussion of the forthcoming holiday. She speaks of strategies that other mothers use to help make the holiday a relaxing time for family activities. When home visitors develop a partnership in their relations with parents, they find that using examples of other mothers is a helpful way of giving suggestions. Mary is comfortable enough to share a recent stressful experience; because she knows that she has often shared with Linnette about how she gets stressed, she can distance herself from the experience and can laugh about it. The conversation ends as Mary reports a successful holiday experience. This Christmas will be better for the children because Linnette helped Mary make it better for herself. When Linnette visited Mary and her boys after Christmas, Mary eagerly shared holiday events—those that were pleasant and festive, as well as those that were stressful. Linnette shared that Mary's level of stress has decreased in each of the 3 years that she has visited Mary. Linnette's support, affirmation, and assistance no doubt helped.

For many families, the preparation time of celebrations may be as important as the actual celebration. Mother and father may spend hours together as they bake Christmas cookies or shop for gifts. Young children love assisting in lighting the menorah or decorating their house for the holidays. Celebration preparations become vibrant patterns of relationship between family members. Often, the elders in a family are the prime keepers of key celebration-making components such as recipes, stories, photos, or other family memorabilia.

Just as everyday rituals give young children a sense of connectedness and security, family celebrations and traditions offer each family member a sense of belonging and shared identity—to the family, the extended family, and the larger culture. Home visitors can assist young parents in recognizing and understanding the value of these celebrations and traditions for their child and each family member's development. With very small children, parents may experience these celebrations and traditions as additional tasks that are not easy to orchestrate and add unwanted stress. In these environments, the home visitor can offer needed support and suggestions. Social relatedness between family members and young children provides children with experiences of nurturance and caring. Regularly occurring family celebrations reflect both unique family and cultural beliefs and values. These celebrations provide family members with a sense of belonging and shared identity.

DIFFICULTIES AND DILEMMAS

As home visitors strive to promote young parents' abilities to create and sustain healthy everyday rituals, celebrations, and traditions, they may encounter several difficulties. First, the modern family's functioning may create obstacles to providing predictable everyday rituals. Second, when parents are trying to bridge two family traditions—each containing unique patterns of everyday ritual, celebrations, and traditions—parents may find that the two patterns are not easy to blend. Finally, home visitors may confront family problems that are unique to single parents or to a recently divorced family.

New family structures offer complexities that challenge our society's taken-for-granted notion of family life and threaten parents' ability to develop predictable daily rituals.[48] Home visitors need to be alert to these changes and develop flexibility in assisting parents in exploring new patterns of everyday rituals. As everyday family life in the United States becomes increasingly more complex, it becomes challenging for parents to provide predictable routines for their young children. It is increasingly rare for one parent to be a full-time homemaker. Only 10% of American families consist of two parents with one parent home full time.[49] About half of the children in the United States will spend time in a single-parent home.[50]

It is not uncommon for family members to have different daily schedules (e.g., older children engaged in sports or other after-school events, parents traveling for business). These patterns often lead to disruption of families' daily rituals; for example, regular dinner times disappear as different family members are involved in their own tasks. No longer is shared family time a given. Family members—even spouses—share less and less of a common reality. As the home visitor and parents share in activities and conversations, the home visitor can help parents recognize their young child's need for predictable, daily, shared family rituals. Once parents understand this need, the home visitor and parent can brainstorm strategies to make certain these daily family rituals take place.

Home visitors also need to be alert to the complexities that spouses experience in joining their two family traditions, which not all couples think out thoroughly prior to marriage. Many people get married without realizing the challenge of uniting two different family traditions. Traditions such as celebrating a holiday or summer vacations may or may not be complementary. In addition, given the pluralistic nature of our society, many couples marry across race, ethnicity, and religion. For these couples, rituals take on added meaning because they must blend the traditions of not only two separate childhoods, but also two racial, ethnic, or religious communities. Some interreligious couples may need to made decisions regarding holidays, such as questions of celebrating Chanukah or Christmas. Parents often see their home visitor as a supportive person with whom they can talk through their decision making as they blend two family traditions.

CONCLUSION

This chapter discussed families' everyday rituals and traditional family celebrations. Rituals consist of repeated, predictable patterns of interactions among family members that give each family member shared beliefs and values, a sense of belonging, and identity. For young children, everyday rituals of eating, sleeping, diapering, and toilet training are the settings for developmental growth. Although this discussion of these daily rituals may seem very detailed, it is the detail of parent–child interaction that has an impact on the child's development and sense of self. Initially, daily rituals of eating and going to sleep allow for the child's biological regulation. Intertwined with the interactions in these rituals is regulation of the child's emotion. Development in all areas (e.g., a sense of self, a sense of relatedness, language and communication, and an understanding of the world) occur within parent and child interaction of everyday rituals.

Each of these areas involves the child's accomplishment. It is the child's task to learn to fall asleep, to decide how much to eat, and to use the toilet. As young children learn to feed themselves, put themselves to sleep, and use the toilet, they are developing increased independence. This process of becoming independent is not always even.

As their child grows, parents learn that the different areas of their child's development are intertwined. With increased language and cognitive skill, toddlers can understand and follow directions in eating, sleeping, and toilet-training activities. Because of the emotional bond with his or her parent, the young child is responsive and eager to please. Successes in these everyday rituals are major developmental accomplishments and become a part of the child's identity.

Predictability is central to each of these everyday rituals. Falling asleep becomes a natural part of everyday routine when there is a calm bedtime ritual. When family members regularly come together to eat, eating is enjoyable and the child feels a sense of connectedness. Regular reminders to use the potty become a part of the child's everyday routine until children can recognize their bodily signals for toileting. In time, the preschooler experiences a predictable rhythm—eating when hungry, sleeping when tired, and toileting according to bodily signals. It is not uncommon for everyday rituals to trigger parents' worry, anxiety, and insecurity.

Within everyday rituals, home visitors can provide important support, affirmation, developmental information, and suggestions to help young parents in their important and challenging parenting tasks. When home visitors prepare parents with information regarding what to expect from their growing baby and young child, parents can develop both confidence in their child's development and confidence in their ability to foster this development. As they observe parent and child behavior, home visitors have the opportunity to interpret the developmental meaning of these actions and to support and affirm the parent. When a parent is feeling insecure or perplexed, home visitors' support and information may assist this parent's understanding of both child and self and thereby offer needed assistance.

Children's Illnesses

I was a healthy child, but now and then in winter I would have a sore throat and tonsillitis, so cold baths were decreed as a daily morning routine—and how I cheated on those baths! Madeleine could not always follow me up, and more hot water went into them than would have been considered beneficial had anyone supervised me.

Eleanor Roosevelt (1989)

WHEN YOUNG CHILDREN ARE SICK, they cannot tell their parents what is wrong with them. Between ages 1 and 3 years, children average eight or nine illnesses per year.[1] Illnesses often make new parents feel anxious, even when the illnesses are minor. Parents can be exhausted by the child's increased needs and by their own lack of sleep. Frequent illnesses include colds, nausea and vomiting, and diarrhea, which usually do not require antibiotics or other medicine. Home visitors support and help parents of sick children when they provide clear guidelines. They can explain that illness may cause fussiness, interrupted sleep, and regression, no matter how skilled a parent may be. Furthermore, they can provide information and suggestions. For example, they can tell parents that clear fluids are important to prevent dehydration if a child has a fever or diarrhea.[2]

These common illnesses cause breaks in the family's predictable everyday routines and rituals. From a developmental perspective, home visitors can help parents understand that they will develop important new rituals with their child during the experience of illness. This chapter will outline common illnesses of young children, debilitating illnesses of young children, and strategies that parents of young children can use when their child is ill.

CAREGIVING AS A SOCIAL EXPERIENCE

Parents' care for their sick child is an intense personal and social experience for both parent and child. A child's illness also is an important experience in social relatedness. When sick, the child's sense of self is changed; he or she may not feel happy, energetic, or curious. When the child recovers, the sense of self is restored, but the child now remembers how bad he or she felt and how nurturing the parent was. During children's illnesses, parents' caregiving changes as well. They more readily accept irritability and make fewer demands on the child. They help reduce the child's discomfort and express empathy. Often, the child's illness is contagious, so children may observe as their siblings or parents go through similar experiences of illness, allowing children to learn how to help in caring for someone else. Illness can be the setting for learning compassion, nurturing, and caring. Initially, the ill child experiences increased empathy and caring. When family members then become ill, the child can develop prosocial behavior such as empathy and assisting others.

ILLNESSES AND MEDICAL CONDITIONS

Home visitors can make certain that parents have basic health and safety knowledge and resources; for example, they understand what is a medical emergency that needs immediate attention, they have phone numbers of a physician and of a poison control center near every telephone in the house, and they own a good first-aid guide. Brazelton defined medical emergencies as those occasions when the child is unconscious, has obstructed breathing, or has convulsions.[3] When children have fever or diarrhea, dehydration is a danger. It is common for children younger than age 3 to have high fever because their body's regulatory system is immature. If children have more than six bowel movements in one day or stop urinating, they are becoming dehydrated.[4] Not all new parents know this information; thus, it is important that home visitors explain the dangers of dehydration.

Ear Infections

Middle-ear infections resulting from colds are quite common during infancy and toddlerhood. Fluid in the middle ear and a loss of hearing often accompany middle-ear infections. With frequent ear infections and accompanying hearing loss, a young child may have immature language skills.[5]

Janice is aware that Greg has had several ear infections. Before he was 12 months old, he had outpatient surgery to put tubes in his ears to assist the fluid drainage. Thus, she regularly initiates a discussion with Greg's mother about this topic.

Janice asks, "Has Greg continued to have ear infections?" Karyn nods yes. Janice explains, "When he has had ear infections, his hearing is not as good. If you notice a pattern that he is not responding to you, check with his pediatrician."

Janice proceeds with play activities with Greg and Karyn. Before she leaves, she returns to the earlier topic. "Even a couple of weeks after an ear infection, babies are not hearing as well. With ear infections, we encourage you to keep close track of his hearing. This can have a major impact on his language development."

Because Janice has a strong commitment to relate to parents as partners, she usually is not as directive as she was here with Karyn. With experience, however, Janice has learned that many new parents do not know this information about ear infections, which is crucial for Greg's healthy development.

The Fussy Baby

About one in five babies has colic.[6] Colicky babies are uncomfortable and cry a lot during the first months of life. Most babies' colic dissipates after the first 3 months of life. Usually this colic is considered a benign condition that is a normal developmental process of postnatal adaptation. Brazelton recommends that parents of colicky babies provide a bottle with warm water every 10–15 minutes, which tends to initiate burps and settle the baby.[7] Fussy babies can increase the mother's risk for postpartum depression.[8]

Sensory and behavioral regulatory difficulties underlie the crying of babies with colic and irritability beyond 5–6 months.[9] These babies are hard to console and highly reactive to sensory stimuli. A longitudinal study of 38 children who were colicky at age 4–12 weeks were followed up at 3–8 years of age. Seventy-five percent of these babies demonstrated atypical behavioral responses to sensory experiences. These children had more attention/hyperactivity problems compared with babies who cried less.[10] Studies like this indicate that excessive fussing beyond 5 months of age can be an early marker for babies at risk of later behavior difficulties.

In 2003, the Erikson Institute began the Fussy Baby Network, which provides preventive service, support, assessment, and intervention. Families with a colicky baby reported that they experienced a high degree of stress and physical exhaustion, isolation and criticism, and a loss of sense of self and baby. This program provides a phone network and home visiting to alleviate parents' stress.

Persistent criers often have feeding and/or sleeping disturbances, mild developmental delay, and organic risk factors.[11] Parents of these babies often have substantive psychosocial risk factors, prenatal emotional distress, a high rate of maternal psychopathology, and postnatal parental conflicts.[12] Babies with regulatory disorder often have excessive crying during their first year. Babies with milk allergies also may vomit, have diarrhea, and have a family history of asthma or eczema.[13]

Dental Disease

Early childhood caries (ECC) is a bacterial, infectious disease that is found in mouths of babies and toddlers, especially those living in poor families. When not treated promptly, ECC can become a chronic disease causing intense pain, eating and speaking difficulties, inability to concentrate due to pain, and accompanying learning problems. ECC can be caused by overuse of bottles, family members using the same eating utensils, or poor hygiene such as not washing a dropped pacifier. About one-fifth of preschoolers have untreated dental decay.[14] Poor or no dental care adds to risk factors for dental disease in young children.

Parents can remove bacterial plaque by cleaning the teeth of babies and toddlers once each day, using a washcloth on gums when the child is young and a toothbrush and floss later. Young children should visit a dentist by the age of 1 year and continue to have regular dental care thereafter.

Iron Deficiency

Iron is necessary for normal red blood cell synthesis and is an essential part of brain tissue. Because iron is so vital for many metabolic processes, iron deficiency can cause many adverse effects. Babies and toddlers get iron in their diet from breast milk, iron-fortified formula, and foods such as iron-fortified cereals, animal tissue, beans, and other vegetables.

A 10-year longitudinal study followed babies who were tested for iron deficiency. Children who were free of iron deficiency grew normally. Children who had iron deficiency or iron deficiency anemia had lower verbal and intelligence quotient scores, as well as lower achievement scores in reading, writing, and arithmetic. Not surprisingly, the children at risk for iron deficiency lived amidst many other risks, such as nutritional deficiencies, intellectual and emotional limitations of parents, and risks of violence.[15] Thus, some of the findings of this study might be attributable to risk factors beyond iron deficiency.

Lead Poisoning

Young children seemingly put everything in their mouths, including paint chips that may contain lead. When young children ingest lead, the long-term effects can be very serious, including intellectual disabilities, hyperactivity and reduced attention span, impaired hearing, decreased growth, and learning disabilities. Young children who are poor are at greatest risk for lead poisoning.[16]

Children should be tested for lead at 1 year of age and every year thereafter if the family lives in a home built prior to 1978, when lead paint was commonly used. Home visitors can tell parents that children who eat enough iron and calcium absorb less lead. Foods rich in iron include eggs, beans, and lean red meat; dairy products are high in calcium. Home visitors need to discuss the possibility of lead paint difficulties to parents living in old homes. They also can tell parents about the agencies that handle lead paint issues.[17]

Obesity

Young children who are overweight are at increased risk for lifelong health problems, including high cholesterol levels, diabetes, orthopedic difficulties, and high blood pressure.[18] One of the most devastating consequences of being overweight is psychosocial; young children may develop negative attitudes about their overweight peers.

Increased weight has been found in all ethnic, gender, racial, and age groups. However, obesity occurs most often among poor African American, Native American, and Hispanic children, particularly girls. The prevalence of obesity is greater among Hispanics than any other racial or ethnic group.[19]

The substantive increase in obesity cannot be accounted for by genetic factors. Between 1976 and 2000, the prevalence of overweight children increased from 7% to 12% for 6- to 23-month-olds and from 5% to more than 10% for 2- to 5-year-olds.[20] Today's overweight children are heavier and are becoming obese at younger ages than they were in the past. A baby who is overweight is not at a great risk of being an overweight adult; however, by age 3 years, an overweight child is nearly 8 times as likely to become an overweight adult.[21] Genetic factors related to obesity include metabolism rates, behavioral predispositions to food, eating patterns, and patterns of physical activity.[22]

Obesity is a result of an energy imbalance; that is, intake is greater than expenditure, such as physical activity. Nutrition also is an indicator of weight. Studies indicate that increasing weight among young children is a consequence of decreasing physical activity rather than more consumption of calories. At the same time, fast food also promotes this obesity trend. Between 1971 and 2001, Americans increased their fast-food consumption from $6 billion to $110 billion.[23]

Child feeding practices also contribute to overweight and obesity in young children. Allowing toddlers to graze when they are hungry, drink sugary beverages, and be rewarded with food are problematic practices. Children as young as 2 years of age can learn food preferences from their peers. Food advertisements on television are powerful for young children; children who are obese are more susceptible to food advertisements on television.[24]

Sudden Infant Death Syndrome

Sudden infant death syndrome (SIDS), or "crib death," is the single leading cause of death of babies less than 4 months old.[25] A baby of any race, religion, ethnic, or cultural group can die from SIDS. The syndrome occurs in healthy, typically developing babies during the babies' sleep. The death occurs quickly; because the baby does not cry, the parents do not know it is happening. Babies who seem to be at higher risk for SIDS include

- Babies who sleep on their stomachs
- Babies whose mothers are younger than 20 years of age
- Babies with low birth weight and/or premature babies
- Babies whose mothers smoked during pregnancy[26]

Since the early 1990s, pediatricians have advised parents to put their babies to sleep on their backs until they are old enough to roll over by themselves, usually at around 4 months old.[27] If a baby is at risk, home visitors can suggest that parents ask their pediatrician about using monitors.

Preventable Diseases

Many new parents do not understand the numerous contagious diseases that young children can acquire and that can cause serious long-term disability. Many home visiting programs have a parent handout on preventable diseases. It is important for home visitors to ensure that parents are getting the correct vaccinations and immunizations for their child. If a home visitor works with teen parents, parents who have intellectual disabilities, parents with mental illness, or parents who abuse substances, the home visitor may need to be rather directive to ensure that the children get their vaccinations and immunizations. Immunizations for the following diseases are most common:

- Polio is a viral disease that can cause permanent paralysis. Polio vaccine is commonly given at 2 months, 4 months, 15 months, and 4–6 years. In the United States, polio was an epidemic disease until the late 1950s when a vaccine was developed. Unfortunately, cases of polio still occur because many parents do not immunize their young children.

- Measles can cause respiratory problems, ear problems, and brain damage that can lead to intellectual disabilities.

- Rubella, commonly called German measles, is a mild infection in children. However, if a pregnant woman becomes infected, it can cause miscarriage, stillbirth, and severe birth defects.

- Mumps is characterized by painful swelling around the jaw and can lead to other complications such as deafness, central nervous system damage, and kidney inflammation.

- Diphtheria is a bacterial infection that can cause pneumonia, heart failure, and nerve damage.

- Whooping cough is a respiratory infection that can cause pneumonia, brain damage, and death. It is especially dangerous to babies less than 1 year of age.

- Tetanus is a noncontagious disease caused by germs found in the soil. It often enters the body through wounds. Tetanus can cause muscle spasms, severe nervous system damage, and death. Individuals should be immunized for tetanus every 10 years.

- Chicken pox is a contagious infection. Symptoms include a fever and an itchy, blister-like rash that can cover most of the body.

- Hepatitis B virus is an inflammation of the liver caused by toxic agents in the body. The vaccine is commonly given at birth, 2 months, and 6 months of age.[28]

Please check The American Academy of Pediatrics web site (http://www.aap.org) or another reliable source for updates.

Asthma and Allergies

Asthma is a chronic disease of the bronchial tubes of the lungs; the airways are inflamed during an asthmatic attack. In the United States, the diagnosis of asthma has increased by 75% over the past 25 years and 160% among preschool-age children.[29] Poor and African American children are twice as likely to have asthma.[30] A young child is at risk for developing asthma if a parent has asthma, the child has a history of eczema, and/or the child has allergies to dust mites, pets, cockroaches, or mold. Indoor air environments have a greater risk than outdoor environments. Current evidence indicates that medical assistance during a child's early years can reduce later disease.

Parents need to watch carefully for possible allergies in their young children. If asthma or eczema begin, parents need immediate help from their doctor. If these conditions are allowed to escalate, young children feel helpless and anxious, which can increase the severity of their illnesses.

If a young child's cold extends beyond 2–3 weeks and congestion seems endless, the cold infection may have developed into an allergic reaction.[31] Over the past few months, when Janice has visited Tracy, Maggie, her toddler, has been congested. Janice helps Tracy understand the possibility of allergies.

Janice asks Tracy if Maggie (age 19 months) has a cold or if it seems to be allergies. Maggie had clear nasal drainage this morning and her chest seems quite congested.

Tracy answers, "Maggie has had a cold for a little over 3 weeks."

"The allergy count has been very high this spring," Janice explains. "It might be helpful to ask the pediatrician about the possibility of Maggie having allergies."

"I never really thought about allergies," Tracy admits.

Janice then explains that when one of her sons was quite young, he had allergic reactions in the spring. Tracy replies that she will ask the doctor and will watch if being outdoors triggers Maggie's congestion. Janice then initiates play activities with Maggie and her old sister, Mia.

Before leaving, Janice initiates a conversation about using a cold water vaporizer to help Maggie's breathing. Tracy replies that occasionally she uses one to help Maggie's congestion.

Janice says, "My son's pediatrician warned me that the cold water vaporizer builds up mold, which was one of the things Tom was allergic to. If Tom had a cold, the allergies would kick in, and he would have an allergic reaction."

During this visit, Janice gave Tracy new information on allergic reactions. The younger the child is, the more successful allergy treatment can be. Once Maggie's allergies were confirmed, Tracy took preventative steps. She eliminated stuffed animals, feather pillows, and throw rugs in Maggie's room. She turned on the air conditioner more often, which protected Maggie from some of the airborne allergens. She also began using antihistamines so that Maggie's breathing would not get obstructed. These steps prevented Maggie from having more symptoms.

Nutritional Deficiencies

Early fetal malnutrition may increase the risk for later development of mental disorders. The timing and duration of malnutrition is very important. Prenatal malnutrition increases the risk for developing internal discord, such as mood disorders and schizophrenia. Children malnourished at 3 years of age have intellectual and verbal cognitive deficits; they continue to have these deficits at age 11 years. Anemia at age 3 years of age is significantly related to low cognitive performance.[32]

Prematurity

Physicians consider a baby born before the 36th week of pregnancy to be premature. In the United States, approximately 1.1% of babies are born prematurely.[33] These babies are often at least 8 weeks premature and usually stay in the hospital until their expected date of birth. Because of the technological improvements and skilled care in neonatal intensive care units, babies born at the 24th to 28th week of pregnancy may survive. Babies born very early, however, may have chronic medical problems that involve the brain and lungs, poorly developed motor skills, and delayed development.

Magnetic resonance imaging studies indicate brain abnormalities in over half of preterm babies.[34] The most severe brain abnormalities occur during the first months of fetal development.[35] For the first 4–6 months, premature babies may have feeding and sleeping difficulties. They frequently are irritable and have difficulty calming themselves. Babies with birth weights of less than 5 pounds may have learning problems such as language and verbal deficits and memory; cerebral palsy; and impairments in sight, hearing, and lung functions. They also are at increased risk of having emotional, behavioral (e.g., hyperactivity and inattention), and temperamental difficulties. Premature babies with no serious physiological abnormality usually are discharged from the hospital when they weigh 4–5 pounds, with gestational ages of 37–40 weeks.[36]

Physicians and parents may not know why a baby is born prematurely, so some mothers feel guilty and blame themselves. Some women with excellent prenatal care have premature babies. However, there are contributing factors to prematurity:

- Toxemia and/or high blood pressure
- Multiple births, such as twins and triplets
- Poor nutrition

- Use of alcohol, tobacco, or other drugs, especially cocaine
- Inadequate prenatal care
- Prior abortions or miscarriages
- Frequent urinary infections[37]

Good maternal health during pregnancy is critical to the health of the fetus, although even the best care cannot guarantee a successful outcome. Healthy prenatal care includes a balanced diet; avoidance of excessive stress, tobacco, alcohol, and other drugs; and a reasonable amount of exercise. During the last 3 months of pregnancy, the fetus gains weight, completes the maturation of organ systems, and develops early responses to sensory stimuli. Because increased neurological development takes place between 24 and 40 weeks of gestation, immature neurological functioning is common among premature babies.[38] As a result, the baby's heart rate, temperature, muscle tone, and ability to process sensory input may be affected.

Some parents may feel anger, grief, or shame because they did not have the perfect baby that they expected. Some parents may become overprotective because of their babies' initial health problems. Mothers of premature babies may show anxiety and low self-confidence in their caregiving competence during the baby's first year of life.[39]

During early home visits with families of premature babies, home visitors can encourage parents to talk about their fears, confusions, or worries. Often, parents have not had the opportunity to share these concerns with another person. A home visitor can invite parents to talk about their baby's prematurity and any lingering questions or concerns they may have. For parents to focus on their baby and promote development, the parents' needs first must be met.

Because premature babies can be easily overstimulated, home visitors can assist parents in reading the language of their baby's behavior to learn what amount of stimulation their baby can tolerate. Because premature babies initially do not give a lot of positive feedback to their parents, some parents can feel that they are not being effective parents. They often need extra support, encouragement, and acknowledgment of their efforts. Home visitors can reassure parents by reminding them that their baby's age is better reflected by his or her due date instead of the delivery date. When home visitors comment positively on the baby's growth and changing behaviors, parents are encouraged and can become more relaxed. In addition, some home visiting programs develop support groups of parents who have had similar experiences with their premature babies.

DEVELOPMENTAL IMPORTANCE OF ILLNESS

New parents, especially parents who find their child's illness a major intrusion in their already complex lives, may not understand the developmental importance of their child's frequent illnesses. Working parents also feel the pull of conflicting demands when their child is sick (e.g., "Do I earn a living or care for my child?"). Home visitors can offer developmental information and suggestions to help parents manage their child's illness as a natural part of growth and development—an experience that provides the child with significant learning about self and others, as well as development of prosocial behavior. In addition, the visitor can be aware of and sensitive to the parents' feelings and concerns, such as feelings of inadequacy in the face of illness, fear of their baby's fragility, or anger over the intrusiveness of this illness.

Times when young children are sick are intense interpersonal periods for both parent and child. Children's illness is a time that can test parents' sense of competence and children's sense of security. However, when parents successfully nurse their child through illness, they gain a sense of competence and the child gains an increased sense of being cared for in a safe world.

SERIOUS ILLNESS

Home visitors and extended family members tend to calm parents' fears when a child runs a high fever, is congested, or has an infection. However, some illnesses are serious, have long-term consequences, and may end with the child's death. The effects of serious illnesses, including death, ripple through the whole family system and affect every member, including children born after the serious illness.

Babies who are born very prematurely begin life precariously close to death. The effects of prematurity, as well as the effects of some of the treatments, may lead to chronic illness. Life-threatening conditions include childhood cancers, birth defects, and heart dysfunction.

Serious illness changes a family's priorities, daily routine, and financial situation. Their relationships with extended family change as they begin extended intensive and extensive interactions with medical, social service, and support networks. A seriously ill child changes parents' interactions with each other and with their other children; siblings' interactions with each other and with the ill child may also change.

Janice has been visiting the Henry family since their 3-year-old daughter's birth. The daughter, Amelia, was born with a malformed heart. She is fragile and is often out of breath after any normal exercise. Within a few moments after Amelia was born, surgery was performed on her heart to keep her alive. The pediatrician told Amelia's parents that over the next 6 or 7 years, Amelia would require several more surgeries. While the pediatrician offered these parents hope that some children with this condition have lived to adulthood and had productive lives, she also has been realistic in mentioning that some children with this condition die.

Amelia has a 7-year-old sister. Prior to her birth, Amelia's mother was working outside the home; she now stays home. This lack of employment has lessened family income and has caused financial distress. Amelia's father had worked very hard to free himself from his own overbearing parents; therefore, he finds it difficult to accept the fact that he now must rely on his parents for continued financial assistance. Being home full time, Amelia's mother is totally consumed by her daughter's care. The father, now sole support of the family, finds that to remain productive at work, he must put aside his feelings and focus on the task at hand. Although Amelia's mother understands this intellectually, she feels that her husband is distant and emotionally unavailable at a time when she needs him most.

The social service department at the hospital sponsors a group of parents whose children have conditions similar to that of Amelia. For Amelia's mother, this group feels like a new family. Amelia's father is pleased with his wife's new relationships and support; he also likes the time with the other fathers, when he can share what his life is like. The hospital social worker keeps in touch with Amelia's mother at least once a week when she does not have to take her daughter to the hospital.

In her family assessment, Janice thinks that the family is doing as well with Amelia's condition as she could hope. However, she is concerned that Amelia's sister, Amy, is often left on her own and has lost the intimate parenting that she once had.

Janice needs to decide what tasks are her job—what has not been picked up by the support network. Her first concern is the older sibling. However, she is also concerned about the one-dimensional life of Amelia's mother. Janice also wants to learn what new forms of assistance she can give this family. Janice has helped Amelia's mother schedule playtimes for Amy, and she has adapted the materials she brings into the home to meet Amelia's limitations. Janice's administrator suggests that she meet with the hospital social worker to coordinate their help with this family.

Many home visitors go into the field because of the joy they experience relating to normal young children and their families. Therefore, it may be difficult to experience the reality of a child's serious illness, especially if a child's health deteriorates and the child dies. In these cases, just as the hospital staff has support services for social workers, the agency should have a rigorous, empathic support system for the home visitor.

DIFFICULTIES AND DILEMMAS

When home visitors work with families with multiple problems, they need to watch for signs of poor growth and development in young babies and toddlers. These signs may be evidence of failure to thrive (FTT) syndrome, in which children have growth and development deficiencies.[40] FTT occurs by 2 years of age, most often in children less than 6 months of age. In addition to failing to gain weight, these babies often have disrupted social-emotional development, delayed psychomotor development, and developmental disabilities. Research has shown that malnourishment, especially during the first 6 months, can cause permanent brain damage. Babies hospitalized during their first year of life for

Table 9.1.   Guidelines for effective communication with parents of young children with failure to thrive (FTT)

---

1. Some parents will not express concern about their child's growth when this child is diagnosed with FTT. Communicating sensitivity to parents' sense of competence while helping parents recognize the needs of their child with FTT requires sensitivity and careful balancing of information.
2. Taking time to learn parents' views of their child's condition is central to parents' trust of the professional.
3. Professionals should expect that many parents will give a medical explanation for their child's failure to gain weight.
4. Professionals should expect that some parents will disagree with the medical diagnosis of FTT, especially when they see their toddler running and climbing.
5. It can be very helpful to focus on the future when discussing the child's condition with the parent. That is, parents can feel supported when a primary focus is how they can improve their child's growth and development.

From Sturm, L., & Drotar, D. (1992). Communication strategies for working with parents of infants who fail to thrive. *Zero to Three, 12*(5), 25–28; adapted by permission.

FTT are likely to be cognitively delayed during later years.[41] Given the individual differences and fluidity of baby development, recognizing FTT is one of the most important responsibilities of home visitors.

People often see weight gain as concrete evidence of good parenting. When their baby or toddler is diagnosed with FTT, parents often respond defensively. No parent wants to hear from others or admit to themselves that they are inadequate parents. Given this pattern, home visitors need to be sensitive when they work with parents of children with FTT. Table 9.1 provides several guidelines for effective communication with parents of young children with FTT.[42]

Many families have no health insurance, which may cause delayed access to a physician, an inability to get medications, and lack of continuity in medical care. In addition, parents of a chronically ill child may be exhausted. In these situations, the home visitor or hospital may need to find respite care for the parents.

CONCLUSION

It is inevitable that babies and young children will become ill. This illness will disrupt a family's daily routine. However, most illnesses last only several days. During that time, parents and older siblings provide loving care to the ill child, who in turn learns new skills in caring.

Some illnesses, however, are serious, debilitating, life threatening, or chronic. In each of these cases, parents have to make major adjustments in personal and family lives. The home visitor should help the parents with the normal developmental tasks of siblings, as well as support the family as they work through the changes needed because of their child's condition.

Siblings

I was the eldest of five children. But I have very few memories of my early childhood in which my brother does not play a part. I remember my second birthday party and I remember spoiling my new red shoes by going out in the snow that winter. Then in spring Richard was born, and very soon Margaret and Richard were expected to do everything together.

We used to have our supper together, wearing white nightclothes (with feet) and eating cereal or, on Sunday night, brownies made of dried remains of Saturday's Boston brown bread and baked beans soaked in hot milk. We were taught to sing the same songs together until it became obvious that while Richard's voice was true and clear, I had no voice at all.

Margaret Mead (1972, p. 61)

RELATIONSHIPS WITH SIBLINGS OFTEN ENDURE LONGER than any other. The sibling bond generates feelings of intimacy, support, and belonging. People attest to the strength of the sibling bond by using the terms *brother* and *sister* in religious groups, sororities, fraternities, unions, and service clubs. The childhood history siblings share allows them to understand one another's strengths and vulnerabilities more fully than they can other people. Older siblings often act as tutors to young children, teaching them games, skills, and what to expect at school. Within this shared history, siblings can provide a lifelong support system, are a source of honest feedback, and can share responsibilities for the care of sick and aging parents.

Siblings differ markedly from early infancy through adolescence. Factors influencing sibling relationships include birth order, gender of siblings, age gap between siblings, personality characteristics of the children, the quality of relationships within the family, and risk factors within the family. Children with secure attachments to their parents are more likely to have positive sibling relationships.[1]

Studies indicate that siblings exert developmental influence on each other. Younger siblings are often more influenced by their older siblings' behavior than vice versa. The most aggressive children have both high levels of sibling conflict and rejecting parent–child relationships.[2]

Siblings can be an important source of support to children facing stressful experiences, such as parental conflict or separation. The sibling bond, however, also contains rivalry and conflict. Although quarrels between siblings are normal, many children in the same family actually spend a large portion of their childhood playing and positively relating with each other. Research indicates that children as young as 3 years old can skillfully understand their younger siblings' actions and feelings and can adapt their speaking to accommodate their younger sibling's developmental level.[3]

Once parents have a second child, they encounter unexpected new experiences that can challenge their sense of competence as parents, change their image of family life, and evoke memories of their own childhood struggles.[4] This chapter discusses themes that emerge in families with children, including

1. Preparation for a new infant
2. Parental expectations and comparisons
3. Valuing different children
4. Sibling relationships
5. Discipline
6. Large families
7. Only children

NEW CHILDREN

Sometimes, parents worry that if they have another child, the older child will suffer because the new baby will distract them from their relationship with the older child. These feelings are strongest before the birth of the second child because the first child has had the parents' exclusive attention. Not surprisingly, the first child may resent the sibling's intrusion and may fear parents' loss of love more than middle children.[5] However, adjusting to a new sibling also offers new learning opportunities.

Brazelton stated that there is no ideal time for having a second child. He claimed that once parents "can handle another, the first child can handle one, too."[6] In contrast, White stressed that the ideal spacing of children is a minimum of 3 years because rivalry and resentment are more problematic for first children younger than 3 years old.[7]

Preparation for the New Infant

The addition of a new child to the family brings significant changes in the older children's everyday life, changes that begin in the months leading up to the birth of the child. It is normal for pregnant women to turn inward and subtly withdraw from their family. Older children notice these changes. Thus, it is helpful for parents to discuss the baby's pending arrival, beginning in early pregnancy, as if the pregnancy were a natural event in the family's development.

Home visitors can offer parents needed support and guidance during this important transition period of family life. As they help parents prepare their first child for the arrival of the new baby, home visitors can also help parents realize that their concerns are normal. The following conversation between Janice and Shelly is illustrative. Shelly is in her second month of pregnancy. She tells Janice that her daughter, Erin (age 32 months), thinks she is having the baby.

Shelly: Erin says, "I'm going to have one and you, too, but not Daddy. He doesn't have milk."

Janice: Erin wants to be like you.

Shelly: I'm concerned because she is with me so much. I'm getting Rob to do more with her, like wash her hair.

Janice: You are going to see her really growing up in the next several months—around 3 years.

Shelly: Everybody tells me we're going to have so many problems when there's a new baby.

Janice: It's always an adjustment, and it's always hardest with the first child. The second child is used to sharing attention when another child comes.

Shelly: We've never even spent a night away from Erin.

Janice: My three children are just about the same distance apart. I remember how well my first was able to entertain himself. Erin also is very skilled at that.

Shelly: Now, I think I'll be more worried than Erin. Erin probably will be fine.

Janice: As long as you know there's an adjustment—that nothing is wrong. As long as you are really sensitive to what she is needing. You and Rob are wonderful parents, and you'll continue to be. We'll talk about it more.

Shelly: It's hard to imagine having another one, hard to think it's possible that you can split the time and have the same feelings for the second one.

Janice: You'll experience a whole range of new feelings. I can't even describe the excitement of seeing the two children together. You'll wonder at it—at Erin's sensitivity and at the baby's response.

In the 32 months that Janice and Shelly have known each other, they have developed a close personal relationship. Shelly feels comfortable sharing her worries with Janice. In turn, Janice offers reassurance: she reminds Shelly of her daughter's strengths and that Erin will develop new skills in the coming months. She compares Erin's strength to that of the oldest of her own three children and thereby lets Shelly know that she has had similar experiences. Janice is able to interpret the meaning of Erin's behavior. She acknowledges that the new baby will be an adjustment for all family members; at the same time, she affirms Shelly and her husband's parenting skills. Two months after the previous conversation took place, Shelly shares with Janice what she has learned when she attended two parent meetings that focused on siblings.

Shelly reports that Rob has arranged time for activities just for Erin and himself, and she sees them becoming much closer. Shelly describes her plans for rearranging the space in their small home.

Janice replies, "A lot will fall into place. Probably you're better off to let Erin have the same space that she is used to. So much else will be new for her."

As the months progress, Shelly tells Janice about the plans she and Rob are making together and about how they are involving Erin in preparations for the new baby. Over time, Shelly shows more confidence in both Erin's and her own ability to adjust to the birth of her new baby. Janice's visits have offered needed support, reassurance, and guidance during this significant transition in the family's everyday life.

Birth of the New Infant

Older children go through many changes in their moment-to-moment experiences with the arrival of a new sibling. It is normal for children to feel a large sense of loss once the new baby is born. As discussed previously, the birth of a new baby sparks older siblings' fear of losing their parents' love. Parents often expect more grown-up behavior, yet they find that suddenly their older child begins acting in babyish ways (e.g., suddenly asking for a bottle, having toileting accidents). Home visitors can reassure parents that it is normal for their older child to regress[8] and suggest possible new patterns of family life in which the older child can participate. For example, parents can create ways in which their older child helps with baby care. Home visitors can call attention to the skills the older child has but that the baby does not; in doing so, they affirm the older child. Home visitors also can help parents reassure the older child of their love by setting aside a few moments each day for alone time with only the older child. Just as they helped parents know what to expect with their first child, home visitors can give information regarding expectations of older siblings' behavior. Janice illustrates this in her conversation with Natalie. Natalie's 3-month-old, Jene, has just fallen asleep in Natalie's arms while Dvonne (age 3½ years) is playing in the backyard.

Natalie: Now [Dvonne] is doing very well. It's helpful that he can enjoy playing outside without me.

Janice: It's nice that he feels that way about his new sister. It indicates what a close relationship you two have. His ability to go play outdoors by himself says good things about your relationship with him. And Dvonne still is in a period of adjustment. His life has changed dramatically and will continue to change, like when she becomes mobile. And he'll sense she is getting more attention because of her doing new things, and how [he has] to adjust again and again.

The first few months can be a relatively easy adjustment period for the older sibling because the new infant sleeps a great deal.[9] Janice is helping Natalie understand that, as her daughter matures, Dvonne will begin to experience more intrusion from his sibling. At the same time, Janice gives a clear affirmation to Natalie regarding her role in her son's healthy adjustment and independence.

In her relationships with older children, Janice repeatedly affirms the first child in relation to the younger sibling. For example, when Maggie began crawling at age 8 months, Janice told Maggie's 26-month-old sister, Mia, "Look at Maggie crawl! Did you show her how to do that? I bet you showed her all you could do, and she thought, `Look at my big sister.'" When Dvonne's 4-month-old sister began fussing, Janice said, "Your sister is saying, `I want to play with you.'" Home visitors often bring special toys for the older child. When Janice begins visiting Marta's second child, Brianna, she brings Brianna's 3-year-old brother, Antoine, a wooden train set. As Janice and Marta chat with Brianna on the floor in the living room, Antoine puts together the train set in the adjoining kitchen. When Antoine joins Janice and Marta, Janice affirms him (e.g., "Only Antoine can play with tiny things because Antoine is old enough to understand. Brianna is still too little").

When another child is born, home visitors usually try to divide their attention between the children. If the home visitor has been working with the family since the first child's infancy, the parents have been exposed to the developmental information on infancy. Often, parents maintain their focus on the oldest child because the behaviors of the oldest child are new to the parent. It can be challenging for home visitors to reintroduce infant material in a meaningful and nonrepetitious manner. Sometimes, home visitors can interpret the infants' behavior for the older sibling. Then, the home visitor is both involving the older sibling in the home visit and still providing information for the parent.

When Janice arrives at Tracey's home, Maggie (age 8 months) is a bit uneasy. Janice explains to Mia (age 26 months), "Maggie knows, `Someone strange is in my house.' When Janice and Carol come, Maggie is not sure yet—they are not Mia, Mommy, or Daddy. She knows she loves Mia, Mommy, and Daddy. She's not sure of those new people."

Janice makes sure that she involves the older sibling, Mia, in the home visit and provides information for Tracy, the girls' mother.

PARENTAL EXPECTATIONS AND COMPARISONS

Every parent has images of what or how they would like their child to be. These images are central to parents' expectations. Parental expectations can be powerful influences on both the parent's and the child's behavior.[10] After the birth of a new baby, parents may expect competency from their oldest child, but they find the child is acting like a baby. When their older child behaves immaturely, parents may respond in anger. This anger is not a response simply to their child but to the difference between unstated expectations and the child's action. When home visitors help parents vocalize their expectations, parents often realize that they are being unrealistic.

Parents unwittingly have different expectations for each of their children.[11] These expectations stem from factors that are unique for different children and parents. For example, more is expected from first children and from sons.[12] Sometimes, the first child sets the standard for younger siblings. Although the second child develops differently, parents may set their expectations according to the development of their first child. When parental expectations are not met, parents may feel overwhelmed and inadequate and the child may sense these feelings. Shelly's comments to her home visitor are illustrative.

Shelly: I remember the parent meetings on siblings and the leader saying that the first-born always knows the rules. We would never let Erin get by with what her younger brother does.

Janice: And she wouldn't try.

Like many young parents, Shelly allows her second child to misbehave more than she had allowed her first.

It is normal for parents to compare their children. As parents make these comparisons in conversations with home visitors, home visitors can let them know that their comparisons and accompanying feelings are normal. Even though all children progress through similar developmental phases, the timing and speed of development varies for each child. Similarly, each child has a different personality and temperament; home visitors can assist parents in understanding that their children are more different than they are alike. Talking about these differences is natural, but comparisons become problematic when they are judgmental—that is, when one child is deemed good or bad compared to the sibling.

Often, the home visitor can make an interpretive comment to help parents to understand their children's behavior and development.

Natalie: When Jene [age 3 months] is in her crib, I hear her making noises as she sucks her fists.

Janice: How wonderful—by herself. The best possible way.

Natalie: Dvonne needed the pacifier to drop off to sleep, and he'd cry whenever it fell out of his mouth. He still needs his pacifier when going to bed.

Janice: She doesn't need it, for she can calm herself without it.

Natalie: She's such a good baby. Dvonne didn't sleep through the night until he was 3.

Janice: Each child is born with a different temperament; that is, different babies have different manners of sleeping, different levels of activity, and different ways of responding to their parents. It seems as if your children each have a different temperament.

Natalie: That's helpful. I keep talking of Jene being a good baby, but I don't mean that Dvonne is bad.

As Natalie spontaneously compared her two children, she unwittingly thought of her second baby as the "good" baby in contrast to Dvonne. She might unintentionally communicate these judgments to Dvonne. Janice introduces the idea that each infant is born with a unique temperament that is expressed in different ways of relating to others and different levels of activity. Therefore, Natalie begins to understand that her children's differences are not a matter of good versus bad.

When Janice returns home after the visit, she writes a note on the home visit form to remember to continue the comparison topic on future visits to make certain that Natalie understands temperament and comparisons. As the months progress, Natalie continues to make comparisons of her children, but in a new manner. She compares Jene and Dvonne in a nonjudgmental way. For example, when Jene is 6 months old, Natalie describes how Dvonne, when a baby, seemed to manage well when different people beyond his parents were present; however, Jene seems to need to have her mother at her side. In response, Janice is able to explain that this is the age when infants learn to be very aware of different people who are not their parents and she notes that every child follows a different path in relating to others.

VALUING DIFFERENT CHILDREN

Studies provide convincing evidence that siblings not only are different from each other, but also do not experience the same family life in the same way.[13] Faber and Mazlish noted that although it is natural for parents to strive to treat their children equally, in reality, parents unwittingly treat each of their children quite differently.[14] Children are sensitive not only to how their parents treat them, but also to how their parents treat their siblings.[15] Studies indicate that there is no straightforward relationship between a child's birth order and how the child is treated by parents or siblings.[16] In reality, siblings do not need to be treated equally by their parents.[17] Rather, each child needs to feel that parents treat him or her uniquely—that their parents value each child as special.

McGuire and Roch-Levecq examined whether mother treated their infant twins differently. Families were studied at 14, 20, 24, and 36 months after birth of the twins. Mothers reported differential attention, discipline, and affection, even as early as 14 months. In addition, mothers of identical twins were more likely to treat the pair as a unit, whereas mothers of fraternal twins were more likely to differentiate between the children. The researchers note that children's characteristics may influence parents' affection and control differently across development.[18]

As home visitors help parents to be good observers of their children and to gain information on the meaning of their children's actions and development, they play an important role in assisting parents to recognize the specialness of each child. When home visitors are relating to the older sibling, they often can model for the parent ways to affirm the older sibling in relation to their younger sibling. For example, they can invite the older child to give the younger one a toy. The following excerpts from Janice's home visits are illustrative.

As Mia (age 21 months) plays at the side of her mother, Tracy, Janice and Tracy discuss Mia's increased vocabulary and ability to express her needs verbally. Janice comments to Mia, "You're teaching Maggie [age 3 months] to talk, too—all those good sounds."

Janice has put on the floor two 10-inch-high cylindrical canisters, each with a circular hole on the lid. Janice empties one canister and dumps out an array of small film cans. Maggie (age 12 months) takes a canister and immediately puts it in her mouth. Mia (age 30 months) skillfully puts the film cans into the canister's circular hole. Janice says to her, "It helps Maggie to learn when you play with what she does. Good, right there in the hole of the can. And Maggie is watching everything you do." Mia smiles proudly as she continues the task.

Janice's comments help Mia feel special. When Janice praises Mia's ability to do things better than Maggie, she helps to counteract Mia's inevitable ambivalent or jealous feelings. As Tracy observes the way Janice helps Mia feel good and how Mia really helps her baby sister learn, Tracy learns to affirm Mia in a more powerful way than she would have if Janice had just made a verbal suggestion. Tracy has not only a clear example but also the concrete results to observe: Maggie's delight.

Tracy spoke to the author about the pleasure she gets when she observes Janice and her children.

Tracy: I like the fact that when she does come into my home, she directly interacts with the kids, rather than just sitting down and just talking to me.

Carol: What part of the home visit do you find most enjoyable?

Tracy: Actually, just watching how my kids respond to what Janice is asking them to do. It's exciting to see that they can do what she asks them to do... and every time Janice leaves, she tells me, "You are doing a wonderful job." And it makes me feel real good for somebody to come and tell me I am doing so good, and my kids are developing so good.

Mia was born 2 years after Tracy and her husband graduated from high school. Janice's ability to involve Tracy's children in play activities and to discuss how their behavior points to their development helps this young mother recognize her children's strengths. She can believe Janice's verbal praise of her children because she has repeatedly observed her children succeed with Janice; these repeated experiences allow Tracy to integrate Janice's verbal praise of Tracy as a mother.

SIBLING RELATIONSHIPS

Siblings need to deal with differences in their temperaments as they learn to get along. A shy 4-year-old may tolerate her older brother's teasing and may need help from her parent to learn to protest. Similarly, the parent needs to redirect the boisterous son to protect his shy younger sister.

Fighting among siblings is normal. Although some parents focus on the fighting, most siblings also spend a lot of time playing together and interacting with each other in many different ways. For example, siblings may do family chores together, walk to school together, join in games with neighborhood friends together, and simply play with each other for hours without fighting. In their hours together, siblings experience a wide range of feelings, both positive and negative. They experience shared interest, affection, caring, and nurturance, as well as jealousy, irritation, control, conflict, and rivalry. The sibling relationship changes as the children's developmental levels change—as each child is able to both enjoy and be frustrated by a sibling in new ways.

Each sibling relationship is unique to each child.[19] That is, each child may experience his or her relationship to a brother or sister quite differently than does the brother or sister. For example, a younger child may view her sister as a good friend with whom she loves to play, whereas the older sister may view the little one as bothersome and intrusive.

The age and developmental level of children is a big factor in the ease with which siblings interact with each other. The most psychologically dangerous period is toddlerhood because when a sibling is born, the toddler is at the age where fear of losing parents' love and being replaced is most upsetting.[20] A 3- to 6-year-old can better understand parents' explanations about the new baby and is more skilled at maintaining focus on play and playing alone. When the youngest child is a toddler, the toddler frequently disrupts the older sibling's play because exploring is the toddler's natural way of relating to the world. Usually, toddlers do not understand their intrusiveness. Because older children can better understand their parents, parents may expect them to be more generous with their younger sibling than is fair or developmentally appropriate. In this case, home visitors can make sure that the parents understand what they are expecting of each child and can help the parent to test whether the expectations are realistic.

Personality and temperament also influence the ways in which siblings interact with each other. An older child's temperamental style and personality influence the child's ability to accept a new baby and later affects how he or she responds to a toddler sibling's intrusions. For example, an even-tempered toddler can be more accepting and patient than a more active, easily frustrated toddler.

As parents respond to their children's sibling rivalry, *ghosts from the nursery*—a parent's strong feeling that stems from their own childhood[21]—may again emerge. Parents need to be aware how old memories may influence their reactions to their child.

Home visitors can assist parents in helping their children get along in many different ways. As previously discussed, Janice modeled affirmations of the older child's skill level in contrast to the younger sibling and in giving the older child small tasks to help her younger sibling. As the second baby develops, Janice asks if the children are playing together more, as parents often enjoy sharing small sequences of their children's play.

Tracy: It's fun to see how Maggie [age 18 months] follows along with Mia [age 36 months] with purses, dolls, stuff like that. The other night, they were playing with a Wiffle ball in their bedroom. Mia was trying to get Maggie to play catch, and Maggie was laughing so hard. In the next room, Dave and I chuckled as we listened to them.

Janice: Now that she is three, Mia is getting better and better [at] playing with Maggie. Three-year-olds understand more.

Janice frames these questions positively; in turn, parents describe their children playing together. Janice's frequent questions help parents become good observers of their children's play together. Seeing over time how Janice enjoys their children, the parents spontaneously share when their children enjoy each other, such as when an infant begins to enjoy watching her brother's play or when an older sibling spontaneously assists his younger brother.

Natalie: Dvonne [3½ years] will get down on the floor with Jene [age 4 months] and tell her to say "Dada" or say "Mama." He plays with her like that.

Janice: Wonderful. A study I recently read showed that when the first child gets involved with the baby, it makes a difference in the second child's language development. It's going to help.

Janice takes pleasure when Natalie speaks about her children. She also provides developmental information to help Natalie understand the value of her son's interactions with Jene. As the months progress, this kind of exchange between Janice and Natalie becomes a natural part of the home visit.

Fighting

It is inevitable that brothers and sisters will be jealous and competitive with each other and will fight. When parents are able to stay out of their children's fights, children have a chance to learn to work out problems together. Letting their children fight without interfering is difficult for most parents. When parents do become engaged in their children's fights, fighting can become the setting for children to manipulate their parents (e.g., by convincing the parents of who is at fault or what a punishment should be).

Home visitors can help parents understand that their children's fights are normal. They also can help parents see these fights as an opportunity for their children to learn social skills, especially conflict resolution skills. Helpful suggestions for parents to respond to their children's fighting are available in the literature.[22]

If one child is dominating the other or if one child has an unfair advantage, home visitors can help the parents to intervene in a constructive way. Parents should learn when to withdraw (e.g., when their children are bickering) or when to intervene (e.g., to separate children when a situation is potentially dangerous). Most important, home visitors can provide helpful suggestions for parents to assist their children in learning how to negotiate. For example, the parent can allow each child to state his or her feelings and intentions or, if the child is quite young, the parent can verbalize feelings and intentions. In this way, the parent can help the children figure out solutions to the problem. As home visitors help parents learn this skill, some parents are having their first experience in recognizing and talking about feelings and intentions. When that happens, parents are learning the same significant social skills as their children. Parents and children are developing an increased ability to recognize the perspective of the other, as well as recognize their own feelings and motivations.

Siblings grow up to be very different from one another. In addition, experiences within the family differ markedly for siblings. Individual differences in temperament, personality, and other characteristics of each sibling elicit different responses from family members and contribute to differences in their responses to others.[23]

Challenges in Sibling Relationships

When a new sibling is born, older siblings often enjoy helping, such as getting mommy a diaper or soothing their sibling. At the same time, some parents expect the oldest child to grow up quickly. No matter how the oldest child acts, that child probably will be a role model for the younger siblings. Younger siblings love to follow their older siblings around like a puppy dog. This behavior is fine in moderation, but older siblings often become frustrated when their sibling interferes with their play with peers.

As they grow older, competition between siblings is inevitable. Grades often become a source of comparison and envy. Opportunities to gain recognition in school usually are limited; thus recognition rarely is distributed evenly across siblings in a family. When a child brings up a teacher's comparison, parents can attentively listen, take these feelings seriously, and help the child recognize her own strengths.

DISCIPLINE

Parents' differences in discipline depend on a child's age, ability, sensitivity, and temperament. If parents discipline their children differently, they can explain the reasons to their children. Without realizing, parents may speak softly to their daughter and be tougher with their son. Different children may need different kinds of discipline; thus, fair discipline does not necessarily mean the same discipline for each child.

Fair and appropriate discipline is described here:

1. The punishment should fit the crime.
2. Consider how much discipline to leave to the children.
3. Balance positives with negatives (i.e., surprise the children with a word of praise).
4. Plan solutions together.
5. Do not compare one child to another.
6. Do not talk about one child to another.
7. Do not humiliate one child in front of another.
8. Discipline should be done in private.
9. Match the discipline to the child by temperament, stage of development, learning style, and thresholds.
10. Find a positive word or activity afterward to balance out necessary discipline.[24]

LARGE FAMILIES

Experiences of siblings in a large family often are very different from those in a small one. Often, the first- and last-born children are seen as having special roles in a large family. In reality, all the children in a large family have a special role. Gender and age differences, along with temperament, can also make for a child's unique role. Children of large families know they are a part of group and often are proud of it. At the same time, they may become "sick" of their siblings who are always around.

Sometimes each sibling has a favorite sibling in the family; this favoritism may be based on gender, temperament, or birth order. Siblings who choose each other as favorites often depend on each other. Rivalry in large families is the same as in small families.[25]

ONLY CHILDREN

Parents may have different reasons for having only one child. Some may think that having more than one child might stretch their financial resources; some may not think they can have a second child because of their age. Some women biologically can have only one child. Others think that when both parents must work, one child is enough.

Parents of only children take socialization seriously. They know that play dates with other children and preschool will help avoid loneliness. However, some only children spend so much time with adults that they, in turn, adopt adult mannerisms earlier than their age would predict.

BALANCING THE HOME VISITOR'S INTERACTIONS

When there are two or more mobile children plus their parent(s) involved in a home visit, the home visitor's job becomes more difficult. This task may be most challenging when the older child is not mature enough to focus on solitary play activities for an extended time while the home visitor focuses on the infant. As home visitors develop their skills, they learn the art of introducing activities that invite extended involvement for both children. Janice demonstrates remarkable talent in orchestrating sustained involvement of Maggie and Mia, siblings with an 18-month age difference.

Janice removes from her bag a box filled with several dozen colored 2-inch diameter circular plastic chips, each with either one, two, or five holes in the center. She also removes two cardboard and two plastic canisters, each with a slot on the lid. As she puts the toys on the rug, she says to Mia (age 33 months) and Maggie (age 15 months), "I brought these today. There's enough so that everybody can play."

Mia immediately takes some chips and places them into one of the holes of the canister as she says, "It's like a bank to put money in."

Janice answers, "You are right. It's like a bank to put money in." Meanwhile, Maggie uses alternate hands to put chips into a canister that does not have a top. Mia puts two chips into a slot at the same time, and Janice says, "Mia, you did that fast, putting two in at the same time. Wow!" As she watches Maggie open and shut the cigar box containing the chips, Janice says, "Close the box, open the box, close the box." Maggie then places a chip through a large slot of another canister. Janice exclaims, "Good, Maggie; you put it right through the slot!"

As Mia watches, she says, "Yeah, Maggie."

Both children stay included in extended play. Because of Janice's repeated affirmation of Mia, Mia is able to enthusiastically praise her younger sister. As Maggie and Mia play, Janice repeatedly describes the children's play. These descriptions affirm the children's involvement, help them recognize their own successes, and model powerful ways for Tracy to help her children develop their self-worth.

Maggie continues to busily dump several chips into a can and then dumps them out and begins the process again (both children have remained focused in play for 15 minutes).

Janice places a 12-cup muffin tin on the floor, and Mia slowly places one chip into each of the muffin tin cups as Janice says with each placement, "One, one, one," and so forth. Mia then begins placing a second disk into each of the cups as Janice comments, "One more makes two."

When Mia seems to tire of filling the muffin tin, Janice gives her a string with a knot on its end and suggests, "Do you think we could put some of these on the string?" Janice holds up two red chips, one with one hole and one with five holes. She asks Mia which chip looks like the one on the string, and Mia picks the chip with the one hole and puts it on the string. They continue this game until Mia has about 10 chips of the string. Janice comments, "Good, you know all of them that have just one hole."

As Mia and Janice play together, Maggie continues to play with the canisters and chips. Janice asks Tracy if Mia understands "two," and Tracy shrugs as she says, "Try it." Janice suggests to Mia that they can string the two-hole chips and shows her how she can put the string in each of the holes as if she were sewing. Mia then successfully chooses the two-hole chips and puts the string through them. Janice then holds up her string as she says, "Look how nice it is. Maggie, isn't it nice what your sister has made? The ones are on the bottom and the twos are on the top." As Janice speaks, Mia smiles.

Janice then removes two large metal spoons from her bag and shows Mia how she can tap the bottom of the canister with the spoon. Mia seems to enjoy this tapping action. She alternately taps the plastic and the metal bottom of the canisters as Janice comments, "Different sounds. The plastic one is not like this one, is it?" Mia nods her head.

During these activities, each child is able to maintain sustained interest in the same toys. With each child, Janice plays several roles—observing, affirming, clarifying, structuring, and extending the children's action, as well as interpreting their actions for the children's mother. These are roles typical of Janice's work with one child and parent, but made more complex with two small children 18 months apart in age.

As the children play, Janice extends and structures new uses of simple materials. She integrates learning into the children's play. Her descriptive comments help these young children learn important concepts. For example, she comments about sameness versus difference of sound and spatial relationships of the one- and two-hole disks on the string. Janice explained her approach.

I think all of that helps parents to see how children's play is legitimate learning. And many times, I can say in a visit, a statement that I heard Burton White say in a training session several years ago, that this is just as serious learning as any child is doing in school. It's neat to see the parents' reaction to that—they'll grin, or say, "Oh, really!" It just makes what the child does seem important to the parents, and it is important.

Although she usually has a general idea of the children's play involvement, Janice also improvises. Janice commented on her visit with Mia and Maggie.

I have to admit, I just thought of that on the spot. I knew that in the visit, I wanted to differentiate the task for Mia and still follow her lead. And once she started threading, I thought this is the time we can start talking about numbers and help her mom realize that she can be aware of those kinds of things. And I thought, "Oh, that's going to work. I can do it some more."

Janice always has some activity plans before beginning a home visit. She chooses activities that are somewhat open-ended so that she can be flexible in use of materials. This flexibility is especially important when more than one child is present because unpredictable occurrences are more likely during the home visit. Beyond having materials, the home visitor constantly observes, interprets, and evaluates ongoing happenings. This internal dialogue, which often is what the home visitor is saying aloud as well, allows the home visitor to shift gears when appropriate. Knowing that relationships are more important in promoting development than any specific activity gives the home visitor the security to be flexible.

In some situations, the home visitor has not worked previously with the family's older children. Because the home visiting experience is relatively new, it is not unusual for the older children to be more demanding of attention. For these families, home visitors need to provide play activities specifically geared for the older children. They should be prepared to devote some time to these older children.

DIFFICULTIES AND DILEMMAS

Each home visitor has a caseload of families of varying sizes and varying patterns of relationships. When focusing on siblings, there are two identifiable problem areas that may provoke challenges for the home visitor. First, parents may be carrying their unresolved childhood sibling conflicts or other unpleasant sibling experiences that left emotional scars. A second difficult area entails making home visits to families with several children present.

Ever since Cain asked, "Am I my brother's keeper?" it has been clear that there is tension in sibling relationships. When parents' childhood feelings are extremely problematic, parents may carry them into their own parenting. For example, they may feel helpless and out of control when their children tease each other or fight because these behaviors trigger the parents' own feelings from negative childhood experiences with continual sibling conflict. Other parents live with feelings of being less competent than their siblings or being excluded; these feelings may also be carried into their interactions with their own children. When these parenting dynamics are operating, the home visitor's role takes on new dimensions. First, home visitors learn to recognize these parent–child dynamics. Once they recognize the dynamics, home visitors need to decide whether this issue can be addressed in the home visitor's work with the parent or whether the family needs a referral to a mental health specialist or other resource.

The home visitor's task can become very challenging when he or she visits homes where there are many children. Sometimes all the children are within one large family; at other times, two different families are living in the same home. To have a successful home visit, the home visitor must be flexible and skilled in working with people of various ages. In these situations, the home visitor often does not know how many people will be present during the visit. Some home visitors go prepared with materials and/or activity ideas for each of the age ranges. Others chose activities that all different ages can enjoy. Cynthia works with many families in which several children always are involved in her home visits and shared her approach.

It's not as hard as it sounds. You just need to have a couple of good books. Books are wonderful because what you can do with a book is settle down. It settles you in hopes of a quiet time. Lots of times, if I have more than one child, I'll start out with a book and read it just to set the tone—a pleasant time.

The hardest thing is working with two babies. If a parent has a toddler and a small baby, that is a high level of difficulty because their attention span is real short. So the baby has to have lots of different activities, lots of things to do. Toddlers demand a lot of attention in that respect. Sometimes I think they get the bulk, and in that case, I may actually plan a time when I know that child is napping so I can spend more time with the baby. And you can have some material for each child. So if you get the kids included in that, then you have time to play with the other child and to work with Mom.

Especially when siblings and parents seem to have difficulty with managing kids, I like to do activities where everybody can play, regardless of their age. Then, what you can show Mom is yes, this 6-month-old can play lotto. And it's a time for Mom to hold the baby. Let the baby hold the cards while Mom is still interacting with the 4-year-old and doing the matching. And the baby wants to eat a card, and that's okay because it's cardboard.

The home where I went the other day, I had a 3-year-old, a 4-year-old, an 8-year-old, a 7-year-old, a 9-year-old, and a 13-month-old, and we all played lotto. Everybody had a card. They took turns. The older kids I used to be the callers, and they took turns calling. The 13-month-old got to walk around holding the cards and stacking them because he had extra cards. You can take one activity and make it apply to all the kids because that is what families do. Families don't get up in the morning and say, "Oh well, you are 12 months old, so you are going to do this activity. Okay, George, you are 15 years old," and so forth. Families do what they have to do, and everybody participates, and they all have a place. That's pretty much what I do with siblings.

Cynthia is skilled in involving all children in home visits, regardless of their age. She understands that if she is not successful in this task, parents will not gain much from her work with them because, as she states so clearly, "That's what families do" (i.e., participate in similar activities, regardless of the age span of family members).

CONCLUSION

The birth of additional children brings new family dynamics for both parents and their older children. Parents and their older children experience the push and pull of feelings, some of which are new and uncomfortable. Parents may experience unexpected changes in their feelings and expectations for their older child, challenges in their sense of parental competence, and unanticipated feelings, which may evoke their own childhood struggles as siblings. The older child's everyday predictability vanishes with the arrival of a new baby and feelings of loss abound.[26] During this transition period of a family, home visitors can listen, affirm both the parents and their children, and provide developmental information and suggestions as needed.

This chapter discussed common patterns of parenting more than one child, such as having different expectations for each child, unwittingly comparing children, and relating to each child differently. We have seen how home visitors can assist parents in comparing their children without judgment and valuing each child as unique and special.

This chapter also examined how sibling relationships involve a complex web of interactions that cross over a wide range of feelings—from admiration, intimacy, and support to jealousy, competition, and rivalry. Each child's unique temperamental style and personality influence the nature of his or her relationships with siblings. Siblings' interactions with each other adjust with changes in their age and developmental level. Fighting usually is a normal part of this relationship; however, it may be quite problematic to the children's parents. Home visitors can help parents understand the different ways their children interact with each other. When parents are uneasy with their children's fighting, home visitors can give helpful developmental information and, when appropriate, assistance in gaining skill in conflict resolution.

Home visitors who deal with families that have more than one child are working in a complex web of relationships—relationships between children, between parents and their children, and between the home visitor and all family members. An essential skill in these situations is the home visitor's ability to orchestrate sustained involvement of young siblings and, at the same time, maintain interactions with their parents.

Two challenges are embedded in the home visitor's work with families with more than one child. First, home visitors need to develop awareness of when parents are bringing unresolved pain from childhood memories of their own siblings into their current parenting and when these parents may need assistance beyond the skills of a home visitor. Second, the balancing of one's interactions in homes with many children during a home visit demands great care and skill.

The Psychologically Vulnerable Family

This uniqueness transforms the minus of the handicap into the plus of the compensation.

Oliver Sacks, *An Anthropologist on Mars*
(1996, p. xviii)

MANY FAMILIES LIVE WITH HIGH LEVELS of acute or chronic stress. A significant number of these families are dealing with more than one stressor. Given this reality, it is not surprising that many home visitors are confronted with babies, young children, and their parents with significant problems. Unhealthy environments and family situations in which many babies and young children are raised can cause them to develop relationship problems and developmental difficulties or delays.

Some parents bring problems into their interactions with the family—internal problems. Internal problems include mental illness, such as depression and bipolar disorder, or substance abuse, either alcohol or drugs. Children who experience maternal mental illness, prenatal alcohol exposure, or prenatal drug exposure are at risk for mental, physical, and emotional disorders.

Some parents find themselves in stressful social-environmental milieus—external problems. These problems include extreme poverty, community violence, or a parent's dysfunctional childhood experiences. Acute stress events are of a short duration, such as when a father has an accident at work. Many families experience acute stress. Chronic events have a long duration, such as living in extreme poverty over many years. Many families live with high levels of chronic stress over long periods of time. Children in these families may be more likely to develop emotional or developmental difficulties. This chapter discusses families who live with chronic stress.

Internal and external problems may push a family toward psychological vulnerability. For example, the Kauai Study, a longitudinal study that followed all children born on one Hawaiian island into adulthood, defined families as high risk if they were exposed to at least four of the following risk factors, including

- Moderate to severe perinatal stress
- Poverty
- Family conflict
- Low parental education
- Parental alcoholism
- Parental mental illness[1]

Adverse conditions often have a rippling effect that creates additional adverse conditions. For example, 22% of American children live in poverty; however, more than 50% of children living in a single-parent home live in poverty.[2] Chronic and multiply stressed children face formidable challenges to successful development.[3]

Socioeconomic status is our best single variable for predicting a child's cognitive ability and social-emotional development because psychologically vulnerable families often live in poverty.[4] At the same time, circumstances of families within the same social class differ quite markedly. Research indicates that the number rather than the nature of risk factors is the best indicator of probable psychopathology.[5] In some cases, between internal and external risks, home visitors will find that psychopathology and poverty often interact; for example, depression and anxiety disorders often interact with poverty. A difficult home environment, however, does not always mean that the child will be unhealthy. Thus, it is important for home visitors to be dual minded. A home visitor should not assume or expect that a child is problematic just because of the child's sociocultural environment. However, home visitors also need to be aware of the potential problems that a difficult home environment can create and be prepared to work with babies and young children who bring problems into the caregiving setting.

In a longitudinal study in Rochester, New York, researchers assessed 10 environmental risk variables when children were 4 years old. One conclusion from this study was that the number of risk factors was the prime determinant within each socioeconomic level, not the socioeconomic level itself. In addition, the same outcomes often were the result of different combinations of risk factors, although income and marital status were major risk factors.[6]

Many families live with high levels of chronic stress, with approximately one-third of the U.S. population at risk, including young children.[7] A significant number of families cope with more than one stressor, such as low income, parental mental illness, domestic violence, substance abuse, and other difficulties. Most prevalent in the United States is acute episodic impoverishment. A major accompaniment of poverty is single parenting, which about half of American children will experience during their first 18 years.[8] Given this reality, it is not surprising that many home visitors are confronted with babies, young children, and parents with significant problems.

Every baby and young child learns to adapt to his or her environment. Healthy development entails adaptation, but in some cases, adaptation is also a limitation. It may be a good thing for a young child living in a violent environment to be fearful. To live a life based on fear, however, seriously inhibits the number of possible trusting relationships that a child may have. As Pawl stated, "Babies learn to adapt, but it may mean they never do the tango, only the 2-step. And in reality, lots of people never learn to do the tango, only the 2-step."[9] A baby's adaptation to a violent home environment may be self-protective for the baby, but this adaptation may severely limit the baby from experiencing his or her full range of potential.

Many home visitors have a hard time finding a way to reach these vulnerable families. Their problems often seem overwhelming. Focus on inner experience is the most effective tool that home visitors can bring to their work with babies and young children who have problems. Home visitors can focus on the child's feelings, the parents' feelings, and on their own inner experience—that is, what each of them is feeling inside. When a baby does not respond or when a toddler has a tantrum, home visitors can ask themselves such questions as "What are these children feeling?" and "What is the child or parent trying to express?" At the same time, home visitors need to consider how their experiences with children and parents make them feel. How does it feel to be vulnerable? How does it feel to be angry? How does it feel to be helpless? The home visitor then can use the energy from the anger to marshal her skills to be patient, nurturing, and respectful in a way that helps the child and parent.

Regardless of income, race, or religion, home visitors should relate to each child and parent as unique individuals. Knowing that each child and family may have different attitudes, values, and behaviors, the home visitor should strive to understand their experiences and lifestyles. When home visitors understand themselves and their own cultural patterns, they can understand and work with others, attending to both nonverbal and verbal communication. The home visitor should strive to focus on strengths rather than the unfamiliar.

This chapter addresses the issues and concerns of families who are psychologically vulnerable and the effect of such a family situation on the children. In particular, the following family issues are discussed: marital/partnership discord and divorce, mental illness, substance abuse, domestic and community violence, and child maltreatment. The reason family problems affect children so much is that the family is the child's main context for interaction and development. Children depend on their families for physical, emotional, social, cognitive, moral, and spiritual development.[10] Children observe family interactions and listen to family stories; in doing so, they develop working models of relationships that then guide their behavior.[11] As children mature, they continue to internalize memories that help to stabilize the parent–child relationship.

MARITAL/PARTNERSHIP DISCORD AND DIVORCE

Family relationships are the first context of development. As discussed in Chapter 1, a baby and young child internalize relationships with parents as the child develops. As the parent–baby relationship matures, the baby continues to internalize memories that help to stabilize the relationship itself:

> The pivotal concept in this perspective is that not only are the coherence, stability, and substance of the relationship represented by these internalized structures, but the stability and coherence of the relationship itself may be located and conserved through time by such structures.[12]

Given the pivotal impact of parent–child relationships on the child's developing self, parental discord, separation, and divorce can lead to young children having problems.

As part of the long-term social, economic, and demographic changes in American society, families have changed dramatically. Since the mid-1980s, nearly half of all children in the United States spent some time in a single-parent home.[13] Many of these families include a single mother and other family members or new male partners. Two-thirds of divorced women and three-fourths of divorced men will remarry.[14] Unfortunately, second marriages are more likely to end in divorce than are first marriages.[15] The uncomplicated family, as depicted on television programs from the 1950s such as *Ozzie and Harriet* and *Father Knows Best,* is never a reality for many children.

Marital/Partnership Discord

Interparental conflict varies widely in impact and on multiple dimensions of adult and young children's behavioral and emotional expression. Conflicts in relationships are inevitable; when children observe conflict, it is not necessarily a negative event, especially if conflicts are resolved.[16] In healthy marriages or partnerships, young children learn that conflicts can be a path to working out differences and learn effective interpersonal coping skills that otherwise would foster resentment or anger.

Interpersonal conflict can lead to psychopathology in both parents and their children. Children from intact families with chronic discord frequently have more behavioral problems than children from separated, but conflict-free, families.[17] These children's negative emotions have been associated with their greater risk for psychological difficulties.[18] Most parents would be surprised to learn how much their children notice about their marital discord. Marital discord often involves subtle changes in mood, habits, schedule, attitudes, and even daily routines. Research indicates that marital discord leads to

1. Poor behavior management techniques reflected in lax monitoring and inconsistent or harsh discipline

2. Greater psychological control, characterized by efforts to control the child through manipulation and exploitation of the parent–child bond (e.g., love withdrawal, guilt)

3. Emotional unavailability, such as diminished responsiveness, sensitivity, and warmth[19]

Disturbances in marriages or partnerships often result in disrupted parenting and withdrawal of parent interaction.[20] Boys seem to be more vulnerable than girls to negative family circumstances.[21] Young children exposed to marital conflict often have feelings of anger, shame, or fear. Children may imagine themselves as either potential mediators or provocateurs of the conflict.[22]

Children of Divorce

Divorce is a transitional process, not a legal relationship; young children are an integral part of the process. Every divorce includes stress and many changes for each family member—some expected and others unexpected. Family systems theory posits that the behavior of each family member has an effect on the behavior of every other family member.[23] Separation and divorce lead to disruptions in each individual's relationships with family members. A family is like a mobile: move one mobile piece and the entire mobile moves. However, family rituals such as daily dinners may serve as a protective factor for families experiencing the transitional process of divorce. The majority of families do not become embroiled in conflict and legal battles over their children.[24]

For many children, the quality and amount of contact with parents decreases substantially because divorce leads to parents' distress and distraction from caregiving. When a child moves, peer social networks are disrupted and the child must adjust to a new school environment. Children who experience multiple postdivorce stressors are susceptible to mental difficulties. Active coping skills such as problem solving and positive thinking are protective for children experiencing divorce stressors.[25] Children's social relationships can promote resilience.

How a divorce affects children varies with the age of the child and how parents handle the divorce. Parents can help babies and young children handle divorce by providing consistent daily routines and limiting spousal fighting in the presence of the children. Even when marital discord occurs in the original family, young children dream of having their parents together with them again. When one parent leaves, a young child might wonder, "If one can leave me, will the other also?" or "Will the parent who left still love me?" Very young children do not have a clear understanding of fantasy and reality or the ability to differentiate clearly between self and other. Thus, a young child might feel somewhat responsible for his or her parents' separation and divorce: "Did the parent leave because he (or she) doesn't love me?"

A young child whose parents are having marital difficulty or separation may regress (e.g., resume bed wetting, have sleep difficulties, suddenly be intolerant of frustration, cling to adults). Parents can help by offering a listening ear, reliability, support, and nurturing. They can reassure their children that they are not to blame for their parents' difficulties and they can protect the children from their fear of desertion. Reading picture books about divorce also can help young children gain understanding of their pain.

Maternal Custody

Most often, mothers gain custody of their children after a divorce. Beyond having difficulty in maintaining a household alone, single mothers may encounter financial problems. Father's nonpayment of child support can contribute to the mother's economic difficulties.[26] Divorced mothers may also have emotional difficulties, particularly in the first year after divorce. Divorced mothers have been found to show less affection toward their children than married mothers.

Father's Involvement After Divorce

In about 10% of divorces, fathers gain custody of their children.[27] Studies indicate that fathers with child custody usually are older, more established, and wealthier.[28] Because it is unusual for fathers to gain custody, they often receive more offers of assistance, such as babysitting.[29] Most of these men handle child-rearing and homemaking without difficulty.[30]

Divorce arrangements often are very difficult for a noncustodial father's relationship with his children. The divorced father's amount of contact with his children varies widely across families and varies with the sex of the child. Studies indicate that over time, fathers have a gradual decline in contact with their children.[31] As contact declines, so does the father's influence.

When a father has limited visitation with his children, he may suffer from the pain of always having to leave his children and pressure to entertain them when they are together. Residential mobility and geographic distance usually decrease visitation. Research shows that the quality of a father's contact with his children is more important than the amount of contact. However, the traditional noncustodial visitation pattern of every other weekend, some holidays, and possibly a month in the summer is inadequate for maintaining a close father–child relationship.[32] Children who grow up apart from their biological fathers are less likely to finish high school, attend college, and keep a steady job and are more likely to become teenage parents.[33]

Joint Custody

Legal joint custody is an arrangement by which both mother and father retain and share responsibility for childrearing. Under joint custody, the children live with each parent for certain periods of time throughout the year. Unfortunately, studies indicate that only about one-quarter of these families are able to cooperate. The remainder are "disengaged," with parents avoiding contact with each other. The degree of parental conflict is the best predictor of a child's adjustment.[34]

Stepparenting

Approximately 40% of U.S. children will spend some time in a stepparent family.[35] Within a blended family, each member has role expectations and gains a concept of self through social interactions. These role expectations and self-conceptions often become problematic in remarriage and accompanying stepparenting. We have no established norms for stepfamilies, so parenting roles are especially ambiguous in these new families. The newly composed family's difficulties often stem from unrealistic expectations because family structures, roles, and interpersonal dynamics are increasingly unpredictable and inconsistent. When role definitions for each family member are ambiguous, family members may experience increased psychological distress.

Children's adjustment to and their relationships with their stepparents have a significant impact on marital adjustment.[36] Stepparent–child relationships often are more distant and have more conflict than relationships in nuclear families. When children living with their stepparents have a good relationship with their nonresidential parent, they are better adjusted.

Common issues in stepparenting include

- Assuming that parenting in a blended family will be the same as in one's biological family
- Assuming that one will have responsibility and authority to discipline one's partner's kids
- Desires to spend time alone with one's own biological children
- Dilemmas about comanaging money and assets
- Relationships with ex-spouses
- Expecting support from extended family

Stepfathers sometimes are uncertain with regard to the amount of authority they should display and confused about appropriate affectionate interaction with their stepchildren. Stepfather–child relationships are often most difficult when the children are adolescents. Still, with all the difficulties, stepchildren usually fare as well as children living with both their parents.

MENTAL ILLNESS

Constantino defined mental illness as "the relative inability (assuming physical health and a reasonable living environment) to experience fulfillment (or happiness) in self, in work, and in love."[37] Babies and young children can be at risk if either parent is mentally ill. This section, however, focuses on mothers' mental illness because they are usually the primary caregivers. A mother's psychological disturbance does not necessarily lead to inappropriate parenting and resulting child difficulties. For some mothers, the bond with her child may be the most stable part of her life. However, the task of child rearing can be more difficult for a mother dealing with mental illness. Research literature also indicates that the children of parents with mental disorders have higher rates of these disorders than do other children.[38]

Approximately 10% of abused young children live with parents with severe mental illness.[39] Research indicates that child rearing by a parent with mental illness may create developmental risks for the child through both genetic and environmental factors.[40] A parent's mental illness can affect their parenting in complex, multiple ways. For instance, the parent's psychiatric thought patterns make it difficult for young children to trust whether what they experience is true or not. For example, the preverbal interaction between baby and mother in routine caregiving may not exist because the mother is in her own world.

The two most common mental illnesses in mothers are depression and schizophrenia.[41] Depression is the most common mental illness among mothers of young children. Studies indicate that twice as many women as men suffer from depression, particularly among women of childbearing age.[42] More than 80% of depressed patients have more than one depressive episode and more than 50% of patients relapse within 2 years of recovery.[43] Thus, babies and young children are especially likely to experience repeated exposures to their mother's depression. Research indicates that depressed mothers' parenting often is impaired in ways that may be problematic for their child's development.[44] Symptoms of depressed mothers include a negative mood, loss of pleasure, low energy, apathy, problems with sleep and appetite, and negative views of self.

How does depression affect parent–child interaction? From birth, babies demonstrate sensitivities oriented toward human stimulation. Caregivers and babies interact both to regulate the babies' biological functions, such as sleep and feeding, and to support emotional and social development. Depressed mothers tend to be less responsive, more critical, and more disorganized than nondepressed mothers.[45] They are also more disengaged, more negative, and less likely to respond to their babies' cues.[46] Clark and Fenichel describe some problematic depressed mother–child interactions:

> Many depressed mothers respond to their babies and toddlers' fussing, tugging or even biting, but not to smiles or positive bids for attention. Babies who have learned from their mothers that only negative strategies get a response are not likely to endear themselves to other adults. Moreover, many passive babies may simply withdraw from social interaction altogether when their depressed mothers don't respond to their bids for attention.[47]

When caregivers experience depression and frequent expressions of sadness, babies also show early signs of derailed emotional development, showing angry and sad facial expressions earlier and more often than babies of nondepressed mothers.[48] Studies indicate that babies of depressed mothers are more drowsy or fussy, less relaxed, engage in less toy exploration, and are less focused in play.[49] Studies indicate that babies, toddlers, and preschoolers of depressed mothers have reduced left frontal lobe activity, usually activated during emotions such as joy, anger, and interest, and increased right frontal lobe activity, usually activated by withdrawal emotions such as sadness and anxiety.[50] By 32 months of age, the child's reduced left frontal lobe activity becomes more permanent.[51] Researchers believe that these findings are not due to genetic factors, but rather from the mother–baby interactions of depressed mothers.[52] However, other studies indicate that genetic influences may play a role in the emergence of depression in young children.[53]

When young babies of depressed mothers develop emotional and behavioral regulation, they repeatedly use their mother's facial expression; thus many of these babies of depressed mothers have a negative emotional expression themselves. Babies of depressed mothers have more difficult temperaments, greater irritability, and more difficulty in self-calming; that is, babies of depressed mothers are depressed.[54] Babies of depressed mothers have psychophysiological alterations such as heart rate variability, right frontal electroencephalogram asymmetry, reduced left frontal activation, and high vagal tone, which is the child's ability to regulate physiological response to stress and a risk factor for the development of anxiety disorders in later childhood.[55]

The literature describes depressed mothers' difficulties in interacting with their young children:

- The mother's depressed mood may lead to her baby mirroring this depressed affect.[56]
- A depressed mother may be insensitive and slower to respond to her child's cues and needs.[57]
- A depressed mother may inappropriately use her baby as a source of comfort.[58]
- Depression can impair a mother's ability to discipline her child appropriately.[59]
- Depression often is associated with family discord. This marital conflict may have an adverse effect on young children.[60]

Research indicates that babies are particularly sensitive to the negative effects of maternal depression between 6 and 18 months of age.[61] When babies are exposed to their mother's depression during this time, they often have emotional and cognitive difficulties during the preschool and early school years, regardless of their mother's depression status during these later years.[62] Parental mental illness can be related to negative child outcomes, such as cognitive deficits, delinquency, or poor social adaptation.[63] Several research studies have indicated that maternal depression has been related to higher rates of insecure attachment.[64]

Stern described how babies have adjusted to living with an emotionally unavailable mother. Some babies learn to "turn their mother on" and are sometimes successful in reaching their emotionally unavailable mother. Sometimes the baby's vocalizing, smiling, and gesturing works and the mother is reanimated, even though depressed. This infrequent response is good reinforcement for the baby's behavior. These babies often develop into charmers who are skilled in capturing people's attention. When the mother is not responsive, some babies turn away, become curious, and seek stimulation elsewhere. These babies develop their own ability to stimulate themselves with external objects and events. Some mothers are aware that they are not responding to their baby enough and thus they make a huge effort to overcompensate in bursts.

Stern suspects that the baby can discriminate these forced interactions from an easy flow; yet they are so eager for relationship that they adjust their behavior accordingly. Although the desires of both baby and mother are very real, a false interaction occurs. Each of these methods sets the child's style of relating to the world and to the self, which may remain throughout the child's life.[65]

When maternal depression occurs in a harmonious marriage, the mothers are more likely to sustain positive, healthy interactions with their babies and young children, who are less likely to develop problematic consequences.[66] When babies of depressed mothers have nondepressed out-of-home caregivers, these caregivers can be a protective factor. These providers can promote healthy social and emotional development, which can compensate for the actions of the baby's depressed mother, as in the example of Gail and her daughter Nancy.

Gail and her family live in a rural town of 3,000 people. Gail, a 26-year-old mother of 11-month-old Nancy and wife of Gary, a short-distance truck driver, has joined the Therapeutic Family Day Care Project. Gail is the 11th child of a mother who committed suicide when Gail was 10 years old. From the time she was an adolescent, Gail has suffered from severe depression; she is hospitalized at least once a year and takes several medications. Prior to Gail's enrollment in the project, Gary had cooked all the family dinners. Nancy was in the playpen alone 100% of the time she was awake.

When family caregiver Jean began caring for 11-month-old Nancy, Nancy had no verbalizations and little if any affect. Jean cared for Nancy 4 days per week. Gail also came to Jean's home one morning per week. Jean cared for Nancy until she entered kindergarten. At that time, Gail began working as a nurse's aide at a nursing home and Jean cared for Nancy in the afternoons after kindergarten.

Sometimes when Jean returned Nancy to her home, she would teach Nancy to bake brownies and cook simple meals. At Jean's home, she cooked for Nancy and the three other toddlers—simple items such as biscuits or muffins. After 1 year in Jean's care, Nancy was spontaneously talking and was emotionally expressive. In fact, by the time she was 3 years old, her behavior showed that she possessed a quick intellect. After 3 years in the project, Gail continued to see her psychiatrist and continued her medication; however, she no longer had any hospitalizations.

Ten years after Nancy and Gail left the project, Jean stated that she sees Nancy a couple times a year and that Nancy seems to be a spontaneous, happy teenager. Jean also says she frequently sees Gary and Gail in town and they exchange friendly brief conversations. Gail continues to work at the nursing home.

In their early contact with families of newborns, home visitors can head off some later problems if they look for postpartum depression. Symptoms of postpartum depression include low mood, tearfulness, irritability, anxiety, and sleep difficulties. Some mothers may experience another episode before their child is 3 years old. Postpartum depression can cause disruptions in mother–baby interaction. However, most women do not require medication and will respond to support from their family, friends, and partner.[67]

Being a new mother is a challenge for all. For some new mothers, however, it can be an overwhelming process. Even in the normal postpartum time, new mothers experience heightened family and family-of-origin issues as they move into parenthood. For example, new mothers need to make adjustments in their sleep schedules, in how they and their spouse allocate roles, and in deciding what employment now means to them. No matter how many children a mother has, each baby has a unique style, needs, and strengths, so every postpartum experience is different.

SUBSTANCE ABUSE

Societal and cultural factors create the likelihood of substance abuse. Living in dense poor neighborhoods with high rates of criminal activity and available drugs makes drug use more likely. In the United States, more than 8 million young children have at least one parent who abuses alcohol or another drug.[68] Many parents who are drug abusers also have psychiatric disorders.

When working with babies and young children of parents who are potential or actual substance abusers, it is important for home visitors to understand the effects of different substances. For example, crack cocaine users tend to be jumpy and full of vitality, whereas alcohol abusers are more likely to be listless with little energy.[69]

The reciprocal interaction between the baby and the baby's social environment influences the developmental outcome in children exposed to drugs and alcohol. In reality, both alcohol and drug abuse have been related to child abuse and neglect. Competent out-of-home caregiving can serve as early intervention that can make a substantial difference. The most optimal environment would be a therapeutic child care environment; however, given today's funding realities, many of these children are mainstreamed into traditional out-of-home caregiving programs.

Home visitors may suspect that substance-abusing parents need a great deal of support. Once home visitors are able to develop a trusting relationship with parents, they may have the opportunity to help a parent use community resources for treatment and other needed assistance. Knowledge of accessible substance abuse treatment centers is necessary. In reality, many of these families need comprehensive, multidisciplinary intervention to assist them with their chronic problems. If the resources are available, the home visitor should make referrals to agencies that can provide the needed help to these families. If a home visitor suspects that a child is in danger in the home, the visitor needs to be vigilant in checking the child for signs of maltreatment, as well as informing her administrator about this concern. Every early educator is a mandated reporter of evidence of child maltreatment.

Parental Drug Abuse

It is hard to say how substance abuse causes problems when it occurs most often in the midst of other problem-creating factors. Many women who use drugs during pregnancy and afterward are suffering from other psychiatric disorders such as depression, anxiety, and personality disorders. Many infants exposed to drugs in the womb are born prematurely; it is not yet known if prematurity, low birth weight, or prenatal drug exposure is what triggers the problems these babies often face. Findings on this issue are mixed.[70]

Prenatal cigarette smoking can cause low birth weight and fetal growth retardation. Researchers estimate that 20%–30% of low-weight births in the United States are attributable to cigarette smoking. Marijuana is the most commonly used illicit drug in the United States and, after alcohol and tobacco, the most commonly used drug during pregnancy. The impact of prenatal marijuana use on birth outcome is not clearly known.[71]

Methamphetamine (meth) use does not decrease with pregnancy.[72] After birth, the health threats to children may be through passive inhalation of meth smoke or through exposure to toxic substances used in the "cooking" process, common among many poor rural families. Meth users usually are of low socioeconomic status, live in harsh neighborhoods, suffer from depression, have family or social systems that promoted substance use, and have a disregard for the law. Researchers found that meth-exposed newborns have lower birth weight, lower arousal, and increased stress of the central nervous system.

Given the surge of cocaine use in the late 20th century, most research on babies who have been exposed to street and prescription drugs prenatally are studies of cocaine-exposed infants.[73] This research provides no consistent pattern of anomalies in prenatally exposed babies. Some studies show the impact of cocaine on child behavior and development, whereas other studies show no impact. Some studies indicate that prenatal exposure may result in birth defects, growth retardation, developmental problems such as difficulty in information processing, and attention difficulties.[74] Norinne is an example of a child living amidst drug abuse.

Norinne, 32 months old, entered Redbud Child Care center on her second birthday. Norinne's mother, addicted to cocaine, lives in a home where there is a steady traffic of drug sellers. Norinne's health record at the center gives no evidence of prenatal drug exposure. Currently, Norinne and her 4-year-old sister Cassie live with their father, Sheldon, his girlfriend, and her three children. Ordinarily, Sheldon brings and picks up all five children. Sheldon reports that at home, Norinne rarely eats. However, Harriet, her teacher, reports that at school she seems unable to get enough to eat. About once or twice a month, Norinne's mother brings her to the center. On these days, Norinne repeatedly asks for her mother.

Harriet reports that often Norinne has no facial expression and seems depressed. Her speech is clear, but she rarely talks. She relates to her peers only with unprovoked aggression. She frequently has urine accidents and puts everything into her mouth. Each day she spends long periods of time playing in the water table. Whenever possible, Norinne clings to her older sister, Cassie. She is quite aggressive with dolls, as in the following observation:

Norinne enters the housekeeping area and picks up a doll. She says, "Sleepy baby." Then she rigorously hits the doll's stomach, saying, "I'm going to hit your butt!" Norinne's teacher, Harriet, enters the area and talks to her softly. They then leave the area, Norinne carrying her doll, and Harriet begins to read a story to Norinne.

Harriet reports that the one time that Norinne is emotionally expressive is when she is alone and playing with the dolls. On most occasions, she is expressing anger and aggression.

Norinne has lived in an environment of drug use and drug dealers. Her teachers do not know if she has experienced or witnessed violence. Norinne's chaotic home life during her first year with her mother caused her a great deal of anxiety, which often is externalized into aggressive behavior, as Norinne demonstrated with dolls. To address Norinne's high level of anxiety, Harriet has water play available; Norinne plays in water quietly each day for about 20 minutes. Harriet also ensures that she gives Norinne focused one-on-one time each day, often reading her a storybook.

Parental Alcohol Abuse

Alcoholism is one of the most common substance abuse problems today; about 6.6 million children live with an alcoholic parent.[75] Alcoholism is both a genetic and an environmental disorder, with studies indicating that the heritable risk for alcoholism is 40%–60%.[76] Approximately 20% of women will drink some alcohol when pregnant, although there is no safe level of alcohol consumption during pregnancy. Risk for negative neonatal outcomes can occur with as little as one drink per day.[77] Alcohol consumed by a mother crosses the placenta and circulates in the bloodstream of the fetus. Similar to children exposed to street and prescription drugs prenatally, babies and children who are prenatally exposed to alcohol frequently live in environments of chronic stress caused by factors other than alcohol, such as low income, parental unemployment, parental mental illness, and so forth.

Researchers have found no exact relationship between the amount of alcohol consumed prenatally and the extent of damage caused by alcohol on the infant. However, alcohol appears to have negative effects potentially throughout pregnancy. The brain and central nervous system of the developing fetus are most susceptible to damage. Studies indicate that major morphological abnormalities are due to exposure early in pregnancy, whereas growth seems most affect by late exposure. Central nervous system damage can occur from exposure at any time during pregnancy.[78]

Fetal alcohol syndrome (FAS) is the leading cause of mental retardation in the United States. Characteristics of babies and young children with FAS include specific physical abnormalities such as a thin upper lip, short nose, flat midface, flattening of the jaw, and low muscle tone, as well as central nervous system dysfunction characterized by mental retardation, hyperactivity, impulsivity, poor attention span, problems in social judgment, and/or seizures.[79] FAS children often are socially engaging, talkative, and affectionate.

[The children are] often alert, talkative, and friendly. They have been described as typically short and skinny, with butterfly movements, but a generally vigorous appearance. These children may have severe temper tantrums and difficulty making transitions. More than half show hyperactivity and many are oversensitive to touch and other stimulation. Attentional deficits, fine motor difficulties and developmental delays also are seen.[80]

Some of the behavior problems seen in FAS children also have been observed in young children prenatally exposed to alcohol. Children with high levels of prenatal alcohol exposure were found to have a negative affect at 1 year of age and depressive symptoms at 6 years, particularly among girls.[81] Children are vulnerable to depression and negative views of self in part because they are likely to experience poor physiological regulation at birth and poor affect modulation during infancy.[82]

Paternal alcoholism has an impact on both family functioning and the mother–baby relationship as early as infancy. Fathers' alcoholism has been linked to maternal depression, marital satisfaction, and the quality of the babies' attachment to their mothers. In one study, wives of alcoholics had higher depressive symptoms and lower marital satisfaction compared to wives of non-alcoholic husbands. About 67% of infants whose fathers were heavy drinkers had insecure attachment with their mothers.[83]

One caregiver reported on her interactions with Brianna, a mother who abuses alcohol. Brianna is a 20-year-old mother of two preschoolers, 3 and 4 years of age. During the day, her children are cared for by Casandra, a therapeutic family child caregiver. After Brianna spends one morning at Casandra's home with her children, Casandra writes in her journal:

Brianna told me that her children need to improve their speech. Throughout the morning, she was quite open about her drinking habits. She says she is trying to "cut down" somewhat. But then she goes on to say that her idea of having a restful day is to get drunk, have the children take naps with her while she passes out. She seems unable to grasp the concept of "what if they get up and hurt themselves while I am sleeping?" Rather, she insists that they always just keep sleeping, so it is okay for her. All morning Darryl (3 years) wanted to sit on my lap.

Some days, the children are ready when I come to take them to her home. On other days, their mother is sleeping, and the 4-year-old is cooking eggs and toast for their breakfast. Some days, mother and children all are asleep together.

DOMESTIC AND COMMUNITY VIOLENCE

Violence is the use of physical force to damage or injure. Gun violence in the United States is the second leading cause of death in 10- to 19-year-olds.[84] One-third of children in certain inner-city, high-crime neighborhoods have witnessed a homicide by age 15 years.[85] Battering of women and child maltreatment occur in as many as 37% of families in the United States.[86] Studies estimate that 40%–80% of children will witness domestic violence.[87] In addition, children see examples of homicide and domestic violence on television. With both the high incidence of violence on television and the increased frequency of homicides in our nation, it is reasonable to speak of violence as being part of the inner psyche of Americans.

Parents who are surrounded by violence frequently describe their sense of helplessness and frustration that they cannot protect their children. For young children and parents exposed to violence, parents' emotion regulation and the development of baby–parent reciprocity can be problematic.

A young child's response to trauma involves multiple factors, such as the nature of the overall circumstances in which the trauma occurs, the child's own history, and the degree of support that the child receives from parents and surrounding environment. Young children's exposure to violence affects them differently, depending on many factors such as the age of the child, the frequency and type of violence exposure, experience of prior trauma, familiarity with the victim or perpetrator, and quality of support provided by significant adults.[88] Although the impact of traumatization differs among young children, research indicates that when trauma occurs during the first 3 years of life, the trauma has a detrimental effect because of the rapid changes that occur in brain development during this developmental period.[89] Adults may think that babies and young children who witness violence are too young to understand what happened and will not remember the violent event. Clear evidence shows, however, that babies, toddlers, and older children do not forget traumatic events.

> The ability to re-see or, occasionally but less frequently, to re-feel a terrible event or series of events is an important common characteristic of almost all externally generated disorders of childhood. Re-seeing is so im-

portant that it sometimes occurs even when the original experience was not at all visual. Visualizations are most strongly stimulated by reminders of the traumatic event, but they occasionally come up entirely unbidden.... . Even those who were infants or toddlers at the time of their ordeals and thus were unable to lay down, store, or retrieve full verbal memories of their traumas, tend to play out, to draw, or to re-see highly visualized elements from their old experiences.[90]

A young child's symptoms of trauma are determined by a variety of environmental and intrapersonal factors that process idiosyncratic symptom patterns. Environmental factors include the nature and chronicity of the trauma, the ways in which parents respond to their child's victimization, the social support available, and the cultural influences that may promote resilience or increased vulnerability.[91] Many practitioners in child welfare may not have extensive training or education in child development or trauma. Thus trauma may go undetected without appropriate early intervention, which can prevent the onset of posttraumatic stress disorder (PTSD) or other difficult outcomes.

Community Violence

Continual violence in a community cause young children to feel helpless and hopeless. Healthy parents provide a holding environment for their babies and young children. However, a constant barrage of violence in a community may result in parents communicating a sense of helplessness to their young children. Child psychologist James Garbarino warned, "Children are growing up in a much more socially toxic environment than every before. They live in a world in which chronic danger displaces the fundamental safety that children need."[92] As a result, many babies and young children are growing up without a basic sense of trust and security, which is the basis for healthy development. When a young child's neighborhood has chronic violent crime, the child's social reality is overwhelming. With the violence that bombards television, videos, and Internet games, the world can be a confusing place to a young child, especially a young child who has experienced trauma.

It is critical for home visitors of young children to be aware of the effects of violence, to be able to note signs of these effects in children, and to have knowledge of how they can work with these at-risk children. The caregiver should

- Provide a calm, safe, nurturing environment for their children who have witnessed or experienced violence

- Ensure that each child under their care has a loving, trusting relationships with them

- Focus on inner experiences and feelings, both their own and the children's

Domestic Violence

Almost half of the calls for police assistance in most areas of the United States are for domestic violence.[93] Studies estimate that 15%–30% of American women are beaten at least once in the course of their intimate relationships.[94] Of those men who abuse their wives, as many as 50%–70% also abuse their children.[95] Similarly, in 60%–75% of families in which a woman is battered, the children also are battered.[96]

Children's emotional responses to trauma are much more intense if they know either the perpetrator or victim.[97] When parents fight over their child, the child's awareness can create a sense of unrealistic power in the child. When a child witnesses parents fight over issues unrelated to the child, the parents are indifferent to the child and the child can feel rejected.[98]

Behaviors associated with young children's exposure to violence include

- Reexperiencing the traumatic event, often in the form of nightmares and in repetitive play sequences
- Trauma-specific fears, such as fear of the dark, strangers, being alone, specific animals, vehicles
- Sleep disturbances
- Enuresis (bed-wetting)
- Low tolerance of frustration, aggression, and impulsivity
- Selective inattention
- Lack of curiosity and lack of pleasure in exploring
- Depression and perpetual mourning
- Lack of a sense of trust and security
- Avoidance of intimacy
- Sensitized hyperarousal state[99]

Studies of young children exposed to violence point to clear associations between the exposure to violence and the occurrence of PTSD.[100] Over time, PTSD solidifies into more enduring patterns such as conduct disorder, anxiety, or depression.[101] Retrospective studies indicate that adults who exhibit violent behavior were exposed to adolescent violence, adult extrafamilial violence, physical abuse of children, and adult aggression toward dating partners and spouses.[102] Prospective studies indicate that parent-to-child aggression is consistently predictive of adult criminality, lower educational and occupational attainment, psychiatric difficulties, and difficulties with intimate relationships.[103]

The youngest case of PTSD in published research was 3 months of age.[104] If experiences with violence are chronic, young children may develop a permanent pattern of hyperarousal or numbing, which can become the precursor to learning and behavior problems. With prolonged stress, the brain's chemical profile can be altered. Parental factors that seem most closely related to PTSD symptomatology in young children include

- Mothers' and fathers' own symptoms of PTSD
- Levels of general parental psychopathology
- The presence and/or extent of denial concerning the child's symptomatology
- Changes in family functioning that may have a powerful indirect effect on the baby's functioning and development[105]

When home visitors work closely with parents, they can learn to be aware of signs of physical adult abuse, such as bruises on any part of the body or swelling. It also is important for home visitors to recognize their own feelings when working with these parents' personal attitudes and feelings. Being impatient with a mother who chooses to continue living with her abusive partner can obstruct the visitor's ability to be caring and supportive of the parent.

The following example illustrates the effects of domestic violence on a child.

Maurice, age 4 years, lives with his single mother who abuses both drugs and alcohol. Maurice was prenatally exposed to drugs. An array of adults are in and out of Maurice's home, with violence frequently erupting. The last time his teacher made a home visit, adults were throwing bricks at each other.

Maurice's teachers report that during eating times, he seems to fear that he will not get enough food and eats as much as is possible. He engages in unprovoked aggression throughout the day. He is unable to participate in any group activity and has nightmares when sleeping during naptime. In the classroom or during gross motor play, Maurice is able to maintain focus in an activity only if his teacher, Jerri, is at his side. Otherwise, he either is running about or engaging in unprovoked aggression. In other words, Maurice can function appropriately when Jerri is able to "shadow" him. This shadowing seems to contain his excessive anxiety and resulting lack of self control.

The child care center is working with the school district to have Maurice evaluated for placement in special education for the following year. Jerri also is assisting Maurice's mother in arranging for a psychiatric evaluation to determine if medication could help him.

Child Maltreatment

Child maltreatment includes neglect (both physical and emotional), physical abuse, sexual abuse, and emotional maltreatment. The most frequent forms of abuse are neglect (45%), physical abuse (15%), and sexual abuse (16%).[106] Young children of different ages, at different developmental stages, from different environments, and with different experiences are exposed to substantially different forms of maltreatment and are likely to manifest vulnerabilities in a wide variety of ways.[107]

Children are physically abused and neglected 15 times as often in homes with domestic violence than in nonviolent homes.[108] Children age 3 years and younger comprise 26% of all indicated child maltreatment reports and 77% of child fatalities of all ages.[109]

Research indicates that child maltreatment causes functional, structural, and biochemical modifications to the central nervous system. Abused children also have disproportionately high levels of depressive disorders.[110] Male children are more at risk of being abused when adult domestic violence is present. Studies indicate that the more severely a mother is battered, the more likely her child is to be abused.[111]

Abusive parents often have very low frustration tolerance, unrealistic expectations of their children, and/or find their children to be particularly stressful and frustrating. Abusive parents may fail to understand their child's individual needs, abilities, and how their child thinks and feels. Often, the parents lack empathy and want their child to meet their needs. Neglectful parents often are permissive but show hostility and little caring. In contrast, abusive parents tend to be very strict and authoritarian. Child abuse often is embedded in a parent's discipline. However, a parent may not intend to hurt the child; injury may occur because of overdiscipline or physical punishment.

Behavior patterns of very young children that most often spark maltreatment are incessant crying, affect regulation deficits, negativism, wetting, and soiling. External signs of physical abuse are bruises, lacerations, scars, and burns.[112] The leading cause of serious head injury to babies is physical abuse.[113] Young children often experience multiple forms of abuse.

The following factors are highly correlated with child maltreatment:

- Negative maternal attitude toward pregnancy
- High level of perceived social stress
- Low socioeconomic status
- Lack of financial resources
- Parent's low intelligence
- Parent's criminal record[114]

Studies indicate that babies who have been maltreated consistently are far more likely to be insecurely attached than are babies who have not been maltreated.[115] Many young children with a history of maltreatment develop not only negative representational models of their attachment figures, but also negative representations of themselves. Moreover, the young children often become disconnected from their actual emotional experience. Toth, Cicchetti, Macfie, and Emde clarified: "[M]altreated children often act compulsively compliant with their caregivers (e.g., ignore their own needs in order to care for and please the parent) and display insincere positive affect."[116]

Research studies report that maltreated young children tend to lack empathy, perspective taking, and ability to focus; they are also more aggressive with peers and siblings. Maltreated children are less likely to show sadness in witnessing a peer's distress or remorse when attention is called to the impact of their aggression.[117] These traumatized children also have difficulties in affect regulation. They seem to be less flexible, less able to adjust their emotions to external cues, and have a "tilt" toward negative emotions.[118] When maltreatment is chronic, young children develop brain pattern changes, as well as changes in behavior similar to those mentioned among children exposed to violence. Some maltreated children respond to anxiety by being hypersensitive, whereas others dissociate.[119] Karr-Morse and Wiley summarized that "Instead of providing the foundation for self-control, for empathy, and for focused cognitive learning, abuse in earliest life undermines all three."[120]

Maltreatment from gestation through the second year of life can be a precursor to violence by children. Violent behavior results from chronic distress or neglect. Maltreatment of a baby may lead to the permanent loss or impairment of key protective factors including intelligence, trust, and empathy.[121] When a maltreated child gains a reliable, accessible relationship with a loving adult and can develop internal representations of this intimate significant other, the child can become resilient and develop into a psychologically healthy adult.

Maltreated children frequently have disturbances in their development of self, form ineffective peer relationships, and manifest difficulties in adapting successfully to school environments. Maltreated young children may talk little about themselves and their internal states. Maltreated children's negative feelings about themselves may hamper their ability to engage in successful peer relationships.[122] In addition, maltreated children have increased rates of behavior problems and psychopathology.[123]

Because of their caregiving experiences, maltreated children are likely to develop negative expectations regarding how others will behave toward them and of how successful they will be in relation to others. As the abused child grows older, their representation of self and self-in-relationship is maintained outside of their awareness; it provides the child with expectations of self and others that influence the child's behavior in relationships. Abused children often expect other people to be rejecting and hostile. When adults have been victimized by aggression in their own childhoods, they tend to reenact these experiences when they become parents.

Abused children break the cycle of maltreatment through

1. The availability of emotionally supportive individuals
2. The mother's stable relationship with her partner
3. Involvement in long-term psychotherapy[124]

Emotional abuse almost always occurs when physical abuse occurs. Emotional abuse includes consistent rejecting, terrorizing, refusing to provide basic nurturance, and failure to give physical, emotional, or mental stimulation. Babies and toddlers may be left in their cribs for long periods of time; they may seldom be talked to or cuddled. A young emotionally abused child is anxious, insecurely attached, and has low self-esteem.[125]

Sexual abuse of children can range from excessive exposure to pornography and living in sexually explicit environments to physical acts of abuse, such as fondling, oral copulation, vaginal intercourse, or sodomy.[126] Sexual abuse can result in children having thoughts pervaded with sexuality, engaging in inappropriate sexual behavior such as excessive masturbation, disturbing toileting patterns (e.g., sniffing underwear, wearing soiled underpants, repeatedly stuffing the toilet until it overflows), or molesting other children.[127] Of families having all types of maltreatment, sexually abusive families have significantly more difficulties regulating anger, more chaotic interactions, and less role clarity.[128] Some families experience physical or sexual abuse as well as emotional abuse or neglect, or both. The story of Charetta illustrates the effects of sexual abuse.

Charetta, age 3 years, is the only daughter of 33-year-old Keona. When Charetta was 8 months old, Keona divorced Charetta's father, Joe, who is a self-employed plumber. Keona worked as an executive secretary for a large corporation. She and Charetta lived in a comfortable home in the suburbs. Charetta's father, Joe, has returned home to live with his parents and four adult brothers, three of whom use and sell drugs.

Keona and Joe attend a parenting group, during which Joe stated that Charetta is "the apple of my eye, my reason for living." On some days, prior to Keona picking up her daughter from the child care center, Joe takes Charetta for an hour or so in the afternoon, then returns her to the center. On Sunday, Joe takes Charetta to his mothers' home to be with him.

During the first week of the parenting sessions, Charetta's teacher, Jean, reported that Charetta was masturbating persistently throughout the day. Jean, Keona, and their home visitor then met together to discuss Charetta's masturbation. Keona commented that she too had noticed Charetta's increasing masturbation.

Keona arranged for Joe to have visits with her daughter only when she was also present. With help from Charetta's child care director, she also arranged for Charetta to have weekly play therapy with a child psychiatrist, which continued for 1 year. Charetta's masturbation ceased. At 7 years old, she is a bright, high-achieving second grader.

When a home visitor suspects that a child has been physically or sexually abused, the first step is to have a confidential conversation with the child's parent. Then, the home visitor can assist the parent in obtaining a medical evaluation of the child and psychotherapy to help heal the child. In most families where child maltreatment occurs, family therapy can assist every family member in healing and the family in becoming whole. Once a home visitor's suspicion regarding a young child's maltreatment has been confirmed, he or she is mandated to report the maltreatment to the state protection agency.

THE RESILIENT CHILD

Not surprisingly, some home visitors may feel overwhelmed when working with the families discussed in this chapter. As home visitors work with these families, they can find comfort in knowing that some at-risk children are resilient.

Most of this chapter has addressed the environmental problems that are part of many babies' and young children's lives. However, young children are not necessarily victims of their fate. Children living in the midst of chronic stress and deprivation have been able to overcome this deprivation and maintain healthy development because they are resilient.[129] *Resilience* refers to an individual's ability to avoid long-term negative or developmental effects from adverse environment and/or experiences. Like competence, resilience changes over time and context. Furthermore, children may be resilient to some stresses but not to others. Some children may manage to avoid failure in the face of poverty or violence but experience real deprivation in the capacity for intimate relationships. Although some children are resilient, some environments are too much for anyone to overcome.

Resilience is not a static condition, but rather a state of dynamic transaction between oneself and another. Wolin and Wolin identified seven strengths that are characteristic of resilient children:

1. Insight: the habit of asking tough questions and giving honest answers
2. Independence: drawing boundaries between self and troubled parents; keeping emotional and physical distance while satisfying the demands of one's conscience
3. Relationships: intimate and fulfilling ties to other people that balance a mature regard for one's own needs with empathy and the capacity to give to someone else
4. Initiative: taking charge of problems, exerting control, stretching and testing oneself in demanding tasks
5. Creativity: imposing order, beauty, and purpose on the chaos of troubling experiences and painful feelings
6. Humor: finding the comic in the tragic
7. Morality: an informed conscience that extends one's wish for a good personal life to all of humankind[130]

Most resilient children have a close bond with at least one caregiver from which they received lots of attention during their first year of life.[131] Resilient children often figure out how to locate allies outside their families; home visitors can serve as these allies. Resilient children often have the capacity to see themselves as separate from their troubled parents and to intuit that their family is not what it is supposed to be. When their home visitors are loving, predictable, and available, these home visitors can be models to help young children learn that there is a different way to relate than the way that they experience at home.

When home visitors recognize that a baby's or a young child's daily life at home is immersed in stress and adversity, they can give these young children loving care and a sense of safety and security. In their interactions, they can provide a trusting, predictable relationship. Many of these children live in homes where they have no control over events. The home visitor can ensure that these children experience a sense of efficacy by being quick to respond to the children's initiatives and by providing opportunities for the children to make choices.

CONCLUSION

Every baby has the right to interact routinely and consistently with an admiring, supporting, and loving caregiver in a relationship that provides security and intimacy. Unfortunately, many babies and young children are at risk for not realizing their humanity, given their families' extreme deprivations. Young children in at-risk families may fail to achieve a strong sense of self and optimal development because their relationship with a primary caregiver is not strong enough to contain and nurture them.

Home visitors have reached a period of accountability. Many parents are hungry for the help and support that home visitors can provide. Home visitors can make a difference in their work with psychologically vulnerable families. They provide support, empathy, active listening, and are a resource for families to gain assistance. Because this work is very demanding, home visitors need support and assistance from peers, supervisors, and administrators. Competent home visiting programs have a family therapist or psychologist meet with home visitors at least once a month to discuss their work with these families and potential strategies to help them.

Person and Profession

Personal History—Professional Competence

Every life has its own significance. This lies in a context of meaning in which every moment that can be remembered has an intrinsic value and, yet, in the context of memory, it also has a relation to the meaning of the whole. The significance of an individual existence is quite unique and so cannot be fathomed by knowledge; yet, in its way, like Leibniz's monad, it represents the historical universe.

Wilhelm Dilthey (1961, pp. 88–89)

IN OUR DISCUSSION OF HOME visiting, it is clear that who the home visitor is as a person plays a large part in each visitor's approach. Home visitors' commitment, perspective, values, decision making, and patterns of relating all have roots in their unique personal histories. In other words, in home visiting, personal and professional identities are intertwined.[1]

In the previous chapters, we observed how Janice and Cynthia conduct home visits. In this chapter, we explore how these two women see their home visiting work as part of the meaning and purpose they find in their lives, how they have grown professionally, and what resources have promoted that professional growth. Then we explore the interaction between their personal history and their home visiting.

The stories of our lives provide meaning and direction to who we are—both in our relationships with others and in our understanding of ourselves.[2] Although we cannot provide a formula for the process through which someone's personal life history influences their professional life, by presenting two life histories as told by the home visitors as they reflect on their own experiences, we perhaps can provide a window into this process.

To learn how home visitors' professional work is connected with their childhood and present personal life as adults, I conducted life history interviews with Janice and Cynthia, two exemplar home visitors featured in this book. Over the course of four interviews, Janice and Cynthia told me about their childhood and adult life.[3] As they progressed beyond their stories of early childhood, their stories expanded to include extended family, friends, schooling, religion, and community. Later they described their adult personal life and career path, from their first jobs to their current work.[4] Throughout the interviews, I occasionally asked a question, either to clarify or to extend their description.

Prior to these interviews, I had observed and discussed Janice's home visits with her for 4 years. I had known Cynthia for 4 years as well, working with her in my role as action researcher for 18 months. While working together, I had many lengthy conversations and several interviews with both women. So, by the time Janice and Cynthia sat down for life history interviews with me, we knew each other quite well.[5] The interviews, structured by these women's remembrance and by their understanding of their personal and professional lives, were informal. As they told me about their life experiences, I felt the freedom to ask questions or to comment on similar experiences in my own life.

These personal and professional histories of Janice and Cynthia should not be regarded as case studies or blueprints. Rather, I present the voices of Janice and Cynthia, as they reflect on their own development as persons and professionals, for readers to use as a resource. By considering how these home visitors reflected on their histories and integrated them into their work, the reader is challenged to think about how this process works, both in the home-visiting profession in general and in the reader's own professional development.

Janice's and Cynthia's self-portrayals begin with a description of the home visiting work. First, each woman identifies the personal meaning and purpose she finds in her work with parents and their children. Second, she describes her growth in understanding and skill. Finally, she discusses what has helped her to grow professionally. Janice's and Cynthia's reflections capture some of the ways that home visiting can be meaningful, how home visitors can grow over time, and how resources can play a role in the home visiting process. There is no single way that home visitors will find meaning in their work, grow as professionals, or use the available resources for professional development, but listening to Janice and Cynthia can provide a range of possibilities and can indicate how one's work and resources can be actively and reflectively used.

Not all competent professionals grew up in families in which parents had strong values and gave their children consistent, loving care. Prior to my interviews with Janice and Cynthia, I was unaware that each woman had a healthy, happy childhood family life, although the families are quite different from each other. Therefore, the chapter closes with a conversation with Karen, a home visitor who uses her recognition and resolution of a painful childhood as building blocks for professional competence, turning childhood pain into professional strength.

JANICE

Personal Meaningfulness of Home Visiting

The strength and happiness of Janice's childhood family life and commitment to her husband and children are themes that blend into her home visiting work. The strongest passions in her personal life are school, babies, and parenting. Home visiting blends these passions.[6]

Serving families as a home visitor in Parents as Teachers [PAT] has been a privilege for me. I believe it to be an extension of who I am as a person, not just as a professional. Family and children always have been—and continue to be—the most important part of my life. Therefore, to be able to promote strong family life and understanding children as part of my career seems at times like a dream.

PAT has given me something in my life that I love to do. I knew all along with my own babies that I really loved that stage of development. And it gives me a change to renew that joy for myself.[7] Work is just fun. It gives me a lift every time I do it. Yes, I get frustrated when things aren't going well with a child. But every situation, and I truly mean this, every child, every situation, there will be parts of the visit that I truly enjoy. There has not been a child, not a parent that I have ever worked with—and I've had some pretty difficult situations—that I've not been able to say "This is good," "That's good," or whatever, because it is there, and I truly enjoy little children. Part of the joy is being with very young children who aren't tainted yet. It helps me to keep a more positive outlook on the rest of my life. It helps me stay happy, when other things are sort of bearing down, I have this picture of Erin in my head, doing something especially darling. It helps alleviate other stresses in my life.

I also am intrigued with child development. Intellectually I find it very fascinating to learn about something in a course, to read about something in a book, and go into a home and see it happen right there in front of my eyes. I truly enjoy education, and being able to convey this and of knowledge is just fun. I mean, I liked it when I was a classroom teacher, but doing one-on-one adult education and have a baby to play with at the same time—what could be better for somebody that loves to teach.

Relationships always have been very important to me. I would never be happy working quietly in front of a computer in a cubicle in an office. I like being a play partner with children. I like getting to know parents better and better over several years of service. I like sharing ideas with my colleagues.

Home visiting continues themes integral to Janice's personal life history and counterbalances stresses that she encounters. She loves home visiting because it is sheer fun for her. Further, this enjoyment can balance those parts of her life that can be stressful. Since she was a young child, Janice has used her intellect to be an active learner and she always has loved teaching. Child development stimulates her intellect and working with parents continues her love of teaching.

Janice also knows that she is making a difference in people's lives, that her work has meaning beyond just herself.

I love the process. You definitely can see results from the information you convey. You get feedback from the parents and from the child. You know it's good. You know that you are making a difference. I think most people like to see results from their work. If you can see that in another human being, that's really valuable.

I have observed Janice working with young parents and their children for 4 years. I can better understand her home visiting style now that she and I have completed four life history interviews. Often, I was impressed at her ease and very soft manner as she relates to a baby and parent, by her spontaneous and genuine delight in a child's action, and by her openness when she shares her own parenting experiences.

Professional Development over Time

Since she first began home visiting, Janice has enjoyed her work. At the same time, she is aware of the many changes in her professional development over the course of 10 years.

I'm getting better at it now that I am aware of more detail and better at understanding development. I understand the significance of certain parts of development better and thus I can convey this better. And my increase in child development knowledge has helped me especially where development is not progressing quite normally. I am better at seeing subtle things that indicate progress, and I can suggest activities that will help that progress. I know it's going to make a difference because with experience, I've seen it.

I don't think my basic approach has changed. From the very beginning, I have conducted my home visits in a very integrated way rather than thinking about specific things I was supposed to accomplish. I was never lesson plan oriented. I always knew there was certain information that I needed to convey, but I didn't have an outline in my head as to how that hour was going to go. I always used the child's action to talk about development—that when I would see the child do something I would point that out. Because from the beginning, I had learned how important it is to hook information to something that is important to the parent. Certainly the baby is very important to the parent. If I can hook developmental information to what we both see as being significant, something they might not have even notice, this will help a mom appreciate her child's development. I've always taught development that way.

The third place my developmental knowledge has changed is in understanding premature babies. The in-service training that I have gotten through Parents as Teachers made all the difference in the world in my ability to provide meaningful service to families with premature babies. It's incredible how much preemies are on their own time table. And working with families of preemies for three full years has given me increased understanding to share with other families.

Also, in the beginning, I thought I had to take a zillion activities, because if something didn't work, I wanted to be sure to have something else to do. I don't take so much stuff anymore because I realize that no matter how much I bring, the child will go through all of it anyway. When they get through all of it, they'll go do their own thing or bring their own toys and we'll play with that. So, since that's going to happen anyway, I might as well not have so much stuff. Also, the other advantage is the child will focus more, and spend more time with an appropriate activity or two that I now bring.

And finally, my relationships with parents have changed. I think my relationships with parents always have been pretty solid. And there always are certain families where it's going to click, and certain families where it's not going to click as well. I know my families are comfortable with me, and I'm not really sure why. I know I always would enjoy staying longer, and I always feel like they would like to have me stay longer. But I don't.

I guess the difference has been sort of in the general comfort level as far as I feel like I don't have anything to prove. The confidence I have in my own ability to do this job sort of takes any pretense away. And I am much more comfortable with silence than I used to be.[8] I used to feel like I needed to talk all the time. Now I realize that the parent can be comfortable and I can be comfortable just watching the child play, and waiting for something to happen that we can talk about. It used to be that I couldn't do that. It would just be too scary. But now I can do it.

The pattern that definitely has changed is the way I respond to parents' questions. It's typical for parents to ask questions about their child's behavior and how to manage this behavior. It used to be that if a parent asked me a question, I thought I had to answer it. Now I usually will remember to say, "What have you tried?" They'll talk about what they have tried, and I'll say, "What else have you tried?" and in this manner let the answer come from the parent instead of from me. Often I can say to them, "That's really a good idea. Just stick with it and give it more time." That's so much more powerful than my saying an answer. And sometimes I'll expand on their idea and give them something to read.

In her 10 years as home visitor, Janice has gained new professional knowledge, skill, and understanding of herself. Gaining increased knowledge of child development and premature infants has helped Janice's skill in observing and interpreting behavior and in giving information to parents. The process of home visiting over time has led to improved skill. For example, visits no longer involve a series of activities. Instead, the child can have extended focus on only one or two activities and Janice can be more involved with the parent as well as the child. Janice speaks of how her increased self-confidence has allowed her to slow down. She is comfortable with silence as she and the parent watch the infant play. Her observations can help the parent understand the developmental meaning of their infant's actions and what to expect next. Being comfortable with herself, she no longer feels that she has to answer each parent's question; rather, a question can be the basis for helping parents solve problems.

I think most difficult for me is talking to men and convincing men of that which I believe in. Yet the first year that I was on the school board, I was the only woman so I had to be forceful, and I found that when I talk about something that I believe in like early childhood education, I can talk to anybody. As a child growing up I was shy with boys. In college I always was shy with boys. I'm just not always comfortable with men. It was fun to have all sons and that has helped me professionally. All of a sudden I was with boys and fathers, doing a lot with boys and fathers in cub scouts and athletics.

Resources for Professional Development

Each home visitor has a different way of knowing and different way of learning. Janice speaks clearly about what she thinks has helped her most over the course of her career. In our chapter on professional development, Janice described how sharing her work with colleagues has helped her. The regularly scheduled PAT in-service sessions have also been helpful for her, both in terms of deepening her knowledge base and in terms of process. Given her keen intellect and love of learning, Janice actively engages in the new learning provided by national experts at these sessions. She thus gains new ways of thinking and new skills in the same way that her parents learn from her.

As discussed previously, professional growth occurs best through doing and reflecting on that doing.[9] Janice thinks of herself as always having been self-reflective.

A lot of my reflection probably is just part of my growing. I always think about situations that have occurred—in my own parenting experience with my own three children. I would think about things and wonder if I could do it better the next time if a similar instance occurred, or do it better the next time with my younger child. That's the kind of person I am.

As a child, Janice's family's daily conversations at dinner and before bedtime were the anchor point of each day. These times in which family members reflected together on daily happenings seem to parallel Janice's ease in being self-reflective about her work and parenting. Now, she often shares happenings with her husband.

I talk to my husband about situations that I find frustrating in my job. Sometimes when you're talking about frustrations, you don't need anybody to give you answers. You just need somebody to sit there and nod their head and give you a hug. It is a skill or an art to be able to shield yourself, given the burdens of the job, because parents sometimes share more than you wish they would share. And if you are a sensitive person, and I am very sensitive, it's hard to just listen and walk away from it. I do listen and I do walk away from it. But I can't get it out of my head a quickly as I wish I could. And that's because it's the kind of job where if you don't have some way to take care of yourself and somebody who will listen, it's too stressful.

Janice talked about the work she and I did together and how it influenced her home visiting.

The kind of observation of my work you did when you would go into a home with me, Carol, was very helpful. You would go into a home with me and with the parents' permission, write down everything that was said during a home visit, and then we'd go back over what you had written. I know I became more aware of giving interpretive comments of the developmental meaning of a child's action, once you pointed this out to me. And then I was able to work towards giving interpretive comments more frequently.

But also it was the time that I could take privately to read through what had occurred during the home visit. It helped me to appreciate what really had gone on. A home visitor doesn't remember everything that she has said or a parent has said. For example, it certainly helped me to appreciate the necessity to wrap up before I leave the home so that the parent really will have a parting thought. Over the course of the hour, she may not have realized, because so much goes on. Our program is now teaching coordinators how to do what you have done.

Janice ended her discussion of influences on her work by returning to her own parenting.

There is always professional development that makes you do your job well, but I think there also is a very personal development that makes you do your job well. I think a lot of why I enjoy the work I do, and why I have confidence in myself doing this job, is because I really enjoyed my own motherhood. I enjoyed my children as babies. I enjoyed them as toddlers, young children, and the teen years that always are a new challenge. And now I'm enjoying them as young adults. I look at my children and see how successful they are in their relationships with other people and how successful they've been in school. It gives me the confidence in this job to think, "Yeah, I think I did a pretty good job as a mother." My children are really great.

So it gives me the confidence to talk about some of these child-rearing issues in a very sincere way. I'm not just talking about it because I've read it in book. I'm talking about it because I've experienced it in my own life and the results have been positive. Because I have the personal experience, I think that makes me more credible.

A give-and-take mutuality seems to characterize Janice's parenting and her work life. Just as her parenting influences her home visiting, her home visiting work influences her parenting. Five years before I conducted these life history interviews, Janice told me how PAT helped with parenting her teenage children.

PAT helps me keep a focus on development, even though my children are older. It helps me structure my thinking about my children in terms of their development. And the parenting techniques I talk about with the mothers of little ones, I find I really use with my teenagers, only adjust up a little. And when I go to parenting workshops at the high school, I hear them saying the same kinds of things that I am telling parents of toddlers. And I can say to the parents of my babies that these are techniques that you will use all the way through your parenting, because you do.

Janice's personal style makes the interplay between her own parenting and home visiting possible. She is quite self-reflective about all her experiences and tends to approach both family and her professional experiences in a cognitive manner.

Personal and Professional History

Janice grew up in Nathan, a middle-class suburb of a large Midwestern city, Centerville. She was the older of two daughters. Janice grew up in a family where children and adults were very close, both within her nuclear and extended family. Janice speaks of her childhood family life as being routine, predictable, and traditional.

I remember growing up in a very modest and predictable environment. My mother was a homemaker; my dad went to the office. My dad went to work at the same time every morning and got home at 5:15 every single night. Mother cooked, cleaned, and dusted the furniture everyday. Dinner was the same time every night, mashed potatoes every night. We'd sit around the table and everyone would share happenings of the day. In the summer, conversation would happen again around 10:00. Everybody would be back out in the kitchen talking again. Lots of sharing about things going on in other families, families within our family, job stories, and Navy stories from dad. And we were very active in the church. Dad was on the vestry so I guess there'd be stories about church activity... just lots of conversation.

And every Sunday, like clockwork, after church we went to my father's mother's house. A ritual. She was my only grandparent. We would always have the same dinners. Even now when I walk into anybody's house and smell pot roast, immediately I think of Sundays walking into my grandmother's house after church. After dinner was over, we would clear the table, do the dishes, and spend the day together. That was Sunday, a family day.

Predictable daily routines, lengthy daily family conversations, and gatherings of extended family each Sunday anchored Janice with a firm sense of connectedness and security. When Janice was 7 years old, her parents adopted a baby girl. Janice described her sister as follows.

We weren't playmates, but I spent a lot of time with her because I loved the way she laughed. I just had fun playing with her, even though it wasn't playmate kind of play. She was my baby sister. She was bright and creative, but she never really could accept the success that I had in school, and felt like she always was trying to be my sister instead of being herself. She was much more resistant to authority. As a teenager, Sherry had a different peer culture than I did—1965 versus 1958. She was incredibly rebellious and my parents did not know how to deal with it. They had some very difficult times. Bottom line is Sherry moved out. She moved to Oregon, and has maintained her distance ever since.

As a child, Janice never questioned her parents' love and adoration for their daughters.

I always had the strong feeling that my parents really adored us. They always spoke to us in a very respectful way. I don't remember any harsh words. I don't remember being punished. We just always understood what was expected.

Shared time with extended family was an important part of Janice's childhood. Her mother was one of seven children and her father had a twin brother. Everyone lived in Centerville. Each year Janice and her family had holiday and birthday celebrations with her mother's siblings, their spouses, and children.

This was a family that truly knew how to have fun, and that probably gave me my sense of family. As I was growing up, we always had family birthday parties for every cousin's birthday, every single year. And there were very large holiday parties that were family-oriented and fun. They had quite wonderful parties because everybody loved music and sang all the time. That's my memory of what it was like to grow up in this family. We'd sing, dance, and party in the front room. And lots of just playing, the old time parlor games like the Pig in the Parlor. That's the context in which I grew up.

I never will understand how some people can buy into what I see as a very narrow view of what it means to be a woman. I think that there is too much setting aside the whole concept of motherhood and marriage. My view of it is that it's so much career, and that is your obligation to yourself to head out in a career. That negates what for me is a very important part of my life. My experience has been that you can have both. I think you can have a rewarding professional experience, take time out for a rewarding family experience, and come back at another stage in your life, and have a rewarding professional experience. I think doing that has helped my family be more stable.

I remained home for 17 years without objection. Granted that's the way I grew up, and that may be more difficult for young women now.

Schooling

People in Janice's childhood community of Nathan were part of the first-generation postwar middle class. Nathan residents valued education. Parents expected that their children would gain more education than they had and, in turn, be successfully employed. Janice spoke of how early schooling influenced her career choice.

Education was valued highly in my family. My mother was one of only two in her family to graduate from high school, the same high school as my dad. As long as I can remember, it was assumed that I would go to college, to Metropolitan University, and as early as second grade, I knew I wanted to be a teacher. It took scholarships and loans and lots of hard work to make it happen, but I graduated as a Phi Beta Kappa.

I loved school. It was just my favorite place to be, my favorite thing to do. I can remember every single teacher I had in grade school. Those grade school teachers—I can remember stories from every single year... Things stick in my mind. Like in kindergarten—all the way through school, I was tall. In kindergarten I was always in the back row. At the tables, I was in the back row. It frustrated me that we always were learning to write other people's names and never got to write my name. That's just the way they taught. They'd demonstrate one person's name on the chalkboard, and everybody would practice, over and over and over again. The fact that my name was Janice didn't matter. We all learned to write Mary.

I had the same teacher for first and second grade. She was wonderful. She absolutely was the person who made me want to become a teacher. She had a wonderful sense of humor and was so much fun to be with. I loved learning.

As Janice talked about her schooling, her detailed description of each of her elementary school teachers, some 30 to 40 years later, was amazing. Two teachers became models who triggered her lifelong love of education. Both her teachers and her parents had high expectations of her and she excelled throughout school.[10]

In high school, Janice was in accelerated classes and she continued to love all aspects of school.

Nathan at that time was considered one of the better districts and my high school education was excellent. People really valued education. Everybody was expected to work. Everybody was expected to do well. Everybody was expected to learn. I was very well prepared for college. I was editor of the high school newspaper. I drove my mother crazy because of the hours I kept. I always was very busy, because I was incredibly active in all kinds of things in high school. I did tons of term papers in high school, and had lots of homework, burning the midnight oil.

Janice also speaks of having fine teachers at Metropolitan University, where she again loved school. Only the education classes were dull and were taught by "uninteresting people." She lived at home.

It never entered my head to go anyplace other than Metropolitan University. I knew how special it was. I was the first person in my family or my extended family who graduated from college.

She graduated Phi Beta Kappa and looked forward to returning to the classroom as a primary teacher.

Friendships

Janice's life revolves around relationships. As a child, she experienced family-like intimacy with close friends. During her childhood, Janice had many special friends, several of whom remain close.

At my last high school reunion, which was the 25th year—or was it 30? We had a group of people from my elementary school at the same table. Several of us still are friends, and several of us were the key people who put together the high school reunion. Suzi is my closest friend, since first grade.

Janice also speaks of creative play with friends in the neighborhood.

Two little girls close to my age lived across the street, until I was about 10. We used to play together all the time, and we usually played things like Office or School. And we played movie stars and dress up. TV and that kind of stuff just wasn't in my life. We had to create our own fun, and it was a very happy time.

Religion

Religion has played a significant role in Janice's childhood and adult life.

My grandmother, Mawie, on my dad's side, was very, very religious, very faithful. We are Episcopalian. I grew up going to Sunday School every single Sunday. I taught Sunday School for years, through high school and college. I think I mentioned earlier that after church we would go to my grandmother's, so that ritual of Sunday was very important.

I started going to church again regularly when we came back to Centerville and returned to church where we absolutely fell in love with the minister. He was both very warm and very humorous. We started going back there every single Sunday. My children were reared going to church every Sunday.

Janice holds faith as important.[11] She speaks of the influence of having a pastor who "could translate religion meaningfully for me."

Janice's grandmother, Mawie, was her model in religious faith. Mawie had a leadership role in the church in a time when it was rare for women to be leaders. Janice describes how Mawie had regular prayers that she recited to give her strength. When Janice was a child, Mawie always told her, "When you can't figure something out, pray about it." And Janice tells me that, in fact, now she feels like she has a very personal relationship with God.

In difficult times in my life, I really will say, "I can't handle this. Please help me." And I gain the strength to deal with the situation.

Marriage, Work, and Parenting

Janice met her husband when they both were sophomores at Metropolitan University.

When I met Joe, I fell for him so fast. He was serious about his studies, an engineering major. And he was very good to me. We went together 3 years, and decided we would get married. He was very kind, always treated me well. We never quarreled. I perceived him as very much like my father. He treated me similarly.

When we married, we moved to Northton, where Joe was in graduate school. We had a wonderful life in Northton. I got a job in the wealthiest suburb on the South shore, Bentley. I taught first grade, and I felt like I had died and gone to heaven. I had a wonderful class, flexibility, good support, and many new friends, other young teachers. I loved teaching!

Janice has been able to continue her love of teaching as she works with parents of infants and young children in home visiting.

In October of Janice's second year teaching at Bentley, she learned that she was pregnant. She had been taking oral contraceptives, so the pregnancy was a total surprise to her and Joe.

The news was like a lightning bolt.[12] I was devastated. I could not imagine it. I was the one teaching with my husband in graduate school. This is not the way my life was planned. When I told Joe, he couldn't believe it either. We couldn't even be excited about it at first, because we were so stunned. It never even dawned on me that I would go back to work after this baby was born.[13] My baby was due the middle of March. And the pregnancy put Joe on the fast track. He finished his Ph.D. three years after graduating from college."

Janice's life was carefully planned by her parents, Joe, and herself. Having a baby was not planned. Once Janice integrated this dramatic life cycle change, her teaching plans were put aside so that she could give total devotion to parenting.

In April, Janice gave birth to a baby boy named Brett. One year later, Joe finished graduate school, and they moved to Centerville, a suburb adjacent to Janice' childhood hometown, where her parents still lived. When Brett was 4 years old, Janice gave birth to another son; then, 3 years later, another son was born. She loved being a homemaker and mother. Janice felt continuity between her own family and the family in which she grew up.

CYNTHIA

Personal Meaningfulness of Home Visiting

I asked Cynthia how her home visiting work was meaningful to her.

I think it's meaningful work. Again, it's not something I consciously chose to do. I think we follow a path that feels comfortable to us. Not that it isn't challenging and frustrating at times. But for the most part, when I go into a home and sit down and talk to people, I feel comfortable. And I can use my intellect. Although it may not seem that way to someone on the outside looking in. I get to use it with the family as I am watching the dynamics and helping people process, and I reflect on what I've done, and how I've done it, why I've done it. I do a lot of that. I will leave a home visit and I can tell by my spirits how that home visit went. Sometimes I fly high out of a home visit. I feel like I made some progress with this person, it was a good experience for both of us. I like to think that the adult and child I leave feel the same way: high. This was a good thing that just happened.

Then there are others that I leave and I feel like the slug of the earth. It just didn't go well. I didn't say the right thing. I should have known better. I missed this. So I know by how my spirit is soaring as to how that visit went. I could leave it at that, or I can take the time—I even do it as I'm driving or as I go out walking. I'll replay the visit in my head. I can almost repeat it verbatim. I remember the look the mom shot the kid or the kid shot the mom. I'll just play it in my head, and I'll think, "Well, what if I'd done this, or what if I'd done that?" Again, the chance to sit and talk to other people who do this kind of work is so important. We never get enough of that.

So I get "stuff" from my home visits, from my interactions with people. It may be a way of correcting the child. I've watched a mom just touch a certain part of the baby's hair to caress, and I've actually gone home and done it with my child. There is a reciprocity. I think there has to be that reciprocity. You have to have an understanding that this is not a one-way street. I'm not just going into a home just to do things with people. I am going into homes to have a relationship. They give me as much as I give them.

I have taken exact words, verbatim from another home visitor, from Janice, words that I read from one of your home visit observations, her explanation of language. I now use it. It's mine. I can't create everything, so I take things from people. My home visits still look very different from Janice's even though we may have several phrases in which we use the exact same words.

I know I make a difference, and parents will tell me that. It's taking the time to sit back and think about it. To think about what that person was like 3 years ago, to be able to do the Denver [Developmental Screening Test] for the child and see that the child is growing, is developmentally appropriate. Maybe it's not the way you want it, but it could have been worse. What has been consistently the most difficult for me is not being able to find the key or not being there when that person needs me.

Professional Development over Time

For the past 5 years, Cynthia has worked as a home visitor with primarily low-income, at-risk families. Cynthia sees home visiting as deepening the level of her involvement with low-income families. She also is aware of her increased level of knowledge and skill. She described how she has grown in her home visiting role.

When I started home visiting, I had been working in early childhood about 12 years. I had some experience working with parents, but not in the home setting. When I first went on home visits, I would talk to parents about their children; my visit was child-focused. The PAT curriculum—the manual—says this is your lesson and this is what you are going to do. I really didn't deal that much with the parents. It was more the child and how the child felt, and how the child was developing. With time, and especially with the kind of families I work with, I still focus on the child and talk about the child, but I'm much more aware of the relationship between the parent and child, and the parent as a person, and how that person deals with everyday life. But as you go, and develop your skill, and become more knowledgeable of development, and of the many different ways to promote development, you merely use the written materials to reinforce information with the parent.

It's such an interesting profession. You are privy to a person's innermost life. You get to see where they live, what possessions they have, how they arrange them, how they arrange their life. Then you watch their interactions with their baby. When I think about that, I get a little afraid sometimes… because it's that person's private world. I don't want to invade that private world and I don't want to be an intrusion into someone's private world. I guess that's where the balance is. Maybe [it's being cautious], but I tend to think of caution as negative. I don't mean fear like, "Oh, my gosh, what am I going to do?" Or I'm going to be hurt, or that kind of thing, but just that I'm very aware that this is a person's private life that I'm seeing. I want the person I'm talking with to know that I value their privacy, that I understand that what they are sharing with me is private. Actually it is a gift when somebody shares something that is private.

Cynthia speaks very specifically about how she has changed her approach with increased experience in home visiting.

My visits have changed over the years. When I first started, I was concerned about how I'd do with the child. You know, would the child respond to me? Would I be able to get the child to play? Over time, I realize that my job isn't to play with the child but to involve the parent with the child so that there's more interaction. Then I'm able to talk with the parent about how the parent interacts with the child.

When I first started home visiting, I spent more time playing with the child. The play would end, and we'd go to the next section of the lessons, which is reviewing what we've been talking about. It was much more step A, step B, step C, step D. Now it melds together. Though I do try to summarize at the end, summarize important things to remember.

I still play with the child and often do model. Not just model. I play with the child because it is fun. And through that play, the parent is more likely to want to participate, because it is fun. And if it looks like fun, and sounds fun, it must be fun. I found that most parents want to play with their kids but they may not be sure exactly how to do it.

So if we can spend 20 minutes where everybody is having fun, and the parent feels successful, and the child is having a good time and parent and child are interacting, then I'll physically back off. We all will be sitting on the floor, and the parent, child and I will be playing. Then I'll back out of the play so that the parent and child are playing together. Then I can observe and can give the parent feedback on what's going on, on what they are doing.

I use the written materials—the parent handouts—to help parents see what they already know how to do, because I'll observe them as they play with their child. Toward the end of the visit, when I summarize, I'll say, "Here are the handouts for language development. Look here, your child already is doing these things. We heard him today." Then I'll summarize, "Remember when he said 'ba ba,' he is using those sounds. Then when you responded to him, that is one of the most important things you can do. It says it right here." I relate the written material back to what has happened in our visit. That's been part of my growth. I wasn't able to do that at first. It makes the parent feel good. 'I must be a good parent if I can do these things.'

When I first started home visiting, I relied on those written materials. I thought it was all in the manual. I felt that if I just read it long enough and memorized it, I'd know every answer to any question any parent would ask me. Now there are all kinds of questions I can't answer. I don't know why that child sleeps 12 hours and then he's awake 2 and then sleeps 8 more. I don't have definite answers for all these things, and that's okay. I'm much more comfortable saying to a parent, 'Well, I'm not really sure. What do you think?' instead of feeling that I have to give the answer. It is not my child. It's their child, and they probably have the answer. They just need some help pulling it out or taking a look at it from a different point of view. Now I'm more aware of what I don't know, and I'm comfortable with that. I used to feel that I alone was responsible for this child's development. Now I'm comfortable with knowing that "No, I'm not totally responsible; what I'm responsible for is supplying information and being there, and interaction with the parent and the child. But it's not my responsibility to make sure that child develops in a certain way. That's the parent's responsibility."

And I have grown in my ability to accept that not all people want my service not all people are ready to accept it. There are homes I'll never get in.[14] There are homes I'll get in once and never be invited back. There are other homes I can be in all the time but never get past a certain point. I really believe that people take from me what they need, not what I want to give them.

When I first started, I thought I had things to give them and they needed to take them. Now I feel I have things to offer and they'll take what they need, what they're able to take at that time. That's what I've learned. Patience is a virtue, one that I've never had. [I've never had] patience with everything. I've learned that when you're working with families over time, changes flow and changes may never come. Giving parents time to be able to do things and giving myself time and knowing that if something doesn't happen tomorrow, that's okay. It may happen the next day, and I've learned to wait for that next day.

Like Janice, when she first began home visiting, Cynthia focused primarily on the baby or young child. With time, Cynthia learned that the greatest gift she could give the parents is to involve them in play with their children, and help them to see the meaning and purpose of this involvement. It is great fun for Cynthia to play with little ones and she skillfully generates this pleasure in parents as she invites them to play. Initially, she moved from one step to another as she followed the lesson plan. Now, like Janice, she has an integrated approach. She involved parent and baby and she shared developmental information and interpretation in terms of the baby's and parent's actions. She also integrated the written materials. As she summarizes the visits, she notes items the parent and baby did that directly relate to the written materials. Cynthia has learned that she cannot be all things to all people; parents will take what they are able to take from her. She can be at peace knowing some families will reject her services.

Resources for Professional Development

Cynthia has been working in the field of early intervention for almost 20 years. She feels that during her first few jobs, she developed skills by "dealing with the task at hand and learning by trial and error." I asked her if over the years other people or experiences have influenced her professional development.[15]

A person who has been influential in my work was one of my professors at graduate school. Every time we moved, there were new courses needed for certification or I even had to repeat a course. When I arrived at Dr. Frank's office at the University of Alabama, I learned that they were going to take away all the hours I had completed at the University of Florida. I sat crying in his office. He made three phone calls and they made some exceptions for me and wrote a special program for me. It wasn't that he did me the favor, but that he cared. I had been in so many colleges at that point, where nobody wanted to listen to my story, nobody really cared, just give me your money and go to class and abide by these state rules. This man was different. The thing I always remember about Dr. Frank was when you walked in that door and he was terribly busy, he took time to listen to what you had to say and responded as a human being. I think he was as pleased as I was when I finally got my master's [degree]. For years after I left there, I sent him a poinsettia every Christmas.

He taught me to slow down and to listen to people and to see people as people, not as a means to an end. That's what I took from that man. It's so easy when you get busy and caught up in things to look at the people you work with as a way to get the job done, rather than a person, a human being with hopes and dreams and problems at home. I think we forget that too often. It helps me to be more compassionate, to remember to stop and say to my Even Start home visitor, Terry, "How is Lori doing? How's the toilet training going?" rather than "Do you have the report done that I need?" Dr. Frank helped me learn to relate to people as people rather than just "coworkers." The truth is, a lot of people have influenced me. I've always been one to sit back, watch, and observe. I take things from others and put them into my own repertoire. But as far as influencing me, I can tell you exactly what Dr. Frank gave to me, his gift to me.

The other thing I want to say about why this work is meaningful to me is because I've made the statement that I go in and have things to offer, and people take from me what they need or are ready to take. I think the same of myself. I take from the people I work with on an everyday basis. I take things for myself. For example, I take your knowledge. I take your ability to synthesize and to look at things from a different perspective, and I make that my own. I play with it. You have given me a new way to look at things. It may be something as simple as the way someone has arranged flowers in a vase, but it catches my eye, and I may use it in my own home. It may be a phrase, the way they put their words together, and I like the way that sounds and it becomes my own.

[I have people with whom I can discuss my work, and] in that respect I have a lot of support. I can share with Margaret (director of the district's early education), with Dan (the clinical psychologist who regularly works with staff), and being able to talk to you has been helpful. I do have people to talk to about certain things. I'm the kind of person who pretty much needs to talk about something to figure it out.[16]

I process by talking. And Bob knows that about me. As I said before, Bob calms me down. And especially when I'm struggling with supervision issues, he helps me process and think things through. Mostly, he listens to me.

I spent a lot of years pretending I could handle anything. Now I am able to say I have a problem. That's my personal development and growth. Many things have contributed to that. The people I've mentioned, different books I've read, and being able to sit and talk about the work with families we do with other home visitors, who often encounter similar problems.

Relationships always have been at the center of Cynthia's life, in childhood, and in her work. Not surprisingly, she sees her professional development emerging through relationships with significant people. Cynthia has learned that she need not always excel, that she need not have all the answers, and in fact, can be comfortable with problems. She knows she needs individuals with whom she can process her work, can talk it through. She feels fortunate to have several colleagues, as well as her husband, who listen and offer supportive feedback.

I asked Cynthia how she avoids burnout and what keeps her going.

I always find a new twist, something new to do within my job. This year it was Early Head Start, a new collaboration to put together. In my 9 years in this district, I have had four different jobs, not significantly different, but enough to give me a challenge. I need a challenge.

I also have learned to recognize my limits. I can recognize my own needs and have become better at voicing my needs, for example, speaking with Janice, the director of early education. I also do things for myself such as leave work on time, walk, and work in the garden. For fun, for just me, I go to the botanical gardens and just walk, or I go to our little library. I smell the books and browse, read the magazines, and go home with 6 or more books.

I then asked Cynthia what she thinks has been her greatest contribution.

I am inordinately positive and caring. In the area of staff development, I have grown many good teachers, caregivers, and home visitors. I'm surprised at my skill almost daily! I have a good sense of what I can do. But I am surprised when I get feedback that I'm good at something. I have had to learn acceptance of others and patience. That's just where some people are. But I still don't accept mediocrity.

I have had to learn not to feel that I have to know and be everything. I seek help, yet it is not easy to do. I had to learn not to feel that I have to know and be everything. In Even Start, Dan, our psychological consultant, and Margaret, our early education director, helped me a lot. Margaret was at each Friday training session, thus I did not feel that I was shouldering all the responsibility. She always was very supportive.

Personal and Professional History

Cynthia, like Janice, grew up in a very close nuclear and extended family. However, the daily life of this family of seven children was not "like clockwork." They lived in a small rural town, Florence, 1 hour from the closest metropolitan area. Cynthia's father owned a bar in town and her mother was full-time homemaker until Cynthia was 9 years old. Then her mother taught Spanish in the town's high school. Cynthia is the fifth of seven children.

Cynthia: I was the start of the second family. My mom had me at 40 and 2 more by the time she was 43. My oldest sister was 17 when I was born. I was raised in an extended family.

Carol: A nuclear family that seemed extended.

Cynthia: Right. But we also had grandmas and grandpas. We lived in this huge house. First my mothers' mother lived with our family, when I was very young. And I also grew up with my mother's father living in our home. And there always was a new baby in our family. And as a teen, I had a lot of experience with young children. I did a lot of taking care of them. That's pretty much how I grew up—in a litter.

Cynthia grew up in a family that loved babies. Thus, she chose a career path continuing her early love of babies and small children.

Family celebrations with singing, laughter, and game playing were a central part of her childhood. While Janice's family rituals stayed about the same, Cynthia's daily family life and celebrations always changed.

Holidays always were celebrated with food, decoration, and ceremony. We were raised Catholic, so Christmas and Easter especially were religious holidays, but also fun holidays. Who was there as a family always changed because of the differences in ages and who was and wasn't available at that time. The celebrations always included a lot of food, a lot of noise, a lot of laughter, playing games and a lot of music. My older sisters both played the piano, had good voices and sang.

Though her parents did not finish college, they valued learning and they instilled that value in their seven children.

Reading was extremely important. My mother read to us from the time we were babies, and my father read to us from about age 6 to 12. He'd take the three of us—"the little ones." Every night after dinner, for a half hour, he'd read nonfiction to us. He had a love of history. I remember all the presidents' lives. He'd read those children's books to us. It was just such a nice, special time.

My mom and dad had such a love of learning. They both were very determined that all of us would grow up well educated and go to college. I always knew, that was the expectation, that you will go to college. And you will do well in school. You had no choice. And that's what we did.

Beyond a love of learning, Cynthia's parents "had a love of their fellow man." Cynthia explains.

They displayed this love in different ways for different things were important to them. I remember when I had my mom as a teacher. She was so understanding of these other kids, especially the ones having difficulty. And when mom died last summer, about 10 of her high school students from about 30 years ago came to the funeral. They loved her. Mom cared about people, understood people, and took time for them.

My dad displayed caring for other people in an entirely different way. He was the local pawn shop. When someone was in trouble, he'd bail them out of jail and pay for it. If someone didn't have money, they'd bring him their TV, and he'd give them 20 bucks and keep it until they could pay him back. In their own way, both mom and dad were very generous people. I grew up with that tolerance of other cultures right from the start. It just always was there, that you are accepting of people who are a little bit different or have different ideas. You don't have to agree with them. But that doesn't have anything to do with the respect you feel for them as a person.

As I listened to Cynthia describe her parents' tolerance, understanding, and assisting people, I reflected on how these themes are central to Cynthia's work as an adult as a home visitor and coordinator of Even Start, a program serving very low-income families.

Although the individual members living in Cynthia's family might change, there was consistency in patterns of her family's daily life. Dinnertime was one of these consistent patterns.

At dinnertime, everyone was expected to be there. You knew you had to be home at a certain time for dinner. Then you had conversation. Sometimes you had arguments, because my mom and dad had such different opinions politically. So we would listen and learn both sides. Mom was a Democrat and dad was a Republican. They would have lively arguments.

Dinner was a time of discussion. My dad might come home with a story from the bar. They were always interesting stories. We learned a lot about human nature and the kinds of things that can happen in families. You recapped day, what was going on, or what was important. It wasn't so much a time of planning what was going to happen next, as a time to be together.

Cynthia grew up in a small town and Janice grew up in a large metropolitan area. As young children, dinnertime for both involved daily extended conversation about ideas and happenings of family members. Both children found a sense of security and connectedness in these daily rituals, yet there were substantive differences between the two families. Janice experienced very predictable, conservative thinking within her family's daily dinner that always involved the same four family members. Cynthia experienced lively arguments and a wide range of perspective taking as she ate with an ever-changing family constellation.

Cynthia had two brothers and four sisters.

My mom was pregnant a very short time after she had me, and then pregnant again. Karen was a sophomore in high school when I was born. The first 3 years of my life she pretty much took care of me. In our family, the older kids always bore responsibility for the younger kids. I got to do all kinds of things that most very young babies don't get to do. I hung out with a teenager, so it was great fun.

We all grew up at a very young age with family responsibility. The daily chores of cooking and cleaning with a very large family take a lot of time and organization. At 8, I started doing the laundry with my older sister, for our weekly responsibility. I couldn't go to movies until I had washed the floors on Saturday morning. Everybody had their jobs.

We used to do all kinds of things we weren't supposed to do. Like, one time we tried to persuade my little sister Annie that there really was a tooth fairy. My sister Liz, who is 5 years older than I am, dressed me up like a fairy, and I went out on a narrow ledge outside Liz's window and tried to convince this kid that I was the tooth fairy. She was maybe 3, and I wasn't very old. She took one look and said, "Oh, that's just Cynthia." I was dancing two stories up on a ledge, and I shouldn't have been doing that.

We did all kinds of things. We'd sneak out at midnight. My older sister would go swimming in the lake in the moonlight and she'd take me. I was 3 years old. They'd swim and I'd sit on the edge and watch. It was wonderful. Then, when the second litter grew up, we'd sneak out of the house while everybody was sleeping, and go down to the lake and swim.

For Cynthia, risk taking was just what you did as a child. As an adult, Cynthia continues be "at home" with risks. At the same time, she sometimes feels fearful.

Cynthia: In my work, I have pursued different kinds of positions with more responsibility, and a chance to do things in a different way. I have actively sought positions and pushed myself. And sometimes there is risk involved. At the time I'm thinking, "You don't want to do that." But there's something inside me that makes me do it. I just do it anyway. Until now. Now I've gotten to the point where I don't think I have to run around taking chances anymore to know who or what I am.

Carol: When you go on home visits in dangerous neighborhoods, do you have the frightening feelings that you remember having as child?

Cynthia: No. It's funny that I don't, because I've thought that I probably should. Why am I not afraid? I know some people who work in dangerous neighborhoods are very afraid, and some just won't do it. Maybe it's just stupidity. I feel safe. No, I'm not stupid about it. I feel aware that there could be danger. I don't go to these neighborhoods at night or after 3 p.m."

Carol: Well, you seem to have had a childhood, beginning at 3 years, involving risk taking.

Cynthia: That's probably true, though I've never thought about it much.

Cynthia speaks of her mother as a very strong woman who had a great influence in her life. She poignantly describes her mother's gifts and how she influenced her own development.

I was crazy about my dad, but I lost him at 19. I said to my son the other night, "I only knew my dad 19 years." I looked at him and said, "You're 13 years old already. I only knew my dad 19 years. That's only 6 more years. But I knew my mom 41 years. So I had more time to know her as a person. I never knew my dad as a person like I grew to know my mother."

My mother had a formidable strength. Yes, she was bossy, and everybody was half afraid of her. But she had love and compassion. I think of her love of life, her sheer delight in a bite of a peach. She would just howl with laughter at things her kids said. No one entertained her more than her own children. She absolutely loved being with them. She waited for the minute we would walk in the door to tell her a story. She would give you her undivided attention at the moment to hear your story. Then she would make sure that everybody else knew about our accomplishments.

And her love of learning. I was able to watch the different things she could do and realize that while your talents are gifts, they also have to be nurtured and take work. She helped me understand that. It doesn't just happen; you have to work to develop your talents.

And she worked hard throughout her life. She worked hard at learning. I mean even up to the bitter end, she played Scrabble and wanted to win. Half-blind, she would get this big magnifying glass to be able to study the dictionary to learn new words to beat May Kabias. They had a Scrabble club. Up to her last day she still was trying to learn new words to beat May Kabias.

And she never lost her love of gardening. She watched birds. She taught me to appreciate nature. When I was growing up, I hated pulling those weeds. I would cry, "You can't make me go out in that garden." But you know, that taught me something too. It taught me that you can bring order to the chaos of weeds. I took great pleasure in how it looked when I was done, when I got all those weeds removed. I learned the names of the plants, and I knew how to take care of them because I spent a lot of time out there with Mom. That has become important in my life. I need my time in my garden.

Though I only observed and interviewed Cynthia for 18 months, as I listened to her describe her mother, I reflected on how the descriptions matched what I know of Cynthia. During several meetings, I listened to her tell me stories of a 39-year-old Even Start mother, who lives with her sister and their 12 children and 4 grandchildren in a home bordering on chaos, and I sense her caring and compassion.

In the fall of 1998, Cynthia became the coordinator of PAT in the same school district in which she had been Even Start Director. For the first 2 years as PAT coordinator, she also was Even Start Director. However with 30 PAT educators, Cynthia did not feel that she could do a good job splitting her time between the two programs. Thus, in the fall of 2000, she requested and obtained a full-time position as PAT coordinator. In late 2000, Cynthia left her position to become Coordinator of At-Risk Families for the PAT National Center. Throughout these administrative positions, Cynthia has continued to serve five PAT families.

Schooling

Cynthia attended a Catholic elementary school and public high school. She speaks of school as being very easy for her. Throughout her childhood, close friendships and time with her large family occupied her far more than did school. There was nothing remarkable about school; it was just something she did; she didn't have to work hard to get all As. Cynthia did not describe her elementary schooling; she began with high school.

I remember my high school years as just a lot of fun. School wasn't hard for me at all. I started working my sophomore year in high school at a pizza place. I worked 1 or 2 nights during the week and on the weekend. That gave me spending money, my clothes money, things like that. I never had to work really hard. I learned things quickly.

Cynthia has a keen intellect that her parents nourished by reading to her since she was a baby and by engaging extended daily conversations and debates at dinner. As I listened to her brief description of school, I thought about how much more stimulating her life at home had been than at school. I also reflected on the stark contrast between Cynthia's and Janice's schooling experiences. Cynthia's small-town schools were unexceptional and she "sailed through" with ease. Janice's teachers had higher expectations and she worked very hard to excel.

Because of her family's income, Cynthia could not choose her college. Her courses in college seemed as unremarkable as her experiences in grade school and high school.

I wanted to go to the main state university, but we couldn't afford it. I didn't want to go into education. Everyone else in my family was a teacher, and I didn't want to be a teacher. But at the time my dad gave me no choice. If he sent me to the main state university then my younger brother and sister couldn't go to school, because there wouldn't be enough money. They had 3 kids to try to get through college, and all of us were going to be in college a year or two together. Dad said that he wanted Western, and he wanted me to take a teacher [education] scholarship, because women need that [background]."[17]

Friendships

Cynthia continues contact with her close friends of early childhood and adolescence, friends whom she shared many happy hours of playful abandon.

I was just talking to one of my childhood friends two nights ago. Her mother is in the hospital dying. It made me think back to my first memory of Lane Kabias. We were both in diapers and were crawling under a dining room table, one of those gate-leg tables where the sides come down. When I think about Lane, that's the first image that comes to me. Our mothers were dear friends. They were gardener friends, in this small town. What the moms had in common was that tolerance of what is different. Lane and I have remained friends. Lane now lives in Chicago and we talk to each other a couple times a year. She was one of my dearest friends.

Even though I came from a big family, I always had friends at school. I had friends from pretty much all walks. I had west-ender friends who were the kids on the wrong side of the track. I didn't really hang around with them because I didn't drink and that kind of thing. But I was respectful of them and they knew it. I would help them with school work.

Already in high school, Cynthia's actions seemed to mirror her parents' tolerance of difference.

Jean Bath became one of my best friends. She was loud and obnoxious and totally hysterical. Jean and I stayed friends through all the years, and I lost her two years ago, when she died at the age of 38 of pancreatitis. She was one of my best and dearest friends.

Another good friend was Rose Matthews. She also became my friend in high school, and ended up at the same college. We were kind of like a "rat pack," Jean, Rose, and I. Rose continues to be a good friend of mine. I see her probably 2 or 3 times a year, whenever I go back to Florence.

All the friends I have mentioned spent hours at my house. Our home was the hang out. Poor mom and dad, how they could stand it I'll never know. I mean, we were the last of 7 kids. Our home was across the street from the pizza place where I worked. So we'd close the pizza place, and everyone would come over to my house. Mom and dad must have been deaf by that point. We would stay up till 1, 2, or 4 in the morning. I remember my high school years as lots of fun.

Throughout childhood and adolescence Cynthia was immersed in a caring and loving web of relationships. Her parents modeled caring and compassion in their personal and work life, teenage siblings were primary caregivers when she was very little, and lifelong childhood friends are remembered within a circle of love and caring.[18]

Religion

Cynthia was raised Catholic and attended a Catholic grade school in Florence.

Cynthia: In grade school, I spent a lot of time in religion class. I went to church every day. My parents were quite active in the church. I loved the old Latin Mass, and the symbolism and incense. The mysticism was to me more prevalent then because you didn't understand the Latin. It's like it was shrouded in a mystery, and to me that made more sense. So when I think of religion and church those are the things come to my mind.

Carol: Symbols, images, and mystery.

Cynthia: Yes. And the celebrations. The Catholic church is great for celebrations. The priests dress up in fancy vestments. They use incense. I think that's important in my life—celebrations in my life. And the religious celebration matched my family life. We carried it into the home. Growing up, religion had a strong influence.

Carol: And sin?

Cynthia: And sin, oh yes, mortal sin. I was scared to death. I remember, growing up scared to death they'd catch me doing something awful. And you know, interestingly, I still have that need to confess. I don't actually go to confession anymore. But if I do something I think is wrong, I have to tell somebody. I still have that ingrained in me. Once I confess, I'm fine.

I do have a strong faith in God. My belief in God has influenced my life. In fact, today I had a conversation with one of our Even Start mothers who has been very depressed. We talked about how hard it is when you're depressed to keep moving forward. I said, "You know, I don't look at this as the only part of my life. I really do believe that something comes after this. And that makes daily life, the troubles, and ins and outs not quite so difficult. They are difficult. But this is just a piece of it, not the whole shebang. If I mess this up, there's still something else out there. I think of life as a dress rehearsal for who knows what comes next. I think that for me that makes a difference, and it helps me put things in perspective." She looked at me and nodded.

I've chosen to work with people in a certain way, and I think that probably the way I was raised and my beliefs in a caring and nurturing God probably influence the kind of work I do.

Carol: Do you and Bob continue the Catholicism of your childhood?

Cynthia: I hate to say this, but I don't like to give up my Sunday morning. But I never miss a Christmas or Easter. Being Catholic is great, because as long as you go Christmas and Easter you've got it made. I've never missed. I have a foot in the door.

Cynthia has a strong faith in a tolerant, caring, nurturing God. She is very clear that she strives to continue to be tolerant and caring in her professional life. Her religion does not have the rational tone of Janice. Rather, it is the mystery, symbolism, images, and celebration that Cynthia embraces. Like Janice, she gains strength through her religion, but in a different way. Janice speaks of God giving her strength through prayer in difficult times; Cynthia speaks of trust in an afterlife helping her come to terms with difficulties.

Marriage, Work, and Parenting

Cynthia and her husband, Bob, both grew up in Florence. Bob's brother was Cynthia's classmate whom she knew well. Bob is $4\frac{1}{2}$ years older than Cynthia. She didn't meet him until she was in college and he was in the Naval Academy.

Bob would come back home for basketball games. Our brothers played on the same team. We met at one of the games, and began dating. I graduated from college in December, and we married in February.

When we were first married, we moved very frequently. First he was stationed in Texas, then the Navy moved him to Germany for three years. So we ended up in this little tiny Navy base. Here I was, 21 years old, Bob was a junior officer, and we were thrown in with older people. I came from a generation that was burning bras and wearing blue jeans. The military was still old guard. Officers' wives were to wear gloves and hats and go to teas. The wives seldom worked. It was awful!

The only job I could find was teaching 4-year-olds. I had no idea how to teach 4-year-olds or what a preschool curriculum looked like. So I "flew by the seat of my pants." I did enjoy this, but even at that time, I knew I didn't want a steady diet of teaching preschool. Actually I've never wanted a steady diet of classroom teaching in any shape or form. For me it's too confining, too limiting. But I do have a genuine affection for children, and I realized that.

The other thing it made me realize is how families affect development.[19] I began that realization in that base nursery. There were so many little kids whose parents were young and poor. I got interested right then in the family, how the family works, and how to help kids with early intervention.

Cynthia's interest in young children, family, and early intervention for at-risk children began with her first position. Yet Cynthia speaks of classroom teaching as being too "confining, too limiting." As I listened to Cynthia telling me that classroom teaching seems too confining, her feelings made sense to me because of the ever-changing daily pattern of her childhood family life and her love of impromptu fun and excitement. In contrast, Janice felt totally fulfilled teaching first grade in a small, very wealthy suburb.

After 3 years in Germany, Bob and Cynthia moved to Florida where they stayed for 10 months.

Cynthia: That's where I taught Spanish in an inner city high school to Cubans—which probably started my risk-taking and living dangerously, because it was crazy. At that time teachers were getting beat up in the hallways. I was about 25 years old, looked 12, wore jeans and platform shoes to school. So I would blend in and look like one of my kids. It also was scary because I hadn't used my Spanish for 3 years, and I had to teach first-year Spanish through fourth-year Spanish.

Carol: A new environment, like Germany, but with a lot more risk taking. And you were able to do well?

Cynthia: Well, yes. But by that time Bob decided that he didn't have much of a career in the Navy, with me as his wife. I mean, that was really part of the decision. At that time, the wife was expected to have parties, not a career. That isn't the only reason for Bob's decision, but it was clear to both of us that I was not going to be just an officer's wife; I wanted a career also. I had one tell me that it was my duty to rub elbows with the big brass. I told him something like, if I could find somebody to watch his kid (because I worked at the nursery), that I'd be there. Otherwise, Bob was perfectly capable of rubbing elbows on his own.

Cynthia was a woman in her early 20s whose life experience prior to moving overseas had been growing up in a small town and graduating from a rural state university. Yet Cynthia knew who she was and felt secure in her values and competence, so she could refuse to act in a manner that she thought violated her temperament and basic principles. As I listened to Cynthia describing her determination to remain true to her self, I reflected on her secure, loving childhood that allowed her to know who she was.

Bob and Cynthia then moved to New Jersey, where Bob worked at a chemical company and Cynthia found a position in Head Start.

Cynthia: Head Start was the only job offered me. I was a home visitor for spe-
            cial needs children. My caseload included Puerto Rican families, so I
            got to use my Spanish. I learned very quickly about families and fam-
            ily dynamics, and child development. And then there was an oppor-
            tunity to move up. So I interviewed and got the job. But then we
            moved again. Bob's company moved him from New Jersey to their
            plant in New Mexico.

            We were in New Mexico for about 3 years. Again I worked for
            Head Start. They hired me as their Handicap Coordinator. I coordi-
            nated services for special needs kids. I could use my Spanish with the
            large Mexican population. Head Start hired me even though I was
            pregnant.

            I liked that job. I did that until our son was born, then I went
            back on a part-time basis. Then I decided I needed to get my
            Master's [degree], so I also started going to the state university. I de-
            cided to major in early education. I completed 6 hours, and then we
            moved again.

            We returned to Florida, and I didn't work for the first 18
            months. I went to school and was a full-time mommy, and didn't do
            real well with it. All my classes did not transfer, so I had to take the
            same classes again.

Carol: Cynthia, given your dislike of the classroom, having to repeat educa-
            tion classes, and our culture's negative stereotype of education, how
            have you dealt with this?

Cynthia: I have real mixed feelings. Part of me wholeheartedly agrees that our
            education system doesn't, for the most part, educate very well. I have
            experienced it first hand. I've been in a lot of different schools. Not
            that I've been in the best schools, but I've hit enough of them that I
            worry about the level of education in this country. Especially now
            that our son is in school, I see that he is getting even less than I did.
            But I have been in education now for so long. Most of the people in
            education that I have met truly care about kids and want to be good
            at what they do, and work hard to do that.

            In every state I have lived, I have to take their courses to be cer-
            tified, and it has been such a waste of time and money. I should have
            three PhDs by now. I've gone to school all but 2 years of my adult
            life, and I'm 42. When I moved here, I had to take six classes to get
            state certification and I already had a Master's [degree].

Carol: Did the teacher education courses you have taken over the years
            make a difference, or influence you, either in terms of knowledge or
            skill?

Cynthia: In my undergraduate work. They just threw in 20 hours of education
            at the very end, and that didn't help a bit. I would say that mostly
            what has helped over the years has been teacher training on the job.

> Once you have a position, you seek information. The one thing my teacher training did supply was some resources, some books that I have used. I doubt it really had much impact on how I think or how I do things.

During their first 10 years of marriage, Cynthia and Bob lived in six very different communities across the United States and in Germany. In each area, Cynthia was able to get an early childhood position working with low-income families. She often was in an administrative role where she could be independent, creative, and could contribute. The positions seemed to match her personal style. Each involved young children and families, and in each she could make a contribution. As a self-reflective, bright young woman, Cynthia was able to develop skills on the job through what she terms "trial and error."

After her son, Andrew, was born, Cynthia worked half time. When Andrew was in first grade, Cynthia began working full time and she always has had the summers off. Unlike Janice, Cynthia never considered being a full-time homemaker. Combining career and family has not been easy.

> It's been difficult. I remember standing on a stranger's doorstep and knocking on that door to ask this stranger, asking if she'd watch my baby, who was about a year old. And it just struck me, "I'm going to ask a total stranger to watch my baby!" I couldn't do it. I went home and told Bob, "We've got to figure something else out." And eventually we found a neighbor who we knew. I remember getting in my car at the end of the day with utter terror in my heart that I would get to that babysitter's and my baby wouldn't be okay. We didn't have car phones then. Now I really like my car phone, because when I'm stuck in traffic, I can call my son.
>
> He answers the phone and I know he's okay. I really sympathize with working moms, because I've experienced that fear myself, and it's awful.
>
> It's also something I chose to do in spite of it's being awful. I chose to work and didn't necessarily have to. Financially we probably could have made it.
>
> I have given up opportunities to do things as far as my career that I'll never get back. But I chose to do that because I wasn't willing to give up the time with my child. I don't regret that, but I mourn it sometimes. I wish I'd had the chance to do whatever I wanted to do. Parenting is important to me. I understand that awful feeling of having to leave your child day after day. I'm a working mother. I have been all along. It's an important piece of me to be able to work and contribute and use my skills. But I also bear the guilt of leaving my kid.

Parenting and relationships are central themes in Janice's and Cynthia's personal history. Both women are exceptionally competent home visitors, but they are quite different in many ways. Each woman also had different personal histories. Both women loved and respected their mothers, though their mothers were very different models. Janice's mother was a quiet, even-tempered homemaker with two daughters. Cynthia's mother was a strong, talented woman who loved lively arguments with her husband, had a passion for writing poetry and gardening, and taught school when three of her seven children were less than 10 years old. Janice's husband changed employers only once in the first 27 years of their marriage, while Cynthia's husband's career brought 7 moves in 15 years.

For the past 7 years, Cynthia has lived 2 hours from Florence. Thus, she often spent weekends with her mother, with whom she remained close throughout her adult life. Her mother died 1 year prior to our interviews. I asked Cynthia if she thought her parenting of her son, Andrew, resembles the parenting she received from her mother and father.[20]

Sure, I think it has. At the same time I made conscious choices not to do some of the things my parents did, but it doesn't always work, such as not lecturing, not yelling. I grew up in a yelling family. So I've had to really work not to do that. I am trying to control myself. But when I'm tired, I feel myself slipping into those old patterns. They are hard to break.

I think the positives I have provided for my child are things I grew up with a strong sense of routine. My mom was a drill sergeant. You did this, and you made sure this happened. Even though she drove me nuts, I also could count on it. It was there. And the feeling that you are special, that you are important in this world, that you can do things in the world. I feel that all that came from my mom and dad. And the love of reading. The importance of education.

The expectation that you will do well. There's no question about it. And with Andrew, I've maintained this stance. But the difference between my childhood and Andrew's is that he can tell me. He will say to me, "I think you care too much about that. Who cares if I get an A or B on that. It's okay, mom. It's okay if I get a B." I wouldn't have dared to say that to my parents.

Cynthia grew up with clear parental expectations of excellence, and she continues this theme in her parenting. In spite of family members coming and going her childhood home, it was a place of daily ritual and routine, like the ritual and routine Cynthia provides for Andrew.

Cynthia speaks of the difference between her husband's temperament and personal style and her own and how he has assisted her personally and professionally.

Bob calms me down. He keeps my feet on the ground. He's very pragmatic and is excellent with people issues. When I'm struggling with how to deal with a supervising issue, he's helpful. He listens to me, helps me process and think it through. He nurtures our son in a way you often don't see in men. He's the one who will put Andrew's vitamin out in the morning. I don't even think about it half the time. He'll take Andrew to the Dairy Queen at 9 at night but I'll tell him to wait until tomorrow.

He gives a lot. He's a very calm man. He doesn't get upset about things, but he doesn't express himself. He stifles his emotions whereas I wear him out screaming sometimes. I think there are times he'd love to just shut me up, just as there are times I would love to make him mad, to see him rant and rave. But he knows me and I know him. He's known me for 20 years and he loves me. Bob listens to me. I guess I'm the kind of person who pretty much needs to talk about something to figure it out. I process by talking and so he knows that about me. We go on walks at night and he lets me talk.

Just as Cynthia's parents had significant differences, Cynthia and Bob also have significant temperament and personal style differences. But as with Cynthia's parents, both have lives where caring, compassion, and tolerance are dominant themes in their lives.

During our first 10 years of marriage, we moved a lot. When we lived in England for 3 years, we loved to explore England every Saturday. We would hit a new small town and a pub for lunch. When [we were] in Germany, we explored Europe. We'd go to a little town and learn the history of the place. Now we have lived in the same city for 11 years. And we continue to enjoy using our weekends to go to a [bed and breakfast] in a small town and explore its history.

Since our son was born, lots of my spare time is with him. He's very athletic, so I go to all his games. I also have been a volunteer in grade school, middle, and high schools.

My six siblings are spread out across the country. I try to see all of them at least once a year. Usually, I am the one going to them.

We have seen that the themes of connectedness and relationships have been central throughout Cynthia's career path.[21] During the last 5 years, these themes have become even more dominant in her home visiting work. Between the spring of 1990 and the fall of 1993, Cynthia was a home visitor. In the fall of 1993, she became Even Start Coordinator. The Even Start program serves approximately 40 low-income families. Beyond administering the program, Cynthia continues to do home visiting with approximately six families.

CHILDHOOD PAIN TO PROFESSIONAL COMPETENCE

Many home visitors do not have happy childhoods like Janice and Cynthia. In fact, some may have grown up in very troubled families. But just because someone's childhood family was troubled, it does not mean that they cannot be competent home visitors. Often, in coming to terms with their own pain, home visitors gain sensitivity to others, and they find insights into their own life that can be a resource when they help others. They may understand and be more sensitive because they could not take anything for granted.

Adults carrying pain from their childhood may have achieved resolution in different ways. For example, some adults may come to terms with their childhood pain through reading ideas and concepts. This process may be varied: some read novels, biography and autobiography, history, or therapeutic literature; some become an intellectual in one specific field of knowledge and practice. Other people may learn alternative attitudes, values, and behavior from those outside their family, such as by spending time with families of childhood friends or by learning from older adults who are role models. Some use psychotherapy to come to terms with their troubled childhood.

Whatever means a home visitor uses to grow, it is important that they understand that each individual must find their own path. For example, an adult abused as a child may find the parent she wished for in God. Her client's path, however, must be the client's own, so the client may not find resolution in a religious faith like that of the home visitor.

Because relationships are central to the process of home visiting, it is common for work with some families to trigger the visitor's own childhood pain. When this happens, home visitors unwittingly may respond more to what has been triggered by their own history than by the needs of the child and parent they are serving. Karen is a home visitor who serves at-risk families. As a child, Karen had a very angry mother who directed much of this anger to Karen. Karen's description of her work with a family illustrates this dynamic.

Karen: One mother is a real challenge to me in lots of ways, and probably the family that comes closest to my situation when I was growing up. The mother is trying hard, but she has a lot of problems. People have said that she has been mentally ill, and she probably still is. She has had some counseling and therapy in the past, but not presently. She is very negative with her daughter, who recently turned 3. This mom has had a really rough time when she was young. And she has become angry and hardened because of it. She is a very rude person. The mother is treating her daughter, I assume, the way she was treated. She is not one who is easy to like. And what I had as a child was a very angry mother.

Carol: So when you are sitting in her living room, Karen, what is going through your mind?

Karen: I really have to detach from it. But when I leave, it hits me. When I get away, the feelings start coming back. I have been this little girl. I identify with what is going on with the little girl. That is tough for me.

Carol: Has there been anyone in the program with whom you can talk about this family?

Karen: Yes, when Dan [a clinical psychologist] was at our team meeting. I found that I ended up needing to say some things about what was going on in that family. When I spoke, I didn't realize it was kind of rolling around in me. I just talked about what was going on in a visit one day, and how that little girl was being affected. And I was very angry. Dan told me that I was blaming the mom, which I was.

At the time, it felt terrible for a professional to say that to me. Dan said, "You can't work with this family if you are blaming the mom and putting guilt on her." I sat back and thought, "Well, she needs to be blamed, for she is wrong."

That was one of the best things that has happened. Because putting blame was exactly what I was doing, and it was getting in the way of things. I stepped back and thought, "I need to be there for this mom and this little girl, and see how we can work with this to make things different." Because the mother has told me several times that she doesn't want things to be the way they are. She doesn't want her daughter to be afraid of her.

And in my next visit, I told this mom that she can change things, that she can make a difference, and I believed it as I told her. I told her that it is very hopeful to see somebody with a daughter this young who has had some problems and is saying, "I don't want to do this." I encourage her and tell her she can change, and make it different, that she doesn't have to keep doing things the way she had been. I feel that when I first told her that, that's when we really connected. I think she holds on to that hopeful talk.

Carol: And you too?

Karen: Yeah, we both do. So I don't know what is going to happen. She is very difficult to talk with, and she can be very rude. But I work hard to find something positive. For example, she told me that sometimes she puts on music and has this dance with her little girl. And I told her that's a great thing to do, and maybe you can do this when you recognize that you are getting angry.

When Karen was able to process happenings with this family with her team, the team leader interpreted her actions and gave her a new understanding, not just of the family, but of her response to this family. Once Karen recognized that she was angry and was blaming the mother, she understood how nonproductive her approach was. She then became proactive and spoke directly to this mother about knowing she could change. Karen's clear statement of hope became the beginning of a new phase in their relationship—a relationship that continued to be difficult, but one in which Karen knew she could help make a difference.

It always is important for home visitors to strive to recognize their vulnerabilities, that is, to be alert for experiences that may trigger unresolved childhood issues. For Karen, being with an unstable mother who raged at her 3-year-old rekindled the feelings of Karen's own childhood memories with her mother. With the help of supervision, Karen was able to step back and ask herself what was happening. Once she recognized her vulnerability, Karen could move forward and approach the mother differently.

Home visitors cannot assume resolutions they have found will fit the parents with whom they work. For example, the home visitor who has achieved resolution of childhood pain may experience vulnerability when she works with a parent or child experiencing pain similar to that of her own childhood. The home visitor may respond intellectually as she strives to problem solve with the parent. Her intellectual approach may protect herself, but may miss where the parent or child is emotionally.

Although parents may look forward to the home visitor's visit, the visitor may dread it because it is too familiar to her own childhood past. For example, one home visitor, Anna, has a sister with Down syndrome. Anna's mother had told her many years ago that God sends special blessings, that these children with Down syndrome are the chosen recipients of God's love because they remain as little children who are fit for the "Kingdom of God." In this religious view, resenting her sister was sinful. As a child, Anna felt anger for her sister's interference, for her mother's preoccupation with her sister, and later for having to remain at home to be with her sister since she could not be alone. She felt guilty for all these feelings because they indicated a lack of faith in God's wisdom.

Now Anna works with a couple who are coming to terms with their 1-year-old child who has Down syndrome. The parents are angry that they do not have a perfect child. They feel cheated because they had waited so long for this child and had dreamed of a perfect child. After amniocentesis showed that his child would have Down syndrome, the father had wanted to abort. The mother briefly considered this idea, but then could not bring herself to do it. She is, however, unable to clearly state religious or philosophical reasons for her choice. These parents' conflict over the abortion continues; the father still thinks he was right even though he is beginning to bond with his daughter. The mother's anger at his request for abortion continues to be strong, even though she knows her child is not the one she had dreamed of having. In this complex network of emotions, Anna discovers that she is having difficulty with these parents' conflicts, for she would like the answers to seem as simple to these parents as they seemed for her mother. At the same time, she has trouble separating the parents' resentment toward their child from the resentment she once felt toward her sister.

Not all home visitors actively work towards ensuring that their own personal history does not confuse them as they relate to the visit. Even if a home visitor is sensitive to this possibility, sometimes it takes an outsider to identify the dynamics. Given this complexity in home visiting relationships, supervision is very important in assisting home visitors' skills in self-reflection and relating to families.[22]

CONCLUSION

In this chapter, we have portrayed the life histories of two home visitors, Janice and Cynthia, how they see their home visiting work as giving meaning to their lives, and how their personal histories are intertwined with their home visiting. Each woman's home visiting grows out of her childhood history. Relationships with family and friends, to whom they continue to relate, were central to their childhood life and are the core of their home visiting work. As an adult, each woman has strong commitments rooted in her childhood. Janice's adult life expresses a strong commitment to education and her family; Cynthia's, to helping others and to her family. Each woman's early life was situated in an environment (e.g., neighborhood, community, and society) that impacted their development. Nathan was a suburb that highly valued education, a dominant theme in Janice's life. Although Cynthia's family highly valued education, their small rural community did not challenge educationally; rather, school was just something you did as a child. Coming from a conservative family and community and being 10 years older than Cynthia, it never dawned on Janice to continue working after she had her first child. In contrast, it never dawned on Cynthia to remain home for an extended time once she had her child.

Each person had her own values, attitudes, beliefs, and way of relating to others. These patterns are rooted in personal history, a history in which childhood relationships are intertwined with present patterns. That means when the home visitor experiences strong emotions before or after a visit, or feels confused or conflicted when there, it sometimes helps to ask if the situation is similar to something the home visitor experienced in his or her own family. For example, we have seen how Karen discovered that in blaming the mother of a 3-year-old, she was actually reexperiencing her own mother's behavior when Karen was 3 years old. Just as a home visitor's problem often is a response to her own childhood, we also have seen a person's strength as part of a childhood pattern. When she shared her childhood history with me, Cynthia discovered that her ability to move in and out of dangerous neighborhoods is similar to the risk taking she and her siblings took as very young children.

Both Karen and Cynthia were able to see these connections between current struggles at work and personal history as they "talked it over" with another person. Most people understand themselves best when they are reflecting on their experiences with someone else. That is why peer support and supervision are central dynamics for promoting high quality home visiting.

Home visiting is a new profession. Builders know what they need to construct a house. When she goes to work, a teacher knows what the day's plans are. In contrast, home visitors never know what to expect as they enter a family's home. Home visiting can be very personally rewarding work while being very difficult and untidy.

Central to the home visiting process is the evolving relationship between home visitor, child, and parent. Development of both parent and child occurs through and within these relationships. The process is different for each family and can be known only as the relationships evolve over time, as each person comes to know the other, and to develop mutuality in their collaborative work together. The child and parent develop in relationship to each other. Parents develop in their relationship with their home visitor. Finally, the home visitor develops in relation to her personal history, to the families she visits, and to her professional peers and supervisors.

Resources

Books for Parents About Parenting

Brazelton, T.B. (1974). *Toddlers and parents: A declaration of independence*. New York: Dell Publishing.

Brazelton, T.B. (1983). *Infants and mothers: Differences in development*. New York: Dell Publishing.

Crockenberg, S., & Leerkes, E. (2000). Infant social and emotional development in family context. In C.H. Zeanah, Jr. (Ed.), *Handbook of infant mental health* (2nd ed., pp. 60–90). New York: Guilford Press.

Gowen, J.W., & Nebrig, J.B. (2002). *Enhancing early development: Guiding parents of young children*. Baltimore: Paul H. Brookes Publishing Co.

Greenspan, S., & Greenspan, N.T. (1989). *The essential partnership: How parents and children can meet the emotional challenges of infancy and childhood*. New York: Penguin Books.

Greenspan, S.I., with Breslau Lewis, N. (1999). *Building healthy minds: The six experiences that create intelligence and emotional growth in babies and young children*. Cambridge, MA: Perseus Publishing.

Imber-Black, E., & Roberts, J. (Eds.). (1992). *Rituals for our times: Celebration, healing and changing our lives and our relationships*. New York: HarperCollins.

Lieberman, A.F. (1993). *The emotional life of the toddler*. New York: The Free Press.

Pruett, K.D. (1997). How men and children affect each other's development. *Zero to Three, 18*(1), 3–11.

Children's Play

Biber, B. (1984). *Early education and psychological development*. New Haven, CT: Yale University Press.

Bruner, J.A., & Sylva, K. (1976). *Play: Its role in development and evolution*. New York: Basic Books.

Carlsson-Paige, N., & Levin, D.E. (1990). *Who's calling the shots? How to respond effectively to children's fascination with war play and war toys*. Philadelphia: New Society Publishers.

Dau, E. (1999). *Child's play in early childhood settings*. Baltimore: Paul H. Brookes Publishing Co.

Erikson, E. (1950). *Childhood and society*. New York: W.W. Norton.

Fein, G., & Rivkin, M.. (1973). *The young child at play: Reviews of research* (Vol. 4.). Washington, DC: National Association for the Education of Young Children.

Galinsky, E., & David, J. (1988). *The preschool years: Family strategies that work— from experts and parents*. New York: Ballantine Books.

Greenspan, S., & Greenspan, N.T. (1989). *The essential partnership: How parents and children can meet the emotional challenges of infancy and childhood.* New York: Penguin Books.

Children's Books About Toilet Training

Allison, A. (1999). *Toddler's potty book.* Los Angeles: Price, Stern, Sloan.
Frankel, A. (1992). *Once upon a potty.* New York: Barrons.

Cultural Diversity

Aber, J.L., Jones, S., & Cohen, J. (2000). The impact of poverty on the mental health and development of very young children. In C.H. Zeanah, Jr. (Ed.), *Handbook of infant mental health* (2nd ed., pp. 113–128). New York: Guilford Press.
Brunson Phillips, C. (1995). Culture: A process that empowers. In J.R. Lally (Ed.), *Infant/toddler caregiving: A guide to culturally sensitive care.* Sacramento: California State Department of Education.
Garcia, E.E. (1994). Addressing the challenges of diversity. In S.L. Kagan & B. Weissbourd (Eds.), *Putting families first: America's family support movement and the challenge of change* (pp. 243–275). San Francisco: Jossey-Bass.
Lynch, E.W., & Hanson, E.W. (Eds.). (2004). *Developing cross-cultural competence: A guide for working with children and their families.* Baltimore: Paul H. Brookes Publishing Co.
Mallory, B.L., & New, R.S. (1994). *Diversity and developmentally appropriate practices: Challenges for early childhood education.* New York: Teachers College Press.
Nai-Lin Chang, H., & Pulido, D. (1994). The critical importance of cultural and linguistic continuity for infants and toddlers. *Zero to Three, 3*(2), 13–17.
Polk, C. (1994). Therapeutic work with African-American families. *Zero to Three, 3*(2), 9–11.

Early Risk

Cicchetti, D., & Lynch, M. (1993). Toward an ecological/transactional model of community violence and child maltreatment: Consequences for children's development. *Psychiatry, 56,* 95–118.
Garbarino, J. (1990). The human ecology of early risk. In S.J. Meisels & J.P. Shonkoff (Eds.), *Handbook of early childhood intervention* (pp. 78–96). New York: Cambridge University Press.
Garbarino, J. (1992). *Children in danger: Coping with the consequences of community violence.* San Francisco: Jossey-Bass.
Goodman, S.H., Radke-Yarrow, M., & Teti, D. (1993). Maternal depression as a context for child rearing. *Zero to Three, 13*(5), 10–16.
Helfer, R., & Kempe, C.H. (1976). *Child abuse and neglect: The family and the community.* Cambridge, MA: Ballinger.

Kaplan, M.D., & Pruett, K.D. (2000). Divorce and custody: Developmental implications. In C.H. Zeanah, Jr. (Ed.), *Handbook of infant mental health* (2nd ed., pp. 533–547). New York: Guilford Press.

Kaufman, J., & Henrich, C. (2000). Exposure to violence and early childhood trauma. In C.H. Zeanah, Jr. (Ed.), *Handbook of infant mental health* (2nd ed., pp. 195–207). New York: Guilford Press.

Kempe, C.H., & Helfer, R. (1980). *The battered child.* Chicago: University of Chicago Press.

Klein, N.K., & Campbell, P. (1990). Preparing personnel to serve at-risk and disabled infants, toddlers, and preschoolers. In S.J. Meisels & J.P. Shonkoff (Eds.), *Handbook of early childhood intervention* (pp. 679–699). New York: Cambridge University Press.

Luby, J.L. (2000). Depression. In C.H. Zeanah, Jr. (Ed.), *Handbook of infant mental health* (2nd ed., pp. 382–396). New York: Guilford Press.

Main, M., & Goldwyn, R. (1984). Predicting rejections of her infant from mother's representation of her own experience: Implications for the abused-abusing intergenerational cycle. *Child Abuse and Neglect, 8,* 203–217.

Schore, A.N. (1998). Early organization of the nonlinear right brain and development of a predisposition to psychiatric disorders. *Development and Psychopathology, 9*(4), 505–633.

Seifer, R., & Dickson, S. (2000). Parental maternal illness and infant development. In C.H. Zeanah, Jr. (Ed.), *Handbook of infant mental health* (2nd ed., pp. 145–160). New York: Guilford Press.

Sugar, M. (1992). Toddler's traumatic memories. *Infant Mental Health Journal, 13*(3), 245–251.

Everyday Routines

Anders, T., Goodlin-Jones, B., & Sadah, A. (2000). Sleep disorders. In C.J. Zeanah, Jr. (Ed.), *Handbook of infant mental health* (2nd ed., pp. 326–338). New York: Guilford Press.

Brazelton, T.B. (1992). *Touchpoints: The essential reference. Your child's emotional and behavioral development.* Reading, MA: Addison Wesley Higher Education Group.

Brazelton, T.B., & Sparrow, J.D. (2003). *Sleep: The Brazelton way.* Cambridge, MA: Da Capo Press.

Brazelton, T.B., & Sparrow, J.D. (2004). *Feeding: The Brazelton way.* Cambridge, MA: Da Capo Press.

Brazelton, T.B., & Sparrow, J.D. (2004). *Toilet training: The Brazelton way.* Cambridge, MA: Da Capo Press.

Cole, J. (1983). *Parents' book of toilet teaching.* New York: Ballantine Books.

Ferber, R. (1985). *Solve your child's sleep problems.* New York: Simon & Schuster.

Jones, S. (1992). *Crying baby, sleepless nights: Why your baby is crying and what you can do about it.* Boston: The Harvard Common Press.

Lansky, V. (1984). *Toilet training.* New York: Bantam Books.

Pediatric Nutrition Practice Group. (1992). *Quality assurance criteria for pediatric nutrition conditions: A model.* Chicago: American Dietetic Association.

Satter, E. (1983). *Child of mine: Feeding with love and good sense.* New York: Bell Publishing.

Satter, E. (1992). The feeding relationship. *Zero to Three, 12*(5), 1–9.

Weissbluth, M. (1987). *Healthy sleep habits, happy child.* New York: Fawcett Columbine.

Welford, H. (1987). *Toilet-training and bed-wetting: A practical guide for today's parents.* Rochester, VT: Thorsons Publishing Group.

Family Rituals and Celebration

Imber-Black, E., & Roberts, J. (Eds.). (1992). *Rituals for our times: Celebration, healing and changing our lives and our relationships.* New York: HarperCollins.

Lieberman, S. (1984). *Let's celebrate: Creating new family traditions.* New York: Putnam Publishing Group.

Wolin, S.F., & Bennet, L.A. (1984). Family ritual. *Family Process, 23,* 401–420.

Guidance and Discipline

Brazelton, T.B. (1992). *Touchpoints: The essential reference. Your child's emotional and behavioral development.* Reading, MA: Addison Wesley Higher Education Group.

Brazelton, T.B., & Cramer, B.G. (1990). *The earliest relationship: Parents, infants, and the drama of early attachment.* Reading, MA: Addison Wesley Higher Education Group.

Clewett, A.S. (1988). Guidance and discipline: Teaching young children appropriate behavior. *Young Children, 43*(4), 26–36.

Gartrell, D. (1987). Punishment or guidance? *Young Children, 42*(3), 55–60.

Gordon, T. (1989). *Discipline that works: Promoting self-discipline in children.* New York: Penguin Books.

Greenberg, P. (1988). Avoiding "me against you" discipline. *Young Children, 44*(1), 24–29

Honig, A.S. (1985). Compliance, control, and discipline. *Young Children, 40*(2), 50–58.

Miller, C.S. (1984). Building self-control: Discipline for young children. *Young Children, 39*(7), 15–19.

Snyder, M., Snyder, R., & Snyder, R., Jr. (1980). *The young child as person: Toward the development of a healthy conscience.* New York: Human Science Press.

Soderman, A.K. (1985). Dealing with difficult young children: Strategies for teachers and parents. *Young Children, 40*(5), 15–20.

Thompson, R.A., & Calkins, S.D. (1996). The double-edged sword: Emotional regulation for children at risk. *Development and Psychopathology, 8*(1), 163–182.

Thompson, R.A., Flood, M.F., & Lundquist, L. (1995). Emotional regulation: Its relations to attachment and developmental psychopathology. In D. Cicchetti & S.L. Toth (Eds.), *Rochester symposium on developmental psychopathology: Vol. 6. Emotion, cognition, and representation* (pp. 261–287). Rochester, NY: University of Rochester Press.

Home Visiting

Bromwich, R. (1981). Working with parents and infants: An interactional approach. Austin, TX: PRO-ED.

Burch, P., Palanki, A., & Thompson, S. (1994). *Home visiting.* Boston: Institute for Responsive Education.

Cochran, M., Deann, C., Dill, M.F., & Woolever, F. (1984). *Empowering families: Home visiting and building clusters.* Ithaca, NY: Family Matters Project, Cornell University.

Doan-Sampon, M.A., Wollenburg, K., Campbell, A., & the Portage Project Staff. (1993). *Growing: Birth to three.* Portage, WI: Portage Project.

Gowen, J.W., & Nebrig, J.B. (2002). *Enhancing early emotional development: Guiding parents of young children.* Baltimore: Paul H. Brookes Publishing Co.

Johnson, E.G., Strickland, C.S., & Thompson, S. (1993). *Home visiting: A tool kit for quilting.* Boston: The League of Schools Reaching Out, Institute for Responsive Education.

Klass, C.S., Pettinelli, D., & Wilson, M. (1993). Home visiting: Building a bridge between home and school. *Equity and Choice, 10*(10), 52–56.

Morra, L.G. (1990). *Home visiting: A promising early intervention strategy for at-risk families.* Report to the Chairman, Subcommittee on Labor, Health and Human Services, Education, and Related Agencies, Committee on Appropriations, U.S. Senate. Washington, DC: U.S. General Accounting Office.

Parents as Teachers. (1989). *Parents as Teachers program planning and implementation guide.* St. Louis: University of Missouri, St. Louis.

Parents as Teachers. (1990). *Born to learn: Prenatal to age three curriculum. Implementation guide.* St. Louis: Parents as Teachers National Center.

Provence, S., & Apfel, N.H. (2001). *Infant-Toddler and Family Instrument.* Baltimore: Paul H. Brookes Publishing Co.

Wasik, B.H., Bryant, D.M., & Lyons, C.M. (2000). *Home visiting: Procedures for helping families.* Thousand Oaks, CA: Sage Publications.

Home Visitors' Professional Development

Almonte, B.E. (1994). Professionalization as culture change: Issues for infant/family community workers and their supervisors. *Zero to Three, 15*(2), 18–23.

Fenichel, E. (1991). Learning through supervision and mentorship to support the development of infants, toddlers and their families. *Zero to Three, 12*(2), 1–8.

Illness

Brazelton, T.B. (1992). *Touchpoints: The essential reference. Your child's emotional and behavioral development.* Reading, MA: Addison Wesley Higher Education Group.

Dawson, P. (Ed.). (1992). Should the field of early child and family intervention address failure to thrive? *Zero to Three, 12*(5), 20–243.

Parmelee, A.H., Jr. (1993). Children's illnesses and normal behavioral development: The role of caregivers. *Zero to Three, 13*(4), 1–9.

Sturm, L., & Drotar, D. (1992). Communication strategies for working with parents of infants who fail to thrive. *Zero to Three, 12*(5), 25–28.

Villarreal, S.F., McKinney, L., & Quackenbush, M. (1992). *Handle with care: Helping children prenatally exposed to drugs and alcohol.* Santa Cruz, CA: ETR Associates.

Infant-Toddler Development and Caregiving

Bernstein, M.H., & Bornstein, H.G. (1995). Caregivers' responsiveness and cognitive development in infants and toddlers: Theory and research. In P.L. Mangione (Ed.), *Infant/toddler caregiving: A guide to cognitive development and learning.* Sacramento: California State Department of Education.

Brazelton, T.B. (1974). *Toddlers and parents: A declaration of independence.* New York: Dell Publishing.

Brazelton, T.B. (1983). *Infants and mothers: Differences in development.* New York: Dell Publishing.

Brazelton, T.B., & Cramer, B.G. (1990). *The earliest relationship: Parents, infants, and the drama of early attachment.* New York: Addison Wesley.

Brazelton, T.B., & Sparrow, J.D. (2003). *Discipline: The Brazelton way.* Cambridge, MA: Da Capo Press.

Brazelton, T.B., & Sparrow, J.D. (2005). *Mastering anger and aggression: The Brazelton way.* Cambridge, MA: Da Capo Press.

Brazelton, T.B., & Sparrow, J.D. (2005). *Understanding sibling rivalry: The Brazelton way.* Cambridge, MA: Da Capo Press.

Chess, S., & Thomas, A. (1987). *Know your child: An authoritative guide for today's parents.* New York: Basic Books.

Field, T. (1995). Supporting cognitive development through interactions with young infants. In P.L. Mangione (Ed.), *Infant/toddler caregiving: A guide to cognitive development and learning.* Sacramento: California State Department of Education.

Lally, J.R. (1995). Discovery in infancy: How and what infants learn. In P.L. Mangione (Ed.), *Infant/toddler caregiving: A guide to cognitive development and learning.* Sacramento: California State Department of Education.

Landy, S. (2002). *Pathways to competence: Encouraging healthy social and emotional development in young children.* Baltimore: Paul H. Brookes Publishing Co.

Pruett, K. (1999). *Me, myself, and I: How children build their sense of self: 18 to 36 months.* New York: Goddard Press.

Language, Communication, and Emerging Literacy

Barclay, L., Benelli, C., & Curtis, A. (1995). Literacy begins at birth: What caregivers can learn from parents of children who read early. *Young Children, 50*(4), 24–28.

Bates, E., O'Connell, B., & Shore, C. (1987). Language and communication in infancy. In J.D. Osofsky (Ed.), *Handbook of infant development* (2nd ed., pp. 149–203). New York: John Wiley & Sons.

Bruner, J. (1985). *Child's talk: Learning to use the language.* New York: W.W. Norton.

Devine, M. (1991). *Baby talk: The art of communicating with infants and toddlers.* New York: Plenum Press.

Dole, J.D., Duffy, G.G., Roehler, L.R., & Perons, P.D. (1991). Moving from old to the new: Research on reading comprehension instruction. *Review of Educational Research, 6*(2), 239–264.

Fields, M.V., & Lee, D. (1989). *Let's begin reading right: A developmental approach to beginning literacy.* Columbus, OH: Merrill.

Galinsky, E., & David, J. (1988). *The preschool years: Family strategies that work— from experts and parents.* New York: Ballantine Books.

Hart, B., & Risley, T.R. (1995). *Meaningful differences in the everyday experience of young American children.* Baltimore: Paul H. Brookes Publishing Co.

Hart, B., & Risley, T.R. (1999). *The social world of children learning to talk.* Baltimore: Paul H. Brookes Publishing Co.

Heath, S.B. (1983). *Way with words: Language, life, and works in communities and classrooms.* New York: Cambridge University Press.

Lee, P. (1989). Is the young child egocentric or sociocentric? *Teachers College Record, 90*(3), 279–291.

Mahoney, B., & Powell, A. (1988). Modifying parent–child interaction: Enhancing the development of handicapped children. *Journal of Special Education, 22*(1), 82–96.

McCartney, K., & Robeson, W.W. (1992). Emergence of communication: Words, grammar, and first conversations. In J.R. Lally, P.L. Mangione, & C.L. Young-Hold (Eds.), *Infant/toddler caregiving: A guide to language development and communication.* Sacramento: California State Department of Education.

Nelson, K. (1973). Structure and strategy in learning to talk. *Monographs of the Society for Research in Child Development, 38*(Serial No. 149).

Nelson, K. (1989). *Narratives from the crib.* Cambridge, MA: Harvard University Press.

Prizant, B.M., Wetherby, A.M., & Roberts, J.E. (2000) Communication problems. In C.H. Zeanah, Jr. (Ed.), *Handbook of infant mental health* (2nd ed., pp. 282–297). New York: Guilford Press.

Sach, J. (1992). Emergence of communication: Earliest signs. In J.R. Lally, P.L. Mangione, & C.L. Young-Hold (Eds.), *Infant/toddler caregiving: A guide to language development and communication.* Sacramento: California State Department of Education.

Shatz, M. (1994). *A toddler's life: From personal narrative to professional insight.* New York: Oxford University Press.

Thal, D.J. (1992). Emergence of communication: Give and take between adult and child. In J.R. Lally, P.L. Mangione, & C.L. Young-Hold (Eds.), *Infant/toddler caregiving: A guide to language development and communication.* Sacramento: California State Department of Education.

Neuroscience

Blakeslee, S. (1995, August 29). Brain's early growth may be crucial. *New York Times*, pp. B5–B6.

Chugani, H.T. (1997). Neuroimaging of developmental nonlinearity and developmental pathologies. In G.R. Lyon (Ed.), *Developmental neuroimaging* (pp. 187–195). San Diego: Academic Press.

Fenichel, E. (2001). From neurons to neighborhoods: What's in it for you? *Zero to Three, 21*(5), 8–15.

Nelson, C.A. (2000). The neurobiological bases of early intervention. In J.P. Shonkoff & S.J. Meisels (Eds.), *Handbook of early intervention* (2nd ed., pp. 204–230). New York: International University Press.

Nelson, C.A., & Bosquet, M. (2000). Neurobiology of fetal and infant development: Implications for infant mental health. In C.H. Zeanah, Jr. (Ed.), *Handbook of infant mental health* (2nd ed., pp. 37–59). New York: Guilford Press.

Schore, A.N. (1994). *Affect regulation and the origin of the self: The neurobiology of emotional development.* Mahwah, NJ: Lawrence Erlbaum Associates.

Schore, A.N. (1998). Early organization of the nonlinear right brain and development of a predisposition to psychiatric disorders. *Development and Psychopathology, 9*(4), 505–633.

Shonkoff, J.P., & Phillips, D.A. (2000). *From neurons to neighborhoods: The science of early childhood development.* Washington, DC: National Academies Press.

Shore, R. (1997). *Rethinking the brain.* Chicago: Family and Work Institute.

Super, C., & Harness, S. (1997). The cultural structuring of child development. In J.W. Berry, P.R. Dasen, & T.S. Saraswathi (Eds.), *Cross-cultural psychology: Vol. 2. Basic process and human development* (pp. 1–40). Boston: Allyn & Bacon.

Pregnancy and Prenatal Care

Abrams, B. (1994). *Eating for two: Nutrition during pregnancy.* White Plains, NY: March of Dimes Birth Defects Foundation.

American Academy of Pediatrics & American College of Obstetricians and Gynecologists (1992). *Guidelines for perinatal care* (3rd ed.). Elk Grove Village, IL: American Academy of Pediatrics & American College of Obstetricians and Gynecologists.

Auman, G.M.E., & Baird, M.M. (1993). Risk assessment for pregnant women. In R.A. Knuppel & J.A. Drukker (Eds.), *High risk pregnancy: A team approach* (pp. 8–35). Philadelphia: W.B. Saunders.

Brott, A.A., & Ash, J. (1995). *The expectant father.* New York: Abbeville Press.

Chamberlain, D. (1998). *The mind of your newborn baby.* Berkeley, CA: North Atlantic Books.

Curtis, G.B. (1997). *Your pregnancy week by week.* Tucson, AZ: Fisher Books.

Driscoll, J.W. (1996). Psychological adaptations to pregnancy and postpartum. In K.R. Simpson & P.A. Creehan (Eds.), *AWHONN's perinatal nursing* (pp. 61–72). Philadelphia: J.B. Lippincott.

Eisenberg, A., Murkoff, H.E., & Hathaway, S.E. (1996). *What to expect when you're expecting.* New York: Workman.

Flanigan, G.L. (1996). *Beginning life.* New York: DK Publishing.

Nilsson, L., & Hamberger, L. (1990). *A child is born.* New York: Dell Publishing.

Remich, M. (1994). Promoting a healthy pregnancy. In E.Q. Youngkin & M.S Davis (Eds.), *Women's health: A primary care clinical guide* (pp. 383–392). Norwalk, CT: Appleton & Lange.

Satt, B.J., Zelen, S.L., & Satgt, L.A. (1995). *A sound beginning.* Agoura, CA: A Sound Beginning.

U.S. Department of Health and Human Services. (1992). *Myself, my baby: Health diary.* Washington, DC: U.S. Government Printing Office.

Wayland, J., & Rawlins, R. (1997). African American teen mothers' perception of parenting. *Journal of Pediatric Nursing, 12*(1) 13–20.

Sexuality Education

Bernstein, A. (1977). *The flight of the stork.* New York: Delacorte Press.

Brick, P., Davis, N., Fischel, M., Lupo, T., Marshall, J., & MacVicae, A. (1989). *Bodies, birth and babies: Sexuality and education in early childhood programs.* Bergen County, NJ: Center for Family Life Education, Planned Parenthood.

Calderone, M., & Johnson, E. (1988). *The family book about sexuality.* New York: HarperCollins.

Calderone, M., & Rame, J. (1982). *Talking with your child about sex.* New York: Ballantine Books.

Gordon, S., & Gordon, J. (1982). *Did the sun shine before you were born?* New York: Ed-U Press.

Gordon, S., & Gordon, J. (1983). *Raising a child conservatively in a sexually permissive world.* New York: Simon & Schuster.

Siblings

Dunn, J., & Plomin, R. (1990). *Separate lives: Why siblings are so different.* New York: Basic Books.

Faber, A., & Mazlish, E. (1987). *Siblings without rivalry: How to help your children live together so you can live too.* New York: W.W. Norton.

Galinsky, E., & David, J. (1988). *The preschool years: Family strategies that work—from experts and parents.* New York: Ballantine Books.

Television

Carlsson-Paige, N., & Levin, D.E. (1990). *Who's calling the shots? How to respond effectively to children's fascination with war play and war toys.* Philadelphia: New Society Publishers.

Jordan, A.B., & Woodard, E.J.H., IV. (2001). Electronic childhood: The availability and use of household media by 2- and 3-year-olds. *Zero to Three, 22*(2), 4–9.

Levin, D.E., & Carlsson-Paige, N. (1994). Developmentally appropriate television: Putting children first. *Young Children, 49*(5), 38–44.

Linn, S., & Poussaint, A.F. (2001). The truth about Teletubbies. *Zero to Three, 22*(2), 24–29.

Endnotes

Chapter 1

1. Bronfenbrenner discussed this type of reciprocal two-person relationship as a primary dyad. In primary dyads, two people coordinate their activities with one another within a mutuality of positive feeling. This mutuality motivates young children to engage in progressively more complex patterns of interaction and increasingly complex learning processes. Bronfenbrenner wrote that the primary dyad continues to exist for both participants even when they are not physically together. Bronfenbrenner, 1979, pp. 56–66.
2. Stern, 1985.
3. Garbarino wrote poignantly of how parenting "depends in large measure on the character and quality of the social environment in which we bear and raise our children" (p. xv). Garbarino identified and discussed the array of relationships connecting child, family, and social environment, and how these relationships influence parent and child development. Garbarino, 1992.
4. Coll & Magnuson, 2000, p. 97.
5. Lewis, 2000, p. 94.
6. Carlson et al., 2004.
7. Lynch & Hanson, 2004, p. 453.
8. A large proportion of community-based home visiting programs use paraprofessional home visitors. Musick and Stott identified dilemmas of paraprofessional helping and explored new methods of educating these individuals. Musick & Stott, 1993, pp. 651–657.
9. Weissbourd provided a provocative overview of traditional parent education and a history of the development of family support programs. Weissbourd, 1987, pp. 38–56. Weissbourd also discussed the emergence of the current family resource moment in Weissbourd, 1994, pp. 28–48. In his historical overview of the first 32 years of parent education in America, Schlossman described U.S. public policy with regard to new knowledge in the behavioral sciences. He also found parallels between parent education of the 1960s and the origin of the parent education movement in the late 19th and early 20th centuries. Schlossman, 1976, pp. 436–467.
10. Pawl, 1995.
11. Weiss argued that home visiting programs are a "necessary but not sufficient" service to at-risk families with multiple problems. Parents whose multiple, complicated problems are so great that they interfere with the parents' attention to their child often are beyond a home visiting program that does not have broader social services. Weiss, 1993, pp. 113–128. Schorr provided detailed descriptions of successful intervention and prevention programs for

at-risk families and discussed the approaches needed to "break the cycle of disadvantage." Schorr & Schorr, 1988.

12. See Chapter 2 for a discussion of networking with community resources.

13. In a discussion of a home visiting program for families at risk with children from birth to 3 years, Bromwich indicated that the reciprocal positive feelings of parent educators and home visitors was strongly related to the effectiveness of their program's intervention. Bromwich, 1981.

14. For further information on the parent–home visitor personal relationship, see Chapter 2.

15. Lussier et al., 2002.

16. Wightman, 2004, p. 40.

17. Lussier et al., 2002.

18. Horn, 2000.

19. Sharp & Ispa, 2006

20. Nelson & Bosquet, 2000.

21. Saffran et al., 2006.

22. Wakschlag & Hans, 2000.

23. Nelson & Bosquet, 2000.

24. Wakschlag & Hans, 2000, p. 134.

25. Luster & Brophy-Herb, 2000.

26. Wasik, Bryant, and Lyons provided an overview of characteristics of teenage parents and effective home visiting approaches for working with such families. Wasik et al., 1990, pp. 193–199. Since 1978, the Prenatal/Early Infancy Project has provided nurse home visiting to new teen mothers and their babies. The program has been helpful in improving mothers' and babies' health and has assisted them in using community resources. The program resulted in a decrease in second pregnancies and an increase in mothers' finishing school and gaining employment. Olds, 1981, pp. 173–197.

27. McDonough has spent many years guiding teenage parents with low incomes in Chicago. McDonough first forms a positive alliance with the parent. She uses educational and behavioral psychology to improve mothers' parenting. Her work always focuses on expanding the parent's strength. After parent and child play together, McDonough and parent watch the videotape of this play sequence. McDonough picks out a positive strength and elaborates on it. Once the positive alliance is formed and the parent can recognize her strengths, the parent often begins talking about her own difficulties nondefensively. McDonough, 1993, pp. 414–426.

28. Smith & Wells, 1990.

29. McDonough, 1993.

30. Brooks-Gunn et al., 2000.

31. Aber et al., 2000.

32. Schon discussed how practitioners, with the help of coaching, learn primarily by doing. He emphasized the power of reflection in action, especially reciprocal reflection in action between coach and practitioner. Schon, 1987, pp. 26–32.

33. Obeidallah & Burton, 1999.

34. Garbarino & Ganzel, 2000.

35. Constantino, 1993.
36. Stern, 1995.
37. Fraiberg, Adelson, & Shapiro, 1975. Pawl and her colleagues Judith Pekarsky and Alicia Lieberman continued Selma Fraiberg's work at the Infant–Parent Program, San Francisco General Hospital, Department of Psychiatry. See Lieberman, Silverman, & Pawl, 2000; Lieberman, 1991; Lieberman & Pawl, 1993.
38. Lieberman, Silverman, & Pawl, 2000.

Chapter 2

1. Bruner discussed how language is the way we "sort out our thoughts about things" (p. 72). He wrote that narratives, or stories, give meaning to experience. If we want to understand people, Bruner claimed, we need to understand the ways in which people construct their world in narrative. Bruner, 1986, pp. 44–78. Anderson wrote that, in telling stories, we are not only informing others but forming ourselves. "When one expresses oneself one is in the process of realizing one's identity." Anderson, 1992, p. 89.
2. Penn discussed how concepts of the future and concepts of change are one. She wrote of the power that families have by imagining new solutions in the future and thus facilitating change. Penn, 1985.
3. Bronfenbrenner explained primary dyads as those two-person relationships in which people are engaged in a joint activity. Bronfenbrenner claimed that, once two people participate in a joint activity, they are likely to develop positive feelings toward each other and engage in mutuality. Joint activity, mutuality, and positive feelings promote the young child's learning and development. Bronfenbrenner, 1979, pp. 56–60.
4. Wasik, Bryant, and Lyons discussed their problem-solving model of home visiting. They identified seven stages of problem solving: defining problems, selecting goals, generating alternatives, considering consequences, decision making, implementation, and evaluation. Wasik, Bryant, & Lyons, 1990, pp. 139–146.
5. Greenspan and Greenspan urged parents of young children to spend 30 minutes each day in "floor time" with their child. Greenspan and Greenspan suggested that parents follow their child's lead so that the child can set the emotional tone of the play and can feel both affirmed and connected. Greenspan & Greenspan, 1989, p. 29.
6. Garbarino described the primary threat to the modern world as the "weakening of traditional sources of social pluralism—a wide range of people and groups surrounding the family which shared basic commitment to the family." Garbarino, 1992, p. 313.
7. Bronfenbrenner, 1979, pp. 209–236; Cochran et al., 1990.
8. Stern found that a mother of a newborn needs a supporting matrix that serves two functions: 1) physical protection of the mother from the everyday maintenance of family life; and 2) a maternal supportive expert force educating the mother on "how to do it," validating and modeling what motherhood is. Stern noted that fathers can fulfill the first function, but only "ex-

perts," women who have "been there before," can fulfill the second function. Stern, 1994.

9. Galinsky & David, 1988.
10. Bronfenbrenner and Neville discussed how the emotional attachment and complexity of the young child and the child's caregiver relationship is enhanced by the other adults who assist, encourage, nurture, and affirm the caregiver. Bronfenbrenner & Neville, 1994, p. 14.
11. Osofsky & Thompson, 2000.
12. Galinsky & David, 1988.
13. Wasik et al., 1990, pp. 69–90.
14. O'Hearn Family Outreach Project Members, 1995.
15. Home visitors learn the Parents as Teachers curriculum when they attend a 1-week training institute sponsored by the Parents as Teachers National Center, 2228 Ball Drive, St. Louis, MO 63146. Home visitors can purchase the Portage Project curriculum through the Chapter 3 Portage Project, 626 East Slifer Street, Portage, WI 53901.

Chapter 3

1. Schon discussed "indeterminate zones of practice" (p. 6), that is, indeterminate, uncertain, and unique situations that are central to professional practice and cannot be handled solely by applying knowledge or strategies stemming from traditional professional knowledge. Schon argued that at the core of competency in these indeterminate zones of practice is artistry, a kind of knowing in action. Conditions needed for professional development, then, become learning by doing, with access to coaches, who help increase skill in reflection on practice (p. 25). Schon, 1987, pp. 3–4.
2. Fenichel, of ZERO TO THREE: National Center for Infants, Toddlers and Families, emphasized that increased understanding of one's own emotional responses in home visiting is a central aspect of professional development. By attending to her own affective experience, the worker may be able to learn more about what children and families are feeling. As the supervisee's own emotional responses are acknowledged and respected, she may become increasingly able to acknowledge, respect, and respond sensitively to the emotional experiences and expressions of infants, toddlers, families and colleagues. Fenichel, 1992b, p. 5.
3. Knapp-Philo et al., 2006, pp. 44–48.
4. Bruner, 1986; Dewey, 1916; Rogers, 1969.
5. Mead, 1934, pp. 135–226.
6. In Holly's report of an interview study of 60 teachers in the United States and England, she noted that what teachers consider most important is the time to discuss with colleagues, and connecting professional development content with their everyday teaching. Holly, 1989.
7. Norton, 1994.
8. Weston, 2005, p. 343.
9. Weston, 2005, pp. 346–347.
10. Cochran and his colleagues compared how networks function in African American and white families in the United States, as well as families in Sweden, Wales, and Germany. Cochran et al., 1990.

11. Garbarino, 2000, pp. 79–80.
12. Gilligan, 1982; Gilligan & Brown, 1992; Loevinger, 1976.
13. Davies & Cummings, 2006.
14. Bullock & Forgathch, 2003.
15. Thornburg & Scott, 2006.
16. Harris, 2006.
17. Harris, 2006.
18. Forest, 1995.
19. Grace et al., 2006.
20. Harris, 2006.
21. Harris, 2006.
22. Thornburg & Scott, 2006.
23. Harris, 2006.
24. Ludlow, 2002.
25. Smith et al., 1991.
26. Larner & Halpern, 1992; Musick & Stott, 1993.
27. Hans & Korfmacher, 2002.
28. Musick & Stott, 1993.
29. Bertacchi & Coplon, 1989; Gilkerson & Young-Hold, 1992; Shanok, 1991.
30. Meisels & Atkins-Burnett, 2000, p. 237.
31. Meisels & Atkins-Burnett, 2000.
32. Meisels & Atkins-Burnett, 2000, p. 232.
33. Weatherston, 2000.
34. Gilliam & Leiter, 2003.
35. Meisels & Atkins-Burnett, 2000.
36. Gilliam & Leiter, 2003, p. 12.
37. Kelly & Bernard, 2000.
38. Weatherston, 2000, p. 13.
39. ZERO TO THREE: National Center for Infants, Toddlers and Families is an interdisciplinary organization of researchers, theorists, and practitioners working with infants, toddlers, and their families. A primary goal of ZERO TO THREE is to promote the continued education of professionals in this field. The organization publishes a bimonthly bulletin, *Zero to Three*. See Fenichel, 1992b.
40. Musick & Stott, 2000.

Chapter 4

1. Stern, 1985.
2. Greenspan, 1992; Sameroff & Emde, 1989; Stern, 1985.
3. Sroufe, 1989.
4. Stern, 1985.
5. Emde, 2001.
6. Emde, Wolf, & Oppenheim, 2003.
7. Winnicott, 1965, p. 39.
8. Emde, 1989; Stern, 1985, pp. 26–33.
9. Emde & Robinson, 2000, pp. 163–164.
10. Greenspan spoke of six developmental levels from birth to 5 years. Greenspan's developmental levels provide indicators of observable behavior

that point to the infant's and young child's increased emotional and behavioral capacities. Greenspan, 1992. Greenspan's developmental levels occur within the same age levels that Stern described as changes in sense of self. Whereas Greenspan's levels are behavioral, Stern's levels point to internal experiences. Stern, 1985, pp. 26–33.

11. Zigler, Finn-Stevenson, & Hall, 2002.
12. Schore, 1998, p. 162.
13. Chugani, 1997.
14. Nelson et al., 2006.
15. Schore, 1994; Shore, 1997; Sroufe, 1996.
16. Schore, 1994.
17. Bugental et al., 2003.
18. Zigler, Zinn-Stevenson, & Hall, 2002.
19. Sieget & Hartzell, 2004, p. 82.
20. Greenspan & Shanker, 2004.
21. Gomez, Baird, & Jung, 2004.
22. Kagan, Herschowitz, & Herschowitz, 2005, p. 19.
23. Nelson, Thomas, & De Haan, 2006.
24. Sieget & Hartzell, 2004, pp. 43–44.
25. Bauer, 2006, p. 416.
26. Porges, 2004, p. 19.
27. Greenspan & Shanker, 2004.
28. Crockenberg & Leerkes, 2000.
29. Izard et al., 2006.
30. Stern, 1995.
31. Kagan, Herschkowitz, & Herschkowitz, 2005, p. 61.
32. Thompson, 2006.
33. Sammons, 1989.
34. Stern, 2004, pp. 32–34.
35. Brazelton, 1992.
36. Brazelton, 1992.
37. Bugental & Grusec, 2006.
38. Saarni et al., 2006.
39. Gowen & Nebrig, 2002, p. 85.
40. Kagan, Herschkowitz, & Herschkowitz, 2005, p. 77.
41. Stern, 1985.
42. Schaefer, 2004.
43. Brazelton & Sparrow, 2003a, pp. 46–47.
44. Brazelton, 1992.
45. Stern, 1985.
46. Emde, Wolfe, & Oppenheim, 2003.
47. Brazelton & Cramer, 1990, p. 98.
48. Brazelton, 1992.
49. Emde, 1989.
50. Sammons, 1989.
51. Sammons, 1989.
52. Villarreal et al., 1992, pp. 103–112.

53. Sameroff & Emde, 1989.
54. Varghese, 2001.
55. Brazelton, 1992.
56. Thompson, 2006.
57. Crittenden, 1993.
58. Pruett, 1997; Glenn et al., 2001.
59. Chess & Thomas, 1987.
60. Chess & Thomas, 1987.
61. Saudino & Cherny, 2001.
62. Kagan, 2001.
63. Caspi & Shiner, 2006.
64. Rothbart & Bates, 2006.
65. Clark, Watson, & Mineka, 1994.
66. Rothbart & Bates, 2006; Emde, Wolf, & Oppenheim, 2003.
67. Hartup & Archer, 2005; Caspi & Shiner, 2006.
68. Wachs, 2004.
69. Kagan & Fox, 2006; Greenspan, 1993.
70. Ainsworth and Bowlby identified infant behaviors such as crying, cooing, smiling, and clinging as proximity-seeking—bringing their parents in closer contact. Bowlby explained that these infant proximity-seeking behaviors are essential for survival. Ethological studies of animal social life support Bowlby's biological explanation for infant attachment behavior. Ainsworth, Blehar, Waters, & Wall, 1978. Bonding is used in the psychological literature to refer to mother's maternally sensitive period, shortly after birth. Bowlby, 1969, 1973. There is some research evidence to suggest a maternal sensitive period immediately following delivery. Klaus & Kennel, 1976. Attachment refers to the parent–infant relation that develops progressively throughout the infant's first year. There also is some research evidence to suggest that, for fathers, early contact also helps to create a stronger initial bond between fathers and their infants. Park & Tinsley, 1981.
71. Thompson, 2006.
72. Stern, 1985.
73. Zeanah & Boris, 2000.
74. Stern and his colleagues in Geneva, Switzerland, conducted microanalytic interviews with mothers, who were asked to recall what they felt, thought, and did during an interaction with their infants. The mother's experiences involved not only their interactions but also their past and future representations. Stern noted, "The mother, in the parenting situation, is necessarily operating in at least two subjective spaces: the behavior interaction and her representational life." Stern, 1995, p. 52.
75. Stern. 1985.
76. Galinsky et al., 1994.
77. Stern, 1985.
78. Thompson, 2006.
79. Greenspan, 1992.
80. Thompson, 2006.
81. Emde, 2001.

82. Greenspan, 1993.
83. Garbarino & Bedard, 2001, p. 39.
84. Thompson, 2006.
85. Greenspan & Breslau Lewis, 2000.
86. Berlin, 2000.
87. Greenspan & Breslau Lewis, 2000.
88. Emde & Robinson, 2000.
89. Kochanska, Aksan, & Carlson, 2005.
90. Zeanah et al., 2000.
91. Moss et al., 2004.
92. Stern, 1995.
93. Bowlby, 1973.
94. Shonkoff & Phillips, 2000, p. 238.
95. Lieberman, 1991.
96. Bowlby, 1973.
97. Kobak et al., 2006.
98. Lieberman, 1991.
99. Stern, 1985.
100. Beebe, 2004.
101. Eisenberg, Fabes, & Spinrad, 2006.
102. Stern, 1985.
103. Stern stated that the developmental leap at ages 7–9 months is a new sphere of relatedness, termed *intersubjective relatedness*. That is, babies discover that their parents also have inner states of experience and that these inner states are shareable (i.e., intersubjectivity). A new form of experiencing connectedness emerges. Stern identified three states of intersubjectivity, or shared mental states: shared joint attention, shared intention, and shared affective states. Stern, 1985, pp. 128–133.
104. Emde, 1989, p. 43.
105. Schaefer, 2004.
106. Stern, 1985.
107. Emde, 1989.
108. Stern, 1985.
109. Emde, Wolf, & Oppenheim, 2003.
110. Thompson, 2006.
111. Eisenberg, Fabes, & Spinrad, 2006.
112. Greenspan & Breslau Lewis, 2000, p. 96.
113. Kagan & Fox, 2006.
114. Stern termed this interactive process *affect attunement*. Stern used the term *vitality* to describe how feeling qualities are communicated. Vitality "is captured in such terms as exploding, surging, fading, fleeting" (p. 11). Stern suggested dance and music as examples of vitality changes. Vitality in this sense can be thought of as the quality of feeling being expressed. Different experiences may be joined as long as they share the same quality of feeling that Stern calls vitality. For example, the baby joins a parent's soothing by voice and by touch because each have the same quality. As these experiences are joined by the same quality of feeling, young babies

experience their empathic responsiveness and thus experience communication. Stern, 1984, pp. 3–4.

115. Stern, 1984.
116. Erikson, 1950.
117. Tronick, Cohn, & Shea, 1986, p. 12.
118. Winnicott called attention to these objects that young children become
       passionately attached to and called such objects *transitional objects*.
       Winnicott, 1971, pp. 1–25. Brazelton termed these objects *loveys*.
       Brazelton, 1992, pp. 171–172.
119. Sammons, 1989.
120. Kagan, Herschkowitz, & Herschkowitz, 2005, p. 149.
121. Schore, 1994.
122. Shore, 1997.
123. Sroufe, 1996.
124. Shonkoff & Phillips, 2000, p. 112.
125. Emde, 2001.
126. Saarni et al., 2006.
127. Greenspan & Shanker, 2004.
128. Saarni et al., 2006; Emde, 2001; Greenspan, 1993.
129. Greenspan and Greenspan discussed how playing as a partner can influ-
       ence the emotional development of one's baby and young child. The
       Greenspans emphasized the importance of the baby's active discovery and
       parents' following their baby's lead in play. Greenspan & Greenspan,
       1989.
130. Kagan & Fox, 2006.
131. Stern called this developmental leap of toddlers the sense of verbal self.
       Stern emphasized that the young child's learning to speak creates "a new
       type of 'being-with,' between adult and child... the infant and mother cre-
       ate a being with experience using verbal symbols—a sharing of mutually
       created meanings about their personal experience." Stern, 1985, p. 172.
132. Erikson, 1950, pp. 80–85.
133. Shonkoff & Phillips, 2000.
134. Robinson et al., 2001.
135. Pelligrini, 2002.
136. Ruble, Martin, & Berenbaum, 2006.
137. Barrera, 2003.
138. Carlsson-Page & Levin, 1990.
139. Greenspan & Benderly, 1997, p. 101.
140. Greenspan & Breslau Lewis, 2000, p. 208.
141. Shonkoff & Phillips, 2000, p. 163.
142. Shonkoff & Phillips, 2000, p. 241.
143. Howes's 3-year study of toddlers' peer relationships in child care indicated
       that very young children, when given the opportunity, can develop a range
       of social skills. In the early toddler period, young children demonstrated
       abilities in give-and-take reciprocal roles as they played with each other.
       These children were ages 16–33 months at the outset of Howes's study.
       As they engaged in social pretend play in the late toddler period, these

children skillfully communicated with each other. Those most socially competent formed friendships that remained stable over the years. Howes, 1988.

144. Rubin, Bukowski, & Parker, 2006, p. 587.
145. Howes, 1988.
146. Rubin, Bukowski, & Parker, 2006.
147. Howes, 1988.
148. Howes, 1988.
149. Dunn, 2004, pp. 6–7.
150. Wigfield et al., 2006.
151. Thompson, 2006.
152. Wigfield et al., 2006.
153. Hart, 2005.
154. Lapsley & Narvaez, 2006.
155. Stern stated that this developmental leap is marked by young children's ability to narrate their own life stories. Stern claimed that this narrative ability is universal across cultures, innate, and no different than walking and talking. Stern stressed the importance of this new developmental leap is that narratives are "a dynamic laboratory in which the child is constantly working on who he is, defining, redefining who he is, and constantly updating." Stern, 1991. Greenspan described the 36-month-old's ability to "create logical bridges between different emotional ideas" (e.g., "Hit bad guy because he did bad thing"). Greenspan, 1993.
156. Piaget called this *lack of perspective-taking egocentrism*. Piaget, 1969, p. 32.
157. Greenspan & Benderly, 1997.
158. Lee, 1989.
159. Saarni et al., 2006.
160. Rubin, Bukowski, & Parker, 2006.
161. Dunn, 2004, p. 60.
162. Zahn-Waxler et al., 1990.
163. Howes, 1988.
164. Rubin et al., 2006, p. 590.
165. Stern, 1985.
166. Greenspan & Greenspan, 1989.
167. Ruble, Martin, & Berenbaum, 2006.
168. Ruble, Martin, & Berenbaum, 2006.
169. Pelligrini, 2002.
170. Ruble, Martin, & Berenbaum, 2006; Greenspan & Benderly, 1997.
171. Vygotsky, 1978.
172. Greenspan & Benderly, 1997.
173. Landry et al., 2002.
174. Thompson, 2006.
175. Erikson, 1950, pp. 90–92.
176. Harter, 2006, p. 515.
177. Greenspan, 2002, p. 20.
178. Fraiberg, 1980; Fraiberg, Adelson, & Shapiro, 1975. The literature of child battering provides evidence that a mother's childhood experience of her

own mother as rejecting is related to her own rejection of her baby. Main, Kaplan, & Cassidy, 1989.
179. Greenspan, 1992.
180. Koenig et al., 2000.

Chapter 5

1. Sameroff & Emde, 1989; Sameroff & Fiese, 2000; Shore, 1997.
2. Sameroff & Emde, 1989; Shore, 1997.
3. Brazelton & Sparrow, 2003a, pp. 1–2.
4. Greenspan & Benderly, 1997, p. 113.
5. *Illustrated Oxford Dictionary*, 1998.
6. Galinsky & David, 1988.
7. Honig, 1985.
8. Brazelton, 1992, p. 254.
9. Random House Dictionary of the English Language, 1973, p. 409.
10. Vygotsky described the social nature of young children's learning and development. He said that the adult guides the young child by providing a *zone of proximal development*. Vygotsky explained that the zone of proximal development "is the distance between the actual developmental level as determined by independent problem solving and the level of potential development as determined through problem solving under adult guidance or in collaboration with more capable peers." Vygotsky, 1978, p. 86.
11. Sammons, 1989.
12. Stern stated that emotions are a temporal experience, not a static event outside of time. Emotional experiences have a temporal contour, which Stern termed a *temporal feeling shape*. The temporal feeling shape depends on which emotions and which motivations are involved in the experience. Stern illustrated the temporal feeling shape with the universal parent game "I'm Gonna Getcha." This game includes increasing suspense, retarding the beat, and then the unexpected "gotcha!" Throughout the game, the baby experiences waves of excitement, suspense, and pleasure. According to Stern, listening to music also is a temporal experience, not a static event. Stern, 1995, pp. 63, 85.
13. McKenna, 2000.
14. Dahl explained that the neurobehavioral systems involved in the regulation of arousal, attention, and emotion overlap with the regulation of sleep. Inadequate sleep influences the emotional state of a baby and young child as well as his or her ability to attend. Babies who experience repeated emotional disturbances or high levels of arousal have difficulty sleeping. Although most babies and young children are deep sleepers, sleep deprivation of young children at risk has substantive effects in weakening goal-directed behaviors and the ability to regulate emotions. Dahl, 1996.
15. Thomas & Chess, 1977.
16. Chess & Thomas, 1987, pp. 56–60.
17. Stern, 1985.
18. Brazelton & Cramer, 1990, p. 123.

19. Stern, 1985, pp. 220–223.
20. Stern, 1985.
21. Reiss, 1989.
22. Greenspan & Greenspan, 1989.
23. Mahler, Pine, & Berman, 1975.
24. Lieberman, 1993.
25. Rothbart & Bates, 2006.
26. Lieberman, 1993.
27. Rothbart & Bates, 2006.
28. Stern, 1985.
29. Nelson, Rubin, & Fox, 2005.
30. Greenspan & Benderly, 1997.
31. Shonkoff & Phillips, 2000, p. 243.
32. McGee and colleagues studied a sample of preschool children during a 12-year period, and their findings indicated long-term troublesome consequences of preschool hyperactivity. Preschool children who are hyperactive show continued problem behavior during elementary school and adolescence. Hyperactivity seems to be significantly related to poor language skills among preschoolers and lower cognition and reading ability in primary school. A strong association thus appears to exist between limited language skills and inattention and difficulties in cognition. McGee et al., 1991. Similar findings are reported by Stattin & Magnusson, 1996.
33. Dodge, Coie, & Lyna, 2006.
34. Kent & Pepler, 2003.
35. Underwood, 2002.
36. Archer & Coté, 2005.
37. Gordon, 1989.
38. Shaw, Gilliom, & Giovannelli, 2000, p. 39.
39. Seguin & Zelazo, 2005, p. 311.
40. Hartup & Archer, 2005.
41. Dodge et al., 2006.
42. Tremblay & Nagin, 2005.
43. Nelson et al., 2005.
44. Boivin, Vitary, & Poulin, 2005.
45. Rudolph & Asher, 2000.
46. Cicchetti, Ackerman, & Izard, 1995.
47. Dodge et al., 2006.
48. Karr-Morse & Wiley, 1997.
49. Garbarino & Bedard, 2001.
50. Garbarino & Bedard, 2001.
51. Thompson, 2006.
52. Greenspan & Breslau Lewis, 2000, p. 275.
53. Dodge et al., 2006, p. 724.
54. Dodge et al., 2006, p. 724.
55. Thompson, 2006.
56. Mayer, 1985.
57. Noll, 1991.
58. Gordon, 1989.

Chapter 6

1. Bates, O'Connell, & Shore, 1987, pp. 151–168.
2. Heath, 1983, pp. 73–148.
3. Volterra et al., 2005.
4. DeBoysson-Bardies, 1999, p. 8.
5. Nelson et al., 2006.
6. Stern, 1995, pp. 59–78.
7. Emde, 1989.
8. Stern, 1985.
9. Emde, 1989.
10. Jervay-Pendergrass & Brown, 2000, p. 28.
11. Jusczyk, 2003.
12. Bateson, 2004.
13. Stern, 1977, p. 74.
14. Bates et al., 1987, pp. 151–169.
15. Jusczyk, 2003.
16. Nelson, 1996.
17. Greenspan & Shanker, 2004.
18. Devine provided a practical guide for parents to understand developmental milestones as well as parenting activities to foster this development. Devine, 1991.
19. Mahoney and his colleagues have developed Transactional Intervention Program (TRIP) for children from birth to 3 years old who have disabilities. TRIP promotes parents' communication and offers an approach to playing with their young children. Turn taking and interactive matching are two instructional strategies used in this program. Mahoney & Powell, 1988. Using a mental health perspective, Greenspan did similar work with parents of very young children. Greenspan termed the give-and-take interaction as *opening and closing circles*. Greenspan, 1992.
20. Stern, 1985.
21. Werker & Desjardins, 2001.
22. Emde, 1989.
23. Nelson, 1996.
24. Clancy & Finlay, 2001; Nelson, 1996.
25. Clancy & Finlay, 2001.
26. Greenspan & Shanker, 2004.
27. Greenspan & Shanker, 2004.
28. Emde, 1989, p. 45.
29. Greenspan & Shanker, 2004.
30. Nelson, 1973.
31. Nelson, 1996.
32. Greenspan & Shanker, 2004, pp. 38–39.
33. Greenspan & Shanker, 2004.
34. Thomas & Chess, 1977.
35. Nelson, 1996.
36. Volterra et al., 2005.
37. Fernald et al., 2001.

38. Greenspan & Shanker, 2004.
39. Greenspan & Shanker, 2004.
40. Marchman & Thal, 2005.
41. Nelson & Gruendel, 1986.
42. Berk & Winsler, 1995, pp. 34–49.
43. Nelson, 1989.
44. Nelson, 1989, p. 16.
45. Huttenlocher, Haiglet, Bryk, Deltzer, & Lynos, 1991.
46. Schachter & Strage, 1982.
47. Bates emphasized that between birth and age 3 years is the window of maximum opportunity for neural development and maximum plasticity for language development. Bates, 1994.
48. Nelson, 1996.
49. Greenspan & Shanker, 2004, p. 71.
50. Lee, 1989.
51. Greenspan & Shanker, 2004.
52. Nelson, 1996.
53. Greenspan, 1997, p. 75.
54. Lee, 1989.
55. Nelson, 1996.
56. Bruner, 2002.
57. Stern, 1985.
58. Emde et al., 2003, p. 6.
59. Tabors, Roach, & Snow, 2001.
60. Dole et al., 1991.
61. Heath, 1983, pp. 190–235.
62. Martens et al., 2004.
63. DeTemple, 2001, p. 48.
64. Katz, 2001.
65. Gest et al., 2004.
66. Beals, 2001.
67. Greenspan & Shanker, 2004; Prizant et al., 2000.
68. Prizant et al., 2000.
69. Carson et al., 1998.

Chapter 7

1. Erikson, 1950, p. 222.
2. Mead, 1962, p. 7.
3. Piaget, 1963.
4. Frost, Wortham, & Reifel, 2001.
5. Katz, 2001.
6. Segal, 2004, p. 38.
7. Stern explained the developmental significance of these microevents: "To the extent that these interactions are purely social with no other goal in mind, they consist of mutual microregulation of affect and activation.... They are the basic step of an interaction regulatory process." Stern, 1995, p. 63.
8. Stern, 1985.
9. Bruner & Sherwood, 1976.

10. Emde, 1989.
11. Stern, 1985.
12. Erikson, 1977, pp. 85–92.
13. Emde, 1989.
14. Sroufe, 1996.
15. Erikson wrote that "dramatic play in childhood provides the infantile form of the human propensity to create model situations in which aspects of the past are re-lived, the present re-presented and renewed, and the future anticipated." Erikson, 1977, p. 44.
16. The role of parent as active participant in young children's play is a relatively new insight among developmental and early education theorists and researchers. Historically, developmental theory promoted adult roles as providers of settings, observers, and periodic participants in children's play who participate as the explicit need arises, for example to implement a rule in conflict situations. Since the mid-1980s, theory and research across the mental health and educational fields emphasize the developmental value of adults' active role in young children's play. Greenspan and Greenspan provided a convincing discussion of how parents' active engagement as play partners with their baby and young child enhances their child's social and emotional self. Greenspan & Greenspan, 1989.
17. Duckworth, 1972.
18. Piaget, 1962.
19. Fabes, Martin, & Hanish, 2004.
20. Zigler, Singer, & Bishop-Josef, 2004.
21. Segal, 2004.
22. Zigler, Singer, & Bishop-Josef, 2004.
23. Smilansky, 1968.
24. Segal, 2004.
25. Pellegrini, 2002.
26. Pellegrini, 2002.
27. Biber, 1984.
28. Frost, Wortham, & Reifel, 2001, p. 102.
29. Rideout et al., 2003.
30. Vandewater et al., 2005.
31. Anderson & Evans, 2001.
32. Jordan & Woodward, 2001.
33. Carlsson-Page & Levin, 1990, p. 12.
34. Jordan & Woodward, 2001.
35. Garbarino & Bedard, 2001, p. 191.
36. Carlsson-Page & Levin, 1990.
37. Linn & Poussaint, 2001.
38. Carlsson-Page & Levin, 1990.
39. Garbarino & Bedard, 2001, p. 203.

Chapter 8

1. Kubicek, 2002, p. 4.
2. Wolin & Bennett, 1984.
3. Reiss, 1989.

4. Imber-Black & Roberts, 1992, p. 4.
5. Fiese, 2002, p. 10.
6. Fiese, 2000.
7. Imber-Black & Roberts, 1992, p. 151.
8. Imber-Black & Roberts, 1992, p. 28.
9. Garbarino & Bedard, 2001, pp. 153, 168.
10. Middlemiss, 2004.
11. Anders, Goodlin-Jones, & Sadah, 2000.
12. Anders, Goodlin-Jones, & Zelenko, 2004.
13. Ferber, 1985.
14. Brazelton & Sparrow, 2004a.
15. Anderson et al., 1999.
16. Brazelton & Sparrow, 2004b.
17. Brazelton, 1992, p. 381.
18. Weissbluth, 1987, pp. 84–87.
19. Ferber, 1985, p. 32.
20. Brazelton & Sparrow, 2003a.
21. McKenna, 2000, p. 16.
22. Brazelton & Sparrow, 2003b.
23. Brazelton & Sparrow, 2003a.
24. Sammons, 1989.
25. Anders, Goodlin-Jones, & Sadah, 2000, p. 328.
26. Ferber, 1985, p. 82.
27. Weissbluth, 1987, p. 119.
28. Brazelton & Sparrow, 2003a.
29. Ferber, 1985, p. 196.
30. Brazelton & Sparrow, 2004a.
31. Brazelton & Sparrow, 2003b.
32. Brazelton & Sparrow, 2004b.
33. Brazelton, 1992, p. 141.
34. Brazelton, 1992, p. 141.
35. Brazelton, 1992, p. 190.
36. Lansky, 1984, p. 9.
37. Brazelton & Sparrow, 2004b, p. 35.
38. Brazelton & Sparrow, 2004b.
39. Brazelton & Sparrow, 2004b.
40. Brazelton & Sparrow, 2004b.
41. Essays in the book *Narratives from the Crib* discussed a 2-year study of mono-
    logues of a child between 15 and 23 months as she was going to sleep. The
    reports showed that monologues have greater complexity than the child's di-
    alogues with her parents just prior to sleeping. The studies find these mono-
    logues help the child to understand her daily experience. Nelson, 1989.
42. Brazelton & Sparrow, 2003a.
43. Middlemiss, 2004, p. 102.
44. Brazelton & Sparrow, 2003a.
45. Gordon, 1989.
46. Fraiberg, 1980.

47. Wolin & Bennett, 1984.
48. Gergen, 1991.
49. Golombok, 2001.
50. Kaplan & Pruett, 2000, p. 533.

Chapter 9

1.   Parmelee, 1993.
2.   Brazelton, 1992.
3.   Brazelton, 1992.
4.   Brazelton, 1992.
5.   Brazelton, 1992.
6.   Brazelton, 1992.
7.   Brazelton, 1992.
8.   Gilkerson et al., 2005.
9.   Drotar & Sturm, 1992.
10. Desantis et al., 2004.
11. Gilkerson et al., 2005.
12. Barr, 2000.
13. Lozoff et al., 2000.
14. Finn & Wolpin 2005.
15. Lozoff et al., 2000.
16. Lozoff et al., 2000; Tomasello, 2001.
17. Lozoff et al., 2000; Tomasello, 2001.
18. Lumeng, 2005.
19. Lumeng, 2005.
20. Lumeng, 2005.
21. Deiner, 2005.
22. Lumeng, 2005.
23. Myers & Chawla, 2002.
24. Myers & Chawla, 2002.
25. Children, Youth and Women's Health Service, November 2007.
26. Children, Youth and Women's Health Service, July 2007.
27. Raising Children Network, 2007.
28. Parmelee, 1993.
29. Wessel & Spain, 2005.
30. Jaber, 2000; Wesell & Spain, 2005.
31. Jaber, 2000.
32. Schmidt & Georgieff, 2006.
33. Minde, 2000.
34. Minde, 2000.
35. Nosarti, Rifkin, & Murray, 2003.
36. Minde, 2000.
37. Minde, 2000.
38. Ward & Beehy, 2003.
39. Minde, 2000.
40. Drotar & Sturm, 1992.

41. Dawson, 1992.
42. Drotar & Sturm, 1992.

Chapter 10

1. Dunn, 2006.
2. Dunn, 1992.
3. Dunn & Kendrick, 1982; Lee, 1989.
4. Dunn, 2006.
5. Dunn, 2006.
6. Brazelton, 1992, p. 199.
7. White, 1985.
8. Dunn, 2006.
9. Dunn, 2006.
10. Dunn, 2006.
11. Dunn & Brown, 1994.
12. Galinsky, 1987, p. 187.
13. Dunn & Plomin, 1990.
14. Faber & Mazlish, 1987.
15. Dunn & Plomin, 1990.
16. Dunn & Plomin, 1990, pp. 283–284.
17. Dunn & Brown, 1994.
18. McGuire & Roch-Levecq, 2001.
19. Dunn and Plomin provided autobiographical and biographical materials of famous people to illustrate remarkable differences in the affection, interest, control, and dominance of brothers and sisters—differences not linked to birth order. Dunn & Plomin, 1990, p. 90.
20. Lieberman discussed the difficulties that toddlers have when displaced by a new baby. Lieberman, 1993, pp. 165–168.
21. Fraiberg et al., 1975; Fraiberg, 1980.
22. Faber & Mazlish, 1987, pp. 162–176; Galinsky & David, 1988, pp. 284–288.
23. Dunn & Plomin, 1990.
24. Brazelton & Sparrow, 2003b.
25. Dunn, 1992.
26. Dunn, 1995.

Chapter 11

1. Landy & Menna, 2006.
2. Wyman et al., 2000; Garbarino & Ganzel, 2000; Cicchetti & Toth, 2002, 2006.
3. Cicchetti & Toth, 2006.
4. Aber et al., 2000; Ispa & Halgunseth, 2006.
5. Sameroff & Fiese, 2000.
6. Sameroff & Fiese, 2000.
7. McDonough and her colleagues implemented an interaction guidance approach in their work with at-risk families with such conditions as poverty,

mental illness, substance abuse, violence, poor education, and inadequate family support. The goals of their interaction guidance approach were to assist families in gaining enjoyment from their child and in developing an understanding of their child's behavior and development through interactive family play experiences that were videotaped and discussed. McDonough, 2000.

8. Garbarino & Ganzel, 2000.
9. Pawl, 1997.
10. Sameroff & Fiese, 2000, p. 144.
11. Stern, 1985; Sameroff, Lewis, & Miller, 2000.
12. Reiss, 1989, p. 192.
13. Kaplan et al., 2000.
14. Kaplan et al., 2000.
15. Golombok, 2001.
16. Cummings & Wilson, 1999.
17. Pellegrini & Notarius, 1988.
18. Davies & Cummings, 2006.
19. Davies & Cummings, 2006, p. 103.
20. McDonough, 2000.
21. Cox et al., 1999.
22. Fiese et al., 2000.
23. Kerr & Bowen, 1988.
24. Jaffe et al., 2001.
25. Jaffe et al., 2001.
26. Parke, 1996.
27. Solomon, 2003.
28. Parke, 1996.
29. Fitzgerald & Montanex, 2001; Bullock & Forgathch, 2003.
30. Pruett, 1997.
31. Parke, 1996.
32. Solomon, 2003.
33. McLanahan, 1999.
34. Parke, 1996.
35. Parke, 1996.
36. Bray, 1999.
37. Constantino, 1993, p. 3.
38. Luby, 2000.
39. Anderson & Seita, 2006.
40. Constantino, 1993.
41. Constantino, 1993.
42. Goodman, 2003.
43. Luby, 2000.
44. Luby, 2000; Berkowitz & Senter, 1987; Dodge, 1990; Murray, 1992; Seifer & Dickstein, 2000.
45. Luby, 2000.
46. Seifer & Dickstein, 2000, p. 150.
47. Clark & Fenichel, 2001, p. 49.

48. Izard et al., 2006.
49. Goodman, 2003.
50. Stern, 1995.
51. Landy & Menna, 2006, pp. 329–330.
52. Seifer & Dickstein, 2000.
53. Goodman, 2003.
54. Stern, 1995.
55. Luby, 2000, pp. 386–387.
56. Coyne et al., 1990; Field et al., 1990.
57. Bettes, 1988; Cox et al., 1987; Stein et al., 1989.
58. Luby, 2000.
59. Davenport et al., 1984.
60. Gottlieb & Hooley, 1988; Rutter & Quinton, 1984; Rutter, 1990, pp. 61–62.
61. Luby, 2000.
62. Nelson & Bosquet, 2000.
63. Seifer & Dickstein, 2000.
64. Seifer et al., 1996.
65. Stern, 1995, pp. 99–105.
66. Shonkoff & Phillips, 2000, p. 254.
67. Luby, 2000.
68. Anderson & Seita, 2006.
69. Jones-Harden, 1997.
70. Behnke & Eyler, 1994; Lester & Tronick, 1994.
71. Chang, 1999.
72. Lester et al., 2006.
73. Mayes et al., 1996; Myers, Olson, & Kaltenbach, 1992; Zuckerman & Brown, 1993.
74. Lester et al., 2000.
75. Wyman et al., 2000.
76. Zucker, 2006.
77. O'Connor, 2001.
78. Fitzgerald et al., 2000.
79. O'Connor, 2001.
80. Olson, Burgess, & Streissguth, 1992, p. 25.
81. O'Connor, 2001.
82. Olson, O'Connor, & Fitzgerald, 2001.
83. Eiden & Leonard, 1996.
84. Osofsky, 2000.
85. Garbarino & Bedard, 2001.
86. Osofsky & Thompson, 2000.
87. Landy & Menna, 2006, p. 25.
88. Osofsky, 2000.
89. Kaufman & Henrich, 2000.
90. Terr, 1991, p. 12.
91. Cameron, Elkin, & Guterman, 2006.
92. Shirk, 1993.
93. Garbarino & Ganzel, 2000.
94. Osofsky, 2000, p. 168.
95. Webb, 2006.

96. Osofsky, 1996, p. 8.
97. Sugar, 1992.
98. Sugar, 1992.
99. Osofsky, 1993.
100. Scheeringa & Greenbauer, 2000; Garbarino, 1992; Osofsky, 1993; Terr, 1991; Zeanah, 1993.
101. Rossman, 2001.
102. Rossman, 2001, p. 40.
103. Rossman, 2001, p. 45.
104. Scheeringa & Greenbauer, 2000.
105. Zeanah & Scheeringa, 1996, p. 13.
106. Kaufman & Henrich, 2000.
107. Cicchetti & Toth, 2006.
108. Mrazek, 1993.
109. Kaufman et al., 2000, p. 195.
110. Rossman, 2001.
111. Edleson, 2001.
112. Mrazek, 1993.
113. Osofsky, 2000.
114. Mrazek, 1993, p. 162.
115. Toth et al., 1997; Kaufman & Henrich, 2000.
116. Toth et al., 2000, p. 783. Toth, Cicchetti, Macfie, and Emde administered 10 narrative story stems to 107 preschool children, 72% of which had experienced multiple subtypes of abuse, and 27% of whom were nonmaltreated children from families receiving Aid to Families with Dependent Children (now called Temporary Assistance for Needy Families), similar to the families of maltreated children. Maltreated children's stories include negative maternal representation, negative self-representation, and were less responsive and more controlling with the examiner.
117. Osofsky, 2000.
118. Kaufman & Henrich, 2000, p. 197.
119. Osofsky, 2000.
120. Karr-Morse & Wiley, 1997, p. 164.
121. Karr-Morse & Wiley, 1997.
122. Osofsky, 2000.
123. Cicchetti, Toth, & Rogosch, 2000.
124. Egeland & Erikson, 1999, p. 7.
125. Cicchetti, Ackerman, & Izard, 1995.
126. Webb, 2006.
127. Gil & Johnson, 1993.
128. Howes et al., 2000.
129. Wolin & Wolin, 1993; Werner & Smith, 1992.
130. Wolin & Wolin, 1993, pp. 5–6.
131. Werner, 1984.

Chapter 12

1. Since the 1980s, there has been a growing literature analyzing the relationship of teachers' careers and their childhood history and adult personal

life. See Ball & Goodson, 1985; Goodson, 1992; Nias, 1989; Raymond, Butt, & Townsend, 1992; Smith, Kleine, Prunty, & Dwyer, 1986.

2. Anderson, 1991; Bruner, 1986; White & Epston, 1990.

3. Bruner described a person's story, or narrative, of his or her life as being a cognitive act of thought involving not only memory but also interpretation. A narrative is a construction in the present. Narratives of past experiences are shaped by experiences and understandings that have occurred since the remembered experience. They also are shaped by anticipations of future experience. Past, present, and future each play a role in the composition of a narrative, and the narrative unites the three. Bruner, 1987, pp. 13–15. This perspective on time was discussed by William Dilthey and his student, George Herbert Mead. Dilthey, 1961; Mead, 1934.

4. Clandinin and Connelly wrote of personal experience methods as focused in four areas: inward (i.e., thoughts, feelings, values, attitudes), outward (i.e., the environmental context), and backward and forward (i.e., past, present, and future). Clandinin & Connelly, 1994, p. 417. Sociologist Mills argued for the integration of biography, history, and social structure. Mills, 1959. The philosopher Dilthey spoke of one's life preserving "the relation between the outer and something inner, which is the meaning of that life." Dilthey asserted that biography cannot capture this relation without including the sociocultural context of that period. Dilthey, 1961, p. 91.

5. Sociological research in the 1980s and 1990s emphasized the central role of the relationship of researcher to participant. Denzin discussed how writing a biography involves both subjective and intersubjective understanding of experiences, of the person studied and of oneself. In other words, understanding is an intersubjective hermeneutic process. Denzin, 1989.

6. Nias emphasized the personal nature of teaching. Following George Herbert Mead's understanding of the inescapably social nature of self, Nias emphasized how teachers' assumptions, passions, and schemata are rooted in experiences from birth. It follows that many of a teacher's satisfactions are tied to the teacher's identity and sense of self. Nias, 1992.

7. Noddings identified joy as the basic human emotion experienced within relatedness and the fulfillment a person experiences when caring for others. Noddings, 1984, pp. 6–7.

8. Schon discussed those fields, such as teaching, in which the worker is a craftsperson, an artist; thus, most of the learning is in the doing. In these professions, framing problems and improvising are essential components of the professional's practice. Schon, 1987, p. 13.

9. Jackson wrote about teachers' development through prolonged reflection on teaching from different perspectives. "The goal is to articulate and broaden the context." Jackson, 1992, p. 73.

10. Bruner argued that most learning is a "sharing of culture. It is not just that the child must make his knowledge his own, but that he must make it his own in a community of those who share his sense of belonging to a culture." Bruner, 1986, p. 127.

11. Butt, Raymond, McCure, and Yamagishi discussed the powerful interaction of person and private and public contexts over time and how this interplay affects a teacher's personal and professional life. Butt, Raymond, McCure, & Yamagishi, 1992, p. 62.

12. Literature on personal biography describes times in a person's life cycle that are termed *critical incidents, turning points,* or *epiphanies.* These critical incidents are key events in a person's life around which pivotal decisions are made, which in turn lead persons in specific directions. Critical incidents may be extrinsic, such as a historical event like the Vietnam War, or intrinsic, like an unexpected pregnancy. For example, Denzin, 1989, pp. 69–71; Measor, 1985.

13. Bruner stated that experience and memory of experience are powerfully structured by deeply internalized cultural notions, what he termed *folk psychology.* He argued that we can interpret meaning only if we situate that meaning in the larger cultural context in which specific meanings are created. Bruner, 1991.

14. Seligman and Pawl discussed four broad categories of obstacles they have experienced when they do therapeutic work in the homes of parents experiencing multiple difficulties. The categories include socioeconomic and sociocultural variables, prior experience with professionals and social agencies, the family situation, and personal history and psychology. Seligman & Pawl, 1984.

15. Schon explained the artistry of good coaching and the importance of coaches "who initiate students into the 'traditions of the calling' and help them, by 'the right kind of telling,' to see on their own behavior and in their own way what they need most to see." Schon, 1987, p. 17.

16. Nias argued that crucial to a teacher's identity are reference groups that help one by offering support in defining the value, meaning, and understanding of one's work. Nias, 1992, pp. 115–116.

17. Bruner discussed how meaning and symbols are public and communal rather than private and individual. He argued that to understand a person is to locate that person in a cultural and historical time and place. Bruner, 1991, pp. 10–11.

18. Noddings argued that "ethical caring depends not upon rule or principle but upon the development of an ideal self… in congruence with one's best remembrance of caring and being cared for." Noddings, 1984, p. 94.

19. Rogers argued that significant learning is acquired through experiencing practical problems. Rogers, 1969, pp. 158–162.

20. Beginning with Freud, therapy literature discusses the transference as the adults' replication of childhood relationship with parents in their relationships with their own children or spouse or with other significant people. For example, Basch, 1980; Fraiberg, 1980; Kerr & Bowen, 1988.

21. Beginning with her classic work, *In a Different Voice,* Gilligan's research explores women's psychological development. Gilligan argues that women have different views of self and morality and different ways of understanding and experiencing relationships than do men. Women see relationships as webs of connectedness, whereas men think in terms of images of hierarchy. Whereas men view morality in terms of the logic of justice, women's view is in terms of the ethic of care. Gilligan, 1982.

22. Shanok discussed the supervisory relationship as the context within which to learn by reflection with a confidante whom one feels secure enough to expose one's vulnerabilities. Shanok, 1991.

References

Aber, J.L., Jones, S., & Cohen, J. (2000). The impact of poverty on the mental health and development of very young children. In C.H. Zeanah, Jr. (Ed.), *Handbook of infant mental health* (2nd ed., pp. 113–128). New York: Guilford Press.

Ainsworth, M.D.S., Blehar, M.C., Waters, E., & Wall, S. (1978). *Patterns of attachment.* Mahwah, NJ: Lawrence Erlbaum Associates.

Anders, T.F., Goodlin-Jones, B., & Sadah, A. (2000). Sleep disorders. In C.J. Zeanah, Jr. (Ed.), *Handbook of infant mental health* (2nd ed., pp. 326–338). New York: Guilford Press.

Anders, T.F., Goodlin-Jones, B.L., & Zelenko, M. (2004). Infant regulation and sleep–wake state development. *Zero to Three, 19*(2), 7–11.

Anderson, D. (1997). Women practitioners counseling men. *Zero to Three, 18*(1), 18–23.

Anderson, D.R., & Evans, M.K. (2001). Peril and potential of media for infants and toddlers. *Zero to Three, 22*(2), 10–16.

Anderson, G.R., & Seita, J. (2006). Family and social factors. In N.B. Webb & J.R. Dumpson (Eds.), *Working with traumatized youth in child welfare.* New York: Guilford Publications.

Anderson, J.W., Johnstone, B.M., & Remley, D.T. (1999). Breast feeding and cognitive development: A meta-analysis. *American Journal of Clinical Nursing, 10,* 525–535.

Anderson, T. (Ed.). (1991). *The reflecting team: Dialogues and dialogues about the dialogue.* New York: W.W. Norton.

Anderson, T. (1992). Relationship, language, and pre-understanding in the reflecting process. *Family Therapy, 12*(2), 87–91.

Archer, J., & Coté, S. (2005). Sex differences in aggressive behavior: A developmental and evolutionary perspective. In R.E. Tremblay, W.W. Hartup, & J. Archer (Eds.), *Developmental origins of aggression* (pp. 425–446). New York: Guilford Press.

Ball, S.J., & Goodson, I.F. (1985). *Teachers' lives and careers.* London: Falmer Press.

Barr, R.G. (2000). Excessive crying. In A.J. Sameroff, M. Lewis, & S.M. Miller (Eds.), *Handbook of developmental psychology* (2nd ed., pp. 327–350). New York: Kluwer Academic Publishers.

Barrera, I. (2003). From rocks to diamonds: Mining the riches of diversity for our children. *Zero to Three, 23*(5), 8–15.

Barrie, J.M. (1911). *Peter Pan.* London: Penguin Books.

Basch, M.F. (1980). *Doing psychotherapy.* New York: Basic Books.

Bates, E. (1994, December). *Normal and abnormal variation in early language development.* Paper presented at the Frontiers of Infancy Research, ZERO TO THREE, National Center for Infants, Toddlers and Families' Ninth National Training Institute, Dallas, TX.

Bates, E., O'Connell, B., & Shore, C. (1987). Language and communication in infancy. In J.D. Osofsky (Ed.), *Handbook of infant development* (2nd ed., pp. 149–203). New York: John Wiley & Sons.

Bateson, M.C. (2004) *Willing to learn.* Hanover, NH: Steerforth Press.

Bauer, P.J. (2006). Event memory. In W. Damon, R.M. Lerner, D. Kuhn, & R. Siegler (Eds.), *Handbook of child psychology: Vol. 2. Cognition, perception, and language* (6th ed., pp. 373–426). New York: John Wiley & Sons.

Beals, D.E. (2001). Eating and reading: Links between family conversations with preschoolers and later language and literacy. In D.K. Dickinson & P.O. Tabors (Eds.), *Young children learning at home and school: Beginning literacy with language* (pp. 53–75). Baltimore: Paul H. Brookes Publishing Co.

Beebe, B. (2004). Co-constructing mother–infant distress in face to face interactions: Contributions of microanalysis. *Zero to Three, 24*(5), 40–48.

Behnke, E., & Eyler, F.D. (1994). Issues in prenatal cocaine use research: Problems in identifying users and choosing an appropriate comparison group. *Infant Mental Health Journal, 15,* 146–157.

Berk, L.E., & Winsler, A. (1995). *Scaffolding children's learning: Vygotsky and early childhood education.* Washington, DC: National Association for the Education of Young Children.

Berkowitz, C.D., & Senter, S.A. (1987). Characteristics of mother–infant interactions in nonorganic failure to thrive. *Journal of Family Practice, 24,* 377–381.

Berlin, L.K. (2000) Understanding parenting: Contributions of attachment theory and research. In J.D. Osofsky & H.E. Fitzgerald (Eds.), *WAIMH handbook of infant mental health: Vol. 3. Parenting and child care* (pp. 135–170). New York: John Wiley & Sons.

Bertacchi, J., & Coplon, J. (1989). The professional use of self in prevention: 1–7. *Zero to Three, 11*(4), 1–7.

Bettes, B.A. (1988). Maternal depression and motherese: Temporal and intonational features. *Child Development, 59,* 1089–1096.

Biber, B. (1984). *Early education and psychological development.* New Haven, CT: Yale University Press.

Boivin, M., Vitaro, F., & Poulin, F. (2005). Peer relationships and the development of aggressive behavior in early childhood. In R.E. Tremblay, W.W. Hartup, & J. Archer (Eds.), *Developmental origins of aggression* (pp. 376–397). New York: Guilford Press.

Bowlby, J. (1969). *Attachment and loss: Vol. 1. Attachment.* New York: Basic Books.

Bowlby, J. (1973). *Attachment and loss: Vol. 2. Separation, anxiety, and anger.* New York: Basic Books.

Bray, J.H. (1999). From marriage to remarriage and beyond: Findings from the developmental issues in stepfamilies research project. In E.M. Hetherington (Ed.), *Coping with divorce, single parenting, and remarriage: A risk and resiliency perspective* (pp. 253–273). Mahwah, NJ: Lawrence Erlbaum Associates.

Brazelton, T.B. (1992). *Touchpoints: The essential reference. Your child's emotional and behavioral development.* Reading, MA: Addison Wesley Higher Education Group.

Brazelton, T.B., & Cramer, B.G. (1990). *The earliest relationship: Parents, infants, and the drama of early attachment.* Reading, MA: Addison Wesley Higher Education Group.

Brazelton, T.B., & Sparrow, J.D. (2003a). *Discipline: The Brazelton way.* Cambridge, MA: Da Capo Press.

Brazelton, T.B., & Sparrow, J.D. (2003b). *Sleep: The Brazelton way.* Cambridge, MA: Da Capo Press.

Brazelton, T.B., & Sparrow, J.D. (2003c). *Calming your fussing baby: The Brazelton way.* Cambridge, MA: Da Capo Press.

Brazelton, T.B., & Sparrow, J.D. (2004a). *Feeding your child: The Brazelton way.* Cambridge, MA: Da Capo Press.

Brazelton, T.B., & Sparrow, J.D. (2004b). *Toilet training: The Brazelton way.* Cambridge, MA: Da Capo Press.

Bromwich, R. (1981). Working with parents and infants: An interactional approach. Austin, TX: PRO-ED.

Bronfenbrenner, U. (1979). *The ecology of human development: Experiments by nature and design.* Cambridge, MA: Harvard University Press.

Bronfenbrenner, U., & Neville, P. (1994). America's children and families: An international perspective. In S.L. Kagan & B. Weissbourd (Eds.), *Putting families first: America's family support movement and the challenge of change* (pp. 3–17). San Francisco: Jossey-Bass.

Brooks-Gunn, J., Leventhal, T.Y., & Duncan, G.J. (2000). Why poverty matters for young children: Implications for policy. In J. Osofsky & H.E. Fitzgerald (Eds.), *WAIMH handbook of infant mental health: Vol. 3. Parenting and child care* (pp. 89–131). New York: John Wiley & Sons.

Bruner, J.S. (1986). *Actual minds, possible worlds.* Cambridge, MA: Harvard University Press.

Bruner, J.S. (1987). Life as narrative. *Social Research, 54*(1), 11–32.

Bruner, J.S. (1991). *Acts of meaning.* Cambridge, MA: Harvard University Press.

Bruner, J.S. (2002). *Making stories: Law, literature, life.* Cambridge, MA: Harvard University Press.

Bruner, J.S., & Sherwood, V. (1976). Peekaboo and the learning of rule structures. In J.S. Bruner, A. Jolly, & K. Sylva (Eds.), *Play: Its role in development and evolution* (pp. 268–276). New York: Basic Books.

Buber, M. (1958). *I and thou.* New York: Charles Scribner's Sons. (Original work published 1923)

Bugental, D.B., & Grusec, J. (2006). Socialization theory. In W. Damon, R.M. Lerner, & N. Eisenberg (Eds.), *Handbook of child psychology: Vol. 3. Social, emotional, and personality development* (6th ed., pp. 300–365). New York: John Wiley & Sons.

Bugental, D.B., Olster, D.H., & Martorell, G.A. (2003) A developmental neuroscience perspective on the dynamics of parenting. In L. Kuczynski (Ed.), *Handbook of dynamics in parent–child relations* (pp. 25–48). London: Sage Publications.

Bullock, B.M., & Forgathch, M.S. (2003). Parenting together after divorce: Navigating the winds of change. *Zero to Three, 23*(3), 38–43.

Butt, R., Raymond, D., McCure, G., & Yamagishi, L. (1992). Collective autobiography and the teacher's voice. In I.F. Goodson (Ed.), *Studying teachers' lives* (pp. 51–98). New York: Teachers College Press.

Cameron, M., Elkins, J., & Guterman, N. (2006). Assessment of trauma in children and youth. In N.B. Webb (Ed.), *Working with traumatized youth in child welfare* (pp. 53–66). New York: Guilford Press.

Carlson, V.J., Feng, X., & Harwood, R.L. (2004). The "ideal baby": A look at the intersection of temperament and culture. *Zero to Three, 24*(4), 22–28.

Carlsson-Paige, N., & Levin, D.E. (1990). *Who's calling the shots? How to respond effectively to children's fascination with war play and war toys.* Philadelphia: New Society Publishers.

Carson, D.K., Klee, T., Perry, C.K., Muskina, G., & Donaghy, T. (1998). Comparisons of children with delayed and normal language at 24 months of age on measures of behavioral difficulties. *Infant Mental Health Journal, 19*(1) 59–75.

Caspi, A., & Shiner, R.L. (2006). Personality development. In W. Damon, R.M. Lerner, & N. Eisenberg (Eds.), *Handbook of child psychology: Vol. 3. Social, emotional, and personality development* (6th ed., pp. 300–365). New York: John Wiley & Sons.

Chang, G. (1999). Tobacco, alcohol and drugs during pregnancy. *Zero to Three, 19*(4), 9–13.

Chess, S., & Thomas, A. (1987). *Know your child: An authoritative guide for today's parents.* New York: Basic Books.

Children, Youth and Women's Health Service. (2007, July). *Infant deaths: Fact sheet.* South Australia: Author.

Children, Youth and Women's Health Service. (2007, November). *Sudden unexpected deaths in infancy (including SIDS).* South Australia: Author.

Chugani, H.T. (1997). Neuroimaging of developmental nonlinearity and developmental pathologies. In G.R. Lyon (Ed.), *Developmental neuroimaging* (pp. 187–195). San Diego: Academic Press.

Cicchetti, D., Ackerman, B.P., & Izard, C.E. (1995). Emotions and emotional regulation in developmental psychopathology. *Development and Psychopathology, 7*(1), 1–10.

Cicchetti, D., & Toth, S.L. (2002). Child maltreatment in the early years of life. In J.D. Osofsky & H.E. Fitzgerald (Eds.), *WAIMH handbook of infant mental health: Vol. 4. Infant mental health in groups at high risk* (pp. 163–196). New York: John Wiley & Sons.

Cicchetti, D., & Toth, S.L. (2006). Developmental psychopathology and preventive intervention. In W. Damon, R.M. Lerner, K.A. Renninger, & I.E. Sigel (Eds.), *Handbook of child psychology: Vol. 4. Child psychology in practice* (6th ed., pp. 497–545). New York: John Wiley & Sons.

Cicchetti, D., Toth, S.L., & Rogosch, F.A. (2000). The development of psychological wellness in maltreated children. In D. Cicchetti, J. Rappaport, I. Sandler, & R.P. Weissberg (Eds.), *The promotion of wellness in children and adolescents (Issues in children's and families' lives)* (pp. 395–426). Washington, DC: CWLA Press.

Clancy, B., & Finlay, B. (2001). Neural correlates of early language learning. In M. Tomasello & E. Bates (Eds.), *Language development: The essential readings* (pp. 307–330). Malden, MA: Blackwell Publishers.

Clandinin, D.J., & Connelly, F.M. (1994). Personal experience methods. In N.K. Denzin & Y.S. Lincoln (Eds.), *Handbook of qualitative research* (pp. 4113–4127). Thousand Oaks, CA: Sage Publications.

Clark, L.A., Watson, D.Y., & Mineka, S. (1994). Temperament, personality, and the mood and anxiety disorders. *Journal of Abnormal Psychology, 103*, 103–116.

Clark, R., & Fenichel, E. (2001). Mothers, babies, and depression: Questions and answers. *Zero to Three, 22*(1), 48–56.

Cochran, M., Larner, M., Riley, D., Gunnarsson, L., & Henderson, C.R., Jr. (1990). *Extending families: The social networks of parents and their children.* New York: Cambridge University Press.

Coll, C.G., & Magnuson, O.K. (2000). Cultural differences as sources of developmental vulnerabilities and resources. In J. Shonkoff & S. Meisels (Eds.), *Handbook of early childhood intervention* (2nd ed., pp. 94–114). New York: Cambridge University Press.

Constantino, J.N. (1993). Parents' mental illness and the primary health care of infants and children. *Young Children, 13*(5), 1–9.

Coyne, J.C., Burchill, S.A.L., & Stiles, W.B. (1990). Interpersonal processes in depression. In G.I. Keitner (Ed.), *Depression and families* (pp. 31–54). Washington, DC: American Psychiatric Press.

Cox, A.D., Puckering, C., Pound, A., & Mills, M. (1987). The impact of maternal depression on young children. *Journal of Child Psychology and Psychiatry, 28,* 917–928.

Cox, M.J., & Brooks-Gunn, J. (Eds.). (1999). Studying conflict and cohesion in families: An overview. In *Conflict and cohesion in families: Causes and consequences* (pp. 1–10). Mahwah, NJ: Lawrence Erlbaum Associates.

Crittenden, P.M. (1993). Characteristics of neglectful parents: An information processing approach. *Criminal Justice and Behavior, 20,* 27–48.

Crockenberg, S., & Leerkes, E. (2000). Infant social and emotional development in family context. In C.H. Zeanah, Jr. (Ed.), *Handbook of infant mental health* (2nd ed., pp. 60–90). New York: Guilford Press.

Cummings, E.M., & Wilson, A. (1999). Context of marital conflict and children's emotional security: Exploring the distinction between constructive and destructive conflict from the children's perspective. In M.J. Cox & J. Brooks-Gunn (Eds.), *Conflict and cohesion in families: Causes and consequences* (pp. 105–130). Mahwah, NJ: Lawrence Erlbaum Associates.

Dahl, R.E. (1996). The regulation of sleep and arousal: Development and psychopathology. *Development and Psychopathology, 8*(1), 3–28.

Davenport, Y.B., Zahn-Waxler, C., Adlend, M.C., & Mayfield, J. (1984). Early childrearing practices in families with a manic depressive parent. *American Journal of Psychiatry, 141,* 230–235.

Davies, P.T., & Cummings, E.M. (2006). Interparental discord, family processes and developmental psychopathology. In D. Cicchetti & D.J. Cohen (Eds.), *Developmental psychopathology: Vol. 3. Risk, disorder, and adaptation* (2nd ed., pp. 86–128). New York: John Wiley & Sons.

Dawson, P. (1992). Should the field of early child and family intervention address failure to thrive? *Zero to Three, 12*(5), 20–24.

DeBoysson-Bardies, B. (1999). *How language comes to children: From birth to two years.* Cambridge, MA: The MIT Press.

Deiner, P.L. (2005). *Resources for educating children with diverse abilities: Birth to eight* (4th ed.). Clifton Park, NY: Thompson Delmar Learning.

Denzin, N.K. (1989). *Interpretive biography.* Thousand Oaks, CA: Sage Publications.

Desantis, A., Coster, W., Bigsby, R., & Lester, B. (2004). Colic and fussing in infancy, and sensory processing at 3 to 8 years of age. *Infant Mental Health Journal, 25*(6), 522–539.

DeTemple, J.M. (2001). Parents and children reading books together. In D.K. Dickinson & P.O. Tabors (Eds.), *Young children learning at home and school: Beginning literacy with language* (pp. 31–52). Baltimore: Paul H. Brookes Publishing Co.

Devine, M. (1991). *Baby talk: The art of communicating with infants and toddlers.* New York: Kluwer Academic/Plenum Press.

Dewey, J. (1916). *Democracy and education.* New York: Macmillan.

Dilthey, W. (1961). Pattern and meaning in history: Thoughts on history and society. In H.P. Rickman (Editor and Introduction). New York: HarperCollins. (Edited from Volume VII of Dilthey's collected works, written in 1910)

Dodge, K.A. (1990). Developmental psychopathology in children of depressed mothers. *Developmental Psychology, 26*(1), 3–6.

Dodge, K.A., Coie, J.D., & Lynam, D. (2006). Aggression and antisocial behavior in youth. In W. Damon, R.M. Lerner, & N. Eisenberg (Eds.), *Handbook of child psychology: Vol. 3. Social, emotional, and personality development* (6th ed., pp. 71–188). New York: John Wiley & Sons.

Dodge, K.A., Lochman, J.E., Harnish, J.D., Bates, J.E., & Pettit, G.S. (1997). Reactive and proactive aggression in school children and psychiatrically impaired chronically assaultive youth. *Journal of Abnormal Psychology, 106,* 37–51.

Dole, J.D., Duffy, G.G., Roehler, L.R., & Pearson, P.D. (1991). Moving from old to the new: Research on reading comprehension instruction. *Review of Educational Research, 61*(2), 239–264.

Drotar, D., & Sturm, L.A. (1992). Personality development, problem solving, and behavior problems among preschool children with early histories of nonorganic failure to thrive: A controlled study. *Developmental and Behavioral Pediatrics, 13,* 266–273.

Duckworth, E. (1972). The having of wonderful ideas. *Harvard Educational Review, 42*(2), 217–231.

Dunn, J. (1992). Sisters and brothers: Current issues in developmental research. In F. Boer & J. Dunn (Eds.), *Children's sibling relationships: Developmental and clinical issues* (pp. 1–18). Hillsdale, NJ: Lawrence Erlbaum Associates.

Dunn, J. (1995). *From one to two: What to expect, how to cope, and how to enjoy your growing family.* New York: Fawcett Columbine.

Dunn, J. (2004). *Children's friendships: The beginning of intimacy.* Malden, MA: Blackwell Publishers

Dunn, J. (2006). *Families count: Effects on child and adolescent development.* New York: Cambridge University Press.

Dunn, J., & Brown, J. (1994). Affect expression in the family, children's understanding of emotions and their interactions with others. *Merrill-Palmer Quarterly, 40,* 120–137.

Dunn, J., & Kendrick, C. (1982). *Siblings: Love, envy, and understanding.* Cambridge, MA: Harvard University Press.

Dunn, J., & Plomin, R. (1990). *Separate lives: Why siblings are so different.* New York: Basic Books.

Edleson, J.L. (2001). Studying the co-occurrence of child maltreatment and domestic violence in families. In S.A. Graham-Bermann & J.L. Edleson (Eds.), *Domestic violence in the lives of children: The future of research, intervention, and social policy* (pp. 91–110). Washington, DC: American Psychological Association.

Egeland, B., & Erickson, M.F. (1999) Findings from the parent child project and implications for early intervention. *Zero to Three, 20*(2), 3–10.

Eiden, L.A., & Leonard, K.E. (1996). Paternal alcohol abuse and mother–infant relationship. *Development and Psychopathology, 8*(2), 307–323.

Einstein, A., & Infield, L. (1996). *The evolution of physics.* New York: Simon & Schuster. (Original work published 1938)

Eisenberg, N., Fabes, R.A., & Spinrad, T.L. (2006). Prosocial development. In W. Damon, R.M. Lerner, & N. Eisenberg (Eds.), *Handbook of child psychology: Vol. 3. Social, emotional, and personality development* (6th ed., pp. 646–718). New York: John Wiley & Sons.

Emde, R.N. (1989). The infant's relationship experience: Developmental and affective aspects. In A.J. Sameroff & R.N. Emde (Eds.), *Relationship disturbances in early childhood: A developmental approach* (pp. 40–47). New York: Basic Books.

Emde, R.N. (2001). The dynamics of development in a unique multidisciplinary collaboration. In R.N. Emde & J.K. Hewitt (Eds.), *Infancy to early childhood: Genetic and environment influences on developmental change* (pp. 3–11). New York: Oxford University Press.

Emde, R.N., & Robinson, J. (2000). Guiding principles for a theory of early intervention. In J.P. Shonkoff & S.J. Meisels (Eds.), *Handbook of early childhood intervention* (2nd ed., pp. 160–178). New York: International University Press.

Emde, R.N., Wolf, D.P., Oppenheim, D. (2003). *Revealing the inner worlds of young children: The Macarthur story stem battery and parent–child narratives.* New York: Oxford University Press.

Erikson, E. (1950). *Childhood and society.* New York: W.W. Norton.

Erikson, E. (1977). *Toys and reasons: Stages in the ritualization of experience.* New York: W.W. Norton.

Faber, A., & Mazlish, E. (1987). *Siblings without rivalry: How to help your children live together so you can live too.* New York: W.W. Norton.

Fabes, R.A., Martin, C.L., & Hanish, L.D. (2004, July). The next 50 years: Considering gender as a context for understanding young children's peer relationships. *Merrill-Palmer Quarterly, 50*(3), 260–273.

Fenichel, E. (1992a). Communication strategies for working with parents of infants who fail to thrive. *Zero to Three, 12*(5), 25–28.

Fenichel, E. (Ed.). (1992b). Learning through supervision and mentorship. In *Learning through supervision and mentorship to support the development of infants, toddlers, and their families* (pp. 1–8). Washington, DC: ZERO TO THREE: National Center for Infants, Toddlers and Families.

Ferber, R. (1985). *Solve your child's sleep problems.* New York: Simon & Schuster.

Fernald, A., Pinto, J.P., Swingley, D., Weinberg, A., & McRoberts, G.W. (2001). Rapid gains in speed of verbal processing by infants in the 2nd year. In M. Tomasello & E. Bates (Eds.), *Language development: The essential readings* (pp. 49–56). Malden, MA: Blackwell Publishers.

Field, T., Healy, B., Goldstein, S., & Guthertz, M. (1990). Behavior state matching and synchrony in mother–infant interactions of nondepressed versus depressed dyads. *Developmental Psychology, 26,* 7–14.

Fiese, B.H. (2000). Family matters: A systems view of family effects on children's cognitive health. In R.J. Sterberg & E.L. Grigorenko (Eds.), *Environmental effects on cognitive abilities* (pp. 390–397). Mahwah, NJ: Lawrence Erlbaum Associates.

Fiese, B.H. (2002). Routines of daily living and rituals in family life: A glimpse of stability and change during the early child-raising years. *Zero to Three, 22*(4), 10–13.

Fiese, B.H., Wilder, J., & Bickham, N.L. (2000). Family context in developmental psychology. In A.J. Sameroff, M. Lewis, & S.M. Miller (Eds.), *Handbook of developmental psychology* (2nd ed., pp. 115–134). New York: Kluwer Academic Publishers.

Finn, E., & Wolpin, W. (2005). Dental disease in infants and toddlers: A transdisciplinary health concern and approach. *Zero to Three, 25*(3), 28–33.

Fitzgerald, H.E., & Montanex, M. (2001). Fathers as facilitators of infant mental health: Implications for Early Head Start. *Zero to Three, 22*(1), 25–28.

Fitzgerald, H.E., Puttler, L.I., Young Mun, E., & Zucker, R.A. (2000). Prenatal and postnatal exposure to parental alcohol use and abuse. In J.D. Osofsky & H.E. Fitzgerald (Eds.), *WAIMH handbook of infant mental health: Vol. 4. Infant mental health in groups at high risk* (pp. 124–159). New York: John Wiley & Sons.

Forest, S. (1995). Rural early intervention training. *Zero to Three, 15*(5), 22–27.

Fraiberg, S.H. (1980). *Clinical studies in infant mental health.* New York: Basic Books.

Fraiberg, S.H., Adelson, E., & Shapiro, V. (1975). Ghosts in the nursery: A psychoanalytic approach to the problems of impaired mother–infant relationships. *Journal of the American Academy of Child Psychiatry, 14,* 378–421.

Frost, J.L., Wortham, S.C., & Reifel, S. (2001). *Play and child development.* Columbus, OH: Merrill/Prentice Hall.

Galinsky, E. (1987). *The six states of parenthood.* Reading, MA: Addison Wesley Higher Education Group.

Galinsky, E., & David, J. (1988). *The preschool years: Family strategies that work—from experts and parents.* New York: Ballantine Books.

Galinsky, E., Howes, C., Kontos, S., & Shinn, M. (1994). *The study of children in family child care and relative care.* New York: Families and Work Institute.

Garbarino, J. (1992). Children and families in the social environment. New York: Aldine de Gruyter.

Garbarino, J., & Bedard, C. (2001). *Parents under siege: Why you are the solution, not the problem, to your child's life.* New York: The Free Press.

Garbarino, J., & Ganzel, B. (2000). The human ecology of early risk. In J.P. Shonkoff & S.J. Meisels (Eds.), *Handbook of early childhood intervention* (2nd ed., pp. 76–93). New York: Cambridge University Press.

Gergen, K.J. (1991). *The saturated self: Dilemmas of identity in contemporary life.* New York: Basic Books.

Gest, S.D., Freeman, N.R., Domitrovich, C.E., & Welsh, J.A. (2004). Shared book reading and children's language comprehension skills: The moderating role of parental discipline practices. *Early Childhood Research Quarterly, 19*(2), 319–336.

Gil, E., & Johnson, T.C. (1993). *Sexualized children: Assessment and treatment of sexualized children and children who molest.* Rockville, MD: Launch Press.

Gilkerson, L., & Young-Hold, C.L. (1992). Supervision and the management of programs serving infants, toddlers, and families. In E. Fenichel (Ed.), *Learning through supervision and mentorship to support the development of infants, toddlers, and their families: A source book* (pp. 113–119). Washington, DC: ZERO TO THREE: National Center for Infants, Toddlers and Families.

Gilkerson, L., Gray, L., & Mork, N. (2005). Fussy babies, worried families, and a new service network. *Zero to Three, 25*(3), 34–41.

Gilliam, W.S., & Leiter, V. (2003). Evaluating early childhood programs: Improving quality and informing policy. *Zero to Three, 23*(6), 6–13.

Gilligan, C. (1982). *In a different voice.* Cambridge, MA: Harvard University Press.

Gilligan, C., & Brown, L.M. (1992). *Meeting at the crossroads: Women's psychology and girl's development.* Cambridge, MA: Harvard University Press.

Glenn, S.M., Cunningham, C.C., & Dayus, B. (2001, February). Comparison of the 1969 and 1993 standardizations of the Bayley Mental Scales of Infant Development for infants with Down's syndrome. *Journal of Intellectual Disability Research, 45*(1), 55–62.

Golombok, S. (2001). New family forms. In A. Clark-Stewart & J. Dunn (Eds.), *Families count: Effects on child and adolescent development.* New York: Cambridge University Press.

Gomez, C.R., Baird, S., & Jung, L.A. (2004). Regulatory disorder identification, diagnosis, and intervention planning: Untapped resources for facilitating development. *Infants and Young Children, 17*(4), 327–339.

Goodman, S.H. (2003). Genesis and epigenesis of psychopathology in children with depressed mothers: Toward an integrated biopsychosocial perspective. In D. Cicchetti & E.F. Walker (Eds.), *Neurodevelopmental mechanisms in psychopathology* (pp. 428–460). New York: Cambridge University Press.

Goodson, I.F. (1992). *Studying teachers' lives.* New York: Teachers College Press.

Gordon, T. (1989). *Discipline that works: Promoting self-discipline in children.* New York: Penguin Books.

Gottlieb, I., & Hooley, J.M. (1988). Depression and marital distress: Current states and future directions. In S. Duck (Ed.), *Handbook of personal relationships* (pp. 543–570). New York: John Wiley & Sons.

Gowen, J.W., & Nebrig, J.B. (2002). *Enhancing early development: Guiding parents of young children.* Baltimore: Paul H. Brookes Publishing Co.

Grace, C., Shores, E.F., Zaslow, M., Brown, B., & Aufseeser, D. (2006). New clues to reaching very young children and families in rural America. *Zero to Three, 26*(4), 7–13.

Greenspan, S.I. (1992). *Infancy and early childhood: The practice of clinical assessment and intervention with emotional and developmental challenges.* Madison, CT: International Universities Press.

Greenspan, S.I. (1993, December). *Toward a new vision for the developmental assessment of infants and young children.* Paper presented at the plenary session of the National Center for Clinical Programs' Eighth Biennial Training Institute, Washington, DC.

Greenspan, S.I. (2002). *The secure child: helping our children feel safe and confident in an insecure world.* Cambridge, MA: Perseus Publishing.

Greenspan, S.I., with Benderly, B.L. (1997). *The growth of the mind and the endangered origins of intelligence.* Reading, MA: Addison-Wesley.

Greenspan, S.I., with Breslau Lewis, N. (2000). *Building healthy minds: The six experiences that create intelligence and emotional growth in babies and young children.* Cambridge, MA: Perseus Publishing.

Greenspan, S.I., & Greenspan, N.T. (1989). *The essential partnership: How parents and children can meet the emotional challenges of infancy and childhood.* New York: Penguin Books.

Greenspan, S.I., & Shanker, S.G. (2004). *The first idea: How symbols, language, and intelligence evolved from our primate ancestors to modern humans.* Cambridge, MA: Da Capo Press.

Grusec, J.E., Davidov, M., & Lundell, L. (2002). Prosocial and helping behavior. In P.K. Smith & C.H. Hart (Eds.), *Blackwell handbook of childhood social development* (pp. 457–474). Malden, MA: Blackwell Publishers.

Gunnar, M.R., Brodersen, L., Nachmias, M., Buss, K., & Rigatuso, J. (1996). Stress reactivity and attachment security. *Developmental Psychobiology, 31*(1), 65–85.

Hans, S., & Korfmacher, J. (2002). The professional development of paraprofessionals. *Zero to Three, 23*(2), 4–8.

Harris, D. (2006). Rural revisiting: A decade-and-a-half of practice. *Zero to Three, 26*(4), 22–29.

Hart, D. (2005). The development of moral identity. *Nebraska Symposium on Motivation, 51,* 165–196.

Harter, S. (2006). The self. In W. Damon, R.M. Lerner, & N. Eisenberg (Eds.), *Handbook of child psychology: Vol. 3. Social, emotional, and personality development* (6th ed., pp. 505–571). New York: John Wiley & Sons.

Hartup, W.W., & Archer, J. (2005). *Developmental origins of aggression.* New York: Guilford Press.

Heath, S.B. (1983). *Ways with words: Language, life, and works in communities and classrooms.* New York: Cambridge University Press.

Holly, M.L. (1989). Teacher professional development: Perceptions and practices in the USA and England. In M.L. Holly & C.S. McLoughlin (Eds.), *Perspectives on teacher professional development* (pp. 172–203). London: The Falmer Press.

Honig, A.S. (1985). Compliance, control, and discipline. *Young Children, 40*(2), 50–58.

Horn, W.F. (2000). Fathering infants. In J.D. Osofsky & H.E. Fitzgerald (Eds.), *WAIMH handbook of infant mental health: Vol. 3. Parenting and child care* (pp. 272–297). New York: John Wiley & Sons.

Howes, C. (1988). Peer interaction of young children [Special issues]. *Monographs of the Society for Research in Child Development, 53*(1, Serial No. 217).

Howes, P.W., Cicchetti, D., Toth, S.L., & Rogosch, F.A. (2000). Affective, organization, and relationship characteristics of maltreating families: A systems perspective. *Journal of Family Psychology, 14*(1), 95–110.

Huttenlocher, J., Haiglet, W., Bryk, A., Deltzer, M., & Lynos, T. (1991). Early vocabulary growth: Relating to language input and gender. *Developmental Psychology, 27,* 236–248.

Illustrated Oxford Dictionary. (1998). New York: Oxford University Press.

Imber-Black, E., & Roberts, J. (Eds.). (1992). *Rituals for our times: Celebration, healing and changing our lives and our relationships.* New York: HarperCollins.

Ispa, J.M., & Halgunseth, L.C. (2006). Raising children. In J.M. Ispa, K.R. Thornburg, & M.A. Fine (Eds.), *Keepin' on: The everyday struggles of young families in poverty* (pp. 157–201). Baltimore: Paul H. Brookes Publishing Co.

Izard, C.E., Youngstrom, E.A., Fine, S.E., Mostow, A.J., & Trentacosta, C.J. (2006). Emotions and developmental psychopathology. In D. Cicchetti & D.J. Cohen (Eds.), *Developmental psychopathology: Vol. 1. Theory and method* (2nd ed., pp. 244–293). New York: John Wiley & Sons.

Jaber, R. (2000). Respiratory and allergic diseases: From upper respiratory tract infections to asthma. *Primary Care, 29*(2), 231–261.

Jackson, P.W. (1992). Helping teachers develop. In A. Hargreaves & M.G.B. Fullan (Eds.), *Understanding teacher development.* New York: Teachers College Press.

Jaffe, P.G., Poisson, S.E., & Cunningham, A. (2001), Domestic violence and high-conflict divorce: Developing a new generation of research for children. In S.A. Graham-Bermann & J.L. Edleson (Eds.), *Domestic violence in the lives of children: The future of research, intervention, and social policy* (pp. 189–202). Washington, DC: American Psychological Association.

Jervay-Pendergrass, D., & Brown, C. (2000). Something happened!: Life stories from birth to three. *Zero to Three, 20*(3), 25–31.

Jones-Harden, B. (1997). You can't do it alone: Home visitation and psychologically vulnerable families and children. *Zero to Three, 17*(4), 10–16.

Jordan, A.B., & Woodard, E.J.H., IV. (2001). Electronic childhood: The availability and use of household media by 2- and 3-year-olds. *Zero to Three, 22,* 4–9.

Jusczyk, P.W. (2003). Chunking language input to find patterns. In D.H. Rakison & L.M. Oakes (Eds.), *Early category and concept development: Making sense of blooming, buzzing confusion* (pp. 27–49). New York: Oxford University Press.

Kagan, J. (2001). The structure of temperament. In R.N. Emde & J.K. Hewitt (Eds.). *Infancy to early childhood: Genetic and environmental influences on developmental change* (pp. 45–51). New York: Oxford University Press.

Kagan, J., & Fox, N.A. (2006). Biology, culture, and temperamental biases. In N. Eisenberg, W. Damon, & R.M. Lerner (Eds.), *Handbook of child psychology: Vol. 3. Social, emotional, and personality development* (6th ed., pp. 167–225). New York: John Wiley & Sons.

Kagan, J., Herschkowitz, N., & Herschkowitz, E. (2005). *A young mind in a growing brain.* Mahwah, NJ: Lawrence Erlbaum Associates.

Kaplan, M.D., & Pruett, K.D. (2000). Divorce and custody: Developmental implications. In C.H. Zeanah, Jr. (Ed.), *Handbook of infant mental health* (2nd ed., pp. 533–547). New York: Guilford Press.

Karr-Morse, R., & Wiley, M.S. (1997). *Ghosts from the nursery: Tracing the roots of violence.* New York: The Atlantic Monthly Press.

Katz, J.R. (2001). Playing at home: The talk of pretend play. In D.K. Dickinson & P.O. Tabors (Eds.), *Young children learning at home and school: Beginning literacy with language* (pp. 53–75). Baltimore: Paul H. Brookes Publishing Co.

Kaufman, J., & Henrich, C. (2000). Exposure to violence and early childhood trauma. In C.H. Zeanah, Jr. (Ed.), *Handbook of infant mental health* (2nd ed., pp. 195–207). New York: Guilford Press.

Kelly, J.F., & Barnard, K.E. (2000). Assessment of parent–child interaction: Implications for early intervention. In J.P. Shonkoff & S.J. Meisels (Eds.), *Handbook of early childhood intervention* (pp. 258–289). New York: Cambridge University Press.

Kent, D., & Pepler, D. (2003). The aggressive child as agent in coercive family processes. In D.B. Bugental, D.H. Olster, & G.A. Martorell (Eds.), A developmental neuroscience perspective on the dynamics of parenting. In Kuczynski, L. (Ed.) *Handbook of dynamics in parent–child relations* (pp. 109–130). London: Sage Publications.

Kerr, M.E., & Bowen, M. (1988). *Family evaluation: An approach based on Bowen theory.* New York: W.W. Norton.

King, M.L., Jr. (1963, August 29). Speech delivered on the steps of the Lincoln Memorial, Washington, DC.

Klaus, H.M., & Kennell, J.H. (1976). *Maternal–infant bonding.* St. Louis: Mosby.

Knapp-Philo, J., Hindman, J., Stice, K., & Turbiville, V. (2006). Professional development that changes practice and programs: Six successful strategies. *Zero to Three, 26*(3), 43–49.

Kobak, R., Cassidy, J., Lyons-Ruth, K., & Ziv, Y. (2006). Attachment, stress, and psychopathology: A developmental pathways model. In D. Cicchetti & D.J. Cohen (Eds.), *Developmental psychopathology: Vol. 1. Theory and method* (2nd ed., pp. 333–369). New York: John Wiley & Sons.

Kochanska, G.M., Aksan, N., & Carlson, J.J. (2005). Temperament, relationships and young children's receptive cooperation with their parents. *Developmental Psychology, 41*(4), 648–660.

Koenig, K., Rubin, E., Klin, A., & Volkmar, F.R. (2000). Autism and pervasive developmental disorders. In C.H. Zeanah, Jr. (Ed.), *Handbook of infant mental health* (2nd ed., pp. 311–325). New York: Guilford Press.

Kubicek, L.R. (2002). Fresh perspectives on young children and family rituals. *Zero to Three, 22*(4), 4–9.

Landry, S.H., Miller-Loncar, C.L., Smith, K.E., & Swank, P.R. (2002). The role of early parenting in children's development of executive processes. *Developmental Neuropsychology, 21*(1), 15–41.

Landy, S., & Menna, R. (2006). *Early intervention with multi-risk families: An integrative approach.* Baltimore: Paul H. Brookes Publishing Co.

Lansky, V. (1984). *Toilet training.* New York: Bantam Books.

Lapsley, D.K., & Narvaez, D. (2006). Character education. In W. Damon, R.M. Lerner, K.A. Renninger, & I.E. Sigel (Eds.), *Handbook of child psychology: Vol. 4. Child psychology in practice* (6th ed., pp. 248–296). New York: John Wiley & Sons.

Larner, M., & Halpern, T. (1992). Lay home visiting programs: Strengths, tensions, and challenges. In E. Fenichel (Ed.), *Learning through supervision and mentorship to support the development of infants, toddlers, and their families: A source book* (pp. 91–99). Washington, DC: ZERO TO THREE: National Center for Infants, Toddlers and Families.

Lee, P. (1989). Is the young child egocentric or sociocentric? *Teachers College Record, 19*(3), 379–391.

Lester, B.M., Arria, A.M., Derauf, C., Grang, P., LaGasse, L., Newman, E., et al. (2006). Methamphetamine exposure: A rural early intervention challenge. *Zero to Three, 26*(4), 30–36.

Lester, B.M., Boukydis, C.F.Z., & Twomey, J.E. (2000). Maternal substance abuse and child outcome. In C.H. Zeanah, Jr. (Ed.), *Handbook of infant mental health* (2nd ed., pp. 161–175). New York: Guilford Press.

Lester, B.M., & Tronick, E.Z. (1994). The effects of prenatal cocaine exposure and child outcome. *Infant Mental Health Journal, 15*(2), 107–120.

Lewis, M.L. (2000). The cultural context of infant mental health: The developmental niche of infant–caregiver relationship. In C.H. Zeanah, Jr. (Ed.), *Handbook of infant mental health* (2nd ed., pp. 91–108). New York: Guilford Press.

Lieberman, A.F. (1991). Attachment theory and infant–parent psychotherapy: Some conceptual, clinical and research considerations. In D. Cicchetti & S.L. Toth (Eds.), *Rochester symposium on developmental psychopathology: Vol. 3. Models and integrations* (pp. 261–287). Rochester, NY: University of Rochester Press.

Lieberman, A.F. (1993). *The emotional life of the toddler.* New York: The Free Press.

Lieberman, A.F., & Pawl, J.H. (1993). Infant–parent psychotherapy. In C.H. Zeanah, Jr. (Ed.), *Handbook of infant mental health* (2nd ed., pp. 427–442). New York: Guilford Press.

Lieberman, A.F., Silverman, R., & Pawl, J.H. (2000). Infant–parent psychotherapy: Care concepts and current approaches. In C.H. Zeanah, Jr. (Ed.), *Handbook of infant mental health* (2nd ed., pp. 472–484). New York: Guilford Press.

Linn, S., & Poussant, A.F. (2001). The truth about Teletubbies. *Zero to Three, 22*(2), 24–29.

Loevinger, J. (1976). *Ego development.* San Francisco: Jossey-Bass.

Lozoff, B., Jimenez, E., Hagen, J., Mollen, E., & Wolf, A.W. (2000). Poorer behavioral and developmental outcome more than 10 years after treatment for iron deficiency in infancy. *Pediatrics, 105*, 2–11.

Luby, J.L. (2000). Depression. In C.H. Zeanah, Jr. (Ed.), *Handbook of infant mental health* (2nd ed., pp. 382–396). New York: Guilford Press.

Ludlow, B.L. (2002). Web-based staff development for early intervention personnel. *Infants and Young Children, 14*(3), 54–64.

Lumeng, J. (2005). What can we do to prevent childhood obesity? *Zero to Three, 25*(3), 13–19.

Lussier, G., Deater-Deckard, K., Dunn, M.J., & Davies, L. (2002). Support across two generations: Children's closeness to grandparents following parental divorce and remarriage. *Journal of Family Psychology, 16*(3), 363–376.

Luster, T., & Brophy-Herb, H. (2000). Adolescent mothers and their children. In J.D. Osofsky & H.E. Fitzgerald (Eds.), *WAIMH handbook of infant mental health: Vol. 4. Infant mental health in groups at high risk* (pp. 369–414). New York: John Wiley & Sons.

Lynch, E.W., & Hanson, E.W. (Eds.). (2004). *Developing cross-cultural competence: A guide for working with children and their families.* Baltimore: Paul H. Brookes Publishing Co.

Mahler, M.S., Pine, F., & Berman, A. (1975). *The psychological birth of the human infant: Symbiosis and individuation.* New York: Basic Books.

Mahoney, G., & Powell, A. (1988). Modifying parent–child interaction: Enhancing the development of handicapped children. *Journal of Special Education, 22*(1), 82–96.

Main, M., Kaplan, N., & Cassidy, J. (1985). Security in infancy, childhood and adulthood: A move to the level of representation. *Monographs of the Society for Research in Child Development, 50*(1/2), 66–104.

Marchman, V., & Thal, D. (2005). Words and grammar. In M. Tomasello & D.I. Slobin (Eds.), *Beyond nature-nurture: Essays in honor of Elizabeth Bates.* Mahwah, NJ: Lawrence Erlbaum Associates.

Martens, J., Strinste, N., Sanchez, S., & Thorep, E. (2004). Stories change a person's heart. ZERO TO THREE's literacy, learning and life initiative. *Zero to Three, 25*(1), 23–30.

Mayer, M. (1985). *I was so mad.* Racine, WI: Western.

Mayes, L.C., Bornstein, M.H., Chawarska, K., Haynes, O.M., & Granger, R.H. (1996). Impaired regulation of arousal in 3-month-old infants exposed prenatally to cocaine and other drugs. *Development and Psychopathology, 8,* 29–42.

McDonough, S.C. (1993). Interaction guidance: Understanding and treating early infant–caregiver relationship disturbances. In C.H. Zeanah (Ed.), *Handbook of infant mental health* (pp. 414–426). New York: Guilford Press.

McDonough, S.C. (2000). Interaction guidance: An approach for difficult-to-engage families. In C.H. Zeanah, Jr. (Ed.), *Handbook of infant mental health* (2nd ed., pp. 485–493). New York: Guilford Press.

McGee, R., Partridge, F., Williams, S., & Silva, P.A. (1991). A twelve-year follow-up of preschool hyperactive children. *Journal of the American Academy of Child and Adolescent Psychiatry, 30,* 224–232.

McGuire, S., & Roch-Leveco, A. (2001). Mothers' perceptions of differential treatment of infant twins. In R.N. Emde & J.K. Hewitt (Eds.). *Infancy to early childhood: Genetic and environmental influences on developmental change* (pp. 247–256). New York: Oxford University Press.

McKenna, J.J. (2000). Cultural influences on infant and childhood sleep, biology, and the science that studies it: Toward a more inclusive paradigm. *Zero to Three, 20*(3), 9–18.

McLanahan, S.S. (1999). Father absence and the welfare of children. In E.M. Hetherington (Ed.), *Coping with divorce, single parenting, and remarriage: A risk and resiliency perspective* (pp. 117–146) Mahwah, NJ: Lawrence Erlbaum Associates.

Mead, G.H. (1934). *Mind, self, and society from the standpoint of a social behaviorist* (Vol. 1). Chicago: University of Chicago Press.

Mead, M. (1962). *A creative life for your children.* (Headliner series no. 1). Washington, DC: Children's Bureau, U.S. Department of Health, Education, and Welfare.

Mead, M. (1972). *Blackberry winter.* New York: Simon & Schuster.

Measor, L. (1985). Critical incidents in the classroom: Identities, choices, and careers. In S.J. Ball & I.F. Goodson (Eds.), *Teachers' lives and careers* (pp. 61–77). Philadelphia: Falmer Press.

Meisels, S.J., & Atkins-Burnett, S. (2000). The elements of early childhood assessment. In J.P. Shonkoff & S.J. Meisels (Eds.), *Handbook of early childhood intervention* (pp. 231–257). New York: Cambridge University Press.

Middlemiss, W. (2004). Infant sleep: A review of normative and problematic sleep and interventions. *Early Child Development and Care, 174*(1), 99–122.

Mills, C.W. (1959). *The sociological imagination.* New York: Oxford University Press.

Minde, K. (2000). Prematurity and serious medical conditions in infancy: Implications for development, behavior, and intervention. In C.H. Zeanah, Jr. (Ed.), *Handbook of infant mental health* (2nd ed.). New York: Guilford Press.

Moss, E., Bureau, J., Cyr, C., Mongeau, C., & St.-Laurent, D. (2004). Correlates of attachment in age 3: Construct validity of preschool attachment classification system. *Developmental Psychology, 40*(3), 323–334.

Mrazek, P.J. (1993). Maltreatment and infant development. In C.H. Zeanah, Jr. (Ed.), *Handbook of infant mental health* (pp. 159–170). New York: Guilford Press.

Murray, L. (1992). The impact of prenatal development on infant development. *Journal of Child Psychology and Psychiatry, 33*(3), 543–561.

Musick, J.S., & Stott, F. (1993). Paraprofessionals, parenting, and child development: Understanding the problems and seeking solutions. In S.J. Meisels & J.P. Shonkoff (Eds.), *Handbook of early childhood intervention* (pp. 651–667). New York: Cambridge University Press.

Musick, J., & Stott, F. (2000). Paraprofessionals revisiting and reconsidered. In J.P. Shonkoff & S.J. Meisels (Eds.), *Handbook of early childhood intervention* (pp. 439–453). New York: Cambridge University Press.

Myers, A., & Chawla, N. (2002). Nutrition and social, emotional, and cognitive development of infants and young children. *Zero to Three, 21*(1), 5–14.

Myers, B.J., Olson, H.C., & Kaltenbach, K. (1992). Cocaine-exposed infants: Myths and misunderstandings. *Zero to Three, 13*(1), 1–5.

Nelson, C.A., & Bosquet, M. (2000). Neurobiology of fetal and infant development: Implications for infant mental health. In C.H. Zeanah, Jr. (Ed.), *Handbook of infant mental health* (2nd ed., pp. 37–59). New York: Guilford Press.

Nelson, C.A., Thomas, K.M., & De Haan, M. (2006). Neural bases of cognitive development. In W. Damon, R.M. Lerner, D. Kuhn, & R. Siegler (Eds.), *Handbook of child psychology: Vol. 2. Cognition, perception, and language* (6th ed., pp. 3–57). New York: John Wiley & Sons.

Nelson, K. (1973). Structure and strategy in learning to talk. *Monographs of the Society for Research in Child Development, 38*(Serial No. 149).

Nelson, K. (Ed.). (1989). *Narratives from the crib.* Cambridge, MA: Harvard University Press.

Nelson, K. (1996). *Language in cognitive development: Emergence of the mediated mind.* New York: Cambridge University Press.

Nelson, K., & Gruendel, J. (1986). Children's scripts. In K. Nelson (Ed.), *Event knowledge: Structure and function in development* (pp. 21–46). Mahwah, NJ: Lawrence Erlbaum Associates.

Nelson, L.J., Rubin, K.H.Y., & Fox, N.A. (2005). Social withdrawal, observed peer acceptance and the development of self perceptions in children 4 to 7 years. *Early Childhood Research Quarterly, 20*(2), 185–200.

Nias, J. (1989). Teaching and the self. In M.L. Holly & C.S. McLoughlin (Eds.), *Perspectives on teacher professional development* (pp. 155–171). Philadelphia: Falmer Press.

Nias, J. (1992). Reference groups in primary teaching: Talking, listening, and identity. In S.J. Ball & I.F. Goodson (Eds.), *Teachers' lives and careers* (pp. 105–119). Philadelphia: Falmer Press.

Noddings, N. (1984). *Caring: A feminine approach to ethics and moral education.* Berkeley, CA: University of California Press.

Noll, S. (1991). *That bothered Kate.* New York: Puffin Books.

Norton, D.G. (1994). Education for professionals in family support. In S.L. Kagan & B. Weissbourd (Eds.), *Putting families first: America's family support movement and the challenge of change* (pp. 401–440). San Francisco: Jossey-Bass.

Nosarti, C., Rifkin, L., & Murray, R.M. (2003). The neurodevelopmental consequences of very preterm birth: Brain plasticity and its limits. In D. Cicchetti & E. Walker (Eds.), *Neurodevelopmental mechanisms in psychopathology* (pp. 34–60). Cambridge, England: Cambridge University Press.

Obeidallah, D.A., & Burton, L.M. (1999). Affective ties between mothers and daughters in adolescent childbearing families. In M.J. Cox & J. Brooks-Gunn (Eds.), *Conflict and cohesion in families: Causes and consequences* (pp. 37–50). Mahwah, NJ: Lawrence Erlbaum Associates.

O'Connor, M.J. (2001) Prenatal alcohol exposure and infant negative affect as precursors of depressive features in children. *Infant Mental Health Journal, 22*(3), 291–299.

O'Hearn Family Outreach Project Members. (1995). When families lead: The Patrick O'Hearn Family Outreach Project. In A. Palanki & P. Burch (Eds.), *In our hands: A multi-site parent–teacher action research project* (pp. 117–134). Boston: Center on Families, Communities, Schools & Children's Learning.

Olds, D.L. (1981). Improving formal services for mothers and children. In J. Garbarino & S.H. Stocking (Eds.), *Protecting children from abuse and neglect* (pp. 173–197). San Francisco: Jossey-Bass.

Olson, H., Burgess, D.M., & Streissguth, A.P. (1992). Fetal alcohol syndrome (FAS) and fetal alcohol effects (FAE): A lifespan view, with implications for early intervention. *Zero to Three, 13*(1), 24–29.

Olson, H.C., O'Connor, M.J., & Fitzgerald, H.E. (2001). Lessons learned from study of the developmental impact of parental alcohol use. *Infant Mental Health Journal, 22*(3), 271–290.

Osofsky, J.D. (1993). *Working with infants, toddlers, and caregivers exposed to violence. Tales from two cities: Boston and New Orleans.* Paper presented at the Eighth Biannual Conference of the ZERO TO THREE National Training Institutes, Washington, DC.

Osofsky, J.D. (1996). Islands of safety: Assessing and treating young victims of violence. *Zero to Three, 16*(5), 5–8.

Osofsky, J.D. (2000). Infants and violence: Prevention intervention, and treatment. In J.D. Osofsky & H.E. Fitzgerald (Eds.), *WAIMH handbook of infant mental health: Vol. 4. Infant mental health in groups at high risk* (pp. 163–196). New York: John Wiley & Sons.

Osofsky, J.D., & Thompson, M.D. (2000). Adaptive and maladaptive parenting: Perspectives on risks and protective factors. In J.P. Shonkoff & S.M. Meisels (Eds.), *Handbook of early childhood intervention* (2nd ed., pp. 54–75). New York: Cambridge University Press.

Park, R.D., & Tinsley, B.R. (1981). The father's role in infancy: Determinants of involvement in caregiving and play. In M.E. Lamb (Ed.), *The role of father in child development* (2nd ed.). New York: John Wiley & Sons.

Parke, R.D. (1996). *Fatherhood.* Cambridge, MA: Harvard University Press.

Parmelee, A.H., Jr. (1993). Children's illnesses and normal behavioral development: The role of caregivers. *Zero to Three, 13*(4), 1–9.

Pawl, J. (1995). The therapeutic relationship as human connection: Being held in another's mind. *Zero to Three, 15*(4), 1–5.

Pawl, J. (1997). Untitled paper presented at the plenary session of the Building a Good Beginning Project for Every Child conference, St. Louis.

Pellegrini, A.D. (2002). Rough-and-tumble play from childhood through adolescence: Development and possible functions. In P.K. Smith & C.H. Hart (Eds.), *Blackwell handbook of childhood social development* (pp. 438–454). Malden, MA: Blackwell Publishers.

Pellegrini, D.S., & Notarius, C.I. (1988). Marital processes as childhood risk factors: Implications for intervention and prevention. In E.D. Hibbs (Ed.), *Children and families: Studies in prevention and intervention* (pp. 497–509). Madison, CT: International University Press.

Penn, P. (1985). Feed-forward: Future questions, future maps. *Family Process, 24*(3), 299–310.

Piaget, J. (1962). *Play, dreams and imitation in childhood.* New York: W.W. Norton.

Piaget, J. (1963). *The origins of intelligence in children.* New York: W.W. Norton. (Original work published 1952)

Piaget, J. (1969). *The mechanisms of perception.* London: Rutledge & Kegan Paul.

Porges, S. (2004). Neuroception: A subconscious system for detecting threats and safety. *Zero to Three, 24*(5), 19–24.

Prizant, B.M., Wetherby, A.M., & Roberts, J.E. (2000) Communication problems. In C.H. Zeanah, Jr. (Ed.), *Handbook of infant mental health* (2nd ed., pp. 282–297). New York: Guilford Press

Pruett, K.D. (1997). How men and children affect each other's development. *Zero to Three, 18*(1), 3–11.

Raising Children Network (RCN). (2007, April). *Preventing SIDS.* Victoria, Australia: Author.

Random House Dictionary of the English language (unabridged). (1973). New York: Random House.

Raymond, D., Butt, B., & Townsend, D. (1992). Contexts for teacher development: Insights from teachers' stories. In A. Hargreaves & M.D. Fullan (Eds.), *Understanding teacher development* (pp. 143–161). New York: Teachers College Press.

Reiss, D. (1989). The represented and practicing family: Contrasting visions of family continuity. In A.J. Sameroff & R.N. Emde (Eds.), *Relationship disturbances in early childhood: A developmental approach* (pp. 191–220). New York: Basic Books.

Rideout, V.J., Vandewater, E.A., & Wartella, E.A. (2003). *Zero to Three: Electronic media in the lives of infants, toddlers, and preschoolers.* Menlo, Park, CA: The Kaiser Family Foundation.

Robinson, J.L., Zahn-Waxler, C., & Emde, R.N. (2001). Relationship context as a moderator of sources of individual differences in empathic development. In R.N. Emde & J.K. Hewitt (Eds.), *Infancy to early childhood: Genetic and environmental influences on developmental change* (pp. 257–268). New York: Oxford University Press.

Rogers, C.R. (1969). *Freedom to learn.* Columbus, OH: Charles E. Merrill.

Rossman, B.B. (2001). Longer term effects of children's exposure to domestic violence. In S.A. Graham-Bermann & J.L. Edleson (Eds.), *Domestic violence in the lives of children: The future of research, intervention, and social policy* (pp. 35–66). Washington, DC: American Psychological Association.

Rothbart, M.K., & Bates, J.E. (2006). Temperament. In N. Eisenberg, R.M. Lerner, & W. Damon (Eds.), *Handbook of child psychology* (6th ed., pp. 99–166). New York: John Wiley & Sons.

Rubin, K.H., Bukowski, W.M., & Parker, J.G. (2006). Peer interactions, relationships, and groups. In W. Damon, R.M. Lerner, & N. Eisenberg (Eds.), *Handbook of child psychology: Vol. 3. Social, emotional, and personality development* (pp. 571–645). New York: John Wiley & Sons.

Ruble, D.N., Martin, C.L., & Bernbaum, S.A. (2006). Gender development. In W. Damon, R.M. Lerner, & N. Eisenberg (Eds.), *Handbook of child psychology: Vol. 3. Social, emotional, and personality development* (6th ed., pp. 858–932). New York: John Wiley & Sons.

Rudolph, K.D., & Asher, S.R. (2000). Adaptation and maladaptation in the peer system. In A.J. Sameroff, M. Lewis, & S.M. Miller (Eds.), *Handbook of developmental psychopathology* (2nd ed., pp. 157–175). New York: Plenum Press.

Rutter, M. (1990). Commentary: Some focus and process considerations regarding effects of parental depression on children. *Developmental Psychology, 26*(1), 60–67.

Rutter, M., & Quinton, D. (1984). Parental psychiatric disorder: Effects on children. *Psychological Medicine, 14,* 853–880.

Saarni, C., Campos, J.J., Camras, L.A., & Witherington, D. (2006). Emotional development: Action, communication, and understanding. In W. Damon, R.M. Lerner, & N. Eisenberg (Eds.), *Handbook of child psychology: Vol. 3. Social, emotional, and personality development* (6th ed., pp. 226–299). New York: John Wiley & Sons.

Sacks, O. (1996). *An anthropologist on Mars: Seven paradoxical tales.* New York: Vintage Books.

Saint Augustine. (1961). *Confessions* (R.S. Pine-Coffin, trans.). New York: Penguin Books. (Written c. A.D. 396–397)

Saffran, J.R., Werker, J.F., & Werner, L.A. (2006). The infant's auditory world: Hearing, speech, and the beginnings of language. In W. Damon, R.M. Lerner, D. Kuhn, & R. Siegler (Eds.), *Handbook of child psychology: Vol. 2. Cognition, perception, and language* (6th ed., pp. 58–107). New York: John Wiley & Sons.

Sameroff, A. (2000). Ecological perspectives on developmental risk. In J.D. Osofsky & H.E. Fitzgerald (Eds.), *WAIMH handbook of infant mental health: Vol. 4. Infant mental health in groups at high risk* (pp. 415–455). New York: John Wiley & Sons.

Sameroff, A.J., & Emde, R.N., (Eds.). (1989). *Relationship disturbances in early childhood: A developmental approach.* New York: Basic Books.

Sameroff, A.J., & Fiese, B.H. (2000). Transactional regulation: The developmental ecology of early intervention. In J.P. Shonkoff & S.J. Meisels (Eds.), *Handbook of early childhood intervention* (2nd ed., pp. 135–159). New York: Cambridge University Press.

Sameroff, A.J., Lewis, M., & Miller, S.M. (2000). *Handbook of developmental psychology* (2nd ed.). New York: Kluwer Academic.

Sammons, W.A.H. (1989). *The self-calmed baby: Teach your infant to calm itself—and curb crying, fussing, and sleeplessness.* New York: St. Martin's Press.

Saudino, K.J., & Cherny, S.S. (2001). Sources of continuity and change in observed temperament. In R.N. Emde & J.K. Hewitt (Eds.), *Infancy to early childhood: Genetic and environmental influences on developmental change* (pp. 89–110). New York: Oxford University Press.

Schachter, F.F., & Strage, A.A. (1982). Adults' talk and children's language development. In S.G. Moore & C.R. Cooper (Eds.), *The young child: Reviews of research* (Vol. 3). Washington, DC: National Association for the Education of Young Children.

Schaefer, W.M. (2004). The infant as reflection of soul: The time before there was a self. *Zero to Three, 24*(3), 4–8.

Scheeringa, M.S., & Greenbauer, T.J. (2000). Posttraumatic stress disorder. In C.H. Zeanah, Jr. (Ed.), *Handbook of infant mental health* (2nd ed., pp. 369–381). New York: Guilford Press.

Schlossman, S.L. (1976). Before home start: Notes toward a history of parent education in America, 1897–1929. *Harvard Educational Review, 46*(3), 436–467.

Schmidt, A.T., & Georgieff, M.D. (2006). Early nutritional deficiencies in brain development: Implications for psychopathology. In D. Cicchetti & D.J. Cohen (Eds.), *Developmental psychopathology: Vol. 2. Developmental neuroscience* (2nd ed., pp. 259–291). New York: John Wiley & Sons.

Schon, D.A. (1987). *Educating the reflective practitioner: Toward a new design for teaching and learning in the professions.* San Francisco: Jossey-Bass.

Schore, A.N. (1994). *Affect regulation and the origin of the self: The neurobiology of emotional development.* Mahwah, NJ: Lawrence Erlbaum Associates.

Schore, A.N. (1998). Early organization of the nonlinear right brain and development of a predisposition to psychiatric disorders. *Development and Psychopathology, 9*(4), 505–633.

Schorr, L.B., & Schorr, D. (1988). *Within our reach: Breaking the cycle of disadvantage.* New York: Doubleday.

Segal, M. (2004). The roots and fruits of pretending. In E.F. Ziegler, D.G. Singer, & S.J. Bishop-Josef (Eds.), *Children's play: The roots of reading.* Washington DC: ZERO TO THREE: National Center for Infants, Toddlers and Families.

Seguin, J.R., & Zelazo, P.D. (2005). Executive function in early physical aggression. In R.E. Tremblay, W.W. Hartup, & J. Archer (Eds.), *Developmental origins of aggression* (pp. 307–329). New York: Guilford Press.

Seifer, R., & Dickstein, S. (2000). Parental maternal illness and infant development. In C.H. Zeanah, Jr. (Ed.), *Handbook of infant mental health* (2nd ed., pp. 145–160). New York: Guilford Press.

Seifer, R., Sameroff, A.J., Dickstein, S., Gitner, G., Miller, I., Rasmussen, S., & Hayden, L.C. (1996, February). Parental psychopathology, multiple contextual risks, and one-year outcomes in children. *Journal of Clinical Child & Adolescent Psychology, 25*(4), 423–435.

Seligman, S.P., & Pawl, J.H. (1984). Impediments to the formation of the working alliance in infant–parent psychotherapy. In J.D. Call, E. Galenson, & R.L. Tyson (Eds.), *Frontiers of infant psychiatry* (Vol. 2, pp. 232–237). New York: Basic Books.

Shanok, R.S. (1991). The supervisory relationship: Integrator, resource, and guide. *Zero to Three, 12*(2), 16–19.

Sharp, E.A., & Ispa, J.M. (2006). The children's fathers. In J.M. Ispa, K.R. Thornburg, & M.A. Fine (Eds.), *Keepin' on: The everyday struggles of young families in poverty* (pp. 203–228). Baltimore: Paul H. Brookes Publishing Co.

Shaw, D.S., Gilliom, M., & Giovannelli, J. (2000). Aggressive behavior disorders. In C.H. Zeanah, Jr. (Ed.), *Handbook of infant mental health* (2nd ed., pp. 397–411). New York: Guilford Press.

Shirk, M. (1993, December 26). They live in a world of chronic danger: Children of today may be most fearful, experts say. *St. Louis Post-Dispatch,* p. 1A.

Shonkoff, J.P., & Phillips, D.A. (2000). *From neurons to neighborhoods: The science of early childhood development.* Washington, DC: National Academies Press.

Shore, R. (1997). *Rethinking the brain.* Chicago: Family and Work Institute.

Sieget, D.J., & Hartzell, M. (2004). *Parenting from the inside out: How a deeper self-understanding can help you raise children who thrive.* New York: Penguin Books.

Smilansky, S. (1968). *The effects of socio-dramatic play on disadvantaged preschool children.* New York: John Wiley & Sons.

Smith, H., Wigginton, E., Hocking, K., & Jones, R.E. (1991). Foxfire teacher networks. In A. Lieberman & L. Miller (Eds.), *Staff development for education in the 90s: New demands, new realities, new perspectives.* New York: Teachers College Press.

Smith, L.M., Kleine, P.F., Prunty, J.P., & Dwyer, D.C. (1986). *Educational innovators: Then and now.* Philadelphia: Falmer Press.

Smith, L.M., & Wells, W.M. (1990, April). *"Difficult to reach, maintain and help" urban families in PAT: Issues, dilemmas, strategies, and resolutions in parent education* (p. 21). Final report submitted to the Smith-Richardson Foundation. St. Louis: Washington University.

Solomon, J. (2003). Caregiving systems for separated and divorcing parents. *Zero to Three, 23*(3), 33–35.

Sroufe, L.A. (1989). Relationships, self, and individual adaptation. In A.J. Sameroff & R.N. Emde (Eds.), *Relationship disturbances in early childhood: A developmental approach* (pp. 70–94). New York: Basic Books.

Sroufe, L.A. (1996). *Emotional development: The organization of emotional life in the early years.* London: Cambridge University Press.

Stattin, H., & Magnusson, D. (1996). Antisocial development: A holistic approach. *Development and Psychopathology, 4*(8), 617–647.

Stein, A., Bucher, J., Gath, D., Bond, A., & Cooper, P.J. (1989). *The relationship between postnatal depression and mother–child interaction.* Unpublished manuscript.

Stern, D.N. (1977). *The first relationship: Infant and mother.* Cambridge, MA: Harvard University Press.

Stern, D.N. (1984). Affect attunement. In J. Call, E. Galenson, & R.L. Tyson (Eds.), *Frontiers of infant psychiatry* (Vol. 2, pp. 3–14). New York: Basic Books.

Stern, D.N. (1985). *The interpersonal world of the infant: A view from psychoanalysis and developmental psychology.* New York: Basic Books.

Stern, D.N. (1991). *Infant observation and the formation of psychic structure.* The Institute for Psychoanalysis Conference. Chicago: Erikson Institute & The Institute for Psychoanalysis.

Stern, D.N. (1994). *The world of infant research and adult psychotherapy.* Paper presented at the eighth annual Cape Cod Summer Symposia, Eastham, MA.

Stern, D.N. (1995). *The motherhood constellation: A unified view of parent–infant psychotherapy.* New York: Basic Books.

Stern, D.N. (2004). *The first relationship: Infant and mother*. Cambridge, MA: Harvard University Press.

Sugar, M. (1992). Toddler's traumatic memories. *Infant Mental Health Journal, 13*(3), 245–251.

Tabors, P.O., Roach, K.A., & Snow, C.E. (2001). Home language and literacy environment. In D.K. Dickinson & P.O. Tabors (Eds.), *Beginning literacy with language* (pp. 75–92). Cambridge, MA: Harvard Graduate School of Education.

Tagore, R. (1958). *Collected poems and plays*. New York: Macmillan.

Terr, L.C. (1991). Childhood traumas: An outline and overview. *American Journal of Psychiatry, 148,* 10–20.

Thomas, A., & Chess, S. (1977). *Temperament and development*. New York: Brunner/Mazel.

Thompson, R.A. (2006). The development of the person: Social understanding, relationships, conscience, self. In W. Damon, R.M. Lerner, & N. Eisenberg (Eds.), *Handbook of child psychology: Vol. 3. Social, emotional, and personality development* (6th ed., pp. 24–98). New York: John Wiley & Sons.

Thornburg, K.R., & Scott, J.L. (2006). Approaches to rural professional development. *Zero to Three, 26*(4), 14–21.

Tomasello, M. (2001). Perceiving intentions and learning words in the second year of life. In M. Bowerman & S.C. Levinson (Eds.), *Language acquisition and conceptual development* (pp. 132–158). New York: Cambridge University Press.

Toth, S.L., Cicchetti, D., Macfie, J., & Emde, R.N. (1997). Representations of self and other in the narrations of neglected, physically abused, and sexually abused preschoolers. *Development and Psychopathology, 9*(4), 781–796.

Tremblay, R.E., & Nagan, D.S. (2005). The developmental origins of physical aggression in humans. In R.E. Tremblay, W.W. Hartup, & J. Archer (Eds.), *Developmental origins of aggression* (pp. 83–106). New York: Guilford Press.

Tronick, E.Z., Cohn, J., & Shea, E. (1986). The transfer of affect between mothers and infants. In T.B. Brazelton & M.W. Yogman (Eds.), *Affective development in infancy* (pp. 11–25). Norwood, NJ: Ablex.

Twain, M. (1947). *The adventures of Huckleberry Finn*. Cleveland, OH: World Publishing. (Original work published 1885)

Underwood, M.K. (2002). Sticks and stones and social exclusion: Aggression among girls and boys. In P.K. Smith & C.H. Hart (Eds.), *Blackwell handbook of childhood social development* (pp. 789–857). Malden, MA: Blackwell Publishers.

Varghese, J. (2001). The role of maternal affect mirroring on social expectancies in three-month-old infants. *Child Development, 72*(5), 1301–1314.

Vandewater, E.A., Bickham, D.S., Lee, J.H., Cummings, H.M., Wartella, E.A. & Rideout, V.J. (2005). When the television is always on: Heavy television exposure and young children's development. *American Behavioral Scientist, 48*(5), 562–577.

Villarreal, S.F., McKinney, L., & Quackenbush, M. (1992). *Handle with care: Helping children prenatally exposed to drugs and alcohol*. San Francisco: ETR Associates.

Volterra, V., Caselli, M.C., Capirci, O., & Pizzuto, E. (2005). Gesture and the emergence and development of language. In M. Tomasello & D.I. Slobin (Eds.), *Beyond nature-nurture: Essays in honor of Elizabeth Bates* (pp. 3–40). Mahwah, NJ: Lawrence Erlbaum Associates.

Vygotsky, L.S. (1978). *Mind in society: The development of higher psychological process* (M. Cole, V. John-Steiner, S. Scribner, & E. Souberman, Eds. & Trans.). Cambridge, MA: Harvard University Press.

Wachs, T.D. (2004). Temperament and development: The role of context in a biological based system. *Zero to Three, 24*(4), 12–20.

Wakschlag, L.S., & Hans, S.L. (2000). Early parenthood in context: Implications for development and intervention. In C.H. Zeanah, Jr. (Ed.), *Handbook of infant mental health* (2nd ed., pp. 129–144). New York: Guilford Press.

Ward, R.M., & Beehy, J.C. (2003). Neonatal complications following preterm birth. *British Journal of Obstetrics & Gynaecology, 110*(2f), 8–16.

Wasik, B.H., Bryant, D.M., & Lyons, C.M. (1990). *Home visiting: Procedures for helping families.* Thousand Oaks, CA: Sage Publications.

Weatherston, D.J. (2000). Infant mental health assessment through careful observation and listening: Unique training approaches. In J.D. Osofsky & H.E. Fitzgerald (Eds.), *WAIMH handbook of infant mental health, Vol. 2. Early intervention, evaluation, and assessment* (pp. 121–155). New York: John Wiley & Sons.

Webb, N.B. (Ed.). (2006). *Working with traumatized youth in child welfare.* New York: Guilford Press.

Weiss, H.B. (1993). Home visits: Necessary but not sufficient. In R.E. Behrman (Ed.), *The future of children* (pp. 113–128). Los Altos, CA: Center for the Future of Children, The David and Lucile Packard Foundation.

Weissbluth, M. (1987). *Healthy sleep habits, happy child.* New York: Ballantine Books.

Weissbourd, B. (1987). A brief history of family support programs. In S.L. Kagan, D.P. Powell, B. Weissbourd, & E.F. Zigler (Eds.), *America's family support programs* (pp. 38–56). New Haven, CT: Yale University Press.

Weissbourd, B. (1994). The evolution of the family resource movement. In S.L. Kagan & B. Weissbourd (Eds.), *Putting families first: America's family support movement and the challenge of change* (pp. 28–48). San Francisco: Jossey-Bass.

Werker, J.F., & Desjardins, R.N. (2001). Listening to speech in the 1st year of life. In M. Tomasello & E. Bates (Eds.), *Language development: The essential readings* (pp. 26–33). Malden, MA: Blackwell Publishers.

Werner, E.E. (1984). Resilient children. *Young Children, 40*(10), 68–72.

Werner, E.E., & Smith, R.S. (1992). *Overcoming the odds: High risk for children from birth to adulthood.* Ithaca, New York: Cornell University Press.

Wessel, L., & Spain, J. (2005). The chronic care model: A collaborative approach to preventing and treating asthma in infants and young children. *Zero to Three, 25*(3), 20–27.

Weston, D.R. (2005). Training in infant mental health: Education the reflective practitioner. *Infants and Young Children, 16*(40), 337–348.

White, B. (1985). *The first three years of life.* New York: Prentice Hall.

White, M., & Epston, D. (1990). *Narrative means to therapeutic ends.* New York: W.W. Norton.

Wigfield, A., Eccles, J.S., Schiefele, U., Roeser, R., & Davis-Kean, P. (2006). Development of achievement motivation. In W. Damon, R.M. Lerner, & N. Eisenberg (Eds.), *Handbook of child psychology: Vol. 3. Social, emotional, and personality development* (6th ed., pp. 933–1002). New York: John Wiley & Sons.

Wightman, B. (2004). Your laughter will be my laughter: Reflections of a grandmother. *Zero to Three, 24*(3), 38–41.

Winnicott, D.W. (1965). *The maturational processes and the facilitating environment.* New York: International Universities Press.

Winnicott, D.W. (1971). *Playing and reality.* New York: Basic Books.

Wolin, S.J., & Bennett, L.A. (1984). Family rituals. *Family Process, 23,* 402–420.

Wolin, S.J., & Wolin, S. (1993). *The resilient self: How survivors of troubled families rise above adversity.* New York: Villard Books.

Wyman, P.A., Sandler, I., Wolchick, S., & Nelson, K. (2000). Resilience as cumulative competence promotion and stress protection: Theory and intervention. In D. Cicchetti, J. Rappaport, I. Sandler, & R.P. Weissberg (Eds.), *The promotion of wellness in children and adolescents (Issues in children's and families' lives)* (pp. 133–184). Washington, DC: CWLA Press.

Zahn-Waxler, C., Ianotti, R.J., Cumming, E.M., & Denham, S. (1990). Antecedents of problem behaviors in children of depressed mothers. *Development and Psychopathology, 2,* 271–291.

Zeanah, C.H., Jr. (1993). The assessment and treatment of infants and toddlers exposed to violence. *Zero to Three, 14*(3), 29–37.

Zeanah, C.H., Jr., & Boris, N.W. (2000). Disturbances and disorders of attachment in early childhood. In C.H. Zeanah, Jr. (Ed.), *Handbook of infant mental health* (2nd ed., pp. 353–368). New York: Guilford Press.

Zeanah, C.H., Jr., & Scheeringa, M. (1996, April-May). Evaluation of posttraumatic symptomatology in infants and young children exposed to violence. *Zero To Three, 16*(5), 9–14.

Zeanah, P.D., Larrieu, J.A., & Zeanah, C.H., Jr. (2000). Training in infant mental health. In C.H. Zeanah, Jr. (Ed.), *Handbook of infant mental health* (2nd ed., pp. 548–558). New York: Guilford Press.

Zigler, E.F., Finn-Stevenson, M., & Hall, N.W. (2002). *The first three years of life and beyond: Brain development and social policy.* New Haven, CT: Yale University Press.

Zigler, E.F., Singer, D.G., & Bishop-Josef, S.J. (2004). *Children's play: The roots of reading.* Washington, DC: ZERO TO THREE: National Center for Infants, Toddlers and Families.

Zucker, R.A. (2006). Alcohol use and the alcohol use disorders: A developmental-biopsychosocial systems formulation covering the life course. In D. Cicchetti & D.J. Cohen (Eds.), *Developmental psychopathology: Vol. 3. Risk, disorder, and adaptation* (2nd ed., pp. 620–656). New York: John Wiley & Sons.

Zuckerman, B., & Brown, E.R. (1993). Maternal substance abuse and infant development. In C.H. Zeanah, Jr. (Ed.), *Handbook of infant mental health* (pp. 143–158). New York: Guilford Press.

Index

Throughout this index, page references followed by a *t* indicate tables and those followed by an *n* indicate endnotes.